Dollars, Distance, and Online Education

The New Economics of College Teaching and Learning

Edited by
Martin J. Finkelstein
Carol Frances
Frank I. Jewett
and
Bernhard W. Scholz

AMERICAN COUNCIL ON EDUCATION ★
ORYX PRESS ★
Series on Higher Education
2000

The rare Arabian Oryx is believed to have inspired the myth of the unicorn. This desert antelope became virtually extinct in the early 1960s. At that time, several groups of international conservationists arranged to have nine animals sent to the Phoenix Zoo to be the nucleus of a captive breeding herd. Today, the Oryx population is over 1,000, and over 500 have been returned to the Middle East.

© 2000 by The American Council on Education and The Oryx Press
Published by The Oryx Press
4041 North Central at Indian School Road
Phoenix, Arizona 85012-3397
http://www.oryxpress.com

Published simultaneously in Canada
Printed and bound in the United States of America

∞ The paper used in this publication meets the minimum requirements of American National Standard for Information Science—Permanence of Paper for Printed Library Materials, ANSI Z39.48, 1984.

Library of Congress Cataloging-in-Publication Data

Dollars, Distance, and Online Education: The New Economics of College Teaching and Learning / Martin J. Finkelstein ... [et al.].
    p. cm.
Includes bibliographical references and index.
  ISBN 1-57356-395-1 (alk. paper)
  1. Education, Higher—Effect of technological innovations on—United States. 2. Universities and colleges—United States—Data processing. 3. Information technology—United States—Finance. I. Finkelstein, Martin J., 1949-
  LB2395.7 .M26 2000
  378'.00285—dc21   00-009259
                                                                 CIP

CONTENTS

CONTRIBUTORS

Judith V. Boettcher is Executive Director of the Corporation for Research and Educational Networking (CREN), a non-profit higher education member organization that provides knowledge services and Internet tools to support research and educational institutions. She has worked in the field of instructional technology for over 20 years, including service at Penn State University, Florida State University, and Control Data Corporation. She has served on various boards for EUIT, Syllabus, the Technology Source, and as a member of the Board of Directors of Seminars on Academic Computing. While at Penn State, she served as the project leader for the EUIT project, which identified 101 Success Stories in Information Technology. She is a Syllabus Scholar, regularly writes columns for *Syllabus Magazine*, and conducts workshops on distance learning.

James Caplan is an organizational psychologist and IT consultant who installs and upgrades networks and computer systems. He is Vice President of Forceware Systems, Inc., which develops database applications. He has conducted extensive research on technology and consumer satisfaction. Dr. Caplan has taught statistics and research methods at Florida International University, the University of Miami, and St. Thomas University. He was a founding partner of Performance Consultants to Education; personnel psychologist at Exxon, where he introduced the first personal computer in 1984; and Chief of the Personnel Psychology Branch and the Personnel Records Branch of the U.S. Office of Personnel Management.

Leroy Dubeck is Professor of physics at Temple University. Dr. Dubeck has taught at Temple since 1965. He is author of four books on higher education budget analysis and teaches an online physics course.

Heather Eggins is Director of the Society for Research into Higher Education; Visiting Professor at the University of Strathclyde; and Honorary Member of the Senior Common Room, Lucy Cavendish College, University of Cambridge. Professor Eggins previously worked for the Council for National Academic Awards, following university teaching posts at the University of Colorado at Boulder, the University of Warwick, and the University of Ulster. Her research interest is in higher education policy and she has edited a number of volumes on different aspects of higher education: *Restructuring Higher Education*, *Higher Education into the 1990s* (with Christopher Ball), *Arts Graduates: Their Skills and Their Employment*, and *Women as Leaders and Managers in Higher Education*. She is currently working on a volume on higher education reform.

Martin J. Finkelstein is Professor of higher education at Seton Hall University. From 1989 to 1997, he directed the New Jersey Institute for Collegiate Teaching and Learning, where he led curriculum development efforts with information technology at Seton Hall's Center for Academic Technology, including establishment of a Small College Consortium for Information Technology and the Curriculum. He also served as Director of Assessment for Seton Hall's online "virtual" university, SETONWORLDWIDE. He recently completed a three-year externally funded project on "The Costs and Benefits of Information Technology in Collegiate Teaching and Learning." Dr. Finkelstein's particular area of interest is information technology's role in redefining academic work and the nature of college teaching. His most recent book is *The New Academic Generation* (The Johns Hopkins University Press, 1998). He is completing, with Jack Schuster, a large-scale analysis of the transformation in college faculty roles and careers; entitled *The American Faculty*, it will appear in 2001. His research and development activities have been supported by the U.S. Department of Education, the National Science Foundation, the Pew Charitable Trusts, and the Exxon Education Foundation, among others.

Carol Frances helped pioneer the development of financial indicators for colleges and universities when she served as Chief Economist of the American Council on Education. Working with the National Association of College and University Business Officers, she directed studies, funded by the U.S. Department of Education and a major foundation, of trends in the financial conditions of the institutions. She is a specialist in the economics and finance of higher education and has published work on the impact of demographic trends on the future demand for college, student financial aid, federal and state budget priorities, and the economic outlook. Frances earned graduate degrees at the Institut d'Etudes Politiques in Paris and at Stanford, Yale, and Duke universites. She is a Senior Associate of the Kaludis Consulting Group, based in Washington, D.C. She is a Visiting Scholar at both Claremont Graduate University and

Seton Hall University where she focuses on the impact of information technology on higher education.

Edward D. Goldberg is President of EHigherEducation.com, a company that provides management expertise and venture capital to universities seeking outside support in planning, establishing, and operating a significant online learning business. Prior to founding EHigherEducation.com, he planned and then headed Seton Hall University's online campus, SETONWORLDWIDE, which has been as a national leader in offering complete degree programs online. His higher education career, spanning three decades, includes service as a faculty member, department chair, dean, and Chancellor of Higher Education for the State of New Jersey. His Ph.D. is from Columbia University.

Kenneth C. Green is Founder/Director of The Campus Computing Project, the largest continuing study of the role of information technology in U.S. colleges and universities. The project is widely cited by campus officials and corporate executives as the definitive source for information about IT issues affecting American higher education. Green is also a Visiting Scholar at The Claremont Graduate University (The Claremont Colleges) in Claremont, California. Green's column on technology and higher education issues, "Digital Tweed," appears monthly in *Converge* magazine (www.convergemag.com). As the author, co-author, or editor of a dozen books and published research reports and of more than three dozen articles that have appeared in academic journals and professional publications, Dr. Green is frequently quoted on higher education, information technology, and labor market issues in print and broadcast media. He is an invited speaker at some two dozen academic conferences and professional meetings each year.

Rachel Hendrickson is Coordinator of Higher Education at the National Education Association, where she has worked since 1991. Her present work centers on part-time faculty, distance education, and organizational change. Her M.A. and Ph.D. in English and her M.S. in industrial relations are all from the University of Rhode Island. She serves on the National Chapter Advisory Committee of the Industrial Relations Research Association.

Frank I. Jewett, an economist and former economics professor, is Special Consultant to Academic Affairs in the Chancellor's Office, California State University (CSU). His assignments there have included large-scale software implementation planning, feasibility studies for three new campuses, state-wide long-range enrollment planning, a benefit-cost study of year-round operation, projection models for physical facilities needs, system-wide faculty budgeting and faculty workload policy, system-wide instructional databases and reporting systems, and higher education faculty staffing and cost simulation models. His interest in the economics of mediated instruction arose from long-range planning work he was doing in the late 1980s. He authored a CSU study on "Removing Barriers to Mediated Instruction" (1992) and wrote the proposal for benefit-cost studies that CSU presented at the National Learning Infra-structure Initiative (NLII) meetings in 1995. He recently completed a three-year assignment as Director of a U.S. Department of Education/CSU-funded research project "Case Studies on the Benefits and Costs of Mediated Instruc-tion and Distributed Learning." The project was jointly sponsored by NLII, CSU, and the State Higher Education Executive Officers (SHEEO). It in-cluded eight campus-specific case studies (state-wide television delivery, multi-media courseware, and Internet applications) and a cost simulation model (BRIDGE) to compare the costs of expanding a campus based on classroom technology versus expanding based on distributed technology (television, Internet distribution). Jewett has made numerous presentations at professional meetings on the benefit-cost case studies, the BRIDGE model, and the costing and productivity implications of mediated instruction.

Dennis Jones is President of the National Center for Higher Education Management Systems (NCHEMS), a nonprofit research and development center founded to improve strategic decisionmaking in institutions and agen-cies of higher education. A member of the staff since 1969, Jones is widely recognized for his work in such areas as the changing environment for postsecondary education and formulation of state and institutional policy in light of this changing environment, strategic planning at all levels of postsecondary education, alternative approaches to budgeting and resource allocation at both state and institutional levels, and use of information in policymaking. Jones has written many monographs and articles on these topics; has presented his work at numerous regional, national, and international conferences; and has consulted with hundreds of institutions and state higher education agencies on management issues of all kinds.

George Kaludis is Chairman and President of Kaludis Consulting Group. Dr. Kaludis has more than 30 years of diverse planning and management experi-ence in higher education. Prior to founding the Kaludis Consulting Group in 1977, he served as Director of Planning and Evaluation at the State University System of Florida and as Vice Chancellor for Operations and Fiscal Planning and Associate Professor of management at Vanderbilt University. Kaludis has held several national leadership positions in higher education, including serv-ing on the National Commission on the Financing of Postsecondary Education, and has spoken and published on a variety of topics related to board and executive leadership in higher education. He holds B.A. and M.Ed. degrees from the University of Maryland and a Ph.D. from Florida State University.

Stephen Landry is a mathematician by training and was a faculty member in the Department of Mathematics and Computer Science at Seton Hall University. Subsequently, he served as Assistant Provost for information technology. For the last three years, he has been the Chief Information Officer of the university. Landry was instrumental in moving the institution towards a major information technology initiative as a member of a Computing and Information Technology Planning and Policy Committee and as the chief author of the 1995 document *Information Technology at Seton Hall University: A Five Year Plan for Excellence*. The university has been rated among the "most wired" campuses in the nation and last year received the EDUCAUSE Award for Excellence in Campus Networking.

Karen Leach has worked in business and education, performing efficiency studies, developing systems, and managing financial, technology, and other resources. She has been at Colgate University, a private liberal arts college in upstate New York, for 13 years, first as Associate Provost, and now as Chief Information Officer. She collaborates with David Smallen from Hamilton College on assessing the cost of information technology in educational institutions. She and Smallen have also collaborated to write on the topic of collaboration—they are avid believers in the benefits of working together in this rapidly changing world.

Christine Maitland is Coordinator of Higher Education at the National Education Association, has worked for the NEA, the California Faculty Association, and the California Teachers' Association for more than 20 years, and is experienced in organizational development, negotiations, and educational technology. Recent projects have included developing a research center for higher education, maintaining a Web site, and producing an interactive CD-ROM on the future of higher education. She has a Ph.D. in education from Claremont Graduate University.

Richard Pumerantz is Vice President of university advancement at Western University of Health Sciences (WesternU). He earned his B.S. in business administration at the University of Southern California, his MBA at the Peter F. Drucker Graduate Management Center of Claremont Graduate University (CGU), and is currently a Ph.D. candidate in higher education at CGU. He has been a member of WesternU committees on budgeting and fiscal management, information technology, and university policies. He is also a member of the President's Cabinet and advises the Financial Advisory and CEFA Bond Committees of WesternU's Board of Trustees. He serves as a consultant to non-profits and financial advisory/investment firms on fundraising, charitable estate planning, endowment management, budgeting, and leadership. He is President of The Webb Schools Alumni Association and a member of the YMCA board and has published collaborative works on the costs of IT.

Bernhard W. Scholz, a medievalist and historian by training, served many years as a tenured faculty member. As Dean of the College of Arts and Sciences at Seton Hall University and later as Chief Academic Officer and Provost, a position he held for 11 years, he focused on improving teaching and learning. These efforts resulted in a highly successful freshman college, various assessment initiatives, and the New Jersey Institute for Collegiate Teaching and Learning. During his tenure as Chief Academic Officer, the university prepared its first strategic plans for information technology, entered into an alliance with IBM, and created a mobile campus and SETONWORLDWIDE, the university's venture into distance learning.

David M. Seldin is Executive Vice President of EHigherEducation.com and President of Catalyst, Inc., a transaction-oriented consulting firm. He serves on the board of directors of NewsAlert, an international Internet-based information company; PeerLogic, Inc., an eCommerce enabling software company; Shoutmail.com, a leader in phone-based Internet applications, such as e-mail by phone; and databid.com, a business-to-business site for data transmission services. He has an MBA from the University of Chicago.

David Smallen is Director of Information Technology Services at Hamilton College, a private, coeducational, liberal arts college of 1,650 students. He provides leadership for information technology resources, including all computing and voice and data communications. He has contributed to the information technology field in higher education through publications and service on the committees and boards of CAUSE, EDUCOM, and EDUCAUSE, and currently as director of the Educause Leadership Institute. Most recently, he has collaborated with his colleague Karen Leach to organize the Costs Project to better understand the financial impact of delivering information technology support services in higher education.

Glen R. Stine is Vice President with the Kaludis Consulting Group. Stine has more than 25 years of experience in higher education. He has served as Vice President for budget and finance at the University of Colorado, Executive Director of Resource Planning and Budget for the University of Pennsylvania, and Vice President for Management at the University of Massachusetts. He has an extensive background in strategic planning, strategic financial planning, and financial and management operations. He is a former member of the Pew Higher Education Roundtable, the Forum for Higher Education Futures, and the Leading Chief Financial Officers. Dr. Stine has a B.S. from Michigan State University, an MPA from the University of North Carolina-Chapel Hill, and an Ed.D. from Harvard University.

FOREWORD

by Barry Munitz

The single most pressing public policy issue confronting American higher education in the 1990s was the "affordability" of a college education for individuals and for society. The question of "who pays, and who benefits" remains as vital as when it was raised by Clark Kerr more than 30 years ago when I served on his staff at the Carnegie Commission. As we enter the new millennium, college costs and prices (a critical distinction) continue to rise at a rate well beyond inflation, threatening our capacity to continue to fuel the optimal growth of a knowledge-based economy. This rise occurs at a moment when higher education confronts the greatest expansion in enrollment in three decades; millions of traditional-age students are joining the even greater numbers of adults and part-timers whose continuing education needs dominated the last decade.

I served for two years as vice-chair of the National Commission on the Cost of Higher Education. Our report, *Straight Talk about College Costs and Prices*, issued in January 1998, identified a number of stubborn factors driving up the cost and price structure of higher education and offered a number of recommendations for public policy. Time and the unavailability of some key data permitted us to list many important issues only as items comprising an "unfinished agenda." It included what has emerged in the last two years as the most significant "wild card" affecting the costs of our colleges and universities—information technology. Many economists and policymakers suggest that electronic connection breakthroughs are the key to increasing productivity and reducing instructional costs. Yet, preparing the infrastructure (physical and human) of higher education for an Internet age appears to others as only the latest institutional "budget buster" or, worse yet, as a philistinean fad, the implications of which most higher education leaders are still struggling to comprehend.

This volume takes a significant step toward promoting that understanding and addresses a major component of the Cost Commission's unfinished agenda. The editors have brought together experts in information technology, public policy, and administrative and faculty leadership to consider what we have learned about the consequences and costs of information technology and what we have yet to learn. From their insights emerge some clear parameters and standards that campuses and higher education systems will find useful for assessing institutional investment in these new tools.

I am particularly pleased that this volume is, in part, a product of an invitational forum co-sponsored by Seton Hall University and the Howard Bowen Institute for Policy Research in Higher Education at the Claremont Graduate University's Center for Educational Studies, where I served for many years on the Board of Visitors. I am also pleased that significant segments of the most relevant work on collegiate instruction patterns were undertaken at the California State University where I served as chancellor during the 1990s. Through such affiliations, I have been privileged to participate in the national conversation on these vital issues—a conversation that this timely volume will help to illuminate and advance.

Barry Munitz is President and Chief Executive Officer of The J. Paul Getty Trust.

PREFACE

The immodest objective of this modest volume is to systematically analyze and assess the costs of information technology (IT) for teaching and learning in higher education. By IT, we refer to that cluster of nonprint electronic communications media that includes radio, television, and, most especially, the digital computer and the Internet.

The general impetus for this stock taking is the accelerating pace at which IT is transforming our society and economy. Such industrial sectors as manufacturing, communications, entertainment, and health services are well into the restructuring process. Other sectors, such as retail and wholesale trade, are at earlier stages in the process, but a major restructuring is emerging. Business-to-business online sales account for billions of dollars in revenues and are growing by the week. Consumers are increasingly turning to the Internet as their primary vehicle for banking, investing, and even shopping. They make travel arrangements and buy cars online, and the online auction has promoted the growth of a whole new generation of small business entrepreneurs. At the center of this revolution is IT's unprecedented capability to facilitate interactive communication.

Within higher education, IT has profoundly affected both the content and the pace of research. Near instantaneous access is now available to documentary materials and resources all over the world, and scholarly communication and collaboration are no longer constrained by barriers of time and geography. IT is also having a major impact upon the structure and operation of the various campus administrative and support functions, including student admissions and records, student registration, class scheduling, finance, and budgeting. However, these important topics are not the focus of the current discussion.

Within the instructional program, the effects of IT are less understood and potentially more problematic. Historically, various nonprint media have been used to augment regular classroom instruction since at least mid-century (e.g., film, TV, computing). To the extent these applications occurred in a few disciplines and were modest in scope, they added a small component to the costs of classroom instruction and were justified by the enhancement of the learning experience. But in recent years, the use of IT, especially in the form of computing and networked communications, has spread throughout the curriculum. Access to a computer and the Internet are becoming a basic component of instruction in all disciplines. Further, employers expect that a college graduate will be knowledgeable in a range of computing applications. Today, failure to provide computer access and related instruction would deny students an essential part of their education. A thorough grounding in the fundamentals of IT is now recognized as an essential part of the undergraduate curriculum. A substantial introduction to the particular disciplinary applications of IT is a vital element in undergraduate major programs.

Moreover, beyond fundamentally strengthening the classroom experience of traditional on-campus students, IT is extending educational access to non-traditional students via distance education and providing a major new avenue for delivering continuing education in the workplace. It is spawning new kinds of education providers (for-profit "edubusinesses") and re-aligning the teaching and learning environment within which colleges and universities compete.

Responding to IT's substantive "educational" potential in contradistinction to its "business" potential is fast becoming the major challenge higher education leaders face in charting the future of their institutions. To date, the response of higher education has been to channel substantial investments into the instructional applications of IT. However knee-jerk or considered, that strategic commitment has been founded on educational and market competitive considerations. While IT can clearly facilitate the "drill and practice" component of education and training as well as the interactive communication between teachers and learners, the promise of IT's contribution to more complex educational processes is widely touted, but less clearly demonstrable. Some argue that IT has facilitated a new and more fundamental centering of the educational process on the learner. It promotes more "active" responsibility among students for their own learning and moves the instructor from the primary role of "information provider and gatekeeper" to that of "guide." It increases time on task and ensures rapid and timely feedback to learners—all conditions that enhance student learning outcomes (TLT Group, 1998). On the other hand, IT is also dislocating traditional arrangements for teaching and learning and raising troublesome issues about faculty workload and ownership of their intellectual property, i.e., their course material.

The issue of costs is at the center of any discussion relating to the use of information technology in teaching and learning. Teaching and learning have always been labor-intensive processes (80-90 percent of higher education operating expenditures are personnel costs). Whether the institutions are public or independent, the pressing issue is how to pay for computing equipment, software, and the network communications capacity required for the instructional program. The funding need is further exacerbated by the fact that computing equipment and software, both of which are properly classified as capital items whose services are rendered over a period of years, have relatively short useful lives on the order of two to five years. The funding need is not simply for a one-time increase in the inventory; once the inventory is built up, it requires a substantial annual expenditure to replace a large share of it each year. Relatively large expenditures on IT are also required for initial training of both faculty and students—although that need should decline over time as students and faculty acquire computing knowledge earlier in their careers—for on-going maintenance of the equipment and software, and for "helpdesk" activities to help users overcome the many problems that arise in daily use of equipment and software. Thus, the word "costs" has a rightful place in the title of this volume.

Indeed, this book focuses squarely on the key question: Where is IT taking the instructional program? And what is it carrying with it? We worry that the necessary debates are not taking place about IT's rightful place within an institution's priorities and educational mission. Moreover, we worry that such conversations are occurring in isolation, with faculty organizations, IT professionals, institutional leaders, and the policy community talking *among* themselves, but not to each other and not with a common framework or foundation of information. The most basic challenge is beginning a national conversation, a taking stock across stakeholder groups, of the transformative effect of IT on our "core" business—teaching and learning. To do so will require that we clarify the basic terms of the discussion, map the domain, and provide a common vocabulary and frame/point of departure.

To launch our analysis of the cost of information technology in collegiate teaching and learning on a clear and common foundation, we have identified 10 "basic" propositions (i.e., ideas, insights, and beliefs that have found wide, although not necessarily universal, acceptance). These propositions undergird the following chapters.

1. The use of information technology, especially in the form of networked and online learning, is now integral to the college curriculum. IT is thus affecting, and will increasingly affect, teaching and learning and their costs.

2. While colleges and universities have been spending enormously—and increasingly—on IT, we as yet have no clear benchmarks of what the costs of IT in teaching and learning are. We know, however, that IT is creating enormous cost pressures for many institutions.

3. Especially outside the academy, a widespread presumption says that the use of IT in teaching and learning will—indeed, must—help reduce the escalating cost of higher education.

4. The cost of IT in teaching and learning varies in line with how institutions plan—strategically and tactically—and manage their IT investment.

5. Methodologies have been developed to identify IT costs and evaluate IT investments, although up to now they seem to have found infrequent application in higher education.

6. As of now, only the most sporadic and limited indicators show that networked and online teaching and learning are saving colleges and universities any money.

7. Certain applications of IT in teaching and learning demonstrate that instructional productivity can be increased. Achieving savings is almost always dependent on realizing economies of scale.

8 Networked and online learning eases access to higher education. Online instruction provides more choices for *all* students (be they commuters or remote) regarding when and where they can accomplish their course work. This increased convenience, together with increased access to heretofore unavailable educational opportunities, will expand the market for higher education as well as enhance classroom instruction.

9. The use of IT in teaching and learning is changing the way faculty work, raising new issues about workload, and affecting the economic position of faculty.

10. Networked and online learning has intensified competition among institutions and spawned new, largely private-sector, competitors for traditional colleges and universities.

Several of the chapters that follow were originally presented as papers at an Executive Forum on Managing the Costs of Information Technology held in Princeton, New Jersey, in April 1999, and jointly sponsored by the New Jersey Institute for Collegiate Teaching and Learning at Seton Hall University and the Howard Bowen Center for Policy Research in Higher Education of the Claremont Graduate University. They represent an attempt to map the IT landscape, to describe not only what we know but also what we don't know, and to suggest how IT may change higher education in the next decades. A substantial amount of work on costs has already been done, and some of it is reported in these chapters. A substantial amount of work remains to be done, and some of these ongoing efforts are also reported in the following chapters. This volume concludes with an annotated bibliography. One value of this edited volume lies precisely in the spectrum of differing views it offers, both among contributors (and even among the editors). We encourage the reader to engage these issues and, in so doing, to contribute to the ongoing dialogue as IT becomes an ever larger component of instructional delivery in higher education.

Martin Finkelstein,   *Frank Jewett,*
South Orange, New Jersey   *Long Beach, California*

Carol Frances   *Bernhard Scholz,*
Claremont, California   *New Hope, Pennsylvania*

ACKNOWLEDGMENTS

For their direct and indirect intellectual contributions to this volume, we are deeply indebted to participants in the Executive Forum for Managing IT Costs in Higher Education held in Princeton, New Jersey, in April 1999 and co-sponsored by the New Jersey Institute for Collegiate Teaching and Learning at Seton Hall University and the Howard Bowen Center for Policy Research in Higher Education at the Claremount Graduate University. These participants include Judith V. Boettcher, Mary A. Burgan, Edmund Cranch, Don Doucette, Heather Eggins, Rhonda Epper, Dennis Jones, George Kaludis, Charles Karelis, Karen Leach, Mark Luker, Bernard Luskin, Christine Maitland, Margaret A. Miller, Christopher N. Oberg, Susan Perry, Anne Savage, Robert Shireman, David Smallen, and Nicholas P. Tworischuk. The organizing team for the Forum included James Caplan, Martin Finkelstein, Carol Frances, Kenneth C. Green, Frank Jewett, Richard Pumerantz, and Bernhard W. Scholz.

Although they were not physically present, the pioneering work of Tony Bates, Sir John Daniel, and Greville Rumble clearly shaped the agenda and the perspectives of participants.

For their financial support, we are grateful to Mr. and Mrs. Albert Merck, who not only financed the Forum, including sponsorship of several of the papers and the meeting itself, but the development of this volume as well. Mr. Merck, a first citizen of New Jersey, served in the legislature and chaired the state Board of Higher Education. A longtime director of the Merck Company, founded by his grandfather, and of the Merck Family Fund, Mr. Merck has, together with Mrs. Merck, over the years provided generous moral and financial support to education at every level and to the arts.

Finally, we are grateful to the College of Education at Seton Hall University which provided a visiting scholar appointment to Carol Frances from January 1999 through Spring 2000; this appointment allowed her to devote time and energy to the preparation of this volume.

Part 1

· · · · · · · · · · · ·

Mapping the Territory

CHAPTER 1

Overview

What Do We Know about Information Technology and the Cost of Collegiate Teaching and Learning?

Martin J. Finkelstein and Bernhard W. Scholz

Higher education in the United States and indeed around the world is in the midst of an expansion that is being driven by demographics and the demands of a knowledge-based global economy. Once the limited province of an intellectual or social elite—less than one-seventh of 18 to 22-year-olds as late as 1945—higher education has become a path for the masses. In the United States, two out of three high school graduates now go on to some form of higher education. Of the many challenges accompanying this growth, one of the most serious for all countries, rich or poor, is how to pay for expanded access. The fiscal challenge is twofold: not only are costs rising in step with rising student numbers, but, certainly in the U.S., costs per student are going up as well. As a result, to make quality higher education widely available at a sustainable cost, societies, both developed and developing, have begun experimenting with alternative ways of delivering higher education, first mainly by radio and television and, more recently, through the personal computer and the Internet.

Up to now, campus computerization of business processes, libraries, research, and instruction have only driven costs upward. When and to what degree will information technology begin to replicate in higher education the productivity gains and cost savings beginning to be seen in the general economy? Is it merely a matter of time, or is the higher education industry a different species—inscrutable in its outcomes as much as in the cost of its production?

All of higher education continues to be changed by information technology. But in the long run, if IT is becoming ubiquitous in teaching and learning, the major IT cost in higher education is going to be in the cost of instruction. Therefore, the focus of this chapter is, first, on the overall impact of IT on the cost of higher education and, second, on the effect IT is having on the cost of teaching and learning. The distinction is fundamental. The issues of cost and productivity are different when we talk about IT in business processes, in the broadest sense of the word, and when we consider IT as an instrument for teaching and learning. As for business processes, one might even claim that the war has been won and IT has proven itself to be a vehicle for greater productivity; at least today's quantities of transactions are inconceivable without IT. As for IT in teaching and learning, the evidence at this point is probably more persuasive for IT improving learning than for reducing costs. However, even in teaching and learning, IT has clearly lowered costs in some areas.

This chapter distills the principal ideas, issues, and findings that have appeared in the literature in recent years, mainly the works listed and abstracted in the "Resources" appendix of this book, to provide a common point of departure for the chapters that follow.

INFORMATION TECHNOLOGY IN THE NEW ECONOMY

The use of information technology is becoming ubiquitous. Half of the investment in larger businesses is now used to buy IT. Its costs are enormous, even though the cost of storing one byte of information has plummeted since 1956 from $10,000 to 10 cents. Some economists—among them Paul A. Strassmann—believe that business in this country and around the world has wasted billions of dollars on information technology with little to show for it, a belief that gives rise to the idea of the "squandered computer."[1] But others are beginning to see a pay-off from information technology. According to a 1999 report of the U.S. Department of Commerce, "The Emerging Digital Economy 2," the IT industry, while only one-twelfth of the total U.S. economy, accounts for one-third of U.S. economic growth. The report also credits the IT industry with calming inflation because of the declining costs of IT products, and with fueling investment through spending on computers and communication.[2] The chairman of the Federal Reserve has credited IT with being the source of recent productivity gains in the U.S. economy.[3] We must see IT and its costs within the context of the role information systems and technologies are playing in the economies of all countries. That global role continues to change as development has moved from IT centered on systems to IT centered on personal computers and then on networks; the next phase—IT focused increasingly on content—is expected to begin with the new millennium. IT is changing everything in the world in which we live and will continue to do so.[4]

Organizations have investments in IT, just as they have portfolios of financial investments. The IT portfolio consists of the various systems and technologies the organization considers necessary to operate and achieve its goals. One economist has proposed a persuasive scheme that sees such investment as a pyramid, at the base of which is *infrastructure* (more than half of the IT portfolio). Above it, *transactional IT* is dedicated to processing basic repetitive transactions, like inventory control. The goal here is to handle high volumes, to replace labor with capital, and to cut costs. Infrastructure and transactional IT support *information* and *strategy*, the apex of the pyramid.[5] Informational IT is an instrument for internal management and control, supporting, for example, planning or accounting. Strategic IT serves to gain competitive advantage, by, for instance, increasing market share, and is at the root of innovation. Key is whether IT investment is in line with current strategies, business goals, and long-term strategic intent, the ultimate destination the organization aspires to. The latter must drive IT investment decisions.[6]

Computing began with a focus on automation and business efficiencies, with an eye to cost savings. The large initial expenditures reinforced the expectation that IT would save money, in the long run if not the short run. A simple unilinear connection became an almost automatic assumption—large expenditures for IT are justified by future savings. This original expectation lies behind what has been called the IT productivity paradox that has occupied economists for more than two decades and generated a mountain of literature.[7] The paradox is simply that despite great investments in IT, there appeared to be no demonstrable productivity gains. The idea of "IT as a financial sinkhole" was born. Even today the specter of the IT productivity paradox is still much with us, and Paul Strassmann only recently argued that "The question of whether information technology has improved productivity is now at the center of the economic stage."[8]

Some economists have come up with persuasive explanations of the IT productivity paradox, including the idea that one should expect a time lag between investment in IT and productivity gains, or that one did not apply the right measures for evaluating the impact of IT. The latter argument is related to another, namely, that the paradox is an invention of macroeconomists who focus on the total economy and base their work on economy-wide data. Such aggregation may allow the productivity gains of some investments to be offset by the loss of others. The argument here is that a redistribution occurred, with greater productivity shifting from some businesses to others. Economists are telling us that the search for productivity gains should take place on the *micro*economic level, i.e., on the level of the organization, the business unit.

Indeed, microeconomic analyses seem to support IT-related productivity gains.[9] Thus, the IT productivity paradox, even if we grant, as we should, that it was more than a nightmare of the macroeconomists, probably describes an earlier reality in the use of information systems and information technology.[10]

Meanwhile, a profound change is afoot in the role IT plays for businesses and other organizations. The for-profit sector, in particular, has gone aggressively beyond using IT as an instrument for achieving efficiencies and redesigning existing business processes. It is interested in the total business value of IT, in creating new business capabilities made possible by IT. This transforms IT from primarily a vehicle for support to an instrument of strategy, a business driver. The big challenge is how best to create value using information technology. What is needed is a continuous alignment between business goals and IT operations. As a result, "there is no such thing as an IT project anymore—only business change programs of which IT is an essential, but often small (5% to 20%) part."[11]

Assessing IT Investments

Investments in information technology have their peculiarities. The rapidity of technological change makes decisions on IT investments difficult. IT has hidden costs; it has been calculated that between 28 and 40 percent of IT expenditure is outside the regular IT budget.[12] Organizations often have not sufficiently defined their objectives to provide a solid basis for IT investment decisions. As IT use becomes more strategic, a larger element of subjectivity enters the picture. While strategic investment in IT is made for many reasons—improving performance and productivity, finding new ways to organize and manage, developing new businesses, gaining competitive advantage—sometimes decisions spring from subjective, superficial, and trivial considerations and are made for the sake of appearances rather than to increase business value. Since 1994-95, networked IT has complicated things, and when evaluating such IT investments, it "becomes crucial to understand the specifics of the risks, cost structures, benefits and time scales that apply."[13]

A gulf seems to exist between theory and practice, between decision-makers and economists. Those making decisions on investment in IT—IT professionals and organization leaders—know that such decisions have to be justified and their value has to be established for increasing efficiency, improving service, and contributing to business. Beyond justifying an individual project, total in-house costs must be tracked, measured, and monitored, tasks made more complex because of the dispersal of IT responsibilities throughout organizations. Potential in-house costs must be compared with the costs and benefits of outsourcing—evaluating whether to outsource, assessing vendor bids, identifying hidden costs, and managing and monitoring contracts. Benchmarking an organization's IT performance, i.e., comparing expenditures with what others are spending, is a technique used by decision-makers, who must also understand the concept of risk and the principles and methods of risk management, for example, in the analysis of software acquisition.[14]

Economists have conducted numerous empirical studies on evaluating investment in IT (although not in higher education). In fact, an extensive literature identifies and explores key issues and problems of evaluating IT investments, including why one should invest in IT, whether IT investment is different from other investment decisions, why there should be evaluation, on what level evaluation should occur (organization? project?), who should do it, who should be consulted, when it should take place (e.g., at the feasibility stage), and whether there are formal or informal procedures. Among the findings of such research is that evaluation is becoming more complex as IT use becomes more strategic, that formal evaluation procedures are often lacking, that identifying and quantifying costs and benefits remain major problems, and that evaluation practice leaves much room for improvement."[15]

IT brings qualitative and intangible benefits that are difficult to measure by traditional investment evaluation methods. Nevertheless, the many existing techniques for evaluating IT investments "are largely an outgrowth of traditional cost-benefit methodologies or are the application of standard accounting techniques to the problem." Objective analysis proceeds by categorizing all costs and applies cost-benefit analysis; subjective analysis, such as user attitude surveys, takes account of the change of computer tasks, e.g., from replacing clerical tasks to supporting decision-making. Evaluation techniques include return on investment (which has its own "formal investment appraisal techniques"), cost-benefit analysis, multi-objective/multi-criteria methods, boundary values, return on management, information economics, critical success factors, value analysis, experimental methods, and others. Evaluation can be improved by matching a particular IT investment with a particular evaluation technique.[16]

Why Must Colleges and Universities Invest in IT?

There are many business and pedagogical reasons for colleges and universities to invest in information technology. Competition is an important consideration. Higher education is now becoming part of "a knowledge and learning industry," in which competition forces every institution to rethink its products and markets.[17] Some believe that half of education beyond high school will soon be online.[18] Competition among institutions has always been a distinguishing feature of American higher education; networked and online learning radically alters the playing field and the stakes. IT exposes colleges and universities to competition across state, regional, and even national boundaries, and offers students unprecedented options to choose courses and programs. Institutions have used "remote site strategies" for a long time but teaching with advanced information technology makes going off campus much easier. As a result, the number of institutions offering distance educa-tion courses and programs has increased dramatically in the last few years.[19] Some try for a global reach; Stanford Online offers 250 courses in computer science and engineering to students around the world.[20] Moreover, competi-tion is no longer drawn solely from within higher education. The nation's 3,600 public and not-for-profit higher education institutions are now compet-ing with the offerings of proprietary and corporate universities. Some of these are long-established degree-granting institutions that are expanding, like DeVry Institute of Technology, which now has 18 campuses in the U.S. and Canada, not counting all its affiliates. Others are new, like the University of Phoenix, and may be divisions of newly emerging knowledge corporations.[21]

Corporate universities, defined as "a strategic umbrella for managing an organization's employee learning and development," date largely from the late 1980s when companies decided "they could no longer rely on institutions of higher education to re-tool their work force."[22] Some profess goals, including "fostering the development of intangible skills such as leadership, creative thinking, and problem solving," that are not unlike what we read in many undergraduate catalogs. Their emphasis on life-long learning and their inter-est in looking beyond internal employees as their target population bring them into direct competition with large segments of higher education. Some are accredited to offer graduate degrees. A 1996 survey involving 100 corporate universities indicated a student body of 4.5 million in those institutions alone. Corporate universities have grown from 400 in 1988 to 1,600 in 1998 and are expected to reach 2,000 in 2000. In 1980, full-time and part-time students in higher education represented 80 percent of the post-secondary market, in 1998, only 56 percent.[23]

Like corporate universities that have a long tradition of computer-based training, the new proprietary institutions, some regionally accredited, are aggressively exploiting new IT-enabled modes of delivering education, some-times eschewing traditional modes altogether. The learning content tradition-ally dispensed by higher education is becoming more readily available and the interested learner need not look to traditional sources. In a decade when the number of students seeking post-secondary education is to rise significantly, competition may not be of overwhelming concern. However, the current reality is that some educational services traditionally monopolized by higher education are being provided more conveniently and at lower cost by enter-prising upstarts.[24] While the service sector of the economy expands, more organizations are offering educational services, and when it comes to the lucrative services, higher education faces significant competition.

Also threatened is higher education's traditional monopoly in credentialing students with respect to their knowledge and competency. In a market overflowing with degree holders and an economy filled with rapidly changing technologies, degrees are often less important than competencies. Certification of special job-related skills is a growth market with increasing shares commanded by non-traditional post-secondary institutions, including professional and industry associations, national commissions, and regulatory boards.[25]

How Are Colleges and Universities Investing in IT?

Colleges and universities are investing increasingly large sums in IT and have at their disposal the requisite techniques for assessing investment in IT that economists have developed. Yet, such investments are generally not preceded, accompanied, or followed by systematic evaluation. The use of IT in its business processes as well as in networked and online learning seems to require every institution to commit to a permanent rise in the cost of doing business. Unfortunately, institutions often do not know precisely how much they are spending, because IT spending tends to be highly decentralized.[26] IT costs, especially involving the application of IT to teaching and learning, for example, the cost of time spent by instructors on developing educational materials, are often not immediately identified and vary considerably by department or program. Hence, the extensive search for the "hidden costs" of IT, especially among researchers in the UK.[27]

Most U.S. higher education institutions have seen IT expenditures rise significantly over the last five years, making such costs a larger component of the institutional budget.[28] Often this rise has been a jump in a given year, as the result of launching a major IT initiative, which has raised IT expenditures to a new and permanently higher level. The majority of the country's institutions may be described as financially constrained, meaning they have little discretionary money. For many of these, staying in the game is a challenge.

Even if institutions do not know the total amount they are spending on IT, many attempts[29] have been made to identify and categorize the different kinds of costs IT imposes on institutions. IT expenditures include the following:

- wiring buildings
- purchasing or leasing hardware, including desktop computers
- purchasing software and obtaining software licenses
- installing hardware and software
- replacing equipment periodically
- maintaining infrastructure
- maintaining networks
- repairing desktop computers
- servicing administrative information systems
- managing distribution of desktop computers
- assisting faculty and staff in the use of desktop computers (help desk)

- training university staff in new applications
- training faculty to apply IT in the curriculum
- developing and maintaining Web sites
- preparing course content for online delivery
- providing design and technical assistance for putting courses and programs online

Comparative data and benchmarks are needed to establish the cost of IT. The Costs project launched and coordinated at Colgate University and Hamilton College is an attempt to identify costs across 100 institutions and to give institutions the data for meaningful comparisons. The *Flashlight Cost Analysis Handbook* is designed to help institutions develop models to measure how the institution's IT enterprise uses such resources as money, space, and time.[30]

As conventional colleges and universities increasingly embrace networked and online learning, they add costs for developing and maintaining online materials, supporting students in online activities, and managing online programs. Greville Rumble of the British Open University, approaching this from the perspective of distance learning institutions, reminds us that "The biggest and . . . the least costed ingredient in the costs of on-line learning is the cost of supporting learners on-line." In the end, these costs might set severe limits to online learning or at least its cost-effectiveness.[31] Colleges and universities also have to consider the large opportunity costs they are incurring by investing in IT because these investments make it impossible to spend on other quality enhancements, such as reducing reliance on adjunct faculty.

How Are Institutions Paying for IT Investments?

The literature suggests many ways in which institutions have attempted to finance higher IT expenditures. The following list is not exhaustive:

- *Re-allocation of resources* appears at first sight to be the poor man's dismal choice, robbing Peter to pay Paul, and paying a high opportunity cost in the bargain. However, it is probably the only way for many institutions to join in the move towards networked and online learning. It also drives institutions to undertake the kind of restructuring and reorganizing that IT-based learning requires to make more autonomous and collaborative learning possible.[32]
- *Drawing on an endowment* is possible only if the endowment has enough funds free of expenditure restrictions. The spectacular performance of the stock market in recent years should help.
- *Capital drives* to secure IT funds from alumni and friends are shortsighted if intended to finance an IT launch, but eminently defensible if aimed at the creation of an IT endowment, like the endowments

institutions have created to provide for institutional financial aid to students.

- *Unpaid faculty labor* is an investment made by early technology converts to take advantage of IT's possibilities in teaching and learning. By all accounts, adopters have to make an enormous investment of time to make possible their own launch into IT-enhanced instruction, and voluntary adopters seem to be universally lavish in their commitment of time. (There must be a paragraph somewhere in *Das Kapital* that applies to these toilers!)

- *Higher student fees*, either direct or incorporated into tuition, may increase student costs by hundreds of dollars in public institutions and by thousands in selective independent institutions. Shifting the costs of IT to students, here and abroad, has raised the serious concern that some sectors of the population will not be able to participate fully in networked learning.

- *Cheap student labor* in the form of student technology assistants is often paid by federal work study funds. Sometimes students arrive on campus without any IT expertise and learn by doing in their first year. Incidentally, the quick training of students to be technology experts is a real teaching and learning success story in higher education!

- *Federal and state grant programs and state bond issues* provide one-time infusions of funds, usually to purchase necessary hardware. An example is a mid-1990s bond issue in New Jersey to equip 39 of the state's 50 higher education institutions with interactive television studios. This was a worthwhile initiative, although it ignored the problems of ongoing support and regular replacement costs. Also, before the facilities were ready, the shift toward Web-based teaching and learning called into question the usefulness of their technology.

- *Permanent higher annual allocations by state governments* can be made to public institutions specifically for IT needs. The arrival of IT in teaching and learning has major implications for higher education financial planning, budgeting, and funding.

- *Inter-institutional collaboration* allows the cost of technology and training to be shared. IT makes it possible to offer joint programs at reduced cost to all. Despite more than 200 examples of formally established consortia in the U.S. aimed at cooperative efforts, from shared transportation to joint degree programs, colleges generally prefer death in solitude to life in alliance with others. Yet, there are a few examples of institutions working together to share the burden of IT costs.[33]

Commercialization or the Rise of Academic Capitalism

Another approach to financing information technology expenditures in higher education has been through strategies traditionally associated with business. Since the 1980s, colleges and universities have been challenged to become more entrepreneurial, meaning to shed traditional ways and be enterprising and innovative in attracting students and resources. A diversified funding base and an entrepreneurial culture have been proclaimed as roads to institutional transformation and the "entrepreneurial university."[34] For the larger research universities, these tendencies have been described as "academic capitalism," defined as "Activities undertaken with a view to capitalizing on university research or academic expertise through contracts or grants with business or with government agencies seeking solutions to specific public or commercial concerns." In part, the quest for entrepreneurship has been an indigenous response of higher education to the global trend toward privatization.[35]

In times of shrinking public funds for higher education, institutions have been called upon to operate on a business model by applying accounting principles and aiming for cost control and maximum revenues. In search of revenues, colleges and universities vie with each other to serve the needs of business and industry, for example, by conducting research for business or by offering programs tailored to the needs of a particular organization. Technology transfer, from universities to the private sector, received governmental blessing when the Bay-Dole Act of 1980 made it possible for universities to own and manage patents resulting from faculty research funded by the federal government. The need for money has driven higher education in this direction. With the high costs of IT investments, many institutions see new needs for commercial ventures, on their own and in partnership with private companies.[36]

Colleges and universities are engaging in e-commerce, as the private sector has done already; they market their services electronically, which is probably no more than doing electronically what colleges and universities have done in other forms for decades.[37] Arrangements with vendors or manufacturers make it easier for colleges and universities to acquire and replace hardware and software. For example, alliances with IBM are assisting institutions in the purchase or lease of equipment in return for various institutional commitments. Private businesses develop IT capabilities for institutions unable or unwilling to do so on their own. Hundreds of institutions, public and independent, have by now contracted with commercial companies, like Campus Pipeline or YouthStream, to provide and maintain Web sites and to operate e-mail at no cost to the institutions. Advertising and commissions on purchases by students from businesses with links on the Web site will pay the costs. As a result, we have now Web pages for colleges and universities with electronic links to online and other retailers, e-mail to users that advertises products, businesses approaching athletic departments to develop pages on sports teams that will also contain messages for certain products, and colleges receiving commissions by using online businesses like Amazon.com.[38]

The high development and marketing costs of teaching software are leading institutions into joint ventures with publishing companies, and other companies provide the technical capability for online courses and programs. The suggestion has even been made that delivery of education should be left to organizations specializing in that business. Charging for access to digitized information "presents new commercial opportunities."[39] Venture capital from external sources is already helping finance major IT initiatives, especially in IT-enhanced distance education. Even well-endowed institutions, like Columbia and New York University, are seeking out venture capitalists for new programs delivered via the Internet. But venture capitalists may increasingly operate outside the existing public and not-for-profit institutions and create their own proprietary enterprises. The likelihood is that unendowed institutions may have no option but to enter into such bargains with business whereas wealthier institutions may be able to remain aloof. However, higher education is at least in part paying the cost of IT by opening doors to commerce in areas where it has not had a place in the past.

How Should Institutions Manage IT Expenditures?

As IT has entered colleges and universities in recent years, it has challenged traditional ways of managing and financing institutional expenditures. Given the prospect of permanently higher costs, institutions need to maximize their return on IT investment. Investing in IT means discarding assumptions and practices that have worked with other assets. The economics of IT are different. Colleges and universities have to know first what impact IT is having on the entire higher education sector. They then must decide what role IT is to have in their institution's mission and what level of IT use they are able and willing to sustain. Such decisions should proceed from a vision of the role an institution is to play in the higher education market over the next five or ten years. A vision will be expressed in a comprehensive institutional plan that spells out the institution's overall goals. Part of the plan should be a carefully developed technology strategy that will drive IT investments. IT must be managed as a strategic asset, not as something that assists a component of the institution here and there, but as an asset that is used by all units and individuals in support of the institution's education mission. A technology strategy will need its own special funding. Because the critical use of IT is now in teaching and learning, resources should probably be shifted from support of infrastructure and administration to supporting instructional uses. A technology strategy that does not envision a transformation of teaching and learning will only increase costs. This also means that the faculty and the institution's academic leadership will have a guiding role.[40]

Individual IT cost items have to be identified as well as the budgets that will pay for them. It must be clear what is being budgeted centrally and what through individual units, such as schools and departments. The accounting methods of activity-based costing and activity-based management provide techniques that are useful for managing the institutional costs of IT. Such techniques identify, measure, and assign all costs incurred in the production and sale of a product or service and are designed "to identify processes and products that add value and those that destroy value." The assumption behind measuring the cost of every product and process is that only in this way can unit costs be reduced, quality enhanced, and products and services redesigned or replaced, especially when IT budgets cannot keep up with expanded or new services.[41]

IT expenditures cannot be covered from year-end budget leftovers, as they have been historically at many institutions. Nor should IT be financed by periodic capital investments. Instead, IT expenditures must be treated as an operating expense. Managers must consider the life-cycles of equipment, i.e., the number of years one should keep hardware or software, and develop a life-cycle budget process that annualizes total technology costs. This need means that amortization in the case of IT should not follow the traditional practice, namely, to amortize for as long as possible. When we compare the costs of conventional teaching and IT-based teaching, we must include all overhead costs because they differ for the two kinds of teaching.[42]

Leasing allows for recycling old technology off campus rather than handing it down to less-favored sectors of the institution, and it assumes regular replacement and life-cycle budgeting. Outsourcing is one way of saving on IT costs, as it may be in other areas, such as bookstores, food services, financial services, and financial aid. Outsourcing can save up to 40 percent on per-computer support costs (the larger the institution, the lower per-computer and per-user support costs). Whether an institution should outsource and in precisely what area are decisions that should be preceded by a thorough cost-benefit analysis. Considerations will include flexibility of contracts and quality control. Whether to outsource support for IT-based courses will depend on how important IT-based teaching is to an institution. In-house capacity is advisable where technology-based teaching is central.[43] As students take advantage of getting parts of their education from different providers, areas that will have to be addressed include collecting tuition and fees, allocating costs to different providers, defining new cost categories, allocating financial aid, and designing new accounting and reporting systems.[44]

What Public Policies Are Needed to Finance IT?

Public support has not kept up with higher enrollments and higher costs per student. An increasingly smaller percentage of the cost of higher education in public (and independent) institutions is covered by public funds. In fact, the prospect now is one of "looming deficits" in higher education, and, according to the Commission on National Investment in Higher Education, millions of students might have to be excluded from higher education over the next 20 years. The answer, it has been suggested, is to re-allocate public resources to higher education and to develop strategic plans for allocating available funds to best meet educational needs. But greater support by government is likely contingent on institutional reforms, which include new governance structures that make possible re-allocation of resources, performance-based assessment, higher faculty productivity, financial accountability, sharpened institutional profiles, and sharing among institutions.[45] In light of this crisis, one wonders what governments can and will contribute to financing IT in higher education, which, as indicated, really means financing higher education at a higher level, not sporadically, but permanently.

IT is generating new forms of higher education as interactive learning systems replace direct instruction, distance loses its meaning, regional monopolies disappear, and colleges and universities are forced to be both more willing partners and more relentless competitors. These trends will demand a restructuring of higher education funding, budgeting, and financial planning. States will have to pool their efforts to develop new funding approaches, so that institutions invest in courses and programs that enhance productivity, use IT strategically to reduce costs and enhance quality, and work with each other in creating and using IT-mediated courses and programs. States will also have to reconsider restrictive residency policies and tuition differentials between residents and non-residents; deregulate and remove barriers to encourage competition, including from new private-sector providers; and base funding on learning outcomes rather than seat-time, but at the same time retain the ability to make system-wide investments in such areas as IT infrastructure or program development.[46]

What is the role of the federal government in managing the cost of IT in higher education? Higher education lacks anything like the e-rate of the 1996 Telecommunications Act to help rural and low-income communities connect to the Internet, representing an infusion of more than $2 billion a year. Nor is there anything like the Snowe-Rockefeller Amendment to the 1996 Telecommunications Act, which provides $4 billion in new money to connect every K-12 classroom in the country to the Internet by 2001. However, the federal government played a key role in the creation of the Internet. The original net was a research project connecting a few sites. NSF grant programs developed that project into the NSFNET, which connected most of higher education. In the last decade, the NSF has provided funds that, together with campus and other resources, assisted over 2,000 colleges and universities to connect to the Internet. Today, the federal government is a partner with industry and academic researchers in working towards the Next Generation Internet and some people are asking for a similar incentive program to bring advanced networking to every college and university.[47] In addition, over the last several decades, the federal government has enabled institutions, through various grants programs, to acquire IT equipment, especially in mathematics and the experimental sciences. It has financed faculty proposals to use IT in innovative ways in teaching and learning (the major flaw here being that such individual efforts usually are not extended to others and thus have done nothing to transform teaching and learning on a broad scale). Recently, the federal government, through special funds authorized by Congress for the National Center for Education Statistics, has begun to provide funds for assessing the cost of IT in higher education. The proposal has been made that the federal government should support IT cost studies through a special institute, or that the federal government should play an initial role in the commercial development of software to be used in high-enrollment basic courses.[48]

Is IT Saving Higher Education Any Money?

As a tentative conclusion to this section, it is fair to say that IT has been an instrument for reducing labor and for saving costs in some parts of higher education—certainly in such areas as administrative and business processes, library operations, and faculty research. For more than three decades, the key business processes of all institutions, such as student records, financial administration, and plant management, have relied on computers and are no longer conceivable otherwise. Computing as automation of business transactions has paid off. According to all accounts, computing and networks have produced greater efficiency in areas like purchasing. Matching classes and rooms, at one time a labor of weeks, can now be done in hours. New ways of saving money through IT are being discovered all the time. Some institutions no longer sell textbooks, which are less profitable than T-shirts and candy bars, through their bookstores, but leave that business to Internet vendors.[49]

IT is transforming our libraries and saving labor for institutions and readers through online catalogues, subscription to online journals, full-text online databases, document delivery by e-mail, or remote access for readers.[50] Additionally, IT has made possible the use of cost-saving strategies, such as sharing of resources with other institutions (e.g., library consortia sharing database subscriptions or cooperating in acquisition of library materials), outsourcing services, or restructuring functional areas. Electronic access to materials, instant communication among scholars, online journals, electronic publishing, or review of articles in traditional journals via the Internet are among the many ways in which IT is saving researchers time and labor and making their work more efficient. Research projects involving the collection and manipulation of large quantities of data are dependent on computers, and some of the truly massive undertakings, such as the Genome Project, would not be possible without the power of advanced information technologies.[51]

IT IN TEACHING AND LEARNING

Many of the changes IT has brought about and many of the problems encountered in higher education are shared by other organizations. The problem of cost in using IT for instruction is also not limited to higher education because other sectors of the economy, as well as other sectors in education, are making heavy use of IT in teaching and training. IT is one instructional technology among many others. Most learning is based on the use of some technology; even pencils and blackboards are tools and are therefore technology. Looking back over the last 40 years, we see that the dominant forms of instruction are the traditional classroom, using relatively simple technology, and distance education, using increasingly more sophisticated technologies. The big change most recently is the emergence of networked and online teaching and learning. Both classroom education and distance education are being transformed in the process. The more revolutionary impact, at least potentially, is on classroom teaching, which has been largely unchanged over decades, if not centuries. This change means that the impact is greatest on traditional colleges and universities. The impact is twofold: (1) classroom teaching is being enriched and transformed by the communications networks and the resources available through the World Wide Web, and (2) the relative ease and low cost of teaching courses or programs over the Internet are inducing many institutions to offer some distance education, usually a handful of courses or a few programs. This is distance education on a small scale. As a result, two cost questions arise: What happens to costs when IT is used in a traditional course? and What are the costs of distance education online if it is offered on a small scale?

Given the inertia of academic practice, and perhaps the proven value of the old ways, the traditional forms of instruction will not soon be gone. Yet, more than 90 percent of college and university instructors already use e-mail, and library use is being transformed by new ways of getting at information, which means that much of instruction is in some way being modified by IT right now. Colleges and universities have no choice but to embrace networked and online learning. Faculty see the possibilities for more effective teaching, and students the possibilities for more convenient and interesting learning. Both know of the expectations of the labor market. Institutions look for ways to differentiate themselves from others and gain a competitive advantage. In all this, there has been little experience of saving on costs; with IT investments, costs have gone up. On the other hand, networked and online teaching and learning already have yielded important benefits for students, such as easier access to learning resources, more program and course choices, and some possible cost saving, for example, by reducing travel. The most positive consequence of networked and online learning is that it is transforming teaching and learning and holds out the real possibility of increasing learning productivity, i.e., increasing learning outcomes while holding costs steady or reducing them (or maintaining current learning outcome levels while reducing costs). We have been told that "the potential for increased learning productivity through technology is too great for higher education to ignore."[52]

Cost Savings in Distance Education

IT has lowered the cost of teaching in some forms of distance education. The two principal forms of distance education that existed in the past—correspondence education (asynchronous) and remote-classroom education (synchronous)—relied for a long time on the technology of print and the postal system.[53] Between 1960 and 1990, other media appeared—the mass broadcast media, radio and television, and telecommunications links to remote classrooms (audio and video teleconferencing technology). The so-called personal media (audio cassette, video tape, personal computer) introduced new technologies, as did recent advances in telecommunications systems (telephone, fax, and computer networks). "The coming together of telecommunications, television and computing" has been called the knowledge media, denoting "the convergence of the learning and cognitive sciences with computing and telecommunications technology."[54]

The rationale for distance education has been to provide broader access to students, but it has always been understood that access had to come at reasonable cost. Access and cost remain the two big issues facing higher education globally. The U.S. met the greater demand for higher education after World War II by vastly increasing the number of conventional colleges and universities. While there was innovation, e.g., in the creation of the community colleges, teaching and learning practices remained the same. Thus an apparent abundance of resources in the U.S. eased the pressure to develop more cost-efficient forms of higher education. In developed countries, demand and supply have been in balance. Not so in the rest of the world, where fewer resources created greater pressure to find more cost-effective ways of bringing higher education to larger numbers. The dozen or so large distance universities around the world today offered a solution providing access to millions—3 million students in 11 mega-universities in 1996—at a fraction of the cost per student in traditional institutions. Greater access and lower cost were achieved through information technology, especially in the form of radio/television.[55]

Numerous studies over the last 20 years have shown that the large distance education systems enrolling more than 100,000 students, which have been called mega-universities, teach more cost-effectively than traditional universities. According to a 1991 review, a degree at the Open University cost only 50 percent of what it cost in conventional UK universities; only 10 percent at Turkey's large distance education system, Anadolu University; and only 5 percent at Korea's National Open University. On the other hand, Canada's Athabasca, offering online degrees to about 2,000 FTE's, produced unit costs in the same range as in traditional institutions. Smaller distance universities or distance programs did not show the cost-effectiveness of the large systems.[56]

Teaching in mega-universities has been compared to industrial production, whereas campus teaching resembles the working pattern of a craftsman. Distance education in the correspondence tradition, using such technologies as radio, television, and personal media, is usually education on an industrial model. This model involved isolating and separating the different functions of the teaching process, let's call them design and delivery, explication and evaluation, and assigning them to different instructors or teams of instructors and other academic support persons.[57] In the traditional model, all these functions are most of the time performed by one instructor.

This arrangement made it possible to teach large classes, often enrolling thousands of students. Even with high design and delivery costs, particularly if television or radio is the medium, costs per student are smaller, given those large enrollments per class. Note that this teaching model implies the use of relatively few full-time academic staff joined by an army of adjuncts. In the Open University, where design and delivery have been of high quality and explication and evaluation are supported by thousands of trained part-time tutors, the ratio of full-time to part-time academic staff in the mid-1990s was 1 to 9.[58] Cost savings in some of the mega-universities have been achieved by limiting teaching and learning support, a fact that probably accounted for enormous non-completion rates in some institutions.

Unit costs diminish after "the necessary level of aggregation" is reached. In other words, distance education costs less than classroom teaching when we are dealing with a large number of students taking a particular course. In this kind of education, the ratio of fixed costs to variable costs is higher than in classroom instruction. For example, in the 1990s that ratio in Great Britain's Open University was 2000:1, whereas in traditional universities it was 8:1.[59] Therefore, the most cost-effective distance learning institutions have been the dozen or so mega-universities, with their students numbering 100,000 or more. In any case, the large distance learning systems developed in the last 40 years demonstrate that transforming the technology employed in teaching and learning can yield greater cost-effectiveness.

IT and Productivity in Classroom Teaching

The high cost of higher education for students and society has led many to look to IT as a means of making college and university teaching less expensive. Governments in particular want IT to "reconcile the paradox of exploding demand and constrained resources."[60] More cautiously, the argument has been made that IT will not shrink budgets but will help avoid additional costs. One underlying assumption seems to be that the projected growth in the U.S. over the next 12 years in the number of students in higher education, both traditional college-age students and adult learners, from 15 to 20 million, cannot be met by teaching the old way and paying for it as before.

We know that IT increases *individual* productivity for students, faculty, and administrators.[61] While economists continue to debate the point, it seems reasonable to believe that IT reduces, or has the potential to reduce, the non-instructional expenses of an institution, thus increasing *institutional* or *administrative* productivity. While *instructional* productivity may be another matter, IT clearly offers the possibility of breaking away from higher education's handicraft tradition. The least efficient (although for many probably one of the most personally stimulating) features of college teaching is the preparation of almost every class and every course by the individual instructor. IT can improve the production processes and the economics of higher education if it becomes a substitute for faculty labor. Where faculty labor is replaced by IT, the capital-labor ratio for instruction is increased, making teaching and learning more capital-intensive. Because of the large costs of IT, faculty costs then become a smaller percentage of total costs, even when the size of the faculty remains the same. This trend can ultimately lead to cost savings; even if total costs for instruction remain the same, a long-term gain results because labor costs rise faster than technology costs.[62]

The irony in attempting to substitute IT for faculty labor as a long-term cost-saving strategy is that more than half of institutional IT costs are actually personnel costs. Thus, to a large extent, we are really replacing faculty not by capital, but by IT professionals. Furthermore, many of these professionals actually command higher salaries than do faculty (although, of course, they don't have tenure). This replacement is not an argument against using IT but against expecting significant cost savings from IT. On the other hand, IT is providing employment opportunities for IT specialists who often have the same disciplinary training as faculty.

The primary effect of IT-enhanced teaching, whether in the traditional classroom or in distance education on the small scale, has been to *increase* the demand for faculty labor. It takes more faculty time (ignoring for a moment the time of designers and technicians), to prepare and deliver an IT-enhanced course. It could not be a cost-saving strategy for a course designed by and only for the individual instructor to be put online or into some sort of IT-enhanced format. If this is worth doing, then it must be for other reasons, such as to make teaching and learning more effective.

Faculty interest in productivity has traditionally meant productivity in research.[63] Although true of many institutions (the point is made on the basis of a survey of 19 research institutions), it could not be true for the majority of the nation's half million faculty members, most of them teaching in institutions where research is not the primary mission. A recent national survey showed that two-fifths of full-time faculty in the U.S. were not currently publishing and the majority outside research universities had not published in the last two years.[64] It is probably reasonable to assume that for most faculty the cost of instruction is an important concern but not as critical as the quality of learning. Making faculty teach more students along established lines, often the idea of administrators when they talk about raising faculty productivity, is an increase in labor (total faculty person hours) not in productivity (unit costs per hour of faculty labor). Increases in productivity are gained mainly by using new technology.

Hundreds of studies done over the last 70 years indicate "no significant difference" in learning outcomes between traditional classroom learning and learning through information technology.[65] Because these studies are typically based on small samples,[66] some argue that their results are largely inconclusive.[67] Moreover, studies on the impact of IT on learning have relied mainly on objective measures, such as test scores and grades, and not on subjective measures, such as student perceptions and preferences; they appear to equate education with information transfer and ignore the human factor. Carol Frances, an editor of this volume, argues that the human factor may be "the most important part of education because it can inspire students to higher achievement and help them make ethical choices."[68]

Using IT in High-Enrollment Courses

Leaders in the IT community have argued for several years that the most cost-effective instructional use of IT may be in certain kinds of high-enrollment introductory courses. In 1996, the Broadmoor Roundtable proposed that a mass market for commercially produced software exists in the relatively small number of introductory courses that usually constitute a large percentage of total credits taken (the extreme example is 1 percent of courses generating 50 percent of total student enrollments).[69] The pedagogical value of the lecture model that is often used in such classes—a lecture presented by a professor and break-out sessions managed by graduate students—seems to be especially dubious; the usual alternative—a large number of small sections—is especially costly. Today the emphasis in redesigning such courses for IT use is on improving the quality of teaching and learning. However, the potential for cost savings had been a consideration initially and remains important. The argument is that these foundation courses, often no more than two dozen or so, account for a large percentage of total enrollments, and that their content—basic information in a field or fundamental skills—is delivered much more effectively via courseware that allows for student involvement in learning, collaboration, individual exploration, and timely feedback. Individualized teaching and learning made possible by IT overcomes the disregard for learning differences, perhaps the single greatest flaw of the lecture method.

To develop a planning methodology and support redesigning high enrollment courses in selected institutions is the aim of the Pew Charitable Trusts Grant Program in Course Design, led by Carol Twigg. Rensellaer Polytechnic Institute has probably the longest history of redesigning basic courses through the development of its "Studio" courses, which reduce lecturing and rely on interactive courseware and collaborative learning. Other institutions that are redesigning courses under the Pew Grant Program are the University of Wisconsin at Madison, the University of Illinois at Urbana-Champaign, Rio Salado College of the Maricopa Community College District [Arizona], and Virginia Tech.[70] All these institutions report substantial reductions in per-student costs. Cost savings are achieved by reducing faculty time on task and replacing faculty by relying on information technology. The model developed under this program uses activity-based costing in comparing traditional and IT courses and calculating cost differences. Determining instructional time devoted to every kind of activity in development and delivery allows one to identify "cost factors that can be altered." The planning model proposed compares operational costs of the traditional course and an IT version; it excludes developmental costs, costs of institution-wide support services, administrative overhead, and the cost of IT infrastructure, which raises questions regarding the validity of this comparison.

The strategy described here raises the possibility of improving teaching and learning in certain kinds of introductory courses as well as the likelihood of significant savings on instructional costs. Admittedly, this strategy addresses a part of the undergraduate curriculum which in the past has been taught in a relatively cost-efficient manner (although not necessarily well) and leaves out a large segment of higher education, including the teaching of upper-level undergraduate and graduate courses. But the plan is, in fact, a promising avenue for both saving costs and improving quality. More self-directed learning and greater reliance on teaching tools and resources made available through computers and networks are going to be part of learning, especially in colleges and universities. Nevertheless, it is probably unwise to raise expectations too high. The effort reminds one a little of the earlier stages of the IT revolution when mechanical and clerical tasks were taken over by computers. This takeover made it possible to do large amounts of repetitive tasks in less time and with fewer people and therefore to work more efficiently. Higher education participated in that stage, and in its business processes probably has achieved the greater efficiencies and cost savings that IT makes possible. Now business appears to take such greater efficiency for granted, and its interest today is less in computers and networks making for higher productivity but as instruments of strategy and means for finding new business opportunities. IT in the form of networked and online learning is primarily about revolutionizing learning, not about savings costs.

Traditional teaching with its emphasis on information delivery and examinations based on memorizing and replicating information is "reproduction technology," which is centuries old. Automating that kind of teaching may do more harm than good. IT can, however, help invent "new kinds of information, knowledge, and truth." It demands a new pedagogy (and perhaps new kinds of professors and universities). It leads to new learning that lets students acquire new skills as workers and citizens.[71]

Impact of IT on Students

A wholesome and probably unanticipated consequence of computer-mediated and networked learning has been its positive effect on college-level teaching and learning. Using IT in college courses presupposes and re-enforces learning behaviors for which teachers in colleges and universities have asked for a long time, such as students being more involved and more autonomous in learning, working with other learners, acquiring the skills and habits of life-long learning, not just taking in information but also developing reasoning and judgment.[72] Computer applications can serve as cognitive tools, rather than just as media of instruction; they can be vehicles for constructing knowledge, and thus develop critical thinking and higher order learning skills.[73] Additionally, IT facilitates convenient access to the instructor, to fellow learners, and to vast quantities of information. As a result, learning can be more efficient and students have more time. Their individual learning styles and problems can receive more attention; their different capacities for learning can be better accommodated. In the case of students of traditional college age, one major challenge remains: Are students sufficiently motivated to take advantage of the greater control over their own learning that IT provides? If so, students could avail themselves of the many choices increasingly at their disposal through the Internet. In the future, more students will be able to build their own programs and obtain its various components from different providers. Students will also be able to choose different modes of learning. Greater learning productivity, more so than lower teaching cost, is the great promise of information technology. For this promise to be fulfilled, students must be willing to make the greater personal effort and psychological investment that more active, autonomous, and collaborative learning demands.

Each generation of students entering college is more accustomed to living, working, and learning in a digital world. As a consequence, colleges and universities must take full advantage of IT in teaching and learning. Yet students are not always supportive of initiatives that integrate IT into instruction, especially if they mean less contact with faculty or make students do more work on their own. There is also the sense that an IT-based education, which is more expensive than the traditional version, is not what students expect. Furthermore, issues of students' rights emerge as their own contributions and communications in the learning process appear on the Internet.

As far as costs are concerned, students have been both winners and losers. Winners because IT makes it so much easier to learn as a result of easier access to libraries and other depositaries of information, to teachers, to peers, and to teaching tools. So many chores in learning, like getting at information, drafting papers, obtaining feedback, are faster and make learning more efficient. Students have been losers in the sense that they have borne a large portion of the new costs IT has meant for higher education. They are paying at least a part—and in independent institutions usually a large part—of growing IT budgets and in addition may be responsible for such expenses as technology fees, purchase or lease of laptops, or access to the Internet. We have no aggregate data telling us how much IT is adding to students' costs. But we know that on average college costs are a greater burden on families. Since 1980-81, college prices adjusted for inflation on average have gone up by 110 percent while average family income rose by 22 percent. There are various reasons for these rising costs to students, but larger expenditures for IT are surely among them.[74] To what extent those added costs contribute to diminished college affordability and to what extent any such contributions are offset by learning benefits remains to be seen.

Information Technology and Faculty Roles

Using information technology can make for better teaching in colleges and universities. What it does precisely has been reported in the pages of *Change* magazine and other publications over the last 10 years, often in the form of confessions by reluctant converts.[75] The following is how five college teachers who kept journals for a semester summed up their experience teaching with laptop computers:

> Teaching with IT is often frustrating. It requires a great deal more preparation than conventional classes. It is dependent on a lot of support. It is often not recognized and rewarded. Classes must be meticulously planned and carefully managed. Assessing what students

have learned is so much easier. The instructor takes on a different role, less omniscient and directive, more that of a fellow learner. The teacher is more exposed, more personally involved, less detached from the student. The student is more engaged, knows better what learning means. Contact between teacher and student is more frequent. There is more sharing among students. There are negatives: technology gets in the way, students produce slick papers from Internet sources, e-mail messages are superficial, and e-mail becomes an excuse for not meeting face to face. Fundamentally we must re-think from the bottom up what learning means for students and what teaching means for us.[76]

To us, one of the most promising consequences of using IT in college teaching seems to be this: There has been a great amount of research in the last decades on student learning and pedagogy, but faculty traditionally have been little interested in the teaching/learning process and in applying the findings of research and successful practice.[77] Only a small fraction of what has been learned has found its way into day-to-day classroom instruction. When teaching and learning with IT, one cannot help but rethink how to teach and how students learn. Thus, IT is building a bridge between research and application, theory and practice.

As IT introduces competing ways to gain information, to practice skills, or to receive learning assistance and tutoring, it takes away from the ancient role of the professor as the foremost source of knowledge, the medieval necessity barely changed in six centuries of print. Faculty continue to be the major producers of new knowledge, and they continue their iron control of the college curriculum. But if software produced commercially or developed by faculty teams plays a greater role in college teaching, control over course content by the faculty member using such products will be reduced. The multiple functions of the teacher in the classroom—being the expert on the subject, determining class content, delivering the course, monitoring what students learn, assessing student progress, certifying what learning has occurred—in the future may often be separated and recombined in new ways, as in distance education offered by the Open University and similar institutions around the globe. Preparing courses not so much individually as collaboratively, especially through project teams, is a more efficient and effective way for faculty to develop courses that make extensive use of information technology.[78] Thus IT is likely to change faculty work.

IT may direct faculty towards activities that play to faculty talents and interests beyond the presentation of information, such as explicating, critiquing, monitoring, and guiding. Moreover, IT may offer faculty opportunities for entrepreneurship, new careers, and new earning sources.[79] The channeling of faculty energies into the production of learning materials may signal a more fundamental change in the relationship to their employers. Heretofore, faculty members have been hired, and have functioned, as providers of a service—teaching courses—and they have been compensated per unit of service or for a given number of units. When faculty begin to create products that can be sold in the marketplace, they are in effect becoming much more independent entrepreneurs, one of whose customers is one's nominal employer. The debate sparked by the professor selling "his" course to another university without his home institution's knowledge or permission may be an isolated curiosity today. But it may indicate where a fundamental re-thinking and restructuring of the relationships of entrepreneurial college faculty to their nominal employers might lead.

Nevertheless, there is fear that IT is moving colleges and universities in a direction where faculty will have less control over their working arrangements, may lose the products of their knowledge and skills, and may be replaced by less qualified personnel—the traditional full-time faculty member may be on the road to extinction. Such fears have been nourished as universities, especially in their extension programs, have created private subsidiaries, often in conjunction with private corporations, to offer online courses and programs, and in the process have asserted exclusive rights to such intellectual products. The faculty at Canada's York University engaged in a two-month strike and secured as a result control and veto power in decisions on the automation of instruction. Copyright and intellectual property rights have become key issues for faculty.[80]

Faculty and national organizations representing them are concerned that greater reliance on information technology in teaching and learning may diminish the use of full-time faculty, threaten tenure, and reduce the economic position of the professoriate.[81] We know that tenure has been questioned for decades, that institutions often prefer to employ faculty on term contracts, and that today over 40 percent of faculty are part-time.[82] These matters predate networked teaching and learning. The massive expansion of higher education since World War II has been sustained to some degree by reliance on low-cost adjunct labor. Except in the case of virtual and proprietary institutions, we do not see indications that IT is replacing full-time faculty with adjuncts. However, in the case of distance education systems like the UK's Open University, instructional costs are lower not just because IT is partially replacing faculty but because part-time tutors are used instead of full-time faculty. In the U.S., over the 20 years from 1975 to 1995, growth in student enrollment has been exceeded by growth in full-time faculty. Even if IT replaces faculty labor to some extent, this trend should not reduce total faculty numbers as long as the higher education market continues to expand as has been projected for the next decade.[83]

Copyright and Intellectual Property

Existing copyright law does not deal with all issues raised by the use of IT in instruction. Additionally, the easy access to and transferral of materials on the Web lead to students and faculty ignoring copyright law on a large scale. Both groups have traditionally supported a liberal interpretation of the principles of "fair use" and "use for educational purposes." Institutions also seemed sympathetic to that point of view, which was easy because the cost of producing such learning materials as books was borne by publishers. The use of IT in teaching and learning is turning both instructors and institutions into producers of learning materials. The issue of copyright comes up again as such products use copyrighted materials from elsewhere. Besides, the creators of these new products, whose use may not be limited to the campus of origin, themselves now seek the protection of their intellectual property. Institutions must make sure they have the expertise to deal with issues of copyright.[84]

Faculty involvement in the production of learning materials for IT-enhanced courses or courses delivered entirely through IT (or, perhaps, in the preparation of courses enhanced by IT or delivered entirely by IT) raises directly the issues of compensation for such work and of ownership of the products. An institution that is truly serious about using IT will look upon such activity as part of the faculty member's work, replacing some other obligations, rather than as an add-on. While faculty play a key role in the production of such courses, they also need the institution's help in the form of instructional design and technical support. Does the participating faculty member or the sponsoring institution own the course? Who owns IT products? Institutions should have clear internal guidelines on the ownership of such materials. However, the proposal has been made that universities should not so much develop special rules for IT products but policies for all intellectual property, proceeding from the principle that a *substantial* and *specific* contribution of the institution—financial, intellectual, or reputational—entitles it to a share in profits and control of use.[85]

This review of the major issues that have been discussed in the literature leaves us with many questions that the use of information technology, especially in its latest forms, raises for college teaching and learning and for all higher education. How higher education reacts to the challenge of information technology will determine the cost consequences. Some consequences already stand out: Many institutions will have a hard time taking advantage of information technology and its considerable benefits. Public moneys will hardly be forthcoming in sufficient amounts to adequately finance the information technology needs of public institutions. A larger share of the postsecondary market will be taken over by new competitors. U.S. higher education shows no signs of going the route of business and achieving higher efficiencies through mergers and downsizing of personnel, meaning, in particular, the million faculty members. These are the questions the editors and contributors of this volume consider most in need of further exploration. While this is more in the nature of a research agenda, from it one can also derive an action agenda.

Higher education is fortunate in the timing of its most recent and perhaps largest challenge. Information technology is transforming college teaching and learning at a time of an exceptionally strong economy and general prosperity. Equally important, higher education is entering a decade during which the number of students in the system is projected to rise from 15 to 20 million. This will accentuate the need for information technology in college teaching and learning, but, for many institutions, it will also ensure the resources to take advantage of this singular instrument and its awesome potential.

ENDNOTES

1. John Thorpe, "Computing the Payoff from IT," *The Journal of Business Strategy* 20, 2 (May-June 1999): 35-39; Michael Schrage, "The Real Problems with Computers," *Harvard Business Review* 75, 5 (September-October 1997): 178, 183-84; Paul A. Strassmann, *Squandered Computer: Evaluating the Business Alignment of Information Technologies.* New Canaan, CT: The Information Economics Press, 1997.

2. Jeff Madrick, "How New Is the New Economy?" *New York Review of Books* 46, 14 (September 23, 1999): 42-50 and see p. 49 for the report of the Department of Commerce. Stephen S. Roach, "Working Better or Just Harder," *The New York Times*, February 14, 2000, p. A21, believes that work time is understated and productivity overstated. A more optimistic view of the new economy is William A. Sahlman, "The New Economy Is Stronger than You Think," *Harvard Business Review* 77, 6 (November-December 1999): 99-106.

3. "Greenspan Now Positive on Prospects of Economy," *The New York Times*, September 9, 1999, p. C8.

4. IT development is divided into these four phases in D. Moschella, *Waves of Power: Dynamics of Global Technology Leadership 1964-2010.* New York: Anacom, 1997. This reference is from Leslie P. Willcocks and Stephanie Lester, eds., *Beyond the IT Productivity Paradox.* Wiley Series in Information Systems. New York: John Wiley and Sons, 1999, p. 12. Paul M. Horn, "Information Technology Will Change Everything," *Research Technology Management* 42, 1 (January-February 1999): 42-57.

5. Peter Weill and Marianne Broadbent, "Four Views of Information Technology Infrastructure: Implications for Information Technology Investments," in Willcocks and Lester, *Beyond the IT Productivity Paradox*, pp. 338-40.

6. Leslie P. Willcocks and Stephanie Lester, "In Search of Information Technology Productivity: Assessment Issues," in Willcocks and Lester, *Beyond the IT Productivity Paradox*, pp. 81, 89.

7. Willcocks and Lester, "Information Technology: Transformer or Sinkhole?," in Willcocks and Lester, *Beyond the IT Productivity Paradox*, pp. 1-12. Each of the 13 chapters in this book has an extensive bibliography.

8. Paul A. Strassmann, "Credit Greenspan, Not Computers," *Computerworld* 33, 23 (June 7, 1999).

9. M.C. Augustus van Nievelt, "Benchmarking Organizational and Information Technology Performance," in Willcocks and Lester, *Beyond the IT Productivity Paradox*, pp.100-02; Willcocks and Lester, "In Search of Information Technology Productivity: Assessment Issues," in Willcocks and Lester, *Beyond the IT Productivity Paradox*, pp. 72-77, 93.

10. Daniel E. Sichel, "Computers and Aggregate Economic Growth: An Update," *Business Economics* 34, 2 (April 1999): 18-24, suggests that business may finally be reaping the benefits of IT.

11. N. Venkatraman, "Managing Information Technology Resources as a Value Centre: The Leadership Challenge," in Willcocks and Lester, *Beyond the IT Productivity Paradox*, pp. 217-44; John Thorpe, "Computing the Payoff from IT," *The Journal of Business Strategy* 20, 2 (May-June 1999): 35-39.

12. Philip L. Powell, "Evaluation of Information Technology Investments: Business as Usual?" in Willcocks and Lester, *Beyond the IT Productivity Paradox*, pp. 152, 177.

13. Powell, "Evaluation of Information Technology Investments," in Willcocks and Lester, *Beyond the IT Productivity Paradox*, pp. 153, 166, 171, 172, 176.

14. Leslie P. Willcocks, Guy Fitzgerald, and Mary Lacity, "To Outsource IT or Not? Research on Economics and Evaluation Practice," in Willcocks and Lester, *Beyond the IT Productivity Paradox*, pp. 293-333 and see pp. 316-17 on benchmarking; Janne Ropponen, "Risk Assessment and Management Practices in Software Development," in Willcocks and Lester, *Beyond the IT Productivity Paradox*, pp. 250-53.

15. Joan A. Ballantine, Robert D. Galliers, Stephanie J. Stray, "Information Systems/Technology Evaluation Practices: Evidence from UK Organisations," in Willcocks and Lester, *Beyond the IT Productivity Paradox*, pp. 123-49.

16. Barbara Farbey, Frank Land, David Target, "Evaluating Investments in IT: Findings and a Framework," in Willcocks and Lester, *Beyond the IT Productivity Paradox*, pp. 154, 157, 184-92; Powell, "Evaluation of Information Technology Investments," in Willcocks and Lester, *Beyond the IT Productivity Paradox*, pp. 154-59.

17. James J. Duderstadt, "Can Colleges and Universities Survive in the Information Age?" in Richard N. Katz and Associates, *Dancing with the Devil: Information Technology and the New Competition in Higher Education*. San Francisco: Jossey-Bass, 1999, pp. 1-25, especially pp. 10-11.

18. Jeanne C. Meister, *Corporate Universities: Lessons in Building a World-Class Work Force*. rev. ed. New York: McGraw Hill, 1998, p. xi.

19. Between 1993/94 and 1997/98, distance learning courses and enrollments doubled; the percentage of institutions offering distance education increased by one-third; the percentage of students in higher education institutions using Internet-based technologies went from 22 to 60 percent. L. Lewis et al., *Distance Education at Postsecondary Institutions: 1997-98*. NCES 2000-13. Washington, DC, 1999. See also <http://nces.ed.gov>.

20. Andy DiPaolo, "Stanford Learning: Worldwide Availability On-Demand at Stanford Online," *T.H.E. Journal* 27, 5 (December 1999): 16.

21. Gordon C. Winston, "For-Profit Higher Education," *Change* 31, 1 (January-February 1999): 12-19; Barbara Goldberg [New Jersey DeVry], "For-Profit Education: A Challenge to Twenty-First Century Higher Education," unpublished paper, 35 pages. Contact author at <DBJRGold@aol.com>.

22. Meister, *Corporate Universities*, p. ix.

23. Jeanne C. Meister, "How the Corporate University Model Works," *AAHE Bulletin* 51, 3 (November 1998):6-9; Meister, *Corporate Universities*, pp. xi, 207, 208. "The entrance of the private sector into the learning business is placing severe pressure for transformation on America's 3,632 institutions of higher education. These institutions need to reinvent themselves for the knowledge economy. This re-invention involves both updating the content as well as altering the delivery system." See especially her chapter "Corporate Universities: Opportunities or Threat to Higher Education," pp. 207-32.

24. Ted Marchese, "Not-So-Distant Competitors: How New Providers Are Remaking the Postsecondary Marketplace," *AAHE Bulletin* (May 1998). See also <http://www.aahe.org/Bulletin>.

25. Alice J. Irby, "Postbaccalaureate Certificates: Higher Education's Growth Market," *Change* 31, 2 (March-April 1999): 36-43.

26. Kenneth C. Green and Robin Jenkins, "IT Financial Planning 101: Developing an Institutional Strategy for Financing Technology, "NACUBO *Business Officer* 31, 9 (March 1998): 32-37.

27. Martin Oliver, Grainne Conole, Lisa Bonetti, "The Hidden Costs of Change: Evaluating the Impact of Moving to On-Line Delivery," at <http://www.shu.ac.uk/flish/oliverp.htm>.

28. Data from the Colgate-Hamilton Cost Project suggest that institutional investment in IT per year has doubled or tripled over the last few years to nearly 8 percent on average

29. Greville Rumble, *The Costs and Economics of Open and Distance Learning*. London: Kogan Page Limited, 1997, pp. 13-73; A.W. Bates, *Managing Technological Change*. San Francisco: Jossey-Bass, 1999, pp. 122-52. For the kinds of costs to be considered in support services, see Karen Leach and David Smallen, "What Do Information Technology Support Services Really Cost?" *CAUSE/EFFECT* 21, 2 (1998): 38-45. The kinds of costs found more specifically when using IT in instruction are considered, e.g., in Frank A. Schmidtlein, "A Framework for Examining the Cost of Instructional Technology." Paper presented at National Institute for Academic Degrees, Yokohama City, Japan, July 24, 1998; by the same author "Assessing the Costs of Instructional Technology." Paper presented at the 39th Annual AIR Forum, Seattle Washington, June 2, 1999; also Carol Frances and Richard Pumerantz, "Costs of Instructional Technology in Higher Education." Paper presented at the Conference of the Congress of Political Economists, Barbados, July 15, 1998. For details, see the "Resources" section of this book.

30. The Flashlight Project is a program of the TLT Group, the Teaching, Learning, and Technology Affiliate of the AAHE, directed by Stephen C. Ehrmann. See <http://www.tltgroup.org/programs/flashlight.html>.

31. Greville Rumble, "The Costs of Networked Learning: What Have We Learnt," at <http://www.shu.ac.uk/flish/rumblep.htm>.

32. A.W. Bates, *Managing Technological Change*. San Francisco: Jossey-Bass, 1999, pp. 157–61.

33. Bates, *Managing Technological Change*, pp.163-80.

34. B.R. Clark, *Creating Entrepreneurial Universities: Organizational Pathways of Transformation*. New York: Elsevier Science, 1998, examines "pathways of transformation" in five European universities.

35. Sheila Slaughter and Larry L. Leslie. *Academic Capitalism: Politics, Policies, and the Entrepreneurial University*. Baltimore: Johns Hopkins University Press, 1997, p. 217.

36. Peggie J. Hollingworth, "Technology Transfer in Higher Education," *American Scientist*, 87, 6 (November-December 1999): 482; Stanley Aronowitz, "The New Corporate University: Higher Education Becomes Higher Training," *Dollars and Sense* 216 (March-April 1998): 32-35; Diana G. Oblinger, "High Tech Takes the High Road: New Players in Higher Education," *The Educational Record* 78, 1 (Winter 1997): 3-37. Also, Eyal Press and Jennifer Washburn, "The Kept University," *The Atlantic Monthly* 285, 3 (March 2000): 39-54. The theme here is that "Commercially sponsored research is putting at risk the paramount value of higher education—disinterested inquiry. Even more alarming . . . . universities themselves are behaving more and more like for-profit companies."

37. Donald M. Morris and Mark Olson, *E-Business in Education: What You Need to Know*. Washington, DC: NACUBO 1999.

38. Lisa Guernsey, "Welcome to College. Now Meet Our Sponsor," *The New York Times*, August 17, 1999, pp. A1, C6.

39. Diana G. Oblinger, "High Tech Takes the High Road: New Players in Higher Education," *The Educational* Record 78, 1 (Winter 1997): 30–37.

40. J. Oberlin, "The Financial Mythology of Information Technology: The New Economics," *CAUSE/EFFECT* 19, 1 (Spring 1996): 21-29; J. Oberlin, "The Financial Mythology of Information Technology: Developing a New Game Plan," *CAUSE/EFFECT* 19, 2 (Summer 1996): 10-17; Paul J. Kobulnicky, "Critical Factors in Information Technology Planning for the Academy," *CAUSE/EFFECT* 22, 2 (1999); Sir John Daniel, *Mega-Universities and Knowledge Media: Technology Strategies for Higher Education*. London: Kogan Page Ltd., 1998, pp. 136-49; Schmidtlein, "Assessing the Costs of Instructional Technology," 1999.

41. "Activity-Based Costing is a costing model that identifies the cost pools, or activity centers, in an organization and assigns costs to products and services (cost drivers) based on the number of events or transactions involved in the process of providing a product or service," according to J. Chutchian-Ferranti, "Activity-Based Costing," *Computerworld* 33, 32 (August 9, 1999): 54; for Activity-Based Costing, see also Rumble, *The Costs and Economics of Open and Distance Learning*, pp. 55-64. See also Christopher S. Peebles and Laurie Antolovic, "Cost (and Quality and Value) of Information Technology Support in Large Universities," *Educom Review* 34, 5 (September-October 1999). See also <http://www.educause.edu/ir/library/html/erm9955.html>.

42. William Graves, "Developing and Using Technology as a Strategic Asset, in Katz and Associates, *Dancing with the Devil*, p. 95; Green and Jenkins, "IT Financial Planning 101," pp. 32-37.

43. Bates, *Managing Technological Change*, pp. 146-48.

44. "Technology and Its Ramifications for Data Systems." Report of the Policy Panel on Technology co-sponsored by the National Postsecondary Educational Cooperative and the George Washington University, August 4-5, 1997 [issued in August 1998]; a summary can be found in *CAUSE/EFFECT* 22, 2 (1999). See also <http://www.educause.edu/ir/library/html/cem9921.html>.

45. *Breaking the Social Contract: The Fiscal Crisis in Higher Education.* Report of the Commission on National Investment in Higher Education. New York: Council for Aid to Education 1997. See also <http://www.cae.org/>. For a summary, see Roger Benjamin, "Looming Deficits," *Change* 30, 2 (March-April 1998): 12-17.

46. Dewayne Matthews, "The Transformation of Higher Education through Information Technology: Implications for State Higher Education Finance Policy." Western Interstate Commission for Higher Education (January 26, 1998). See also <http://www.wiche.edu/IT&Finance.htm>. Also in *Educom Review* 33, 5 (September-October 1998): 48-57. See also <http://www.educause.edu/ir/library/html/erm9854.html>.

47. George O. Strawn and David A. Staudt, "Toward a National Policy to Broaden Academic Participation in Advanced Networking," in Mark A. Luker, ed., *Preparing Your Campus for a Networked Future.* Educause Leadership Strategies 1. San Francisco: Jossey-Bass, 1999, pp. 71-80.

48. Schmidtlein, "A Framework for Examining the Costs of Instructional Technology," p. 14; Carol Twigg, "Academic Productivity: The Case for Instructional Software." A Report from the Broadmore Roundtable, Colorado Springs, Colorado, July 24-25, 1996. See also <http://www.educause.edu/nlii.keydocs/broadmoor.html>.

49. Lisa Guernsey, "Bookseller Is Ready to Offer Textbooks On Line" and "Buy the Book: On Line Stores Vie for Students," *The New York Times,* July 5 and August 26, 1999.

50. Paul Chao, Associate Dean of Libraries, Seton Hall University, provided a useful perspective. Clifford A. Lynch, "The Academic Library in the Information Age," in Luker, *Preparing Your Campus for a Networked Future,* pp. 15-28; Suzanne E. Thorin and Virginia D. Sorkin, "The Library of the Future," in Oblinger and Rush, *The Learning Revolution,* pp. 164-79.

51. See Peebles et al., Modeling and Managing," pp. 50-53 on the value of information technology.

52. W.F. Massy and R. Zemsky, "Using Information Technology to Enhance Academic Productivity." Paper sponsored by NLII, Wingspread Conference on Enhancing Academic Productivity, June 1995. An NLII Monograph published by EDUCAUSE. See also <http://www.educause.edu/nlii/keydocs/massy.html>.

53. Sir John Daniel, *Mega-Universities and Knowledge Media: Technology Strategies for Higher Education.* London: Kogan Page Ltd., 1998, pp. 47–56.

54. Daniel, *Mega-Universities,* p. 55.

55. Daniel, *Mega-Universities,* pp. 8, 39-40.

56. See the table in Daniel, *Mega-Universities,* p. 31.

57 Daniel, *Mega-Universities,* p. 41; R. Zemsky and W.F. Massy, "Expanding Perimeters, Melting Cores, and Sticky Functions: Towards an Understanding of Current Predicaments," *Change* 27, 6 (November-December 1995): 41-49.

58. Daniel, *Mega-Universities,* p. 31. The actual numbers are 815 versus 7,376.

59. Daniel, *Mega-Universities,* p. 61.

60. Dwayne Matthew, "Transforming Higher Education: Implications for State Higher Education Finance Policy," *Educom Review* 33, 5 (September-October 1998): 48-57. See also <http://www.educause.edu/ir/library/html/erm9854.html>.

61. Kenneth C. Green and Steven W. Gilbert, "Expectations: Content, Communications, Productivity, and the Role of Information Technology in Higher Education," *Change* 27, 2 (1995): 8-18.

62. Massey and Zemsky, "Using Information Technology to Enhance Academic Productivity," June 1995. See also <http://www.educause.edu/nlii/keydocs/massy.html>.

63. William F. Massey and A.K. Wilger, "Improving Productivity: What Faculty Think about It—and Its Effect on Quality," *Change* 27, 4 (July-August 1995):10-21.

64. Martin J. Finkelstein, Robert K. Seal, and Jack H. Schuster, *The New Academic Generation.* (Baltimore: Johns Hopkins University Press, 1998), p. 76.

65. T. Russel, *The No Significant Difference Phenomenon.* Raleigh: North Carolina State University Office of Instructional Communications, 1999.

66. Alfred Bork, "Is Technology-Based Learning Effective?" *Contemporary Education* 63, 1 (1991): 6-14.

67. *What's the Difference? A Review of Contemporary Research on the Effectiveness of Distance Learning in Higher Education.* Washington, DC: The Institute of Higher Education Policy, April 1999.

68. Carol Frances, Richard Pumerantz, and James Caplan. "Planning for Informaation Technology: What You Thought You Knew Could Lead You Astray," *Change* 31 (July/August 1999): 25–33.

69. Twigg, "Academic Productivity: The Case for Instructional Software," July 24–25, 1996. See also <http://www.educause.edu/nlii.keydocs/broadmoor.html>.

70. Carol Twigg, "Improving Learning and Reducing Costs: Redesigning Large-Enroll-ment Courses," at <http://www.center.rpi.edu/PewSym/mono1.htm>. For details on cost savings in the institutions involved, see under this item in the "Resources" section of this book.

71. Paul Michael Privateer, "Academic Technology and the Future of Higher Educa-tion: Strategic Paths Taken and Not Taken," *The Journal of Higher Education*, 70, 1 (January-February 1999): 60-79.

72. R.B. Barr and J. Tagg sum up and contrast the salient features of the traditional "instruction paradigm" and the desired "learning paradigm" in "From Teaching to Learning: A New Paradigm for Undergraduate Education," *Change* 27, 6 (November-December 1995): 12-25, especially pp. 16, 17; R.B. Kozma and J. Johnstone, "The Technological Revolution Comes to the Classroom," *Change* 23, 1 (January-February 1991): 10-23, describe seven changes of learning (and teaching) when we use technology: (1) from reception to engagement, (2) from the classroom to the real world, (3) from text to multiple representations, (4) from coverage to mastery, (5) from isolation to interconnection, (6) from products to process, and (7) from mechanics to understanding in the laboratory. A. Chickering and S.C. Ehrmann, "Implementing the Seven Principles: Technology as Lever," *AAHE Bulletin* (October 1996): 3-6, discuss how IT supports teacher-learner contact, student collaboration, active learning, prompt feedback, time on task and learning effi-ciency, setting of high expectations, and giving due consideration to differences in talents and learning styles. Patricia Senn Breivik, *Student Learning in the Information Age.* ACE Series on Higher Education. Phoenix: Oryx Press, 1997, examines "resource-based learn-ing," which makes students gather their own learning materials from "real-world resources," and thus induces them to take greater responsibility for their own learning. T. Batson and R. Bass, "Teaching and Learning in the Computer Age: Primacy of Process," *Change* 28, 2 (March-April 1996): 42-47, detail the shift towards process when we go from a print culture to a digital culture for six elements of epistemology: knowledge, teaching, collaboration, publication/authority, thinking, and classroom; see especially p. 46.

73. D.H. Jonassan, "Computers as Cognitive Tools: Learning with Technology, Not from Technology," *Journal of Computing in Higher Education* 6, 2 (1995): 40-73. This is based on the new theory of constructivism. "Learning theory and instructional technology are in the midst of a scientific revolution" (p. 41). Active learning here means "that learners must participate and interact with the surrounding environment in order to create their own view of the subject" (p. 44).

74. The College Board, *Trends in College Pricing 1999*. Washington, DC: The College Board, 1999, p. 3. The decline of federal and state funds as a percentage of total institutional revenues explains in part why students have to pay more. In 1980-81, tuition and fees were 21 percent of institutional revenue, in 1995-96, 28 percent.

75. See note #71. Lee R. Alley and Philip C. Repp, "Technology Precipitates Reflective Teaching," *Change* 28, 2 (March-April 1996): 48-57, note how teaching with IT focuses instructors on understanding motivation and learning processes, assessing prior learning, learning styles, learning outcomes, and using problem-based and collaborative learning. Wendy Ricky, "Can Information Technology Improve Education? Measuring Voices, Attitudes and Perceptions," *Educom Review* 33, 1 (January-February 1998): 50-54, reviews changes in teaching introduced by the winners of the Educause Medal and quotes John Etchemendy, Stanford University, as follows: "Computers are far and away the most flexible tools ever created by mankind and as such they will eventually revolutionize how most subjects are taught."

76. From an unpublished 1998 report on a project directed by Martin Finkelstein at the New Jersey Institute for Collegiate Teaching and Learning and carried out by Mary Balkun, Carolyn Bentivegna, Charles Carter, Dolores Thompson, and Angela Weisl.

77. Massy and Wilger, "Improving Productivity: What Faculty Think about It—and Its Effect on Quality," pp. 10-21.

78. Bates, *Managing Technological Change*, pp. 66-75.

79. William F. Massy, "Life on the Wired Campus: How Information Technology Will Shape Institutional Futures," in Oblinger and Rush, *The Learning Revolution*, pp. 198, 202, 208, 209.

80. David F. Noble, "Digital Diploma Mills: The Automation of Higher Education," October 1997 at <http://www.journet.com/twu/deplomamills.html> and "Diploma Mills Part II: The Coming Battle over Online Instruction," March 1998, at <http://chass.utoronto.ca/~buschert/noble/>.

81. See Chapter 14 by Christine Maitland, Rachel Hendrickson, and Leroy Dubeck.

82. C. Frances, "Enrollment Trends and Staffing Needs." TIAA-CREF *Research Dialogues* 55 (March, 1998): 9-10.

83. Frances, "Enrollment Trends and Staffing Needs," pp. 9, 12. Fulltime faculty grew by 19.1 percent from 1975-89, and by 5.0 percent from 1989-95; student FTE rose by 15.3 percent and 5.6 percent during those same periods.

84. Bates, *Managing Technological Change*, pp. 107-17.

85. Dennis P. Thompson, "Intellectual Property Meets Information Technology: An Olive Branch in the Debate over Who Owns IT Products," *Educom Review* 34, 2 (March-April 1990): 14-21; Jaques Steinberg and Edward Wyatt, "Boola, Boola: E-Commerce Comes to the Quad," *The New York Times*, February 13, 2000, Section 4, pp.1, 4.

CHAPTER

Conceptual Framework and Terminology

Frank Jewett

Our topic, the cost (and benefit) impacts of digital electronic technology on higher education, is vitally important. The topic is so large, so diverse, so amorphous, and changing so rapidly that one despairs of coming to grips with it, much less of coming to agreement on a set of terms that can be used to consistently describe and analyze the phenomena. Nevertheless, without a consistent vocabulary, we cannot debate the issues, much less understand them, and we cannot analyze the potential (and the threats) inherent in the use of these media for instructional purposes.

First, an issue related to the use of the word "technology" must be addressed. "High technology" is a popular term that refers generally to the applications of modern science that stem from the digital computer and from related developments in digital electronics, especially as applied in communications and computer networks. Within the higher education community, the term "high technology" often refers to instructing students by using digital electronic technology (i.e., computers and computer networks—the Internet— or the various forms of television that are also migrating to a digital format). At times the term is shortened to just "technology" or "hi-tech," as, for example, "What are the implications of *technology* for the future of higher education?"

Within a specific higher education context, these shorthand terms should be understood as references to the longer versions. Unfortunately, the shorthand version is sometimes taken as the actual name of the activity, e.g., "we are going to use *technology* to teach this course." If taken literally, the use of the word "technology" to describe the employment of digital electronic media to offer a course produces a nonsensical interpretation. Technology is a term with a general meaning; it refers to the way things are done, or the way resources are combined to produce goods and services (its economic meaning). Thus, it is impossible to offer a course without using some type of technology. And, because alternative technologies use different combinations of resources, the costs of providing instruction are significantly affected by the particular technology employed.

INSTRUCTIONAL TECHNOLOGIES

Before plunging into a list of terms that have been used to describe the various ways information technology (IT) is used in the instructional process, it is useful to look at the process from a broader perspective. Understanding that technology refers to the way things are done generally, e.g., the way resources are combined to produce instructional services in higher education, allows us to list and describe the alternative technologies by which instructional services can be provided. Such a list is useful because it defines the context within which the various implications of IT use for collegiate instruction can be examined.

Classroom Technology

"Classroom technology" is the primary means by which courses (instructional services) are currently provided in higher education. Such technology is familiar; its resources include a live instructor and a classroom equipped with tablet armchairs and a chalkboard. The course is scheduled in a given classroom at a given time (e.g., Econ I, Founder's Hall, Room 109, MWF at 9 AM) and is offered for credit to the group of students who are formally enrolled. The technology also includes a textbook, a course syllabus, and access to a library.

Laboratory courses represent a variation on classroom technology in that students are scheduled to meet with an instructor in a more specialized room at a certain time and place to do experiments and engage in other practical activities to gain a better understanding of the topic they are studying. Yet another variation on classroom technology is the large lecture section (usually given by a prominent professor) accompanied by several quiz sections (wherein graduate teaching assistants work with smaller groups of students to answer questions and elucidate the material presented in the lecture).

All these variations incorporate the common practice of students meeting with individual instructors at given times and places. Course section enrollment is limited by the size of the physical facilities. In many cases, the sizes of the classrooms have, in turn, been influenced by judgments about the number of students an individual instructor could reasonably be expected to instruct in a given type of course.

As the basic means of providing instruction, classroom technology defines the environment within which higher education has developed; it literally permeates the culture. The need for classrooms, including specialized labs, provides the rationale for a campus.[1] The campus is the site where scholars congregate and where students come to learn. "Going to class" defines the rhythm of life for both students and faculty during the academic year. Teaching classes is the basis for faculty instructional workload (i.e., the number of preparations or courses per term and the enrollments in these courses).

The classroom culture is decentralized. Administrative tasks related to courses at the department level consist primarily of scheduling instructors to offer course sections at given times and places.[2] What happens in any given course section is primarily the responsibility of the individual instructor who is responsible for all the following basic functions required to provide formal instruction of any type:

1. planning and preparation of course materials (including selection of a text and other reading materials)
2. presentation of course materials (in a classroom)
3. interaction with students both inside and outside the classroom
4. evaluation of student performance and assignment of grades

One-on-One Tutoring

The technology whereby one individual simply instructs another was probably the first teaching approach ever used. Its application is obvious and adaptable to many situations. It requires a teacher and a student, but beyond that, it is flexible as to time, place, frequency, and level of formality. In terms of the four basic functions listed above, there may be less emphasis upon specific preparation and presentation and more emphasis upon interaction and evaluation. The disadvantage of one-on-one tutoring is that if several students need instruction, the teacher must repeat the same material for each. The "class," a group of students needing instruction in the same topic, probably developed as an extension of one-on-one tutoring. The trade-off for the time saved by the instructor lies in the difficulties inherent in scheduling a group to be in a given place at a given time, and the need for an adequate meeting place.[3]

Field Work and Clinical Practice

In this situation, an instructor/supervisor observes, monitors, and advises advanced students who are beginning to apply their learning and practice to their discipline. The site could be a public school, a hospital, an accounting office, or a village in the Andes. The instruction may be more or less intense and may involve some tutoring and classroom sessions.

Correspondence Technology

This technology involves developing a set of instructional materials for a course separate from and prior to delivering the materials to the students. Once the materials have been developed they are distributed, e.g., by mail, to all students enrolled in the course. Students study the lessons, complete exercises, and return them by mail to the school to be graded, commented upon, and returned with a new set of lessons. This process, which is sometimes augmented by term papers and other activities, repeats until, in conjunction with examinations, a course is completed.

Correspondence technology has basic differences from classroom technology. Instructional materials are produced independent of the process of delivery and presentation. Once the materials are produced, they can be distributed to all individuals who enroll. Enrollment is not limited by the size of a classroom because there is no classroom, and is not limited by the amount of work an individual faculty member can handle because several faculty can be assigned to the interaction and evaluation components. Students study at times and places of their own convenience and do not necessarily need to be in close proximity to a campus. No one presumes that the course materials are produced and the exercises and exams are graded by the same faculty member. The materials are likely produced by a team of specialists and the exercises and exams are probably graded by another group.

Distributed Technology

I coined this term to describe the basic elements of a correspondence course except that information technology rather than the post office serves as the delivery and communication media for the courses. The concept is not trivial. By including the following elements, it represents a way of doing business that is fundamentally different from classroom technology:[4]

1. Instructional materials are prepared (developed and maintained) by teams of faculty.
2. Materials are presented (distributed) to students via IT media, and students accomplish course work at times and places (which may be remote from a campus) convenient for them.
3. Some (if not all) student interaction occurs via IT media with faculty who are not necessarily the same as those who prepared the materials originally.
4. Student performance on course assignments and examinations is evaluated and grades are assigned by faculty who are, again, not necessarily those who prepared the course materials.

EXAMPLES OF APPLICATIONS OF THE TECHNOLOGIES

Below are examples of the application of technologies.

Classroom Instruction as a Pure Case: If one defines media to include the chalkboard and printed materials, all classroom instruction uses media. If print media are excluded, examples of pure classroom technology (i.e., a live instructor and a room equipped with tablet armchairs and a chalkboard) abounded in the early part of this century but are less frequently observed today.

Classroom Instruction Augmented with Electric Media: Slide projectors, over-head projectors, 16-mm film, VCRs, and tape recorders are examples of electric media that came into classroom use from the 1920s onward.

An illustration of the relationship between total direct costs of classroom instruction and annual enrollment in a single course is illustrated in Figure 2-1. The primary direct cost of classroom instruction is the cost of putting the instructor in the classroom ($7,000 to $12,000 per course section depending upon faculty salaries and the number of courses expected for a professor teaching full time) plus a modest amount representing the imputed cost of the classroom and, say, an overhead projector. The heavy black line labeled "clsrm inst" starts at the origin and rises (or steps up) at a constant rate as additional sections of the course are added.

Classroom Instruction Augmented with Digital Electronic Media (IT): The advent of the digital computer in the 1940s and its widespread adoption on college campuses in the post-World War II period marks the threshold of the use of digital electronic media in higher education. In the early years, the computer was used to do research (much of which was supported by the U.S. Department of Defense). By the early 1960s, two other uses of computing had developed in higher education: (1) for administrative processing of student records and budget and financial data, and (2) for augmenting classroom instruction.

All these uses of the computer emphasized its capacity to perform complex numerical calculations accurately and quickly and to maintain, manipulate, and analyze large data sets. During the 1960s, student research and homework assignments in many disciplines (e.g., physical sciences, mathematics, engineering, and accounting) migrated from use of logarithms, slide rules, electric calculators, and accounting ledgers to the use of computer programs employing FORTRAN or COBOL. During this same period, the general purpose campus computer center evolved as the preferred means to provide access to mainframe computers for research, administrative, and instructional purposes.

The direct costs of this instructional application of IT are illustrated in Figure 2-1 by the wide gray line labeled "clsrm+IT." This line lies above and parallel to the "clsrm inst" line. The vertical distance between the two cost schedules represents the imputed cost of the computing capacity required by the students enrolled in the course.

During the late 1960s and the 1970s, the use of computing spread across virtually all academic disciplines in parallel with its adoption in a myriad of scientific, business, and administrative applications. The "stand alone" computer also changed as software that was initially developed for the DARPA Network (Defense Advanced Research Projects Agency) became more generally available to facilitate communication between computers. A third development during this period, as transistors became both smaller and more powerful, was the desktop or personal computer. During the 1980s, use of desktop computers became widespread and the DARPA Net began evolving into the Internet. During the early 1990s, e-mail came into general use. By 1995, the World Wide Web was accessible via the Internet to anyone who had a computer, a telephone line, and access to a network server.

Electronically Mediated Instruction, Classroom Format: To this point, the uses described for digital electronic media have been to augment classroom instruction, to add activities and experiences that enrich and extend the classroom but that do not replace it.[5] As the personal or desktop computer became more common and network access became available to all students (at least through campus computer labs), and as computing became more dynamic and interactive, the potential emerged to move some of the coursework that would ordinarily occur in a classroom to a Web site.

A search of the Internet will reveal many examples of these "Web based" or "online" courses. Trained in various workshops and assisted by various software vendors, faculty are putting their course materials on Web sites, assigning students work at the Web site, and reducing the meeting schedules of their courses. At the Web sites, the students use bulletin boards, do assignments, participate in chat rooms and threaded discussions, and use e-mail for communications among themselves and with the instructor. This arrangement has many of the characteristics of distributed instruction—students access course materials at times and places of their own choosing and interact with each other and the instructor on the network. However, this instruction is still predicated upon the classroom technology model to the extent that a single instructor is responsible for the materials for the course section and for all the interaction and evaluation activities of the students enrolled in that section. Instruction of this type has led to the suggestion that class size should be reduced for "online courses" to compensate for the increased workload of maintaining the Web site materials and of interacting with the students.

The direct costs of this type of instruction are illustrated in Figure 2-1 by the broken line labeled "clsrm+IT+wkld" that starts on the "clsrm+IT" line and then diverges, rising above it. If it is assumed that instructors absorb the extra workload associated with this type of instruction on a volunteer basis, the

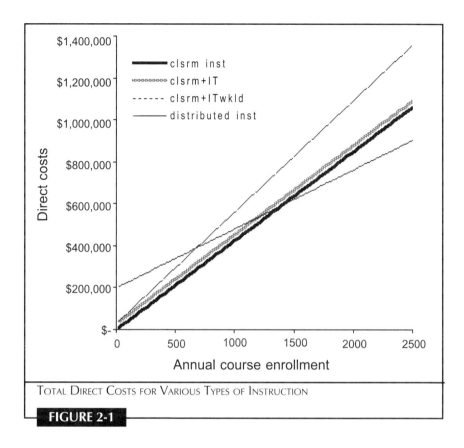

TOTAL DIRECT COSTS FOR VARIOUS TYPES OF INSTRUCTION

FIGURE 2-1

institution has no additional cost over and above the "clsrm+IT" line. But simply assuming that individual faculty should work more hours per term (or devote a greater share of their effort to instruction and a smaller share to research or shared governance activities) avoids dealing with the true costs of this type of instruction. The correct interpretation is that the increased workload associated with additional course preparation time and interaction time per student is recognized. This can be accomplished in several ways, including (1) extra pay or additional staff assistance, (2) a reduction in the average number of courses an individual teaches per year, or (3) a reduction in average class size. In any case, the effect is to increase the costs per student as shown by the divergence of the two graphs.[6]

Distributed Instruction as a Pure Case: The pure case of a network distributed course involves a team of faculty and media specialists who produce (prepare and maintain) the materials for an entire course; the materials are placed (presented) at a Web site where students who are enrolled in the course do all of their work and all (or at least some) of their interaction with other students and with instructors (tutors). As discussed above, the fundamental differences between this and classroom instruction are that the design, production, and maintenance of course materials is accomplished by a team of individuals who may be different from the group of faculty who interact with and evaluate students enrolled in the course. In principle, there is no upper limit on course enrollment because additional faculty can be assigned to cover the additional student interaction and evaluation workload as enrollment increases. Course preparation workload does not increase as additional enrollments are added because the course materials are accessible to all students on the network (course preparation workload is a fixed cost). The incremental cost of additional students is the cost of additional interaction and evaluation associated with those students.

The direct costs of distributed instruction are shown in Figure 2-1 as the line labeled "distributed inst." This line starts above the three classroom graphs because of the substantial amount of fixed costs necessary to produce and maintain the course materials and to provide the server and network capacity to distribute the materials. The line rises more slowly, however, because the incremental cost represents only the costs of interaction and evaluation associated with additional student enrollments and does not include the duplicative costs of preparation and presentation time that is incurred every time an additional classroom course section is added.

Because the graph of distributed instruction costs rises more slowly, it eventually intersects all the various classroom graphs. In Figure 2-1, it intersects the classroom graph at about 1,400 annual course enrollment. Beyond that enrollment, distributed instruction is less expensive than all the classroom alternatives.

Television and "Distance Education"

At about the same time the digital computer was being developed, broadcast television was emerging as another electronic media technology. Television has also had an effect upon higher education but it has been both functionally and organizationally different from that of computing.

One of the primary uses of television in higher education since the 1960s has been to provide "distance education," to broadcast live courses from campuses to remote sites. It has also been used to provide specialized high school courses to students in remote schools. A typical format is to bring an instructor and live students into a studio classroom on campus from which the course is transmitted to one or more remote sites where additional students are enrolled. Remote sites may include off-campus centers, classrooms located at other educational institutions, work sites, military bases, and homes. Communication back to the studio classroom may be by telephone (one-way video, two-way audio) or by a return television signal (two-way video or video conferencing).

Because TV applications have historically been the most common form of non-traditional instructional delivery using electronic media, the term distance education (DE) is the one most often encountered; see, for example the recent NCES report on distance education.[7] Reference to DE is often found in campus policy documents, faculty union contracts, and legislation.

The instructional use of television has been moderately successful in providing access to university courses for students who, because of work or family responsibilities, cannot afford to relocate to or to take the time to commute to a remote campus. Although instructional TV does not provide the same "anytime, any place" options of the Internet, it does provide some alternatives in regard to the place where the instruction can be accessed and, if one uses a VCR, some choice as to when the materials are viewed.

Although TV as a separate category of IT is not illustrated in Figure 2-1, its cost implications can be approximated as follows: If the TV course is the sole responsibility of one faculty member and enrollment is limited, we are dealing with something that approximates the "clsrm+IT" graph. If individual faculty are provided assistance in preparation and presentation of materials as well as additional personnel to assist with student interaction and evaluation, we have something that approximates the "distributed inst." graph.

An important constraint on the use of TV for instructional purposes has been the relatively small number of broadcast channels available for such purposes. Even if augmented with ITFS circuits, satellite uplinks, and local cable feeds, there is insufficient capacity to enable an institution to offer a broad range of degree programs. However, this situation is changing because TV can also be transmitted via a digital signal over a computer network. This convergence of computing and television technology further enhances the instructional potential of computer networks that are not constrained by the limits of the broadcast spectrum.

In contrast to computer applications that have been introduced primarily at the initiative of individual faculty in their courses, the need for a dedicated TV circuit and studio classroom has often placed the initiative for television instruction in an administrative unit, such as Continuing Education, or in an academic department, such as Engineering, where the need to reach groups of students at remote sites has been recognized.

TERMS USED TO DESCRIBE ELECTRONICALLY MEDIATED INSTRUCTION

her name was McGill
    she called herself Lil,
        but everyone knew her as Nancy
            (from "Rocky Raccoon," the Beatles, 1966)

As discussed above, "distance education" is the term that has been used most commonly to describe electronically mediated instruction that does not occur in a regularly scheduled classroom (whether the application involves TV or computers).[8] The following terms have been developed as alternatives to distance education partly to avoid the somewhat negative connotation associated with the word "distance," partly to avoid the fact that the "distance" is sometimes short (e.g., an online course available in a computer lab or the dorms), and partly to distinguish applications based upon computer media from those based upon television:

- *Mediated instruction*, an alternative to distance education, can apply to either television or computer applications. (I was once asked by a layperson if mediated instruction involved bringing in a third party to mediate between the students and the instructor.)
- *Distributed learning*, another alternative to distance education, implies that networked computers are involved.
- *Online courses/online instruction/online learning* are best thought of as synonyms that refer to learning materials that students access through a local network or the World Wide Web. A pure online course, where all course work is done online, could qualify as a distributed course if its component parts (production, presentation, interaction, and evaluation) were unbundled. *Web course* and related variants indicate that the Web is the delivery vehicle.
- *Telelearning/networked learning* are terms of English or European origin. The first is approximately a synonym for distance education and the second is a synonym for distributed learning or online instruction.

DIMENSIONS OF INSTRUCTIONAL TECHNOLOGY

Because the vocabulary is not standardized, it is more important to understand how instruction is being delivered than to know what it is called in a given situation. The basic dimensions of instructional technology involve questions of when, where, and how instructional materials are made available to students and what medium is used to contain and transmit these materials. A description of a course in terms of the following characteristics should allow two individuals to agree on what is occurring even if they do not agree on what it should be called:

- *When does the instructional activity occur?* Is it regularly scheduled (instructor and students face-to-face, synchronous) or not scheduled (materials accessed any time by students, asynchronous)?

- *Where does the instructional activity occur?* Is it in a scheduled class-room on campus, in a non-scheduled lab on campus, at off-campus centers, at other off-campus sites, or in students' homes or dorms?
- *How is the course produced and delivered?* Is an individual faculty member responsibile for everything, do individual faculty with gradu-ate/student assistants share responsibility, or is there a complete unbundling of course production, student interaction, and student evaluation activities, i.e., each activity handled by different indi-viduals?
- *What synchronous medium is involved?* Is it a live instructor in a classroom, a live instructor via one-way TV, a live instructor via videoconferencing, or a live instructor via "RealVideo?" The use of recording devices such as VCRs allows synchronous TV or computer materials to be converted to asynchronous materials.
- *What asynchronous medium is involved?* Is it print materials, audio tapes, video tapes, CD- ROMs, or courseware on a server?

The technology's several dimensions allow courses to share many characteris-tics yet still be fundamentally different. This situation is especially true for the "how is the course produced" dimension. For example, a course can be 100 percent asynchronous, delivered online, and still be produced and delivered by an individual faculty member. From the perspective of the medium, the course may be almost indistinguishable from another online course produced by a team of faculty and managed, e.g., by the Open University. From a cost perspective, however, the former course should be considered based upon classroom technology (because enrollment is constrained by what an indi-vidual faculty member can handle) while the latter is an example of distributed technology (individual workload is not a constraint upon enrollment), and the individual who has management responsibility for the course is not the individual assigned to teach the course because no one is assigned to "teach" the course.

None of these dimensions should be thought of as either-or propositions. Combinations of asynchronous media such as books, CD-ROMs, and online materials can be used in one course, while live classes can be combined with one-way TV in the same course. An instructor in a live TV course (or a large lecture course) may have total responsibility for preparation and presentation of the course materials while student interaction and evaluation is handled by a team of tutors who are in contact with the faculty member.

THE MIX OF PROGRAMS AND COURSES IN THE FUTURE

In addition to considering the different technologies that can be used to offer a particular course, it is also important to consider the different types of courses individual students might encounter during their educational careers. In the recent past, typical college graduates may have taken 90 to 100 percent of their undergraduate instruction in classroom format. To the extent there were other types of instruction, they were supervised reading or research projects with some clinical or field work in some disciplines.

With the advent of "electronically mediated instruction, classroom format," "distributed instruction," and "distance education," it is apparent that the average proportion of courses taken by students entirely in the traditional classroom format is declining. There are today students who have completed upper division degree programs entirely via televised courses, and graduate programs, especially the MBA, that can be substantially completed with online courses.

However, it would be an overestimation to conclude that the entire university curriculum will *only* be available online within a year or so. What is more likely is that an increasing amount of the curriculum will be available online but it will also continue to be available in classroom format. If this is so, the stage is now being set for a "grand experiment." Students will have greater opportunity to choose among different formats for their courses. Some will opt for more online instruction and some will prefer the classroom environment, but most will take some of each.

Whether, when, and where the mix of classroom, classroom plus IT, and distributed courses will stabilize remains to be seen. The outcome will be influenced within a broad social context and will be especially affected by where digital technology is taking the economy and the occupational mix of the workforce. Within the narrower context of higher education, the outcome will be significantly influenced by considerations of quality (and relevance as perceived by students and their families) and cost (to both students and the public), and by the availability, accessibility, and convenience of the instruction.

ENDNOTES

1. The need for a library is another rationale that probably predates classroom instruction.

2. Other related tasks include maintenance and development of the curriculum and coordination of the hiring and evaluation of faculty.

3. The observed result, that classroom instruction is predominant, suggests that the trade-off was worth it, that classroom technology within the administrative structure of a campus offers a cost-effective means of providing instructional services to students.

4. A good example of "distributed technology" in practice is the instructional delivery approach used by the United Kingdom Open University. Useful references are A.W. Bates, *Technology, Open Learning, and Distance Education*. London: Routledge, 1995; John S.

Daniel, *Mega Universities and Knowledge Media*. London: Kogan Page, 1996; and Greville Rumble, *The Costs and Economics of Open and Distance Learning*. London: Kogan Page, 1997.

5. This enrichment is often described as "bolt-on technology." Its importance to student learning should not be overlooked. To a large extent, the enrichment gives students an opportunity to learn about digital technology and computing and to be better prepared for their working careers where such knowledge is necessary.

6. I am indebted to Charles Karelis, Director of FIPSE, whose challenging questions about the interpretation and application of this cost model led to the development of this particular example. See his article, "Education Technology and Cost Control: Four Examples," *Syllabus* (February 1999): 20-28.

7. Laurie Lewis, Kyle Snow, Elizabeth Farris, and Douglas Levin, *Distance Education at Postsecondary Education Institutions: 1997-1998*. NCES 2000-013. Bernie Greene, project officer. Washington, DC: U.S. Department of Education, National Center for Education Statistics, 1999.

8. The NCES report on distance education referred to earlier, *Distance Education at Postsecondary Education Institutions: 1997-1998*, defines DE as "education or training courses delivered to remote (off-campus) locations via audio, video (live or prerecorded), or computer technologies, including both synchronous and asynchronous instruction." Courses conducted *exclusively* on campus or by written correspondence are excluded as are courses where an instructor travels to a remote site to deliver a regular classroom course (p. 2). Because on-campus instruction is excluded, it is not entirely clear whether the report would include as distance education a Web-based course that conducts half of the work in a regular classroom.

CHAPTER 3

What Is Information Technology in Higher Education?

Kenneth C. Green

C hildhood parables often yield new meaning and insight as we age. So it is that the old story about the blind men and the elephant seems an apt reference point to begin almost any discussion about information technology (IT) in higher education. Describing and defining the role of technology in the academic enterprise depends much on context and reference points—technology means different things to faculty across the academic disciplines, to administrators responsible for "managing" the academic enterprise, and to the growing numbers of increasingly heterogeneous students who seek courses, certification, degrees, and more from some 3,700 two- and four-year public, private, and for-profit colleges and universities in the United States.

Moreover, the shadow cast by the annual *Yahoo! Internet Life* ratings of the most wired American colleges <www.zdnet.com/yil> means that campus IT issues now take on special significance for admissions officers, campus PR personnel, and prospective students. Finally, during the closing months of academe's fiscal year, technology discussions among IT support staff, academic and administrative computing personnel, faculty, and campus officials often focus on funding. All are eager to leverage the year-end money—the

Note: This chapter was originally prepared for the Executive Forum on Managing the Costs of IT in Higher Education, sponsored by Seton Hall University and the Claremont Graduate University and convened at the Chauncey Conference Center, Educational Testing Service, in Princeton, New Jersey, on April 15-17, 1999. This work was supported, in part, by a grant from The New Jersey Institute for Collegiate Teaching and Learning (NJICTL) at Seton Hall University. © Kenneth C. Green 2000.

"budget dust"—into technology resources that will help fuel digital aspirations and sustain the IT infrastructure in academic departments and on college campuses across the country.

The many potential forms of information technology and technology initiatives on college campuses, coupled with the accidental history of computing in higher education[1] help explain, in part, why the higher education enterprise continues to struggle with all aspects of IT—definitions, planning, funding, and implementation.[2]

Like the blind men touching the different parts of the elephant, students, faculty, and administrators also touch (experience) different parts of the IT enterprise on college and university campuses. And like the elephant and the blind men's efforts to describe it, IT is also a *gestalt*—it is more than the sum of the parts, more than the accumulation of bits and bytes, the aggregation of hardware and software, the linkage of networks and servers, or the presence of the Internet and the Word Wide Web. Moreover, information technology on college campuses also involves more than the aggregation of institutional aspirations and individual experiences. We need to identify and understand the parts to move forward with an enhanced understanding of the whole.

ASPIRATIONS AND IMPLEMENTATION

Academe has long held great aspirations for the potential role of technology. Writing in *Scientific American* more than three decades ago, Stanford professor Patrick Suppes, one of the early innovators in the use of computers in instruction, outlined a vision for the role of technology in education that still rings true for many today.

> Both the processing and the uses of information are undergoing an unprecedented technological revolution. Not only are machines now able to deal with many kinds of information at high speed and in large quantities, but it is also possible to manipulate these quantities so as to benefit from them in new ways. This is perhaps nowhere truer than in the field of education. One can predict that in a few more years millions of schoolchildren will have access to what Philip of Macedon's son Alexander enjoyed as a royal prerogative: the services of a tutor as well-informed and as responsive as Aristotle.[3]

In the era of Internet time, some of Suppes's language seems dated. But the vision remains compelling—technology as a comprehensive and interactive source of content and as a catalyst for learning. With minor modification, Suppes's vision works well as the anchoring statement for a campus technology plan or a policy report from a state or federal agency or philanthropic organization interested in IT issues affecting both K-12 and postsecondary education.

Suppes provides but one example of how academics and educators have long held great hopes for the potential role of technology. At the turn of the last century, Thomas Edison believed that film would supplant books as the medium for instruction in schools by the end of the 1930s. However, it was the experience of film as a propaganda and training tool during the Second World War, coupled with the funding unleashed by Sputnik and the Cold War (remember "new math"?) that finally brought film into elementary and secondary classrooms during the late 1950s and early 1960s. For those of us who sat in those classrooms some 30 to 40 years ago, film then was much like the Internet today. Heralded as a great innovation and as an essential instructional resource, film (for example, *Hemo the Magnificent* from the Bell & Howell Science Series and *Donald in Mathemagic Land* from Disney) brought new, rich, and engaging "multimedia" into our classrooms—content that teachers could not provide.

Following film, educators and others also flirted with television, mainframe computers (remember Plato?), microcomputer courseware, and computer-aided instruction (CAI). In each instance, aspirations usually exceeded the capacity for implementation. In each instance, costs usually surpassed the financial resources of both the provider/developer and the buyer/user.

The emergence of the Internet and the World Wide Web over the past decade have fostered a new set of aspirations, accompanied by a new set of IT resources and a new level of IT infrastructure requirements. The proliferation of student and faculty Web pages suggests that this time around the technology may eventually deliver on some aspirations—a larger proportion of the aspirations—to a larger proportion of the potential beneficiaries.

Over the past five years the World Wide Web and the Internet have become ubiquitous not just in education, but across a wide spectrum of daily activities. Internet metaphors are no longer the sole domain of the *digerati*; Web references are now understood and appreciated by a growing proportion of the "unwired" population, including some of the most "tweedy" academics who *do not* spend large portions of their professional lives in cyberspace.[4]

A casual stroll on almost any college campus today provides ample visual evidence to document the seeming ubiquity of technology as part of the college experience. Additional evidence about technology activities and resources comes from The Campus Computing Project. As of fall 1999, more than half (53.4 percent) of all college classes use e-mail, compared to 44 percent in 1998 and just 8 percent in 1994 (Figure 3-1). Almost two-fifths (38.6 percent) of all college courses now use Internet resources as a component of the syllabus, up from one-third (33.1 percent) in 1998, one-fourth (24.8 percent) in 1997, and just 15.3 percent in 1996. And more than one-fourth (27.8 percent) of all college courses are using "WWW pages for class materials and resources," compared to just over one-fifth (22.5 percent) in 1998, less than one-tenth (8.4 percent) in 1996, and only 4 percent in 1994. Campus officials also estimate that more than half of all undergraduates (55.1 percent) access the Web at least once a day, up from 45.1 percent in 1998; three-fifths of all faculty (60.8 percent) also make daily use of the Web, compared to 51.6 percent in 1998. Additionally, an estimated one-fifth (18 percent) of all faculty have a personal Web page, independent of Web sites for their classes.[5]

Yet our fascination with and aspirations for IT run head on into the challenge of instructional innovation. We in academe all offer knowing smiles when we hear the old joke that "one can measure the pace of innovation in higher education by noting the 40 years it took to move the overhead projector out of the bowling alley into the classroom." And those of us who will admit to having been bowling recently have often found more computer projection capacity at the bowling alley than we have in our campus classrooms. Bowling really has gone "high tech" by installing computerized scoring and projection systems at every lane in the alley. In contrast, most of us who want to project computer graphics in our classes continue to wait for a work-study student to arrive with the crash cart that houses an overhead (or maybe even an LCD) projector.[6]

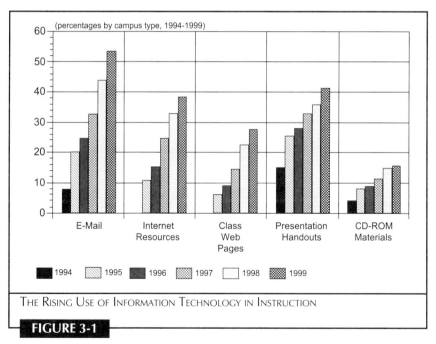

THE RISING USE OF INFORMATION TECHNOLOGY IN INSTRUCTION

FIGURE 3-1

Source: The Campus Computing Project; Kenneth C. Green, *Campus Computing 1999: The Natural Survey of Computing and Information Technology in U.S. Higher Education.* Encino, CA: Campus Computing, December 1999.

The "going high tech" issue poses a new instructional conundrum. On one hand, many in the academic community are committed to a *high-touch* (if increasingly mythical) model of education best symbolized by the widely cited "Mark Hopkins and the log" comment attributed to Williams alumnus (and later U.S. president) James A. Garfield more than 150 years ago.[7] On the other hand, some faculty and administrators, at times supported by public officials, have a *high-tech* vision of the future in which technology saves the American educational enterprise (from itself!). In between resides the vast majority of faculty and campus officials; neither Techies nor Luddites, they simply want and badly need accessible software tools, reasonable levels of user support, a viable campus technology infrastructure, and online content to support their instructional and scholarly work. Those in the middle seek a hybrid solution, one that fosters individual efforts to integrate high tech and high touch, bringing the best from both sides into their classrooms and course syllabi.

Going high tech raises an array of implementation issues that involve individual faculty, institutional aspirations, curriculum plans, campus infrastructure, library resources, campus networks, and more. Going high tech also involves lots of money—sustained investments of millions of dollars for most campuses.

Clearly, market pressures require virtually all campuses to invest in IT; after all, what college today will say it *does not* have computers and IT resources for its students? Still, going high tech involves an act of faith. Significant questions remain about the potential promise and probable limits of technology-based (or IT-enhanced) instruction in postsecondary education (and in other educational contexts). The continuing discussions about what is IT and how to use technology effectively—questions raised by faculty, administrators, technical support personnel, college trustees, state authorities, and corporate patrons of higher education—cluster around the following three core issues:

- *Content:* How can technology expand access to and improve the quality of information resources that might be incorporated into teaching, learning, and instruction? What content is critical to support the enhancement of scholarship and research?

- *Delivery:* How will information technology be used to enhance the delivery of instruction in both traditional and non-traditional contexts, for both traditional and non-traditional learners?

- *Infrastructure:* What kind of infrastructure (hardware, software, networks, technical support, user support, financing, etc.) is essential to make technology accessible, available, and effective over a wide range of educational contexts?

Against the backdrop of rising expectations and dynamic technologies, some significant questions remain about the potential and appropriate role of IT in collegiate teaching, learning, and instruction. Does the broad (or even the focused) application of information technology as (1) content in the syllabus, (2) an online resource for a campus community (3) a delivery vehicle for instruction, or (4) a component of the campus infrastructure yield significant, cost-effective benefits that affect both the educational experience and enhanced learning outcomes?

Finally, we also must acknowledge that the discussion about IT in higher education increasingly has less to do with technology products per se, and more to do with implementation experience.[8] Data from the Campus Computing Project reveal that campus officials view "instructional integration" and "user support" as the key IT issues confronting their institutions (*see* Figure 3-2). Two-fifths (39 percent) of the 530 two- and four-year colleges and universities participating in the 1999 Campus Computing Survey identified "instructional integration" as the single most significant IT challenge for their campuses, up from 33.2 percent in 1998 and 29.6 percent in 1997.

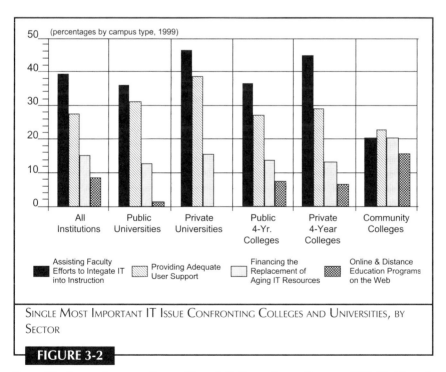

SINGLE MOST IMPORTANT IT ISSUE CONFRONTING COLLEGES AND UNIVERSITIES, BY SECTOR

FIGURE 3-2

Source: The Campus Computing Project; Kenneth C. Green, *Campus Computing 1999: The National Survey of Computing and Information Technology in US Higher Education*. Encino, CA: Campus Computing, December 1999.

"Providing adequate user support" ranked second in the 1999 Campus Computing Survey; just over one-fourth (27.5 percent) of the survey respondents identified user support as the most important technology challenge confronting colleges and universities, up from 26.5 percent in 1998 and 25 percent in 1997. Placing third was "financing the replacement of aging hardware and software," which was cited by one-seventh of the survey respondents (15.2 percent) as the single most important IT issue for their campuses. "Providing online/distance education via the Web" ranked fourth across all sectors. Four other response options (mandating student ownership of computers, using IT effectively in distance education, solving Y2K problems, and restructuring IT organizations) registered low responses from survey respondents across all institutional sectors.

Taken together, these data document the growing campus awareness that the key IT challenges in higher education involve people, not products. For many institutions, user support and instructional integration are two sides of the same coin—complementary components of a broad challenge that involves the effective and innovative use of technology resources in colleges and universities.

These data also suggest that fully two decades after the first desktop computers arrived on college campuses, college and university officials have recognized that the campus community's major technology challenges involve human factors—assisting students and faculty in their efforts to use new technologies in ways that will support teaching, learning, instruction, and scholarship.

The 1999 survey data also suggest that despite some dire predictions on both sides of the issue, the real future of technology in higher education is not about a winner-take-all competition between high tech and high touch. The data suggest that most students and faculty will experience some kind of hybrid learning in which technology supplements, not supplants, both the content and the discourse that have been part of the traditional college experience. This prediction applies as much to the traditional undergraduate who lives on campus as it does to commuter students in undergraduate and graduate programs. It also applies to the growing new clientele of (typically) older students who are eager for both content and certification and who increasingly expect educational opportunities and services to be available online.

Ultimately, the discussion focuses on technology as a *process* that enhances higher education. The core long-term questions are not about *which* technologies (e.g., notebook computers, Unix workstations, instructional software, e-mail, or wired classrooms), but about *how* technology—as a resource, process, and experience—affects academic work, learning outcomes, and the culture of the academic enterprise.

A DUAL TWO-CULTURE PROBLEM

The academic experience with IT over the past decades resides under the shadow of a dual "two-culture" problem. At the top level, institutions typically divide computing and technology into the separate domains of administrative and academic computing. The operational focus of administrative computing—student records, accounting and finance, human resources—parallels the MIS services of a mid-sized business or a large corporation. Indeed, many of the nation's larger universities installed administrative service units well before the emergence of campus-wide "academic computing" offices in the mid-1960s.

In contrast, the history of academic computing has been less linear, the activities less focused and less accessible to a broad range of students and faculty. Academic computing at most institutions began as computing resources for a small group of academic departments, primarily in the sciences and engineering. The early initiatives in academic computing—computing as a tool for research and scholarship, with little emphasis on instruction—expanded beyond the sciences as new kinds of statistical software for the social sciences and modeling and forecasting software for business drew new kinds of users to the emerging campus computing centers. Somewhat ironically from the current perspective, academic users often had to beg for time on the administrative system at many smaller colleges during these early years.

Yet the two-culture issues that separate academic and administrative computing pale in comparison to the two-culture chasm within the academic side of the house—the computing and technology cultures that separate the technical from the "tweed" disciplines. Academic humanists and social scientists are only beginning to realize both the technology resources and accompanying corporate goodies that have often showered down upon their nominal colleagues in the sciences and engineering. The growing decentralization of academic computing means that money and decisions that previously resided within central services and computer center offices now operate at the departmental level; individual faculty in the humanities and arts are making decisions about technology that previously would have been handled by administrators (i.e., former faculty) with degrees in science and engineering.

The legacy of these competing computing cultures continues to pose major challenges for most institutions. The sciences and technical areas demand more resources, even as the social sciences and humanities struggle to stay current with current technologies. The sciences and engineering benefit from more grant and contract funds, which provide more IT resources. The external funds also foster greater autonomy in the areas of technology policy, planning, and resources—an autonomy rarely experienced in most social science and humanities departments.

THE PRODUCTIVITY CONUNDRUM

Some of the difficulty the campus community experiences in attempting to define and describe information technology stems in part from academe's problems with the much-dreaded P-word—*productivity*. For many in and around higher education, academic productivity is an academic oxymoron. For others, given rising costs and new technologies, academic productivity is the new organizational imperative. Yet much like Robert Persig's complaint about quality in higher education, productivity also eludes us; it is at the same time personal and consensual.[9] Quality is also a decidedly amorphous concept when applied to academic institutions. And like the blind men touching the elephant, our experience is usually severely limited by context.

The January 1998 report of the National Commission on the Cost of Higher Education identified productivity as a top priority for American colleges and universities. While not explicitly citing technology as a potential solution for some of the productivity challenges confronting higher education, the language of the Commission's recommendations points in that direction.

> The Commission recommends the creation of a national effort led by institutions of higher education, the philanthropic community, and others to study and consider alternative approaches to collegiate instruction which might improve productivity and efficiency. The Commission believes significant gains in productivity and efficiency can be made through the basic way institutions deliver most instruction, i.e., faculty members meeting with groups of students at regularly scheduled times and places. It also believes that alternative approaches to collegiate instruction deserve further study. Such a study should consider ways to focus on the results of student learning regardless of time spent in the traditional classroom.[10]

But what does productivity really mean, besides the Commission's suggestion to reduce costs? From economics, we know that productivity occurs under any one of the following three conditions:

1. Quality remains constant while production (output, units) increases with no additional increase in costs (i.e., constant quality and lower unit costs).
2. Quality improves while production (output, units) remains constant, with no increase in costs (i.e., improved quality and no change in unit costs).
3. Quality improves *and* production (output, units) also increases with no increase (and perhaps a potential decline) in costs (i.e., enhanced quality and lower unit costs).

What troubles many in and around academe about the building productivity debate is the concern about which definition will dominate and which authorities (e.g., faculty, college administrators, public officials) will define the parameters of campus discussions, institutional initiatives, and public policy. For professors, technology assumes an understandably qualitative dimension; faculty advocates affirm that IT improves their scholarly work, enhances the resources they bring to the syllabus, enhances their interactions with students, and expands their accessibility to students.[11] But these admittedly qualitative enhancements may not reduce costs; some may even increase operating costs.

In contrast, administrators concerned about rising costs see technology-linked productivity as a way to leverage a huge investment in faculty time and campus infrastructure. For administrators (and many public officials), the discussion about technology in the classroom and in instruction increasingly assumes a quantitative dimension: How will technology help increase units (i.e., teach more students) and thus reduce costs?

Technology has brought both enhanced quality and reduced costs ("productivity") to parts of the academic enterprise. Like many corporations, colleges and universities routinely and effectively use technology in many administrative areas. As in the corporate domain, computers and technology resources have improved productivity in a wide range of data management and transaction-processing activities (e.g., student and personnel records, accounting and financial management). Growing numbers of colleges and universities are placing more information on their Web sites—admissions and financial aid information, course schedules, campus event schedules, employee handbooks, course materials, and more.

In some parts of the academic enterprise, technology has helped increase productivity and reduce operating costs. For example, a generation of faculty have come into academic positions with little or no secretarial assistance from their departments and institutions; these faculty routinely use a computer to write papers, prepare syllabi, draft grant proposals, and write research reports and scholarly manuscripts. Faculty may be unhappy about the demise of secretarial support; but from an economic perspective, their departments are more productive in some administrative areas because the investment in capital (desktop computers, servers, networks) has replaced an investment in labor (departmental secretaries). However, more than a dozen years into the so-called "computer revolution in higher education," technology shows little evidence of having either aided or impeded instructional productivity, of having reduced costs of instruction or enhanced learning outcomes. Much like the corporate sector, hard data about the linkage between technology and productivity remains elusive for higher education.

Yet the terms of the productivity debate are changing, much as they have in the corporate sector in recent years. Efforts to identify a productivity lift from corporate investments in information technology during the late 1980s and mid-1990 often led to inconclusive results. More recent analysis of the corporate data for the mid- and late 1990s suggests that business and industry experienced direct productivity gains linked to IT investments once those investments reached a critical mass and became an integral part of the organizational infrastructure.

While the corporate data do not predict what will happen in academe, the more recent findings linking IT investments and productivity certainly foster expectations for some productivity-linked benefits in education as instructional resources and campus infrastructure improve.

These are significant issues for academe. The demographic factors that drive growth over the next two decades, outlined by both Carol Frances[12] and Cliff Adelman,[13] among others, point to a future of exploding demand accompanied by inadequate capacity, at least as measured by current standards. As well-intentioned but perhaps not so well-informed public officials seek to substitute technology for physical plant, questions about costs, impacts, benefits, and productivity will cast a large shadow over many critical aspects of the public discussion about the role of IT in higher education.

MONEY MATTERS

Finally, the discussion about IT in higher education must confront the challenge of IT funding and costs. Money remains one of the most difficult issues for colleges to address in the broad discussion about technology. Data from the annual Campus Computing Survey (*see* Figure 3-3), reveal that as of fall 1999, two-fifths (39 percent), down from 52 percent in 1998, have a financial plan for IT. Additionally, less than half (44.9 percent) report a financial plan to "acquire and retire" technology resources, compared to 37.3 percent in 1998 and just 16 percent in 1990.[14]

The survey data have shown some improvement on these issues in recent years as more campuses report strategic and financial plans for IT. Although the gains are impressive and no doubt reflect real improvements in campus planning on IT issues, the self-reported data may also overstate the real levels of IT strategic and financial planning on college campuses. For example, true strategic planning should include a financial plan that addresses and fully funds the "acquire and retire" cycle for computers, software, network services, and related technology resources. Yet as shown in Figure 3-3, within each sector of higher education more campuses report a "strategic" plan than a financial plan.

Why, then, do colleges struggle with IT funding, especially on the academic side of the enterprise? Why does budget dust (i.e., year-end money) play so large a role in the IT spending among so many academic departments and at so many institutions—large and small, rich and poor, public and private?

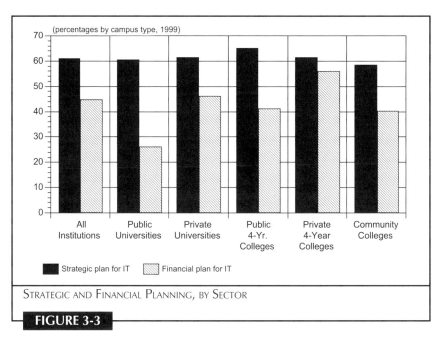

STRATEGIC AND FINANCIAL PLANNING, BY SECTOR

FIGURE 3-3

Source: The Campus Computing Project; Kenneth C. Green, *Campus Computing 1999: The National Survey of Computing and Information Technology in US Higher Education*. Encino, CA: Campus Computing, December 1999.

It is easy (and perhaps appropriate) to blame the funding and financing models that drive higher education and, by extension, not-for-profit organizations. Stated simply, we miss the benefit (or discipline) amortization imposes on the management of key capital resources, including IT infrastructure. The organizational mind-set is too often to make do; we seem to define amortization as the willingness of the most recently hired humanist to use a 14-year-old IBM Selectric typewriter.[15] Institutional budgets appear to be the last place in the academic enterprise to recognize the ubiquity of IT across the college campus; too much of the true IT funding at too many campuses is based on the budget dust money we hide for nine months and then rush to spend before the close of the fiscal year. Some of this budget dust behavior stems from the initial arrival of desktop computers in the late 1970s and early 1980s; deans often allocated some year-end money for small experiments using the early Apple IIs, IBM PCs, and Macintoshes. But while campuses have moved beyond the experimentation phase, the budget models for IT have not.

Just how badly academe manages the financial side of IT is reflected in the growing tendency of both public and private institutions to use bonds to finance IT infrastructure enhancements. Stated simply, bonds are bad, at least for IT investments. Unlike buildings, which last (almost) forever, the useful life of the technology investment (desktop computers for faculty, wire for campus networks) may be one-quarter to one-half of the life of the bond (often issued for 10 years).

Moreover, the higher education community—at least at the board/presidential/vice presidential level—is only beginning to recognize the full cost of the human resources required to support an adequate IT infrastructure.[16] The 1999 Campus Computing Survey reveals that personnel expenditures account for 40 to 50 percent of IT spending at most institutions, a figure equal to or more than the annual aggregate campus expenditure on hardware and software.[17] Yet this number grossly understates true personnel costs because it fails to account for the undocumented time many faculty and staff spend responding to informal requests for assistance from peers and colleagues.

Additionally, IT support in the campus environment is well below levels found in comparably complex corporate environments; the ratio of users to support staff on college campuses runs 2 to 10 times higher than the levels typically found in large corporations and small businesses.[18] Finally, given the growing demand across the economy for personnel with IT skills, colleges will experience still more competition for good IT staff. IT salaries on college campuses are often 25 to 40 percent below comparable salaries in the corporate environment.

Rising demand for IT resources and support notwithstanding, the absence of a capital investment policy, the inability to amortize, a reluctance to lease, the underpayment of IT personnel, and the general tendency to use technology tools well beyond their useful life means[19] that most colleges and universities will continue to underfund the operating and infrastructure costs of information technology. Some of the problem is structural, inherent in the financial operations of public or not-for-profit organizations and the legal restrictions on the ways these entities can handle their money. But some of the problem is also conceptual, a direct consequence of how campus officials fail to address the true costs of IT as part of the long-term strategic and financial plan.

WHAT *IS* IT IN HIGHER EDUCATION?

We end as we began—partially sighted observers touching the IT elephant, attempting to define the whole from various, vaguely defined parts. IT in higher education is many things—hardware, software and networks, the tangible manifestations of technology that appear as budget expenditures. IT is administrative and academic computing, reflecting the organization of the academic enterprise. IT represents computer and technical resources that support research and scholarship within the respective academic disciplines, a shrinking chasm that separates the "technical" from the "tweed" fields of inquiry.

Information technology is also instructional technology, a set of expanding digital and online resources that many academics hope will help enhance teaching, learning, and instruction. Information technology is the campus infrastructure of hardware, software, networks, user support services, and personnel. IT is digital content, used by students and faculty. IT is the money colleges spend on computers, software, network servers, and personnel. IT is curriculum resources such as courseware, online tutors, class Web pages and resources, CAI, and more. For many, IT may be the key to academic productivity. IT is the implementation challenge that will affect many traditional processes and practices on college campuses and in college classrooms. IT is also lots of money spent to support computing, content, research, scholarship, and instruction.

Finally, IT reflects a set of long-held aspirations in and around academe that computers and related digital resources will enhance the educational experience and improve learning outcomes. These are great, perhaps even unfair, aspirations. However, they cast a prominent shadow over any discussion about "what is IT in higher education."

ENDNOTES

1. Robert Gillespie. *The Accidental Revolution.* A report prepared for the National Science Foundation. Seattle, WA: University of Washington, 1980.

2. Kenneth C. Green. *Campus Computing 1998: The National Survey of Desktop Computing and Information Technology in US Higher Education.* Encino, CA: Campus Computing, March 1999; Kenneth C. Green, *Campus Computing 1999: The National Survey of Computing and Information Technology in US Higher Education.* Encino, CA: Campus Computing, December 1999; Laurie Lewis, and others. *Distance Education at Postsecondary Education Institutions, 1997-1998.* Washington, DC: National Center for Education Statistics, U.S. Department of Education, 1999.

3. Patrick Suppes. "The Uses of Computers in Education." *Scientific American 215* (October, 1966): 206-20.

4. The instant recognition and popular appeal of an oft-cited (and several years old!) *New Yorker* cartoon—"On the Internet, no one knows you're a beagle"—documents the diffusion of Internet metaphors.

5. Green, *Campus Computing 1999.*

6. Kenneth C. Green. "Go bowling!" *Converge* (October 1999).

7. Frederick Rudolph. *The American College and University.* Athens: The University of Georgia Press, 1990.

8. Green, *Campus Computing 1999.*

9. Robert Persig. *Zen and the Art of Motorcycle Maintenance.* New York: Bantam Books, 1975.

10. National Commission on the Costs of Higher Education. *Straight Talk About College Costs and Prices. Final Report.* Washington, DC: GPO, January 1998.

11. See Robert Kozma, and Jerome Johnson. "The Technology Revolution Comes to the Classroom." *Change* (January/February 1992).

12. Carol Frances. *Higher Education: Enrollment Trends and Staffing Needs.* New York: TIAA-CREF, 1998.

13. Clifford Adelman. "Crosscurrents and Riptides." *Change* (January/February, 1999).

14. Green, *Campus Computing 1999.*

15. For the record, the market value of a 15-year-old IBM Selectric typewriter is greater than the resale value of a 3-year-old (first generation) IBM Pentium-class notebook or desktop computer.

16. Katherine Selleck. "Big Picture Questions Produce Bottom-Line Answers." *Trusteeship*, Special Issue on Information Technology (October, 1997). Also, Kenneth C. Green, and Robin Jenkins, "IT Financial Planning 101." *NACUBO Business Officer* (April 1998).

17. Green, *Campus Computing 1999.*

18. Green, *Campus Computing 1999.*

19. The 1999 Campus Computing Survey reveals that 35 percent of college campuses routinely use a four- or five-year replacement cycle for institutionally owned computers in student labs; 62 percent use a four- to five-year cycle for computers in faculty offices. In contrast, corporations routinely use a 24- to 30-month replacement cycle for similar equipment.

CHAPTER 4

Costing Technology-Based Education

Research Studies from the UK, Canada, the European Community, and Australia

Heather Eggins

A curious phenomenon of the research community is the way in which the exploration of particular topics arises spontaneously in different countries at about the same time. Work on the costs of networked learning proves the old adage exactly. Groups of researchers in the U.S., the United Kingdom (UK), Canada, Continental Europe, and Australia have been simultaneously conducting separate studies to find a satisfactory methodology to cost technology-based education, without, until recently, being aware of each other's endeavors. This chapter provides a survey of key developments in the UK, Canada, the European Community, and Australia, so that readers in each country can judge how these findings align with those of projects in other countries.

Underlying the worldwide interest in this topic is the global technological revolution and its steadily growing influence on how learning is delivered around the planet. This chapter surveys the major work in the field of costing in each of these countries outside the U.S.

Acknowledgments: The author would like to thank Charlotte Ash and Paul Bacsich of Sheffield Hallam University for much information and helpful advice in the preparation of this chapter. Thanks also to Pieter de Vries of the EU Telelearn Project for providing information.

UNITED KINGDOM

The pioneer in large-scale distance education is the Open University of the UK which was specifically founded in the 1960s to deliver higher education using the tools of modern communications. The Open University is thus unusual in that, as a distance learning university, it naturally turned its attention earlier than others to examining the costs of delivering distance education.

Greville Rumble of the Open University has been publishing works on the costs of distance learning since the late 1980s.[1] Tony Bates, also then at the Open University, edited a volume in 1990 on *Media and Technology in European Distance Learning*,[2] and subsequently published a book entitled *Technology, Open Learning and Distance Education* in 1995.[3] This book is considered by some to be a seminal work for those seeking to make sense of the cost of networked learning.

Bates recognized that it is essential to have a clearly defined planning process and to develop a "framework for decision-making." He specified that the framework should have a number of necessary features, namely:

- It would work in a variety of contexts;
- It should allow decisions to be taken at both a strategic or institution-wide level, and at a tactical or instructional level;
- It should give equal attention to instructional and operational issues;
- It would identify crucial differences between different technologies, so enabling an appropriate mix of technologies to be chosen for any given context; and finally,
- It would accommodate new developments in technology.

This proposed framework, coming when it did at the early stages of the development of the use of the Internet for teaching and learning, has been very influential. It is usually referred to as the ACTIONS framework which can be spelled out as the following headings:

- Access
- Costs
- Teaching and Learning
- Organizational Issues
- Novelty, and
- Speed.

As time has passed, the importance of the novelty criterion has somewhat diminished but the other headings still provide a valuable approach.

Greville Rumble published his very useful book, *The Costs and Economics of Open and Distance Learning*, in 1997.[4] This book specifically examined the costs of technology-based education. Then, in a follow-up paper entitled "The

Costs of Networked Learning: What Have We Learnt?"—presented in May 1999 at the Flexible Learning on the Information Superhighway FLISH99 Conference at Sheffield Hallam University—Rumble gave a wide-ranging survey of the current state of knowledge on the topic.[5] The change that has engendered intensified interest in the cost of technology-based education is set out clearly in Rumble's paper. Investment by governments and institutions had, by the late 1990s, become a major financial commitment. The Dearing Report of 1997, *Higher Education in the Learning Society*, estimated that of the total budget spent on higher education in the UK, about 10 percent (equal to between £800 million and £1.1 billion) was allotted to Communications and Information Technology (CIT).[6] Future costs are likely to be higher. Much of the money is absorbed by the national universities' networks—JANET and SUPERJANET—but a small though growing amount goes into online courseware.

In the UK, as elsewhere, there is a strong desire to make the business case for online learning, to establish costs and benefits, and to model the relationship between them. Rumble recognizes that the problem has not yet been satisfactorily solved, and worries that much of the expended costs might be borne by the students, thus impacting adversely those students from deprived socio-economic sectors who might find themselves, as a result, barred from participating in online learning.

The Sheffield-Hallam Study: A UK Research Project on the Cost of Networked Learning

The leading team in the UK working on the planning and costing of networked learning is led by Dr. Paul Bacsich, Professor of Telematics at Sheffield Hallam University. Bacsich's earlier work was financed by the European Commission and by the Finnish government. The recent report on "The Costs of Networked Learning" by Paul Bacsich, Charlotte Ash, Kim Boniwell, and Leon Kaplan, issued in October 1999, was produced by a project funded by the Joint Information Systems Committee (JISC) of the UK Higher Education and Research Councils.[7] The original JISC circular issued in September 1998 spelled out the committee's position as follows:

> Many of the costs of developing and supporting Networked Learning are hidden: unrecorded academic staff time, increased demands on technical support, more complex administration, additional telephone costs, etc. The Committee on Awareness, Liaison and Training (CALT) wishes to fund a study that will more accurately document the costs of a number of different approaches to Networked Learning. CALT wishes to see the study lead to a planning checklist for Networked Learning and a schema for estimating costs.[8]

An outline of the team's approach to its task and the methodology employed is presented here. The definition of networked learning for the purposes of the project was "using a networked computer for the purposes of learning, blurring the boundaries between on-campus, distance and flexible learning."[9] This definition aligns exactly with other terms such as "online learning," "technology-enhanced learning," and "technology-based education."

The aim of the study was two-fold: The first aim was to "document the overall cost factors, with special reference to unrecorded or hidden costs." The problem of hidden costs had been slowly surfacing as on-line learning was expanding. This was, however, the first study to focus on unrecorded costs, and as such has provided valuable information for higher education worldwide.

The second aim of the study was to establish a planning framework that takes account of cost analysis in order to estimate "actual costs of different approaches to networked learning."[10] This framework could provide a very useful tool for making decisions affecting the future of networked learning in institutions of higher education.

The methodology used by Bacsich and his collaborators included a literature review, and a Sectoral Survey of 173 higher education institutions in the UK, including traditional universities, new universities, and university colleges. The purpose of the survey was to "establish a representative view of the approach to and extent of networked learning activity" and to assess how costs were recorded, if at all.

The researchers noted that "It became clear at an early stage that many of the hidden costs were being absorbed by students." A student questionnaire was therefore developed to gather information on their attitude toward networked learning and the associated costs. An earlier National Union of Students survey had already established that students were paying an average of £571 a year towards general education costs, which included IT costs that had not been made apparent to them at the beginning of their courses.[11]

The final part of the study focused in depth on seven case study institutions where detailed data on costs could be gathered. The institutions selected were representative of all countries in the UK, of both traditional and new universities, and at various stages of networked learning development. Sheffield Hallam University was included in the study as "representative" but Oxford, Cambridge, and the Open University were excluded as atypical. The team used public documentation to draw up a profile of each institution, and a series of 44 questions was prepared for its visits to the campuses. Over two- or three-day periods, the study team met with a range of staff whose views and knowledge would be helpful. Additional consultation was broad, with a one-day workshop attended by five experts from higher education and industry. Also, the international conference held in May 1999 at Sheffield Hallam on

"The Business Case for On-Line Learning" featured presentations on various aspects of the project. The final draft of the project report was delivered in August 1999 and the completed report was made available in October.

Conclusions of the Sheffield Hallam Study

Costs

The Sheffield Hallam study was launched with a literature review that included case studies from Australia, the United States, and Canada.[12] The research findings from the case studies were in general agreement as to the difficulties in accurately costing educational technologies. The Australian work undertaken by Alexander, McKenzie and Geissinger had pointed out that multiple stakeholders—students, staff, departments, institutions, and society itself—were affected by the development and use of information technologies. The Sheffield Hallam study reported on three categories of costs—those for institutions, staff, and students.

Institutional Costs

The main institutional costs are the major investments in infrastructure, especially the investment in secure and reliable networks, and increased technical support for online learning programs. There are also huge hidden costs borne primarily by institutions, including the costs of development, particulary the time taken by staff to develop resources, as well as the additional technical support and related training costs that tend to be absorbed into existing budgets for staff development and academic planning. An often overlooked institutional charge is the cost of accessing the Internet via an institution's own servers.

Staff Costs

The major problem in assessing staff cost is that academics are not paid in relation to the time spent working on specific activities, and there is little incentive to quantify and cost all staff activities. Academics normally work well over 50 hours a week, often over 55, and frequently have no number of hours specified in their contracts. It is therefore difficult to attribute their time to particular activities. However, the hidden cost of time invested by staff includes becoming familiar with new technologies, integrating computer-based learning materials with teaching, and developing course materials for technology-enabled learning. The huge amount of energy and effort needed to produce these results should not be underestimated.

It was not unusual for institutions to encourage academic staff to develop electronic learning materials to enhance and extend the reach of their courses, but institutions usually did not want to relieve these staff of other responsibilities.

The Australian report issued by Alexander, McKenzie and Geissinger in 1998 also noted that staff incurred a high personal cost in terms of time.[13] This cost could lead to loss of research and personal time, which in turn could result in loss of tenure and promotion, as well as increased work-related stress. Many academic staff had purchased their own computers to use at home, and put in considerable hours there on their academic work, thus lengthening their work day considerably.

The Sheffield Hallam report noted that staff identified overtime and time for developing materials as problem areas. No workable method of recording and assigning staff time to particular activities has yet been found, hence costing time remains unsatisfactory.

KPMG Management Consulting and the Joint Funding Councils conducted a study in 1997 entitled "Management Information for Decision Making: Costing Guidelines for Higher Education Institutions."[14] The Higher Education Funding Council for England (HEFCE) highlighted the "cultural difficulties" in getting academic staff to complete accurately an activity-based time sheet, which is an added problem.

Student Costs

The widespread practice in the U.S. of charging students separately for computing facilities, an average of $120 a year according to K.C. Green's 1998 *Campus Computing Survey*, has only just begun to take hold in the UK.[15] However, the 1997 Dearing Report suggested that all students should be expected to own personal computers by the year 2005-2006. No university has yet required this for all its courses, but in many cases students are strongly encouraged to buy their own computers. In effect, this expense, when added to insurance, maintenance, and running costs for the computer, represents a hidden cost in the neighborhood of £80 average per annum.

The student survey, undertaken as part of the study, indicated that some 68 percent of students believed that networked learning was increasing their costs, but the main cost as they saw it was *time*—to gain familiarity with software, lost to delays in logging on, in queuing for printing, and lost to system crashes. Students considered the cost of printing high and on-campus facilities as frequently inadequate. On the other hand, students judged that networked learning did enable them to learn more effectively.

Development of a Model

Following their review of the literature and consultation with colleagues, the research team developed a five-phase working model (Figure 4-1) for the lifecycle of a course, which was tested during case study interviews and at the workshop attended by experts. The model had an outer ring of five linked learning environments: planning, developing, providing, managing, and main-

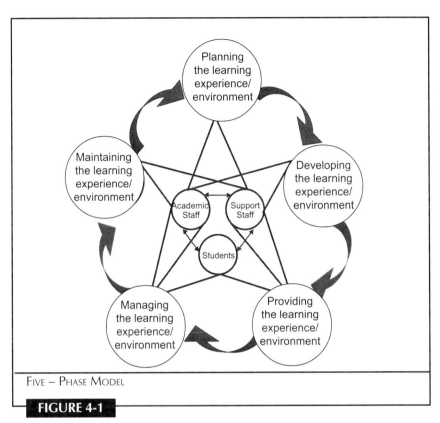

FIVE – PHASE MODEL

FIGURE 4-1

Reproduced with permission from *The Costs of Networked Learning* Bacsich, P., Ash, C., Boniwell, K., Kaplan L., Mardell, J., and Caven-Atack, A. (1999) Sheffield: Sheffield Hallam University.

taining. Within the model were three cross-linked inner units for the stake-holders: students, academic staff, and support staff.

The use of the model in discussions enabled those taking part to focus on the learning environment and explore how best to strengthen it. Both those interviewed at institutions and the experts at the workshop noted some omissions in the model—including additional stakeholders beyond students, academic staff and support staff; management evaluation; strategic planning; quality assurance; and flexibility and sustainability. In recognition of the desire for simplicity, however, it was decided to move towards a less complex three-phase model that would make apparent the hidden costs the team hoped to identify.

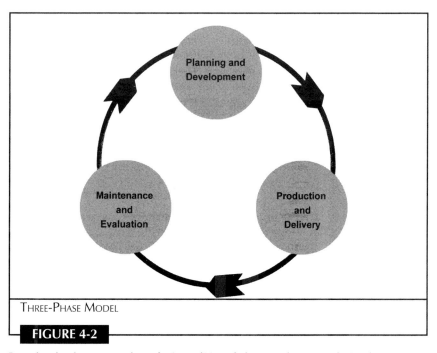

THREE-PHASE MODEL

FIGURE 4-2

Reproduced with permission from *The Costs of Networked Learning* by P. Bacsich, C.Ash, K. Boniwell, L. Kaplan, and A. Caven-Atack, Sheffield Hallam University, Sheffield, England, 1999.

The new model (Figure 4-2) includes evaluation and quality assurance but assumes that strategic planning envelops the whole. This three-phase model of the course life cycle revolves around three nodes: planning and development, production and delivery, maintenance and evaluation.

The team reported that the tests undertaken so far indicated that the model had functioned well as a framework for discussions of costs. The model was then used as one of the bases for the planning document and financial scheme.

Developing a Planning Framework and Financial Schema

The Sheffield Hallam team drew on many resources including the work of Bates, referenced earlier in this chapter, and the framework that KPMG and the Joint Funding Council laid out in their report,[16] as well as the work of the Flashlight project on costing methodology in the U.S.,[17] and the "classical" costing work of economists such as Rumble. Combining this earlier work with its own insights, the team produced a planning framework. The report refers with approval to the 1999 HEFCE document "Appraising Investment Decisions," which was reinterpreted so that the language is that of the educator, not the planner.[18]

The key steps in the framework are as follows:

1. Defining the objectives, which includes identifying the need or the problem, considering the strategic context, and deciding on the objectives.
2. Identifying the options.
3. Assessing basic costs and benefits.
4. Analyzing the information, which includes selecting a preferred solution and making an initial assessment of affordability.
5. Presenting the results.

If a full business case is to be developed, the report suggests that the following additional considerations be added:

- confirming assumptions of the basic business case
- considering procurement routes
- assessing financing options; and
- reassessing and selecting the preferred solution.

A useful further section puts forward an appraisal checklist which, in the view of the Bacsich team, could provide a very valuable tool for institutions. This list reworks Annex A of the HEFCE report in the language of teaching and learning and identifies the following five steps in the appraisal process: (1) identifying the objectives, (2) valuing costs and benefits, (3) assessing affordability, (4) presenting the results, and (5) monitoring and evaluating. The report also developed a set of questions for each of these stages which are quoted in full.

1. Specifying the *Objectives:*
   - How does this appraisal relate to the strategic aims of the department?
   - Is the teaching and learning requirement clearly defined?
   - Are the objectives supported by a strategic plan?
   - Identifying the options:
   - Has a sufficiently wide range of options been considered?
   - Has the "do nothing" or "do minimum" option been explicitly considered?
   - Have all the realistic procurement options been appraised (including innovative forms of procurement, such as buy-in of content, or use of consultant writers)?
2. *Valuing Costs, Benefits, Timing, Risks, and Uncertainties:*
   - Has account been taken of all the direct costs and benefits accruing to the department?
   - Are there any wider considerations?

- Have all relevant costs, income streams and benefits (over the life of the course) been included?
- Has allowance been made for running costs over the life of the course?
- In particular, have course maintenance (including running update) costs over the life of the course been taken into account?
- Does the appraisal take account of assets that are already owned (sunk costs), or could be used in other ways (opportunity costs)?
- Is there any double-counting of costs and benefits?
- What allowance has been made for non-financial aspects?
- Have uncertainties in key assumptions been identified and tested?
- Have risks been assessed and valued?

3. *Assessing affordability:*
- Has the impact on the department's overall financial position been assessed?
- Can the department accept the best and worst case scenarios?

4. *Presentation of results:*
- How does the chosen option compare with the alternatives?
- Are the results set out clearly, in an appraisal report, in a logical order, and with all relevant assumptions made clear?
- Are tables available showing the details of costs and benefits for all options?
- Do they show the effects of risks?
- Do they show the influence of sensitivities?
- Is the overall financial impact clear?

5. *Monitoring and evaluation:*
- Is provision made for monitoring throughout the course lifecycle?
- Are proposals included in the appraisal report for evaluating the course once implemented?
- Is the timescale for evaluation defined?[19]

Conclusion

In summary, the work of the Sheffield Hallam team has provided the UK with the first comprehensive and detailed study of the best way to establish the true costs of networked learning. Bacsich's foreword to the report rightly states that "the only way forward is to have a framework to understand the costs of teaching and learning, and in turn, the costs of universities, together with costs falling on the wider society of stakeholders." He argues convincingly that "educators need to imbue and enliven financial and planning tools with a modern educational viewpoint, so as to facilitate the creative dialogue be-tween pedagogues and planners."[20] The Bacsich team has recently been asked to undertake further work on its findings which will, hopefully, lead to practical working tools that institutions will be able to use.

CANADA

When we look at the western hemisphere beyond the United States, distance learning via electronic technology has played an important role in South America and Canada. For several decades, radio has been an instrument of distance learning for secondary education in Latin American countries. Important initiatives in distance education and especially in online teaching and learning have been taken by such Canadian institutions as the University of British Columbia and Athabasca University. Scholars in Canadian universities, such as A.W. Bates now at the University of British Columbia, have been key contributors to the research on teaching with technology, measuring its impact, and managing the costs of distance education. Also, the most outspoken demonstration of faculty reservations about certain trends in online teaching has been at Canada's York University.

In recent years, the Canadian government has created the TeleLearning Network of Centers of Excellence, which is responsible for a project called NCE-Telelearning. Telelearning is defined as "the use of multimedia learning environments based on powerful desktop computers."[21] This initiative is funded at $13 million and involves universities, colleges, schools, and other public and private organizations across Canada. Headed by Linda Harasim of Simon Fraser University, its purpose is to examine the effects of telecommunications on teaching and learning.[22]

Part of this larger initiative is a project under the auspices of *Distance Education and Technology,* an entity in the Department of Continuing Studies at the University of British Columbia that focuses on how technology affects learners. The project is directed by A.W. Bates and is called "Developing and Applying a Cost-Benefit Model for Assessing Telelearning."[23] Its purpose is "to develop and test a methodology that will allow decision-makers to analyze objectively the costs and benefits of using networks to provide education and training." It proceeds from the assumption that different educational technologies have different cost structures. The plan is to test and adapt an existing methodology to telelearning, to collect data on costs and benefits, look at the opportunity costs, and better understand costs in different areas of telelearning. Apart from producing guidelines for decision-makers using telelearning and a methodology for establishing the costs of telelearning, the project is expected to lead to a better understanding of why different forms of telelearning have different cost structures. Another objective of this project is to apply cost-benefit analysis to other NCE-Telelearning projects.

The ACTIONS model, developed by Bates a decade ago, is to guide the assessment of costs and benefits. It suggests such questions as: Where will students access education? What technology is suitable given the costs? What are the required approaches to teaching and learning? What are the mode and quality of student-teacher interaction? What organizational changes may be necessary? What innovation is apparent? and How speedily can learning materials be produced, changed, and accessed?

Bates had earlier developed a methodology for assessing the costs of distance education. This same methodology will serve in this project as the foundation for assessing the costs of telelearning. It includes the distinction between fixed and variable costs, production and delivery costs, and capital and operating costs. It considers the variables affecting costs, such as amount of material to be produced, number of students, length of time materials are to be used, as well as the costs of capital, operating, production, and delivery. Assumptions differ by institution. In making a decision to use a particular methodology, managers must consider "total costs over the whole life of a course . . . for different numbers of learners . . .; the marginal cost of increasing the volume of teaching by one unit . . .; the marginal costs of adding an additional student to a course . . .; the average cost per hour of study material for a particular technology . . ., [and] the average cost per student study hour." The ACTIONS model is also to guide the assessment of performance-driven benefits, such as learning outcomes; value-driven benefits, such as increased access; and societal benefits, such as reduced traffic.

The project at the University of British Columbia includes six case studies at Canadian institutions: Simon Fraser University, the Ontario Institute for Studies in Education/University of Toronto, Kwantlen University College, Southern Alberta Institute of Technology, LICEF Tele-Universite/University of Quebec, and the University of British Columbia. These case studies are intended to be cost-benefit analyses of different types of courseware used for course development, including *HyperNews* for asynchronous conferencing via the Web; *Virtual-U* which provides a course shell; *WebCSILE* which provides a communal database for asynchronous student/teacher exchanges; *Lotus Notes* for e-mail and "threaded discussion conferencing"; *NetMeeting* for Internet video and audio conferencing; and *Lernlink-I-Net* whose applications include support for administration of the learning environment.

In his 1999 book, *Managing Technological Change: Strategies for College and University Leaders*, A.W. Bates addresses a topic that is broader than the cost of information technology, but he deals with many of the cost issues of teaching with technology.[24] He stresses that the new technologies will not reduce cost but can improve cost-effectiveness, and that the costs of technology-based teaching can be measured accurately using activity-based costing (ABC). The book has much to say about the different cost structure of teaching with technology as compared with face-to-face teaching, the need for re-allocation of resources, and the need for organizational re-structuring. The author argues that direct costs of technology-based teaching compare favorably with the direct costs of conventional teaching. He also believes that a shift from spending on infrastructure and IT applications in administration to spending for IT in teaching and learning may be advisable. Cost-sharing through collaboration, partnerships, and consortia can ease the burden of IT costs.

EUROPEAN COMMUNITY

The Telelearn Study

The Telelearn Study, conducted from spring 1997 to 1999, differed fundamentally from the Sheffield Hallam study. The Telelearn Study focussed on the costing issue in relation to the use of learning technologies in vocational training and adult education, rather than in higher education. The project was partially funded as one of the Transnational Survey and Analysis Projects of the Leonardo da Vinci Program of the European Commission. It was carried out by a group of researchers drawn from the Netherlands, Italy, Spain, Sweden, and the UK. The impetus for the project came from the recognition that not enough was known about education and training costs to make informed decisions. The aim was to gather information to develop decision-making and costing analysis tools that would help organizations in the field of vocational training and adult learning decide how they might make use of technology to offer more flexible and easily accessed services.

Two main reports have been produced as a result of the two-year study undertaken by CINOP (Centrum voor Innovatie van Opleidingen), the Telelearn Project Report and the Case Study Report.[25] The work undertaken here predated the Sheffield Hallam study discussed above, but provided a useful basis for the broad question of costing. It created a corpus of relevant literature references and commissioned a number of case studies. A common resource base on costing issues was drawn up from a variety of national and international sources. Several case studies were developed which in their turn helped to create a Europe-wide community of interest in the topic. In addition, an online discussion group was established to stimulate further interest, understanding, and research on the subject.

The study used concept management tools to organize the data and a list of key cost factors was created, based on a review of earlier frameworks and models for costs of online training, and an analysis of the resources and case studies. The findings were disseminated through workshops, conferences, and publications at regional, national, and international levels. The main conclusions of the project were as follows:

1. Online training can be cost effective in certain circumstances.
2. The key cost factors can be discovered in the standard costing frameworks and highlighted.
3. Far too little accurate costing data is available.
4. The project had encountered great difficulty in getting accurate cost information from companies using online learning; in future projects, the report recommends that a commitment to provide *accurate* costs must be gained from key industrial and commercial stakeholders.
5. Work on the costs of online training needs to be carried out internationally and linked closely with work on costing online education.

The last point is of particular interest in the context of this volume. It is generally agreed that the more researchers on education costs are able to exchange information internationally, the more valuable are likely to be the findings. A new project, which is again under the auspices of the European Commission, to take this work forward has now been approved.

AUSTRALIA

Australian Studies on the Costs of Technology-Based Teaching and Learning

The Australian government introduced important policy changes affecting higher education in its 1996-97 budget. These changes placed universities in a much more competitive environment which made the need for accurate measurement of costs increasingly apparent. As a result, the Australian government's Department for Education, Training and Youth Affairs (DEETYA) launched a project charged with (1) publishing a report identifying the major cost issues in Australian higher education institutions and (2) developing a costing methodology for use by the institutions.[26]

This issues report, published in September 1998 is, by definition, broad-based. While the principal objective was to develop a sound costing methodology, this was to be achieved in close consultation and cooperation with interested universities. Great respect was paid to institutional autonomy, and universities were at liberty "to adopt, modify or reject the methodology developed [in line with] their own assessment of its usefulness to them."[27] The study assured institutions that no methodology would be imposed on them, regardless of whether a university participated in the study. Of course, the authors of the report hoped and expected that the new methodology would result in better ways to establish costs than traditional approaches.

The study had two stages: the first stage was the preparation of the discussion document on the issues which were then considered at a workshop attended by the eleven participating universities. The second stage was the

development of a costing methodology for distribution to university participants and testing it in the participating universities.

Because the Australian study was wide-ranging, the costs of technology-
based education were to a great extent subsumed in the broad sweep. Yet the
"Issues Report" specifically identified the costs of alternative delivery methods—distance education, including by correspondence and the Internet—as
key issues.[28]

The Australian report, which pre-dated the Bacsich study, makes reference
in some detail to work done in the UK. The Australians pay particular
attention to a parallel general study undertaken by the Scottish Higher
Education Funding Council that suggests comprehensive and accurate costing
methodologies that would help institutions meet their educational objectives.[29]

The report, *Costing Methodology for Use within Australian Higher Eductiton
Institutions was* published in September 1998. It recommends an activity based
management (ABM) approach to cost management. It argues that this ABM
appears to be the most productive approach to cost management, and the only
tool currently able to deliver what institutions require. "An activity describes
what an institution does—the way time is spent. First, you determine the costs
of significant activities. You then assign the cost of these activities to cost
objects such as courses. This approach also involves attributing all the overhead and support costs down to the predetermined cost objects."[30]

The report explains that activity-based management is built on the following components:

1. Establishing the project scope and start-up
2. Costing the activities
3. Costing the cost objects
4. Reporting

Data needs to be gathered from a wide range of areas: "financial, personnel,
records of orders, calls, problems; in addition to self-reporting of what activities are performed and percentage of time spent on each activity."[31]

The report is enthusiastic about this approach, expecting that it will
generate information which will provide universities with a distinct competitive advantage by enabling them to gain greater flexibility and be more
responsive to change. Some Australian universities are developing and delivering networked learning very effectively and in some respects are the world
leaders in this area.

The challenge of cultural resistance, touched on in the first of the Australian reports, resonates with other studies. This first Australian study concludes
that the key challenge to implementing an improved costing methodology is
that of confronting and overcoming cultural resistance. The ability of univer-

sities' managers to deliver successful change management strategies is crucial to acceptance of those strategies by employees. If universities are unsuccessful in dealing with this change, then employee resistance to all change develops. The report quotes Rosabeth Moss Kanter's 1989 book, *When Giants Learn to Dance*. She identified in social and psychological terms the specific sources of such resistance. Among the behaviors which she enumerated were the loss of control linked to sudden, unprepared changes; loss of staff confidence; and fear of loss of status.[32]

The report recognizes that if the universities are to introduce improved costing methodologies, their success will depend on the skill with which change management strategies are put in place. Currently, the follow-up work involves studying each of three pilot areas for one year—estates, catering, and arts. It will be interesting to revisit this topic in a few years to determine if the pilot studies are successful and if the costing methodologies are working smoothly.

CONCLUSION: TAKING TECHNOLOGY COSTING FORWARD

Work is progressing in the UK, Canada, the European Union (EU), Australia, and the United States to look further into costing technology. Projects in the UK, Canada, Australia, and the EU have already been commented on in this chapter. The U.S. work is the subject of the rest of this volume. One study that is proving influential to those outside the U.S. is the Flashlight Project linked to the TLT Group at One Dupont Circle, in Washington, D.C. There is much interest also in the Technology Costing Methodology Project being undertaken by the Western Interstate Commission on Higher Education (WICHE) and the National Center for Higher Education Management Systems in Boulder, Colorado, which is also producing a costing methodology for calculating technology costs both within an institution and across institutions. This methodology is currently (2000) being pilot tested in Montana, New Mexico, Utah, and Washington.

The Sheffield Hallam team is involved in bidding for or undertaking several relevant projects. Sheffield Hallam has bid for a study to identify the real costs to staff and students for the procurement and implementation of computing and IT systems in higher education institutions. The emphasis of the study will be on non-technical costs, such as human effort, and resources and retraining and rewriting of materials. It will examine what lessons can be learned from elsewhere, both domestically and internationally, and from both the private and public sectors.

The Sheffield Hallam team is undertaking a study to evaluate the Further Education National Learning Network, with a particular focus on "Value for Money" in evaluating the effectiveness of investment, especially investment in technology at further education colleges.

Another study is Phase 2 of the Costs of Networked Learning, which was discussed in detail earlier in this chapter. The aim is to develop the current theoretical framework into a practical handbook that can be employed by universities to cost all types of learning. The methodology will be based on three stages:

1. A draft handbook will be developed and written based on the outcomes of Phase 1.
2. Liaison will be established with industry partners and trials will be held. Focus group meetings with stakeholders participating in the trial will take place.
3. The handbook will be rewritten in light of the results of the trial.

One key activity during this study will be analysis of the trials of other methodologies, such as *The Flashlight Costing Handbook* and the recent Australian Costing Methodology. An industry partner will be engaged to assist with the more complex costing issues and to evaluate the activity-based costing software.

Like other researchers, Bacsich still has concerns about the reluctance of the higher education sector to engage in any form of intrusive costing research. However, it is hoped that by the production of the final handbook most of the controversial issues will have been satisfactorily resolved. Realistic explanatory figures based on real data, but with suitable scaling and protection of the confidentiality of the sources of the data, will be used in the trial of the draft handbook. The draft handbook will then be used by two faculties for pilot studies. The final outcome should be a handbook that takes into account the research findings and methodological frameworks being developed in other countries as well as experience drawn from the UK. The need, then, is for the staff throughout the sector to be persuaded, institution by institution, that such an approach is to everyone's advantage in providing the information on which sound decisions on the use of technology-based education can be made.

In an age when every week brings news of new global partnerships relating to technology and to transworld university collaborative arrangements to maximize the use of technology-based education, knowing what it costs is absolutely essential. It is a global necessity, which it behooves each country and each group of countries to address to its own satisfaction.

ENDNOTES

1. G. Rumble, "Online Costs: Interactivity at a Price" in R. Mason and A. Kaye, eds. *Mindweave: Communication: Computers and Distance Education*. Oxford: Pergamon Press, 1989.

2. A.W. Bates ed., *Media and Technology in European Distance Education*. London: Milton Keynes, 1990.

3. A.W. Bates, *Technology, Open Learning and Distance Education*. London: Routledge, 1995.

4. G. Rumble, *The Costs and Economics of Open and Distance Learning*. London: Kogan Page Ltd., 1997.

5. G. Rumble, "The Costs of Networked Learning: What Have We Learnt?" Paper presented at the FLISH 99 Conference, 1999. See <http://www.shu.ac.uk/flish/rumblep.htm>.

6. National Committee of Inquiry Into Higher Education (NCIHE), *Higher Education in the Learning Society*. London: HMSO, 1997.

7. P. Bacsich, C. Ash, K. Boniwell, L. Kaplan, J. Mardell, and A. Caven-Atack, *The Costs of Network Learning*. Sheffield: Sheffield Hallam University, 1999.

8. *Joint Information Systems Committee Circular*, September 1998.

9. Bacsich et al., *Costs of Networked Learning*, p. 4.

10. Bacsich et al., *Costs of Networked Learning*, p.7.

11. National Union of Students, unpublished document..

12. S. Alexander, J. Mckenzie, and H. Geissinger, *An Evaluation of Information Technology Projects for University Learning*. 1998; Arizona Learning Systems, *Preliminary Cost Methodology for Distance Learning*. Report dated August 21, 1998, Arizona Learning Systems and the State Board of Directors for Community Colleges of Arizona, 1998; A.W. Bates, *Assessing the Costs and Benefits of Telelearning: A Case Study from the University of British Columbia*. 1998. See <http://research.cstudies.ubc.ca>.

13. S. Alexander, J. Mckenzie, and H. Geissinger, *An Evaluation of Information Technology Projects for University Learning*. 1998..

14. KPMG Management Consulting and Joint Funding Councils, *Management Information for Decision Making: Costing Guidelines for Higher Education Institutions*. Bristol: Higher Education Funding Council for England (HEFCE), 1997.

15. K.C. Green, *Campus Computing 1998: The Ninth National Survey of Desktop Computing and Information Technology in Higher Education*. The Campus Computing Project, 1999.

16. Higher Education Funding Council for England (HEFCE), *Appraising Investment Decisions*. HEFCE Guide 99/21. Bristol: HEFCE, March 1999; Bacsich et al., *Costs of Networked Learning*, pp. 63-64.

17. L. Delinger, S.C. Ehrmann, and J.H. Milam, *Flashlight Cost Analysis Handbook, Version 1:0: Remodelling Resource Use in Teaching and Learning with Technology*. Washington, DC: American Association of Higher Education, 1999.

18. Bacsich et al., *Costs of Networked Learning*, p. 65.

19. Bacsich et al., *Costs of Networked Learning*, p. iii.

20. Bacsich et al., *Costs of Networked Learning*, p. 65.

21. See <http://www.telelearn.ca/access/front.html>.

22. See <http://research.cstudies.ubc.ca>.

23. A.W. Bates, *Technology, Open Learning, and Distance Education*.

24. A.W. Bates, *Managing Technological Change: Strategies for College and University Leaders*. San Francisco: Jossey-Bass Publishers, 1999.

25. P. Vries and S. Hertogenbosch, "The Telelearn Project Report" and "Case Study Reports," 1999. See <http://www.ellinet.org/telelearn>.

26. S. Robertson, G. Applebee, R. Bernasconi, N. Forshaw, and G. McKay, *Issues Report on Costing within Australian Higher Education Institutions.* Like the following item, this is an Ernst & Young report prepared for Australia's Commonwealth Department of Employment, Education, Training and Youth Affairs—DEETYA (now Department of Education, Training, and Youth Affairs—DETYA), September 1998, 82 pages. See <http://www.deet.gov.au/highered/otherpub/costme.pdf>. S. Robertson, G. Applebee, R. Bernasconi, N. Forshaw, N., and G. Mckay, *Costing Methodology for Use within Australian Higher Education Institutions.* DEETYA, September 1998, 50 pages. See <http://www.deet.gov.au/highered/otherpub/costme.pdf>.

27. Robertson et al., *Issues Report,* paragraph 2.

28. Robertson et al., *Issues Report,* paragraph 23.

29. Scottish Higher Education Funding Council, unpublished report.

30. Robertson et al., *Issues Report,* paragraph 36.

31. Robertson et al., *Costing Methodology,* p. 6.

32. R. Moss Kanter, *When Giants Learn to Dance.* New York: Simon and Schuster, 1989.

Part 2

· · · · · · · · · · ·

Analytical Frameworks and Empirical Findings

CHAPTER 5

A Framework for the Comparative Analysis of the Costs of Classroom Instruction vis-à-vis Distributed Instruction

Frank Jewett

INTRODUCTION

The material in this chapter contains some innovations that, to the best of my knowledge, appear here for the first time: (1) the use of an index of average learning outcomes to adjust FTE (or student credit units) as a measure of educational output (we can't sensibly discuss costs and productivity until we have defined output in terms of total learning outcomes), (2) the derivation of an average cost function for higher education institutions that includes measures of learning productivity and faculty and staff productivity, (3) functional definitions of "classroom technology" and "distributed technology," and (4) a fundamental result regarding the faculty resource needs of distributed instruction relative to classroom instruction.

Note: The preparation of this chapter was supported by a grant from the New Jersey Institute for Collegiate Teaching and Learning. The content of the chapter draws, in part, from the author's work as director of a project entitled *Case Studies in Evaluating the Benefits and Costs of Mediated Instruction and Distributed Learning*, which was funded through a Field-Initiated Studies Educational Research Grant by the National Institute on Postsecondary Education, Libraries, and Lifelong Learning, Office of Educational Research and Improvement, U.S. Department of Education, with additional funding provided by Information Resources and Technology in the Chancellor's Office of the California State University.

Contributor's Note: I owe a major debt to Tony Bates, Dennis Jones, Jim Mingle, and Tom West, the four individuals who served on the advisory board of the benefit cost project that I recently completed. Their suggestions, advice, and encouragement have had a major effect upon the substance of this chapter. Other individuals who reviewed drafts of the chapter and provided helpful comments include Chuck Wilmot, Frank Young, Lorie Roth, Philip Garcia, Chuck Schneebeck, Maryanne Bakia, Jim Hightower, Russ Utterberg, Judith Boettcher, Patricia Cuocco, Carol Twigg, and Carol Frances.

THE QUEST FOR INCREASING PRODUCTIVITY IN HIGHER EDUCATION

Total expenditures for higher education have grown substantially in the past 40 years. The growth has been driven by increases in both student enrollments and increases in the rate of expenditure per student. Increases in student enrollments occur because of population growth[1] and because of the shifting occupational structure in the labor market in favor of educated individuals,[2] thus providing an incentive for increased participation in higher education from any given population.

Escalation of Per-Student Costs

Expenditures per student grow for a variety of reasons. During the 1960s, 1970s, and 1980s, colleges and universities assumed an increased range of activities, including outreach, recruitment, and remedial programs, and were required to meet occupational health and safety, disabled access, and environmental regulations. In addition to new programs and legislative requirements, costs also grow because of increased wages and salaries (including the costs of fringe benefits) and increases in the prices of goods and services purchased by the institutions. Increases in the prices of products purchased can be directly attributed to the effects of inflation. Increases in salaries can also be attributed to inflation in the sense that the decision to ask for, or grant, a pay increase can be motivated by the desire to provide employees with constant purchasing power (e.g., a 2 percent increase in consumer prices requires a 2 percent increase in income to maintain constant purchasing power).

In the funding of public higher education, there is tension between the perception that the increase in education associated with enrollment growth is basically a good thing for the society and economy and should be funded, and the reluctance to fund growing enrollments at a continuously increasing cost per student, especially in light of other pressing social priorities, such as K-12 education and health care. Because a major component of this financing problem is the growth in cost per student (or per FTE), an understanding of the relationship between productivity and costs is crucial. The basic definition of productivity is output per unit of labor input. If output per unit of input is constant (productivity is constant) and the cost of labor inputs (e.g., wages and salaries) increases, it follows that the average unit cost of output must also increase. Alternatively, improvements in productivity can act directly to offset increases in input costs.

What Is Productivity?

Before further pursuing the relationship between costs and productivity, it is necessary to clarify the relationship between technology and productivity. *Technology*[3] is a description of the way things are done, how tasks are accomplished (one dictionary definition is "applied science"). The economic definition, consistent with the dictionary definition, refers to how resources (inputs) are used to produce products—goods and services. Manufacturing technology provides good examples, e.g., in the automobile industry where the inputs (workers, semi-processed materials, factories, equipment) come together using assembly line technology to produce automobiles. The economic concept of technology is not limited to manufacturing. It has relevance to understanding production activities in all sectors of a modern economy, including education.[4]

Within the higher education sector, the predominant technology for producing educational services can be described as "classroom technology," which literally requires a classroom, a teacher, tablet armchairs, and a chalkboard to instruct students. Important supporting materials include textbooks, a syllabus, other course handouts, and access to a library.

Labor productivity is defined as a ratio of units of output per unit of labor input. Examples of productivity are contained in such statements as "He can bake 10 pies in an hour," or "It takes 0.10 work-year to build an automobile." In both examples, the output is a tangible product and the input is a measure of labor effort. If there are several different ways (technologies) for producing pies of equal quality, one would usually choose among them by selecting the technology associated with the lowest cost per unit of output—the lowest average cost. That technology can be characterized (in an over-simplified way) as the most efficient, i.e., most efficient in terms of producing the most output per unit of expenditure on inputs.[5]

The relationship between technology and productivity is fundamental. Within a given technology, the flexibility to increase productivity is limited. Major improvements in productivity tend to occur when there is a major change in technology (e.g., the change in transportation technology from horse and wagon to railroad). The implementation of productivity enhancing technology generally involves augmenting labor effort with more and better tools, equipment, and facilities. Although these capital investments are often expensive, a commonly observed result is an increase in labor productivity sufficiently large so that the average cost of output (taking account of all inputs including the new equipment and facilities) declines.

The incentive for individual business firms in the private sector to use the most productive technology is to increase profits and to protect against other firms with lower costs gaining market share by undercutting prices. In the public sector, the incentive for government agencies is weaker because government services are not ordinarily sold to consumers. However, the executive and legislative branches of government have an incentive to urge agencies to use the most productive technology as a means of minimizing the government tax burden. Within individual government agencies, the incentive to adopt more productive technology probably has more to do with most effectively using the agency's budget revenues.[6]

Input Costs, Output Costs, and Productivity

A simplified general relationship between input and output costs can be derived based upon an expression for calculating total costs and average costs of production. Total cost (TC) is the sum of all input costs, e.g., labor costs plus all other costs, associated with the production process in some time period, e.g., a month or a year.

$$(1) \quad TC = wL + OEX$$

TC = total production costs for a given product in a given time period
w = hourly wage rate for labor
L = number of labor hours
OEX = all other expenses including the costs of materials, utilities, equipment, leases, loan payments, and overhead

Average cost (AC) is total cost divided by the number of units produced in the time period.

$$(2) \quad AC = \frac{TC}{Q} = \frac{wL + OEX}{Q} = \frac{wL}{Q} + \frac{OEX}{Q}$$

AC = average cost of a unit of output
Q = units of output produced

Thus, the average cost of a unit of output can be interpreted as the sum of labor cost per unit of output plus all other expenses per unit of output. Equation (2) can be rearranged to show labor productivity explicitly.[7]

$$(3) \quad AC = \frac{w}{Q/L} + \frac{OEX}{Q}$$

Q/L = units of output per unit of labor input, a standard definition of labor productivity

The implications of these average cost relationships are further summarized in Table 5-A. The table and the equations illustrate the important results that increases in wages or other production expenditures tend to increase average costs while improvements (increases) in productivity tend to reduce average costs. One implication is that the effect of wage increases on average costs can be offset by a productivity increase. Another implication is that investments in new equipment (an increase in "all other expenses") that embodies new technology may allow both wage increases and reductions in average costs provided the new technology increases labor productivity sufficiently.

COSTS AND SCALE EFFECTS: A COMPLICATION

There is an important qualification to the preceding discussion about costs and productivity improvements. Most productivity improving technology changes require additional equipment and capital facilities to be implemented. These

TABLE 5-A

EFFECTS OF CHANGES IN INPUT COSTS AND PRODUCTIVITY UPON AVERAGE COSTS

Increases in:	Cause (AC) the average cost of a unit of output to:
Costs of labor (wages, salaries, fringe benefits) **(w)**	Increase
Costs of materials (part of **OEX**)	Increase
Costs of utilities/communications (part of **OEX**)	Increase
Costs of equipment and capital facilities (including loan payments—part of **OEX**)	Increase
Costs of other items including overhead (part of **OEX**)	Increase
Productivity (output per unit of labor input) **(Q/L)**	Decrease

capital expenses, often treated as the payment to amortize a loan to purchase the equipment (included above as part of OEX), are fixed in regard to the amount of output produced. As a result of these added fixed costs, it is unlikely that the implementation of the new technology will result in lower average costs at *all* levels of production.

Figures 5-1 and 5-2 illustrate the situation. The improved productivity flattens the new total cost line TC(1) relative to the old one TC(0) but the increase in OEX (associated with the additional equipment that increases labor productivity) causes TC(1) to shift up relative to the total cost (TC) axis. Thus, in the example, the technology change reduces total costs only when produc-

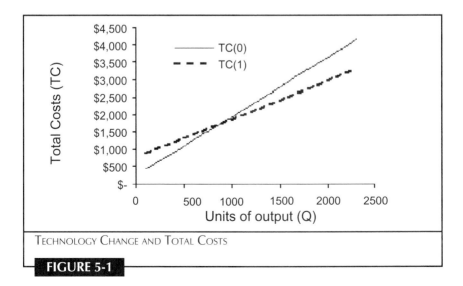

TECHNOLOGY CHANGE AND TOTAL COSTS

FIGURE 5-1

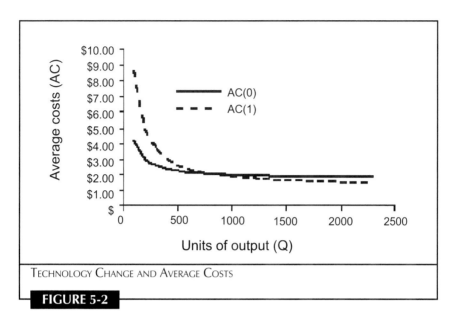

TECHNOLOGY CHANGE AND AVERAGE COSTS

FIGURE 5-2

tion exceeds approximately 900 units. Figure 5-2 shows exactly the same result except it is cast in terms of average costs (AC) instead of total costs.

The trade-off between lower average costs (above some level of output) and higher fixed costs (due to more investment in equipment and facilities) is often described as a "scale" effect. In some situations, demand for the product may be insufficient (e.g., less than 500 units) to warrant implementation of more capital-intensive technology because the scale of operation is insufficient to achieve the potential cost savings, i.e., the higher fixed costs are spread over too few units of production. Alternatively, at a production level of 1,500 units, the scale effect is operable; the higher fixed costs associated with the newer technology have been spread over enough units of output to allow the more efficient production process to have an effect.

Measuring Labor Productivity—Another Complication

Within a manufacturing or agricultural environment, it is plausible to measure productivity in terms of units of output per hour of labor input. Even here, however, such measures encounter difficulties. Output must be a single, homogeneous product of constant quality. The hours of input must also be homogeneous and of constant quality. In a dynamic economy, these assumptions are often violated; changes in technology often involve changes in the quality of the product and a concomitant change in the necessary skill levels of the workers.

The result is that precise measurements of labor productivity over time are possible only in narrow and carefully controlled environments. Measures of productivity at the industry level are usually based upon aggregate indices of both output and labor inputs; they are approximations that involve many assumptions.[8] Measures of productivity at the national level are even more tenuous in that they involve aggregations across all, or most, industrial sectors, a changing mix and quality of products, and a changing mix of labor skill levels.

In spite of these measurement difficulties, the concept of labor productivity survives and has credibility for at least two reasons: (1) from a theoretical standpoint, it plays a key role in understanding how changes in technology (changes in the way inputs or resources are combined to produce goods and services) relate to changes in the costs of production, and (2) in spite of the difficulties of measurement, the results of productivity improvements are observable phenomena that explain, for example, how the real value of U.S. agriculture production continues to grow while agricultural employment has been declining throughout this century or how manufacturing production continues to grow while manufacturing employment has been essentially constant for several decades.

TECHNOLOGY, PRODUCTIVITY, AND COSTS IN HIGHER EDUCATION

Measuring Output in Higher Education

Higher education provides educational services to students.[9] The services can be thought of as providing structured experiences that give students the opportunity to learn.[10] Alternative ways for providing educational services to students include older technologies, such as one-on-one tutoring, correspondence courses, and the current "classroom technology." Newer technologies include televised transmission of classroom materials, including lectures and discussions for students at remote sites and so-called asynchronous modes where video or computer-based media are accessed by students at times and locations more-or-less at their own convenience.

A basic question is whether these electronically mediated technologies have any potential to increase productivity in higher education. An important secondary issue is whether it is possible in a practical sense to measure output so that productivity ratios (and costs) associated with different technologies can be validly compared.

Because educational services are intangible, they are more difficult to measure than manufactured products. While it is possible to measure the number of individuals who receive the services (e.g., the number of students enrolled in a course), it is difficult to obtain a direct measure of the quality of those services in terms of what individual students learn. Given the absence of agreed-upon outcomes measures, it is still possible to make some progress in measuring productivity in higher education, provided we are willing to work with comparisons of learning outcomes (as measured by course grades, examination scores, surveys of students, faculty, etc.).

The standard measure of instructional activity and output in higher education is full-time equivalents or FTEs. FTE is defined in various (equivalent) ways as the number of students if all were enrolled for 15 units of course work, or all course units enrolled by all students divided by 15, or all units generated by enrollments in all courses divided by 15.[11] As an aggregate measure of instructional activity at an institution, FTE has the advantage of counting all course enrollments weighted by course credit units. However, FTE is considered a defective measure of instructional output because it measures input (nominal student work effort) rather than student learning. FTE is also artificial in the sense that few students carry a full 15-unit workload. This latter problem can be rectified simply by dropping the reference to 15 units. The problem of measuring student learning is addressed by introducing a factor that adjusts for changes in the quality of learning outcomes.

Measuring Output for a Single Course (or Course Section)

It is best to begin by considering the measurement of instructional activities from the perspective of a course that enrolls several students. Student credit units (SCU) in the ith course (section) are the product of the course's credit units (CCU) and enrollment (ENR).

$(4)^{12}$ $SCU_i = CCU_i \times ENR_i$

For example, a three-unit course enrolling 25 students generates 75 SCU.[13]

An adjustment factor for the amount of individual learning that occurs in the course can be introduced as a term representing average learning outcomes (ALO_i) for students enrolled in the course. An immediate problem with ALO is that a general objective measure of "learning" does not exist. It is possible, however, to define ALO in a comparative or relative sense. Based upon some set of criteria or indicators, one might conclude that for some given course the quality of learning outcomes, ALO, has increased, decreased, or remained constant between two adjacent years, i.e., $ALO(t+1) > ALO(t)$, $ALO(t+1) < ALO(t)$, or $ALO(t+1) = ALO(t)$. Alternatively, the comparison could be made between learning outcomes associated with different technologies for delivery of the course content, i.e., that the ALO associated with some particular form of distributed instruction are greater than, less than, or about equal to those associated with classroom instruction, e.g., $ALO(distributed) >$, $<$, $= ALO(classroom)$.

Defining ALO in a relative sense, as a comparison between two situations, allows it to be expressed as an index with an initial value of 1 (associated with some initial time period or with an initial mode of course delivery) and subsequent values greater than 1, less than 1, or equal to 1 depending upon the outcome of the particular comparison. A measure of total student learning outcomes (TLO) in the course can then be obtained by using the ALO index to adjust the student credit unit calculation.

(5) $TLO_i = ALO_i \times CCU_i \times ENR_i$

The result is a measure of total student learning outcomes that is sensitive to (1) the number of students enrolled in a course, (2) the number of credit units for which the course is offered, and (3) an adjustment factor that takes account of whether there has been a change in the quality of learning outcomes. For example, if course enrollment increased by 10 percent between year 1 and year 2 and there was reason to believe ALO had remained constant, $ALO(t) = 1 = ALO(t+1)$, one could conclude that TLO (and SCU) had increased by 10 percent. Alternatively, if enrollment went up 10 percent and there was reason to believe that ALO had declined by about the same amount, $ALO(t+1) = 0.9$, SCU would increase but there would be essentially no change in TLO.

The TLO equation does not provide an absolute measure of total learning outcomes. If only one observation of course units and enrollment is possible, e.g., the first time a course is offered, ALO = 1 and TLO = SCU. ALO can only take a value other than 1 when there is a basis to make a comparison between two versions of the course, such as between two different years when the course was offered, or between offering the course in classroom mode and some specific electronically mediated mode.

In view of the difficulty of measuring ALO, a more practical approach for comparing two values of TLO is to work with inequalities, $ALO(t+1) \ge ALO(t)$, that eliminate the need for conclusions to the effect that ALO is up or down by some percentage amount.[14] For example, if the inequality holds and enrollment is constant between two periods, it can be concluded that $TLO(t+1)$ is *at least* as large as $TLO(t)$, or if the inequality holds and enrollment grows by 5 percent, it can be concluded that TLO has grown by *at least* 5 percent.

Introduction of the ALO index adds a quality dimension to the measurement of the production of educational services. It provides a basis in some situations for a calculation of educational productivity and the conditions under which it may be concluded that such productivity has changed. This potential exists even if actual measurements of changes in ALO are difficult and cumbersome to accomplish.

Measuring Output for All Courses Across a Campus

Equations (4) and (5) can be aggregated to obtain campus-wide measures by summing across all courses.

$$(4a) \quad SCU = \sum_i CCUi(ENRi)$$

$$(5a) \quad TLO = \sum_i ALOi(CCUi)(ENRi)$$

SCU (without the subscript) refers to campus total student credit units and TLO refers to campus total learning outcomes (student credit units weighted by the ALO indices). Equations (4a) and **(5a) can be combined** to obtain a campus-wide weighted index of average learning outcomes across all courses.

$$(6) \quad ALO = \frac{TLO}{SCU} = \frac{\sum ALOi(CCUi)(ENRi)}{\sum CCUi(ENRi)}$$

Evidence Regarding the Benefits of Electronically Mediated Instruction

Learning Outcomes

Learning outcomes for students are the primary direct benefit of providing instruction. The issue here is how do the learning outcomes associated with various forms of mediated instruction compare with those of classroom instruction. Basing studies on comparisons of classrooms with mediated instruction has the advantage of not requiring a fundamental definition and measurement of learning, only a relative comparison.

A series of eight benefit cost case studies conducted by the author in 1997-1998 involved comparisons of learning outcomes for students taking the same or similar courses in both classroom and various technology-mediated settings. These studies showed a consistent pattern of no significant difference for the comparisons that were made, including grades, exam scores, student attitudes, and faculty attitudes.[15]

These results are similar to those reported by Thomas Russell in "The 'No Significant Difference' Phenomena," which reviews over 200 comparison studies spanning the period 1928-1996.[16] Greville Rumble also reported on a series of studies done outside the U.S. that had essentially similar findings regarding learning outcomes.[17] Finally, James Kulik reported on a series of studies on the effectiveness of computer-based instruction[18] and concluded that computer-based instruction is generally effective in grades K-12.

The "no significant difference" finding has been challenged recently by Merisotis and Phipps, who raise questions about the methodology used in the studies. The Merisotis and Phipps critique has been answered by Brown and Wack and, perhaps most perceptively, by Peter Ewell in an editorial in *Change* magazine.[19] As Ewell pointed out, a basic problem is that critiques of the individual studies ignore the fact that all the studies show no significant difference. The piece of the critique that is missing, the piece that would make the case most convincing, is a list of studies showing that there is a significant difference and that it is in favor of classroom instruction.

The preponderance of evidence at this point is consistent with the working hypothesis put forward above that average learning outcomes for distributed instruction are at least as good as those of classroom instruction, i.e., that $ALO(distributed) \geq ALO(classroom)$.

Other Benefits

Two other benefits associated with distributed instruction were identified in the case studies previously mentioned: improved student access and institutional renewal and growth. In the Maine and Virginia (Old Dominion University) case studies, listed as c and e in footnote #15, where television was used to provide instruction to remote students throughout the state, the author estimated increases in statewide participation rates on the order of magnitude of 4 percent. Such increases suggest that making instruction more convenient for individuals does provide an incentive for more students to participate. Convenience and access turn out to be different sides of the same coin.

In terms of institutional renewal and growth, all the cases reported opportunities for faculty development in terms of learning to use the media for instructional purposes. Another important result relative to institutional growth was how the delivery of instruction to other campuses required cooperation among campuses regarding course and program sharing; see especially the case studies on the joint MSW program in Ohio, at Old Dominion, and the SUNY Brockport cases (items d, e, and g in footnote #15). The results for these other benefits reinforce the conclusion stated above.

Input Costs, Output Cost, and Productivity in Higher Education

The general equations for total and average cost (equations (1) and (2), above) can be adapted to an institution of higher education by using a model that includes faculty positions, staff positions, and expenditures for other operating expense and overhead.

Total operating cost (TC) for this model is as follows:

(7) $TC = s1(FP) + s2(SP) + OEX$

FP = faculty positions

SP = staff positions
s1 = average faculty salaries (including benefits)
s2 = average staff salaries (including benefits)
OEX = operating expenses and overhead

Taking campus total learning outcomes (TLO from equation (6), above) as the measure of output, average costs are as follows:

$$AC = \frac{TC}{TLO} = \frac{s1(FP) + s2(SP) + OEX}{TLO} = \frac{s1(FP) + s2(SP) + OEX}{ALO(SCU)}$$

This equation can be rewritten to show the dependence of average costs (per TLO) upon various productivity measures.[20]

$$(8) \quad AC = \frac{1}{ALO}\left[\frac{s1}{sfr} + \frac{s2}{ssr} + \frac{OEX}{SCU}\right]$$

sfr = SCU/FP, the "student faculty ratio"
ssr = SCU/SP, the "student staff ratio"
ALO = the campus-wide weighted index of average student learning outcomes, an index of learning productivity

The "sfr" defined above is the familiar student faculty ratio except that its numerator is student credit units (SCU) instead of FTE. The student staff ratio, "ssr,"[21] is defined in a manner parallel to the "sfr." Although the "ssr" is not as familiar and direct a relationship as that expressed by the student-faculty ratio,[22] non-faculty staff in all departments and offices of the campus contribute indirectly to the production of total learning outcomes in the sense that if the various support functions were not provided, the campus could not function and instruction could not occur.

The two ratios, sfr and ssr, relate student credit units to faculty and staff position inputs and can be interpreted as "volume of output" productivity measures. The ALO index can be thought of as a "learning productivity" measure in the sense that it adjusts for changes in the average quality of individual learning outcomes. Taken together, the three productivity measures account for changes in both quantity and quality. In parallel with the earlier discussion of productivity, equation (8) defines a comprehensive relationship between average cost of output, labor input costs (s1 and s2), faculty, staff, and learning productivity, and all other expenditures. Increases in labor input costs and other expenditures act to increase AC, increases in any of the three productivity measures act to reduce AC, simultaneous increases and decreases have offsetting effects.

Two Examples

The following examples apply the concepts of productivity, ALO, and TLO to (slightly) fictionalized situations.

Example #1: Funding in a Period of "Normal Times"

Background: The state and the nation have experienced a mild business expansion for the past five years (since 1993). State tax revenues have grown in pace with the state's economy. Consistent with the growth of the population and the economy, enrollment in the state university system has grown at about 1.5 percent per year (about 7.73 percent for the five-year period).

Changes in ALO: The ALO index, measured across all campus courses, was 1 in 1993. Given that the campuses (1) have experienced normal turnover in the ranks of faculty and staff, (2) had no difficulty in hiring qualified new employees, (3) have been able to bring new building and equipment capacity online as needed, (4) have not instituted any major changes in curriculum requirements, and (5) have not instituted any changes in the way courses are offered, one might conclude that the ALO index has, at least, remained constant over the entire time period. One might argue for some positive trend in the index based upon the introduction of more computer-related elements in the curriculum that allow students to communicate more effectively with faculty and each other, and that provide access to a broader range of application programs and information resources. (Without specific evidence to substantiate the claim, it would be difficult to argue that the trend in ALO has been negative.) This example satisfies the inequality requirement on ALO discussed above—ALO (1994, 1995, 1996, 1997) ≥ ALO (1993). The conclusion is that FTE has grown by 7.7 percent *and* TLO has grown by at least 7.7 percent.

Budget Projection If Productivity Is Constant: Assume the inflation rate is 2 percent. The legislature has authorized university expenditures for the next fiscal year, including a 2-percent increase to make up for inflation (including an across-the-board pay increase—about 85 percent of the institution's budget is salary and wage costs, 15 percent is other operating expense.) In addition, enrollment growth of 1.5 percent is projected. The necessary funding increase (with constant productivity—constant "sfr" and "ssr" as defined above) is about 3.5 percent.[23]

Budget Projection If Productivity Improves: If productivity (sfr and ssr) were projected to increase by 2 percent, the 2-percent increase in salary costs would be entirely offset. The necessary expenditure growth would be 1.8 percent (1.5 for enrollment increase and .3 for the non-personnel cost increase), less than the rate of inflation.

There is little evidence of (average) cost reducing productivity improvements in higher education over the past 40 to 50 years.[24] Perhaps the best evidence to support this is that technology has not changed in any basic way during this period. Thus, in ordinary times, the full cost increase of 3.5 percent would occur with the result that the expenditure budget would increase faster than inflation. This situation raises concerns that the public higher education budget will absorb an ever larger share of general fund public revenues.

Example #2: Funding in a Situation that Involves a "Budget Cut"

> *Background:* Occasionally, the times are not normal. The national recession that began in 1990 provides an example. In many states, recession-induced declines in tax revenues led to reductions in public higher education budgets in 1991-92 and 1992-93. The question is whether the legislature can mandate an increase in productivity by arbitrarily reducing a campus's funding level (e.g., increase the student faculty ratio) and thereby reduce costs per FTE. It is argued here that such changes in productivity are difficult or impossible to mandate.

When such a budget cut occurs, institutions are faced with several difficult alternatives.

> *Institutional Response #1—Reduce Enrollments, Protect the Funding Rate:* In this case, campuses manage enrollments and course offerings so as to reduce the FTE actually accommodated. This practice protects quality by maintaining the funding rate at which the instructional program is operated (keeping costs per FTE and per ALO constant) but this is accomplished by restricting student access (it is more difficult for new students to get admitted and more difficult for continuing students to enroll in courses).

> *Institutional Response #2—Increase Tuition, Protect the Funding Rate:* This response involves raising the tuition and fees paid by students to make up for the shortfall in public funding. Again, this action tends to protect quality by maintaining the funding rate (keeping costs per FTE and per ALO constant) for the program. It may also reduce costs to the state, but this is accomplished by shifting more of the financial burden to students and their families and again has a negative impact upon student access.

Responses 1 and 2 are unpopular with the legislature. They are also unpopular with students and their families who are likely to find themselves in the position of either finding it more difficult to enroll in classes (choice 1), paying more (choice 2), or, because the choices are not mutually exclusive, some combination of the two (finding it more difficult to enroll in classes *and* paying more). Nevertheless, campuses are likely to institute some mix of these two policies as a response to budget reductions because of a recognition of the difficulties associated with attempting to actually implement the increased student faculty ratio.

Institutional Response #3—Accept the Reduced Funding Rate: In this situation, the campuses accept the increased student faculty ratio. This acceptance will reduce costs per SCU (or FTE). Within the context of classroom technology, this means the faculty, on average, must literally instruct more students in the classrooms. As explained below, this situation may not increase productivity. This choice is unpopular with faculty who are faced with the lose-lose situation of either increasing their work efforts or allowing educational quality to decline (or both).

Faculty Response A: One possible faculty response is to spend more effort on instructional activities to insure individual student learning outcomes (ALO) don't decline even though a larger number of students are instructed. Costs per SCU do decline but there is no real improvement in productivity (ALO/FP) because faculty work hours (the real measure of inputs) have increased. In effect, the increased output per position is obtained by increasing the input (the work hours associated with a position). The state obtains its objective of reducing costs per FTE and TLO but it does so because faculty either are working harder or have redirected their efforts (e.g., from research or public service to teaching).

Faculty Response B: Another possible response is to maintain work effort at a constant level. This response leads to a decline in faculty time per individual student, on average, and the likelihood that the quality of individual student learning outcomes (ALO) will decline. There is no real increase in productivity because the increase in students instructed (SCU) is offset by a decline in individual learning outcomes, ALO(after cut) < ALO(before cut), and TLO per position remains about constant.

SUMMARY AND EXTENSION

- During periods of stable funding, normal operating conditions, and constant technology, a campus-wide index of ALO is likely to remain approximately constant and changes in SCU (or FTE) provide relatively good indications of changes in total learning outcomes (TLO). However, the combined effects of inflation and enrollment growth in situations such as this are likely to result in institutional budgets that grow faster than inflation.
- Abrupt budget reductions by the state are more likely to result in a reduction in student access than a reduction in costs per SCU. This outcome occurs because institutional incentives to protect quality (maintain ALO) result in policies to manage enrollment down and to increase student tuition.

- Within the context of classroom technology, where an increased student-faculty ratio literally requires faculty to instruct more students in the classroom, the potential to increase productivity is limited. If a reduction in costs per SCU is achieved, the result is more likely to be caused by a reduction in ALO than by an improvement in productivity. Even in the case where faculty choose to increase their instructional efforts to maintain ALO, the increased TLO is achieved at the cost of an increase in effort and does not represent a real gain in productivity.

These two examples are relevant to an examination of the more complex issue alluded to previously—a situation where there is long-run growth in enrollments coupled with the reluctance of the state to fund the growth at a constant real cost per TLO. Example #1 demonstrates the situation the state wants to avoid, funding of growth where budgets grow faster than the rate of inflation such that higher education's share of total state tax revenues increases.

Example #2 suggests the possible responses to what could be thought of in the long-run growth context as a series of small budget cuts, i.e., a 3.5-percent funding need and a 3.2-percent funding increase. Institutional responses include assertions that the growth potential is really not as large as it was thought to be (equivalent to managing enrollment down) and that students should pay a larger share of the costs (increasing fees and managing enrollment down). To the extent these two responses are effective, enrollment growth is slowed or stopped. Given the pressures of the public funding arena, it is also likely that some of the small cuts will become effective in which case faculty are faced with a bleak future that involves steadily increasing course enrollments and workloads and the potential of participating in a process of declining quality of learning outcomes. Growth in SCU, to the extent it occurs, will overstate the growth of TLO because of the declines in ALO. Improvements in productivity associated with changes in technology may provide a way out of this dilemma.

TECHNOLOGY CHANGE AND PRODUCTIVITY CHANGE IN HIGHER EDUCATION

Whether it is possible to improve labor productivity by changing technology depends upon whether another technology is available that can produce more TLO (with ALO at least constant) holding faculty instructional effort constant. The following model defines the characteristics of such a technology.

Model for Comparing "Classroom Technology" with "Distributed Technology"

Choosing an efficient technology, one that minimizes average cost of output, necessarily requires comparisons among alternatives. The survival of classroom technology over the centuries testifies to its effectiveness and adaptability. It constitutes the baseline against which alternative technologies should be compared.

Classroom Technology

Classroom instruction is generally structured so that an individual faculty member is responsible for performing all three components of the instructional tasks listed above. Once the course materials are prepared, they are presented only to the students enrolled in the course section taught by that faculty member.

Faculty effort is the most important component in the provision of instructional services. The first step in developing the model is to define the parameters of faculty workload and distribution of effort as they apply in the case of the current classroom technology. The model is then used to project faculty positions needed to instruct a given number of students in a given classroom course.

Within classroom technology, faculty are individually responsible for the three basic functions involved in teaching a course—preparation of instructional materials for presentation, the presentation of those materials in the classroom, and student-related workload (interaction regarding course content and evaluation of homework, quizzes, examinations, projects, and papers, up to and including assignment of course grades). Effort devoted to these activities is distributed as follows:[25]

$p1$ = proportion of instructional effort on course preparation

$p2$ = proportion of effort on course presentation

$p3$ = proportion of effort on student-related workload (interaction and evaluation)

The functional relation between the number of student enrollments in a given course and the number of faculty positions needed to instruct those students depends upon the number of students who enroll annually, average section size (the class size), and the number of courses taught per faculty position per year.

$$FPc = \frac{1}{k}\,ns$$

$$ns = \frac{ENR}{ase}$$

FPc = faculty positions for classroom instruction
k = the workload expected of a full-time faculty position (FP), the number of course sections per year
ns= number of sections of the course offered per year
ENR = annual course enrollment
ase = average section enrollment

$$(9) \quad FPc = \frac{1}{k(ase)} \, ENR$$

For example, if 150 students enroll in the course in a given year, a faculty position taught eight course sections, and average section enrollment was 25, six sections and 0.75 FP would be required.[26] Assuming faculty effort is evenly distributed among the three basic teaching functions, $p1 = p2 = p3 = 1/3$, the equivalent of .25 position would be devoted to course preparation, .25 to course presentation, and .25 to student-related workload.

The educational output of the instructional services provided is defined as total learning outcomes (TLO), the product of course credit units (CCU), annual enrollment (ENR), and a relative index of average learning outcomes (ALO). The ALO quality index converts student credit units (course credit units times enrollment) from a measure of instructional activity to a proxy for the learning outcomes that are produced.

$$TLO = ALO(CCU)(ENR)$$

Solving for ENR, we get

$$(10) \quad ENR = \frac{TLO}{ALO(CCU)} \quad \text{substituting into (9)}$$

$$(11) \quad FPc = \frac{1}{k(ase)(ALO)(CCU)} \, TLO$$

If, for example, $k = 8$, ase = 25, ALO = 1 (if average learning outcomes are constant, the index is constant over a period of time), and CCU = 3

$$(11a) \quad FPc = 0.00167 \, TLO$$

This last equation can be checked by recalling that an annual workload of eight courses implies 0.125 of a faculty position to instruct one three-unit section of 25 students, which is equivalent to 75 SCU which, in turn, is equal to TLO because ALO = 1. Multiplying 0.00167 by 75 results in 0.125 positions.

Distributed Technology

The essential characteristic that distinguishes distributed technology from classroom technology is that once the instructional materials are prepared and presented, they are *potentially* available to all students enrolled in the course. The particular media and related protocols by which the materials are made available to students defines the various types of distributed instruction, e.g., one-way television, video conferencing, asynchronous network, etc.

An initial estimate of the faculty effort required for preparation and presentation of the course materials, based upon classroom technology, is given by

$$\frac{(p1 + p2)}{k}$$

This estimate is the average amount of effort each faculty member spends preparing (p1) and presenting instructional materials (p2) to students in a course section, although this level of effort may be insufficient to prepare and present materials that will be available to a substantially larger group of students (an issue discussed below). The important point here is to recognize that for any course with a given set of characteristics, the workload of preparing and presenting the materials is independent of the exact number of students involved.

The first approximation for faculty positions (FPd) for the distributed version of the course is

$$FPd = \frac{p1 + p2}{k} + \frac{p3}{k} \, ns$$

The first term in the equation above represents the effort to prepare and present the materials and the second term represents the share of faculty effort devoted to student-related workload. The number of course sections (ns) is explicitly introduced in the distributed technology equation to maintain the same amount of faculty effort (attention) per individual student as was available in the classroom version.

The equation can be simplified by substituting the definition of ns

$$= \frac{p1 + p2}{k} + \frac{p3}{k(ase)} \, ENR \quad \text{and then substituting (8) for ENR}$$

$$(12) \; FPd = \frac{p1 + p2}{k} + \frac{p3}{k(ase) \, (ALO)(CCU)} \, TLO$$

Equation (12) is a distributed technology version of the faculty need equation defined in such a way as to maintain the same amount of faculty effort (attention) per individual student as was provided in the classroom version of the equation.

Taking the derivatives of equations (11) and (12)

$$\frac{dFPc}{dTLO} = \frac{1}{k(ase)(ALO)(CCU)}$$

$$\frac{dFPd}{dTLO} = \frac{p3}{k(ase)(ALO)(CCU)}$$

$$(13) \quad \frac{dFPc}{dTLO} > \frac{dFPd}{dTLO} \quad \text{because } 1 > p3.$$

The classroom version of the function has a *steeper* slope than the generic distributed function (classroom faculty position need increases at a greater rate as TLO increases). Equation (13) is a fundamental result that establishes a smaller incremental faculty resource need associated with distributed technology. The result (1) is independent of specific assumptions about faculty workload in terms of the number of courses taught or research assignments (except for the requirement that faculty instructional effort devoted to student-related workload under classroom technology is less than total effort related to all instructional activities), (2) does not depend upon providing less faculty attention to individual students (it is predicated upon providing the same amount of effort per student as provided by classroom technology), and (3) is independent of any assumption about salary costs.

An intuitive grasp of this fundamental result regarding relative incremental resource need probably underlies much of the support distributed technology has enjoyed over the years. The result occurs because distributed technology has the potential to avoid the duplication of effort that occurs when course materials are prepared and presented to several sections of the same course on a campus during an academic year.

This fundamental result establishes that distributed technology can make more efficient use of one of the basic resources (faculty positions) required to produce learning outcomes. Such an improvement in efficiency is a necessary, but not a sufficient, condition for distributed technology to be less expensive than classroom technology.[27] Distributed technology is not inherently less expensive than classroom technology, but, under appropriate conditions, it can possibly be less expensive. To investigate the possibilities, it is necessary to make some modifications to equation (12).

Assuming $p1 = p2 = p3 = 1/3$, and the same values for the other parameters as were used above, the numerical values of the coefficients in (12) are

FPd = 0.08333 + 0.00056 TLO

One might be concerned that the value 0.08333, which represents the share of a faculty position associated with the preparation and presentation of course materials for a classroom enrollment of 25 (where there is the potential for discussion and immediate feedback), is inadequate for preparation of materials that will be distributed to a potentially larger group of students where feedback is more difficult. An ad hoc adjustment to allow increased preparation effort can be rationalized as a means to maintain the value of average learning outcomes on a par with classroom technology (ALO=1). Instructors teaching live television courses commonly receive additional time for preparation (usually by means of relief from other classroom teaching). Assume such an assignment is made in the form of relief from one other course. Adding 0.125 to the constant gives

(12a) adj FPd = 0.20833 + 0.00056 TLO

Equations (11a) and (12a) are plotted in Figure 5-3[28] where the classroom graph is shown as a bar chart to recognize the step increments in resource need (both for faculty and rooms) as additional sections are added. The graph of the distributed version of the course is shown as a line because it is possible to recognize workload in relatively small increments as additional students are added (e.g., in increments of TLO associated with an additional individual student).

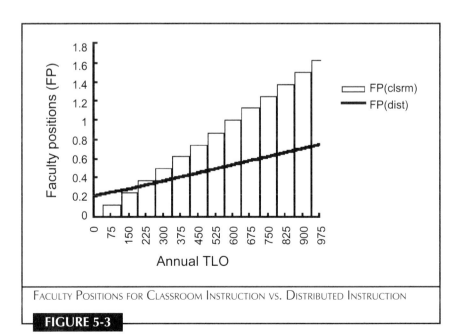

FACULTY POSITIONS FOR CLASSROOM INSTRUCTION VS. DISTRIBUTED INSTRUCTION

FIGURE 5-3

The graphs in Figure 5-3 illustrate the basic differences between the two technologies. As discussed above, distributed technology has a lesser need for additional faculty positions as TLO (and enrollment) increases than classroom technology; the slope of the distributed technology line is flatter (this result does not depend upon the assumption that p3 = 1/3, only that p3 for distributed technology is less than 1). Distributed technology has a greater initial faculty start-up cost than classroom technology (changes in start-up costs shift the graph vertically, but do not affect its slope).

Without reference to costs, the graphs illustrate the scale effect that was discussed above, i.e., because of the greater start-up costs of distributed technology, it will only be most efficient in terms of faculty positions for values of TLO to the right of the intersection or "crossover" point. For TLO to the left of the crossover point (for courses with small annual enrollments), classroom technology is the most efficient.[29]

Technology Change and Student Faculty Ratios

The graphs in Figure 5-3 can be used to derive the student faculty ratio that appears in the higher education average cost function, equation (8), which is repeated below. The result also provides a transition from faculty position requirements to a more complete discussion of costs.

$$(8) \quad AC = \frac{1}{ALO} \left[\frac{s1}{sfr} + \frac{s2}{ssr} + \frac{OEX}{SCU} \right]$$

Using Figure 5-3, it can be demonstrated that

$$sfr(dist) > sfr(clsrm)$$

for all values of TLO to the right of the crossover point where the two graphs intersect.

sfr(dist) = TLO/FPd, the "student faculty ratio, adjusted for learning outcomes" associated with distributed technology

sfr(clsrm) = TLO/FPc, the "student faculty ratio, adjusted for learning outcomes" associated with classroom technology

The result is established by choosing FPc and FPd to the right of the crossover, for example, at TLO = 750

$$sfr(dist) = \frac{750}{FPd} > \frac{750}{FPc} = sfr(clsrm) \text{ because FPd} < FPc$$

The terms sfr(dist) and sfr(clsrm) represent alternative values of the productivity ratios used in equation (8) to calculate average cost per TLO. This improvement in faculty productivity associated with the larger value of sfr(dist) contains the potential to reduce average costs. It cannot be concluded, however, that

$$AC(dist) < AC(clsrm) \text{ simply because sfr(dist)} > sfr(clsrm).$$

The overall effect upon average costs (AC) that occurs with the adoption of any particular distributed technology depends upon the increase in the sfr and whether such an increase is sufficient to offset the increases in OEX that are associated with the adoption of distributed technology, i.e., it also depends upon the relative values of OEX(dist) and OEX(clsrm) as expressed in the average cost equation.

There are other complications, as will be seen later in this chapter. In addition to increases in fixed costs (OEX), distributed technology may also entail additional incremental costs associated with students. And, as illustrated by equation (8), the productivity of faculty positions is only one productivity component in the average cost equation. The gross productivity of all other campus positions is also in the equation in the form of ssr, the student staff ratio. The effect of improvements in faculty productivity upon average costs is attenuated to the extent the value of the ssr does not change in a parallel manner.

VARIATIONS ON THE THEME: THE TRANSITION FROM THEORY TO PRACTICE[30]

The model can be used to address questions relating to the costs of various forms of electronic media that have been incorporated into the instructional/ teaching process during the past several years. The discussion will also be used to illustrate that between "pure" classroom technology and "pure" distributed technology there are combinations of the two approaches, some closer to the classroom mode, some closer to the distributed mode.

Total direct costs for instruction delivered via the various modes will be stated in terms of course enrollments. Average costs will be calculated based upon total learning outcomes (TLO). The number of faculty positions to instruct a given number of students using classroom technology is given above by equation (9):

$$FPc = \frac{1}{k(ase)} ENR$$

This equation can be converted to a cost equation by multiplying by average faculty salaries (s1):

$$(14) \quad DCc = s1(FPc) = s1\frac{1}{k(ase)} ENR$$

DCc = direct cost of classroom instruction[31]

Equation (14) is simply another version of the straight line graph illustrated in Figure 5-3 except it is in terms of dollars that represent the cost of faculty positions instead of the positions themselves.

Equation (14) is a special case of a more general direct cost function. In the more general function, other direct costs are incorporated simply by adding other terms, for example, as follows:

$$(15) \quad DC = sl(FP) + cl(ENR) + FC$$

c1 = an additional cost incurred per student enrolled in the course
FC = a fixed or start-up cost that must be incurred to offer the course without regard to student enrollments

Average direct costs per TLO are

$$AC = \frac{DC}{TLO} = \frac{sl(FP)}{ALO(CCU)(ENR)} + \frac{cl(ENR)}{ALO(CCU)(ENR)} + \frac{FC}{ALO(CCU)(ENR)}$$

which can be simplified to an expression similar, but not identical, to equation (8), above.

$$(16) \quad AC = \frac{1}{ALO}\left[\frac{sl}{sfr} + \frac{cl}{CCU} + \frac{FC}{SCU}\right]$$

The difference between equations (7) and (8) and equations (15) and (16) is that the latter apply at the course level while the former refer to an entire campus. The important point to note is that equation (15) allows one to plot total direct costs against course enrollments while equation (16) allows a plot of average costs against total learning outcomes (i.e., DC/TLO). The final format of equation (16) provides a basis for making explicit adjustments to average costs based upon changes in learning productivity, as will be seen below.

Computers Are Used to Augment Classroom Instruction

The advantage of the digital computer in the late 1950s and 1960s was its ability to make rapid and accurate calculations involving complex mathematics and large amounts of data. It quickly became an integral part of disciplines in the physical sciences, mathematics and statistics, engineering, and business and accounting. It became necessary to introduce students in these disciplines to computing so that they could be properly trained for entry level positions and careers in these fields.

The mainframe computers that were available during this period were best suited for student exercises and projects that augmented classroom instruction.

As such, the cost of computing became an "add-on" to the other direct costs of classroom instruction. At the course level, this cost could be estimated from the annual cost of the campus computer center (including equipment lease costs, software, and staff costs), appropriately adjusted to remove the costs of administrative computing, and then allocated to course sections based upon the number of course sections (and enrollments) that could be accommodated. For a single course, the fixed computer cost (imputed computer cost[ICC]) is included as the fixed cost term in equation (15).

Adding the constant has the effect of shifting the classroom cost curve upward by the value of ICC as shown in Figure 5-4. The computer-related costs in Figure 5-4 also illustrate a capacity constraint such that for each additional 400 enrollments, the computer capacity must be upgraded. The costs of these upgrades account for the "steps" in the classroom plus ICC cost line.

Although the data that underlie the graph are only an example, the effect of augmenting classroom instruction with access to main frame computing clearly has the effect of increasing the total costs of classroom instruction when measured against course enrollments. But the change may have occurred because average learning outcomes went up, thus increasing total learning outcomes.

Some of the alternatives are illustrated in Figure 5-5, which shows average costs per unit of total learning outcomes (TLO) where, as before, total learning outcomes for the course are course credit units times course enrollment times average learning outcomes. The dashed horizontal line represents the average costs of classroom instruction before the introduction of computing in the course. The heavy curved dashed line (Clsrm+) is the average costs of class-

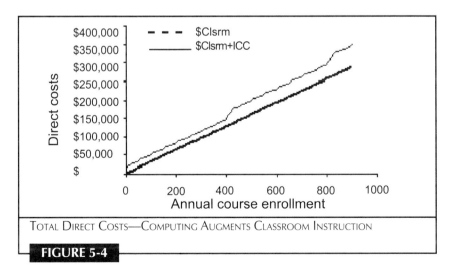

TOTAL DIRECT COSTS—COMPUTING AUGMENTS CLASSROOM INSTRUCTION

FIGURE 5-4

room instruction plus ICC without any change in ALO. The other two curved lines represent classroom plus ICC with a 15-percent and a 30-percent improvement in ALO, respectively. The average cost curves clearly illustrate that if learning outcomes for students are not improved, the introduction of computing simply results in increased costs (both per student and per total learning outcomes). If ALO are increased by 15 percent, the increased costs are offset such that for TLO of about 1,000 (enrollments of about 330) the increased costs are approximately offset by increased quality (improvements in ALO) per student to make costs comparable with classroom instruction. If ALO increases by 30 percent, at about 200 students (600 TLO) the increases in learning quality put the average costs per TLO below that of classroom instruction.

Even though costs per student increase, the additional expenditures to add computing to the curriculum could be considered a bargain in terms of the improved quality of learning outcomes. Such a result may come close to being true by definition because of the role educational institutions play in preparing young people for their careers and their working lives. Consider the situation within a discipline when there is a major breakthrough in theory or a fundamental change in the way an operation or process is performed. In such situations, existing instructional methods must change quickly to reflect the new knowledge and technology regardless of the additional costs that might be incurred. In terms of average learning outcomes, the additional costs are justified and to do otherwise than incur them would result in a failure of the institution to serve its educational purpose.

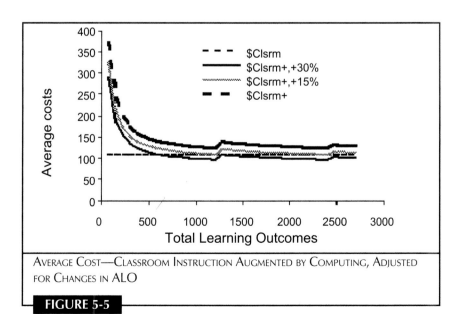

AVERAGE COST—CLASSROOM INSTRUCTION AUGMENTED BY COMPUTING, ADJUSTED FOR CHANGES IN ALO

FIGURE 5-5

The WWW Is Used to Augment Classroom Instruction

This situation is a further extension of the use of computers to augment classroom instruction. It incorporates elements of the previous example plus others as described below. It is a practice that has developed and grown within the past several years. It is predicated upon the existence of the Internet and broad access to desktop/laptop computers for students. It involves a wide range of applications, including e-mail, Internet resources, WWW home pages, computer simulations and exercises, and chat rooms and threaded discussions.

In effect, instructors make substantial portions of their course materials available at a course home page. Students ask questions and respond to assignments via e-mail. Student assignments may be posted on the homepage for other students and the instructor to review and critique. Chat rooms may be used to generate general discussions about the course content among students and with the instructor. Threaded discussions involve students and the instructor in exchanges focused upon particular topics.

Such course work allows students more flexibility regarding when and where they participate in the course. It requires that students express more of their thoughts in writing, provides expanded opportunities for students to work together on problems and projects, and provides opportunities for all students to have direct communication with the instructor outside the context of examinations and papers.

As with the introduction of mainframe computers in the curriculum, the exact applications of the Internet to instruction have been left, for the most part, for individual instructors to determine. Experience with the resultant applications strongly suggests that the design of the courses has tended to increase faculty workload. This increase in workload arises from the effort required to produce and convert course materials for use on the Web and from the increased interaction with individual students who now have more convenient access to the instructor and who may now be required to provide more exercises that the instructor must evaluate. The suggested solution is to offset the increased workload per student by reducing average class size.

The graph of the resultant total direct cost for this mode of instruction is compared with regular classroom costs in Figure 5-6 where a constant is added to account for fixed costs related to provision of the computer network (in a manner similar to that shown in Figure 5-4 above) and average class size is adjusted downward (from 25 to 20 in this example). The two cost curves diverge as annual course enrollment increases because the incremental cost of instructing the course has been increased with the reduction in average section size.

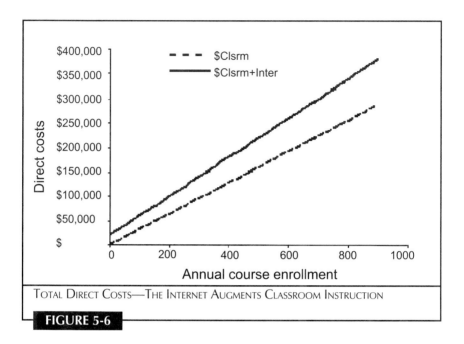

TOTAL DIRECT COSTS—THE INTERNET AUGMENTS CLASSROOM INSTRUCTION

FIGURE 5-6

Figure 5-7 shows the average cost curves plotted against total learning outcomes. As with the previous example, the horizontal line represents the average costs of regular classroom instruction. The heavy dotted topmost line represents average costs unadjusted for changes in average learning outcomes per student. It lies relatively higher above the regular classroom average costs than the case illustrated in Figure 5-5 because here there is an increase in incremental costs as well as in the fixed costs of providing computer access.[32] As a result, an adjustment in the ALO index in the range of plus 20 to 40 percent is required to obtain average costs per TLO that bracket classroom average costs at enrollment levels above 330 (TLO = 1,000).

Again, as with the use of the mainframe computer to augment classroom instruction, one can argue that the benefits in learning outcomes are substantial and the change in instructional method is absolutely necessary for the institution to properly educate its students. But at this point, a question arises: Are there alternative ways to achieve the same learning outcomes without incurring the higher costs?

The WWW Is Used to Provide Distributed Instruction

Because of the initial absence of computer networks, the use of mainframe computers in instruction could be accomplished only by using them to augment classroom instruction. However, the advent of networks and desktop comput-

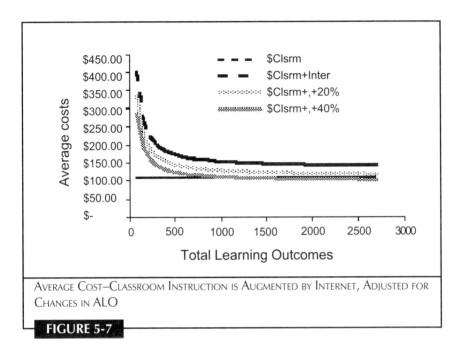

AVERAGE COST–CLASSROOM INSTRUCTION IS AUGMENTED BY INTERNET, ADJUSTED FOR CHANGES IN ALO

FIGURE 5-7

ing suggests that the electronic media might serve as the basis for alternative instructional delivery modes that are not predicated upon classroom technology. It was argued above that distributed technology has the potential to increase faculty productivity and, under appropriate circumstances, reduce the average cost per TLO below that of classroom instruction.

An "asynchronous network" (AN) online course serves as the basis for the discussion.[33] Such a course has the following characteristics:

1. It is designed and produced by a group of subject matter faculty and learning theory and media professionals.

2. It incorporates substantially all the course material in a format that is accessible from a network server, including, in addition to the course syllabus and handouts, interactive exercises and computer simulations, course projects (including team projects), and various evaluation exercises.

3. It provides for student-faculty interaction in both electronic and face-to-face format; faculty who are involved with the production of the course materials may or may not be involved with the interaction.

4. It provides for student-student interaction in both electronic and face-to-face format.

5. It provides for evaluation of student performance in the course and assignment of final grades by faculty.

Because the functions of production and presentation of course materials are separated from the functions of student interaction and evaluation (e.g., testing), the workload that can reasonably be expected of an individual faculty member is not a constraint upon the course enrollment. Once the course materials are produced, course enrollment determines the number of faculty positions needed for interaction and evaluation.

The costs of producing an AN course are likely to be substantial, from $200,000 and up. In addition, the courseware must be maintained, which requires a continuing expenditure to keep the material up-to-date. These costs could be incorporated at the campus level as an initial capital cost and a continuing maintenance cost. But it is more likely that the costs would be incurred by a third party (either a consortium of campuses or a private vendor, i.e, a publisher). These costs are combined below by assuming that the course is leased from a third party.

In addition to course production and maintenance, the costs of providing computer and network access capacity for students is another fixed cost. Student access to computer networks may also include a line charge that varies with the number of students.

Once the course is available on a server, the cost of interacting with and evaluating students varies with the number of individual students enrolled in the course. The problem is to determine a reasonable estimate of the per-student cost of such interaction and evaluation. Faculty workload surveys suggest that full-time faculty spend between 20 and 33 percent of their effort on student-related workload. Assuming a student faculty ratio (defined above as SCU/FP) of 600 and three semester unit courses implies that an average full-time faculty position teaching regular course sections in a classroom works with 200 students per academic year.[34] If between a fifth and a third of faculty effort is devoted to interaction and evaluation, a full-time interaction-evaluation assignment could accommodate between 600 and 1,000 student course enroll-ments per year (300-500 per semester). Taking $80,000 as an average faculty salary, including fringe benefits, results in an average faculty cost for interaction and evaluation of $80-$133 per student enrollee.

Two things should be noted immediately. First, the faculty cost of interaction and evaluation per course enrollee is dependent upon all the parameters—a smaller student faculty ratio will give a larger per-student cost, a smaller average faculty salary and a smaller percent of effort devoted to interaction and evaluation will give a lower per-student cost.[35] Second, the results are predi-cated upon classroom instruction and can only provide a baseline for estimating the costs of interaction and evaluation of the AN course.

In the cost estimates shown in Figure 5-8, a faculty salary of $80,000 is assumed for both the classroom and the AN versions of the course. For the AN course, a minimum faculty interaction and evaluation cost (the baseline cost

[BL]) per student is based upon one-third of total effort devoted to this function in the classroom mode. Other AN cost parameters are set at $100,000 for the annual lease of use rights to the course (this cost covers the initial capital and maintenance costs) plus a charge of $40 per student enrollee to cover communications and line costs associated with network use. The resultant cost schedule is shown as AN Crs (BL for [baseline]) in the figure. Another AN cost schedule is derived and plotted on the assumption that twice as much faculty time (the equivalent to two-thirds of a position instead of one-third in classroom mode) is devoted to interaction and evaluation (AN Crs[adj]).

As Figure 5-8 shows, the crossover point where AN course costs are less than classroom occurs at about 450 student enrollments for the baseline case and at 900 for the case with adjusted (increased) interaction and evaluation costs. A similar result is shown in Figure 5-9 for the average costs of the three cases. The important result illustrated here is that it is not necessary to make any adjustment for increased learning outcomes associated with the distributed instruction to demonstrate that, with sufficient enrollments, average costs of distributed instruction are less than average costs for classroom instruction. In other words, under the right circumstances, distributed instruction can be a bargain even if learning outcomes as measured by ALO are constant. It becomes an even better bargain if ALO is improved, as was argued for in the previous two examples.

SUMMARY AND CONCLUSIONS

The findings and conclusions drawn from the foregoing analysis can be summarized in nine basic propositions that ought to form the core of our mental set as we address the challenges and opportunities that information technology presents to American higher education.

1. Expenditures in higher education grow because of enrollment growth and increases in average costs per student. Improved labor productivity is the basic remedy for increases in average costs. Changes in technology are one of the major ways of improving labor productivity.

2. Classroom instruction (based upon classroom technology) has been the primary mode of instructional delivery in higher education for many years. The advent of electronic media (especially TV, computers, and computer networks) is facilitating the development of alternative instructional delivery modes.

3. "Distributed technology" is a term adopted to describe a specific electronically mediated alternative to classroom technology. In a pure case of distributed technology, instructional course materials are prepared once by a team of faculty and other professionals and placed on a server; all students enrolled in the course can access these materials at times and places convenient for them.

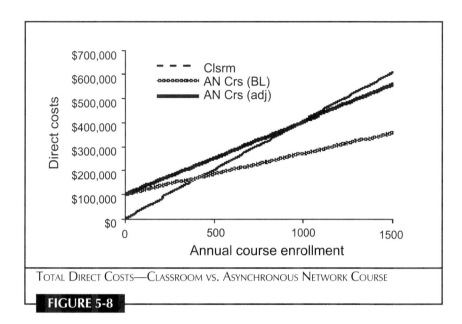

TOTAL DIRECT COSTS—CLASSROOM VS. ASYNCHRONOUS NETWORK COURSE

FIGURE 5-8

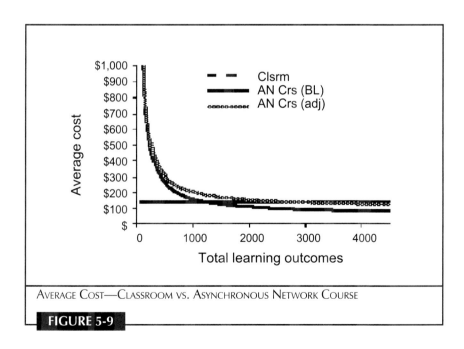

AVERAGE COST—CLASSROOM VS. ASYNCHRONOUS NETWORK COURSE

FIGURE 5-9

4. Within distributed technology, student-faculty interaction on the subject matter materials can be assigned to faculty separately from course production and maintenance activities. Similarly, evaluation of student performance can be a separately assigned function. This "unbundling" of the components of faculty workload represents one of the key differences between distributed instruction and classroom instruction where the various instructional activities (prepare, present, interact, and evaluate) have usually been performed by the individual faculty member teaching the classroom courses.

5. A measure of total learning outcomes can be derived based upon student credit units (or FTE) weighted by an index of relative learning outcomes. A substantial amount of evidence suggests that learning outcomes (and other benefits) associated with mediated instruction are at least as good as those associated with classroom instruction. A conservative working or planning assumption is that the learning outcomes and other benefits of mediated instruction are at least as good as those of classroom instruction.

6. Distributed technology has a different cost structure than that of classroom technology. Distributed instruction has larger start-up or fixed costs and lower incremental costs (for adding more students) than classroom instruction. The basic reason for this is that distributed technology eliminates the duplication of faculty effort involved in preparing and presenting materials for multiple classroom sections of the same course in a given term. At relatively low levels of course enrollment, classroom instruction is less expensive. At some enrollment level, distributed and classroom instruction costs are equal (the "crossover point"). At greater enrollment levels, beyond the crossover point, distributed instruction is less expensive than classroom instruction.

7. Because of the cost structures described in #6, distributed instruction is subject to economies of scale. Controlling for the quality of learning outcomes and at sufficiently large enrollment levels, it can be shown that distributed instruction has lower average per-student costs than classroom instruction.

8. The adoption of distributed technology has the potential to increase productivity and reduce average costs in higher education. To achieve this potential will require fundamental changes in the way courses are designed and provided to students. One possible arrangement is that courses will be produced by teams of faculty and shared among several campuses. In any given term, faculty may specialize in course production and maintenance. In another term, these same individuals may devote a substantial amount of their time to interacting with and evaluating students enrolled in the courses.

9. Although the mix of courses will shift away from classroom instruction toward distributed instruction, it is likely that a substantial amount of classroom instruction will be continued. Most students will, therefore, continue to take at least part of their programs in a classroom setting.

ENDNOTES

1. The population of the United States is projected to grow from 265 million in 1996 to over 325 million in 2021, a change of about 60 million individuals. See U.S. Bureau of the Census, "Resident Population Projections of the U.S., Middle, Low, and High Series, 1996-2050," March 1996. The numbers quoted are from the Middle Series.

2. See U.S. Department of Labor, *Monthly Labor Review*, "Employment Outlook: 1996-2006, Occupational Employment Projections to 2006," November 1997, pp. 58-83. Also see David Autor et al., "Computing Inequality: Have Computers Changed the Labor Market?" NBER Working Paper 5956, March 1997, which argues that a substantial amount of the growing earnings differential for college educated workers can be attributed to the growth in computer use in the industries hiring college educated workers.

3. "High technology" is a popular term that refers to the applications of modern science that have been so profoundly influenced by the advent of the digital computer and related developments in digital electronics, especially in communications. Properly understood, high technology refers to modern scientific research and applications based upon "digital electronic technology." Within the context of higher education, "high technology" is commonly used to refer to instructing students through the use of digital electronic technology (i.e., computers and digital communications, including various forms of television that are also migrating to a digital format). At times, the term is shortened to just "technology" or "hi-tech," as, for example, "what are the implications of *technology* for the future of higher education?" Within a specific higher education context these shorthand terms are generally understood as references to the longer versions.

4. The other sectors in the Standard Industrial Classification system published by the federal government include agriculture, mining, construction, transportation and public utilities, wholesale and retail trade, finance, services, and government, as well as manufacturing. Education appears in this framework as a component of the service sector, which produces a wide range of products (services), including legal, accounting, and medical services.

5. The most efficient technology is that which produces a maximum output for a given expenditure on all inputs or, what amounts to the same thing, a minimum expenditure on inputs to produce a given level of output. Also see the section below entitled "Costs and Scale Effects: A Complication." Formal discussions of this proposition can be found in any intermediate textbook on microeconomic theory, e.g., Jack Hirshleifer and David Hirshleifer, *Price Theory and Applications*, 6th ed. Englewood Cliffs, NJ: Prentice Hall, 1996.

6. Whether made in the private or public sector, all the individual decisions about technology have a cumulative impact at the national level. For any given society at any given time, there exist many ways to combine resources to produce the entire range of the nation's goods and services. To the extent the most productive technologies are chosen, the society will enjoy a higher material standard of living.

7. The labor cost term (wL/Q) in (2) can be rearranged by dividing numerator and denominator by L, as follows:

$$AC = w\left(\frac{\frac{L}{L}}{\frac{Q}{L}}\right) + \frac{OEX}{Q} = \frac{w}{\frac{Q}{L}} + \frac{OEX}{Q}$$

8. See, for example, U.S. Department of Labor, Bureau of Labor Statistics, *Handbook of Methods*, Chapter 11, "Industry Productivity Measures," 1997.

9. The following discussion does not deal with the potential complication that research and public service may also be produced as joint products with educational services.

10. This perspective focuses upon the effects on students of the services produced (i.e., learning associated with taking a course) rather than the consequences of taking a series of courses (i.e., a degree). This is not to deny that educated individuals, as typified by those with degrees, are an important primary output of higher education. Courses are probably the better practical focus, however. From an operational standpoint, it is courses (and the related FTE) that are budgeted, produced, and managed by the institutions, not degrees. Course activities may also be a proxy for degrees in that courses represent building blocks leading to degrees.

11. Division by 15 generates term FTE. Annual FTE is the average of two semesters (divide by 30) or three quarters (divide by 45).

12. A single numbering sequence is used for all equations whether in footnotes or text.

13. If the discussion were to be conducted in terms of FTE, at this point the 75 SCU would be divided by 15 to obtain 5 term FTE (or by 30 to obtain 2.5 annual FTE).

14. Basing a decision upon the weak inequality is also consistent with the criteria established in the 1998 FIPSE grant application, *Controlling the Cost of Postsecondary Education*, where cost control is defined to include "reducing the amount spent to bring 100 freshmen to the *same level of understanding* achieved by comparable groups in earlier years" (emphasis added, see p. 4). Such a criterion precludes the often stated rationale for an increase in total expenditures that will increase productivity by substantially increasing ALO. It is not intended to argue here that productivity increases of this latter type are unimportant. It is argued, however, that productivity increases of the former (cost controlling) type are also important, especially in a fiscally constrained environment.

15. See the following studies:

a. Frank Jewett, "Courseware for Remedial Mathematics: A Case Study in the Benefits and Costs of the Mediated Learning System in the California State University."

b. ———, "Teaching College Literacy: A Case Study in the Benefits and Costs of Daedalus Courseware at Baruch College."

c. ———, "The Education Network of Maine: A Case Study in the Benefits and Costs of Instructional Television."

d. ———, "The Master's Degree in Social Work at Cleveland State University and the University of Akron: A Case Study of the Benefits and Costs of a Joint Degree Program Offered via Videoconferencing."

e. ———, "TELETECHNET—Old Dominion University and 'Two Plus Two' Programs at Community Colleges in Virginia: A Case Study in the Benefits and Costs of an Intercampus Instructional Television Network."

f. ———, The Human Computer Interaction Certificate Program at Rensselaer Polytechnic Institute: A Case Study in the Benefits and Costs of a Joint Industry/University Designed Program Featuring Integrated Delivery Methods."

g. ———, "The WESTNET Program—SUNY Brockport and the SUNY Campuses in Western New York State: A Case Study in the Benefits and Costs of an Interactive Television Network."

h. ———, Course Restructuring: A Case Study in the Benefits and Costs of Restructured Courses Following an Instructional Development Initiative at Virginia Polytechnic Institute and State University."

All case study reports were completed in 1998 and published by the California State University Chancellor's Office, Seal Beach, California. Copies are available at the benefit cost project Web site at <www.calstate.edu/special_projects/>.

16. Thomas Russell, *The No Significant Difference Phenomena as Reported in 355 Research Reports, Summaries and Papers.* Raleigh: North Carolina State University, 1999. The materials are also available at <http://tenb.mta.ca/phenom/phenom1.html>.

17. Greville Rumble, *The Costs and Economics of Open and Distance Learning.* London: Kogan Page, 1997.

18. James A. Kulik, "Meta-Analytic Studies of Findings on Computer-Based Instruction," in Eva Baker and Harold O'Neil, eds., *Technology Assessment in Training and Education.* Hillsdale, NJ: Lawrance Erlbaum, 1994.

19. J. Merisotis and R. Phipps, *What's the Difference?: A Review of Contemporary Research on the Effectiveness of Distance Learning in Higher Education.* Washington, DC: Paper prepared for the AFT and the NEA by the Institute for Higher Education Policy, 1999; G. Brown and M. Wack, *The Difference Frenzy and Matching Buckshot with Buckshot.* 1999. Paper available at <http://horizon.unc.edu/ts/reading/1999-05.asp>; P. Ewell, "No Significant Difference?" Editorial in *Change* magazine (May/June 1999).

20. $AC = \dfrac{TC}{TLO} = \dfrac{s1(FP) + s2SP + OEX}{ALO(SCU)}$

Moving ALO to the front of the expression

$$AC = \frac{1}{ALO}\left[\frac{s1(FP)}{SCU} + \frac{s2(SP)}{SCU} + \frac{OEX}{SCU}\right]$$

Dividing both numerator and denominator of the first term in parentheses by FP and the second term by SP

$$AC = \frac{1}{ALO}\left[\frac{s1}{SCU/FP} + \frac{s2}{SCU/SP} + \frac{OEX}{SCU}\right]$$

21. The term was suggested by Frank Young.

22. Which, for classroom technology, literally invokes an image of a faculty member in a classroom instructing students.

23. Strictly speaking, the increase is 3.53 percent: 2 percent (to pay for the increased costs of existing inputs) plus 1.5 percent (to pay for the additional resources needed to accommodate the enrollment growth at the old pay rates and prices) plus 2 percent times 1.5 percent (to pay the new rates and prices for the added resources).

24. While it is possible that productivity has improved because students are better educated (e.g., better library collections, better access to computing resources), still these increases in TLO are associated with increases in ALO. Individual students are more expensive to educate because of the increase in resource costs (OEX).

25. Each of the proportions is a positive number, $0 < p < 1$ such that $\sum p \leq 1$. If the inequality holds, other formal assignments, such as research, can be accounted for. Faculty effort associated with shared governance is appropriately treated as overhead (necessary workload that arises as a consequence of the instructional mission). If research is not separately funded, it is also treated as overhead with the result that all activities can be allocated back to instruction. If research is funded separately, activities associated with the research component will result in the above sum being less than 1.

26. Because it is not possible to offer a fraction of a section, equation (7) holds only if ENR≥ase. If ENR<ase, a decision based upon curriculum considerations must be made as to whether or not to offer a single section of the course. This complication is not serious. As will be shown below, for low enrollment courses, classroom technology is generally the least expensive.

27. As a moment's reflection will reveal, to reduce costs, a change in technology must improve productivity of at least one input to the production process (or eliminate the input altogether). The cost reduction potential is enhanced to the extent the input whose productivity is improved represents a large share of total costs.

28. Figures of this type can also be found in Tony Bates, *Technology, Open Learning, and Distance Education*. London and New York: Routledge, 1995; Greville Rumble, *The Costs and Economics of Open and Distance Learning*. London: Kogan Page, 1997; and Sir John S. Daniel, *Mega-Universities and Knowledge Media*. London: Kogan Page, 1996.

29. The location of the intersection or crossover point relative to the TLO axis is sensitive to all the workload parameters incorporated in both the FPc and FPd graph. The crossover point moves to the right, for example, as average section enrollment increases. It also moves to the right as the start-up effort associated with distributed technology increases.

30. I am indebted to Charles Karelis, director of FIPSE, whose penetrating questions regarding the crossover graph led me to formulate these specific examples.

31. The imputed cost of the classroom is another direct cost of classroom instruction. It is excluded from the present discussion but can easily be incorporated. Capital costs, on a per course section basis, are relatively small, e.g., $90,000 to construct a classroom with a useful life of 30 years and 24 course sections per year results in an imputed cost per section of $125.

32. In Figure 5-5, the "Clsrm+" (computer) average cost curve converges with the "Clsrm" average cost curve. In Figure 5-7, the "Clsrm+Internet" average cost curve always lies above the "Clsrm" average cost curve (it converges upon a Clsrm average cost with an enrollment of 20).

33. Historically, various forms of television have served as the predominate form of distributed instruction (wherein an individual faculty member prepared and presented the course material and then received extra compensation or graduate assistance with student questions and examinations). The AN type course is chosen here because it is now possible to incorporate live television as part of the AN course format.

34. SCU/FP = 600 = 3CCUxENR. Solving for ENR gives 200 student enrollments.

35. A basic issue related to the percent of faculty effort devoted to interaction and evaluation is the treatment of faculty effort related to research and shared governance. Faculty effort devoted to funded research should be accounted for in making the calculation (e.g., if 50 percent of a position is funded for research and one-sixth of effort is devoted to student interaction and evaluation, on a full-time teaching equivalent basis, $1/3 (= (1/6)/.5)$ of effort is related to interaction and evaluation). Efforts devoted to unfunded research and shared governance should be treated as an overhead expense (e.g., if approximately one-fifth of effort is devoted to course preparation, course presentation, student interaction and evaluation, unfunded research, and shared governance, respectively, the allocation of effort including overhead, is one-third to preparation, presentation, and interaction and evaluation, respectively).

CHAPTER 6

Understanding the COSTS of Information Technology (IT) Support Services in Higher Education

Karen Leach and David Smallen

Many institutional leaders are concerned that expenses relating to the support of information technologies are a growing percentage of the institutional budget. Informed institutional leaders realize that unbounded growth of such expenses is not possible, but continuing expenses are necessary. Perceptive institutional leaders are looking for ways to manage instructional technology (IT) expenses similar to other significant parts of their budgets. A key to effective management of information technology resources is the availability of understandable and relevant benchmarks, and comparative data for other institutions. This chapter discusses the current state of such knowledge and a collaborative project—COSTS—designed to inform the planning process for information technologies in higher education.

The ultimate goals of the COSTS Project are to provide useful data to participants, establish benchmarks for providing IT services in an educational environment, and identify exemplars. Data are collected through a template completed by participants. The data are then analyzed and summaries, as well as complete data sets, are shared among participants. The COSTS Web site can be found at <http://www.its.colgate.edu/kleach/COSTS/costs.htm>.

THE PROBLEM

Information technology investments in higher education have been criticized as "bolt-ons" to the curriculum, increasing the overall cost of higher education, and putting a college degree out of the reach of many. Others hold that IT investments are the best hope of achieving greater productivity in higher education—an industry that rarely views improved productivity as a measure of success. But calls for accountability are increasing in all areas of institutional management.[1]

In the for-profit sector, where increases in productivity are often synonymous with financial success, investments in information technology were widely questioned in the 1980s. In the 1990s, economic prosperity was often cited as evidence of the value of those same investments in IT. Economists, including Alan Greenspan, theorized that "technological gains and investment are producing sweeping changes in the way portions of the economy operate and raising prospects for continued robust economic growth in the future."[2] The Giga Information Group reported that "online technology cut $15.2 billion from corporate cost structures in the U.S. in 1998, while annual savings will reach $600 billion in 2002."[3] Service industries such as higher education may simply be lagging behind the industrial world in technological evolution. What seems like the "black hole of information technology" in education today may pay off handsomely in the future, finally quelling the questions being asked now. In the meantime, we must continue to try to find ways to understand the costs, benefits, and best practices associated with the use of IT.

At a recent conference of small liberal arts colleges, a program director at a prominent foundation suggested that one of the most challenging problems facing colleges is knowing how to make good decisions about information technology expenditures. This pronouncement is a glaring indication that IT expenditures are not yet planned for in the same way as other more established areas of the budget. IT spending is still mystifying and worrisome to many educational leaders and managers.

As a component of most college budgets, the percentage of spending on information technology is growing rapidly. In many institutions it is seen as a threat to traditional programs. The Consortium of Liberal Arts Colleges, a group of 58 well-known liberal arts colleges, collects annual data that provides evidence of this growth. The IT share of the educational budget ballooned from 2.1 percent in 1990-1991 to 3.9 percent in 1997-1998.[4] This growth threatens other campus initiatives. As the threat grows larger, more questions are asked about the costs and benefits of IT versus other uses of institutional resources.

And, it is not only cost that raises questions about information technology. People are often frustrated by IT. Their anxiety makes them question their IT investments. In November 1996, for example, Steven Gilbert, moderator of the American Association for Higher Education's (AAHE) technology listserv, was experiencing a personal technology support crisis. His laptop computer was down for repairs, his office server was experiencing problems, and he found himself unable to function in the Internet world on which he depends. In a posting to the listserv, he wrote

As I've been suffering the effects of my own personal "support service crisis," I've realized that there are a lot of people who want the same thing I do. We want powerful, effective tools that are utterly reliable, available, and easy to use. We want to spend our time figuring out how to use these tools to improve teaching and learning—how to do our work more effectively and efficiently. We don't want to spend much time figuring out how to use these tools and their successors . . . or how to cope with unexpected limitations or anomalies. We especially don't want to spend time trying to get our machines fixed or dealing with software packages that interfere with each other in mysterious ways. And we want the full costs associated with these capabilities and services to be highly predictable. We're willing to pay a premium for all this, but we'd like that premium to be as low as possible.

A reasonable request. But what is really known about the cost of providing these support services or about the relationship between cost and quality?

The challenge is to develop a simple way to understand the costs of information technology today. The life cycle of IT equipment and software is extremely short and recognized improvements in productivity and quality are slow. This situation makes rational and reliable cost-benefit analyses difficult. However, even under these adverse terms, understanding IT investments can be dramatically improved by developing and using tools that support other strategic decision-making activities.

We believe that inter-institutional collaboration to create accepted IT benchmark figures is the key to the rational assessment of the cost of information technology in higher education. Educational leaders are familiar with benchmarks that, while not perfect, capture the essence of a situation. Measures such as endowment per student, cost per dollar raised, student/faculty ratio, comparative staffing levels, average faculty salaries by rank, and so on are used by senior administration to compare their institution to peers. Similar approaches can be used to compare IT expenditures. Collaboration using valid data could increase understanding.

While data collection and analysis in the IT area is not without difficulties, the approach used in the COSTS Project is aimed at gathering comparative data that is comprehensive and reliable *enough* to inform high-level institutional planning. Understanding IT expenditures in the COSTS framework also gives IT managers needed tools for evaluating their own spending against practices at other institutions. By collecting, comparing, and analyzing data across educational institutions, IT directors, financial officers, and campus strategic planners can begin to speak the same language. They can bolster confidence in their investments. These activities are especially important at small colleges, which make up two-thirds of the country's institutions of higher education. Small schools are often better able to capture and track IT expenditures.

The COSTS approach is not the first effort to study information technology expenditures. Other studies of IT costs in higher education fall into two main categories. The first category includes detailed case studies of particular institutions. These studies shed light on the efficiency and effectiveness of strategies for providing services at that institution. An ongoing study at Indiana University,[5] for example, captures cost *and* quality measures for a vast array of IT services. The resulting comprehensive data reflect the complexity and idiosyncrasies of a large institution.

A second type of study develops broad parameters for institutional expenditures on IT but does not relate these to particular support services. These studies deal with ratios such as the percentage of institutional budgets that are spent on IT, but do not provide a sense of how those expenditures are being made. They are useful for the highest level comparisons, but do not provide any detail on what total spending includes and do little to help IT managers understand the alternatives available for delivering key support services.

Fully comprehensive studies of the total cost of ownership, such as those conducted by the Giga Information Group (formerly the Gartner Group) and others, are not necessarily useful to college administrators. They are geared toward application in industry and it is costly for colleges to participate in the study. These studies also inflate costs by including overhead and items such as the cost of employees doing personal work on office equipment. The kinds of tools that IT managers and college financial officers need involve more practical assessments of incremental costs.

The COSTS Project bridges the gap between these types of studies. The study is a cost-free collaboration between institutions. Only direct expenditures are captured. They are divided into a small number of traditional categories and over a range of core support services.

The short-term goals of the COSTS project are to

- identify and understand examples of IT services at institutions of higher education,
- develop ranges for the unit costs of providing IT services based on institutional characteristics, and
- test simple hypotheses about the unit costs of providing IT services.

The long-term goals are to

- identify core IT services that should be common to most institutions of higher education,
- identify exemplars for each IT service (i.e., institutional approaches that deliver exceptionally high levels of service at given cost levels),

- develop benchmarks that are useful for comparing the costs of providing IT services among various institutional categories, and
- determine components of the total cost of ownership (TCO)[6] for desktop computer equipment in higher education.

Among the hypotheses tested for each service area are the following:

- *Economies of Scale:* The unit cost of a service will decrease as the number of units increases.
- *Outsourcing:* The unit cost of providing services decreases with the degree to which they are outsourced.
- *You Get What You Pay For:* As service levels increase, the unit cost of providing the service increases.
- *Complexity:* The unit cost of a service increases with the complexity of the environment in which that service is provided.

PILOT PROJECT (1997-98)

The initial COSTS Project began in 1997 and attempted to develop an understanding of IT support services costs. It focused on three common IT support services offered on college and university campuses: repair of desktop hardware, network support, and support for centralized administrative information systems. This effort was, by design, limited in scope and intended to demonstrate the efficacy of the approach. For each of these services, we defined a data set of institutional characteristics and budget categories related to the cost of providing the service. We then recruited institutions to provide the data, with the incentive that only participating institutions shared the results.

Early returns were sparse, numbering approximately 25 institutions. However, after preliminary results were reported in December 1997, the number of participating institutions rose to over 100, including a few from outside the United States. The number of services studied was expanded to include the helpdesk and training services. Participants received summarized results and analyses and detailed data on what other schools are doing to facilitate their own specialized analyses. The goal of the analyses was to develop *ratios* that are comparable across institutions and *ranges* of unit costs that provide insight into the viability of different approaches to meeting campus needs.

EARLY RESULTS

This section shows examples of types of analyses developed from the early efforts. These early results led to a larger study, currently underway, and described later in this chapter.

To understand the data, we focused our analyses not on the average result, but on a typical range of expenditures between the 25th and 75th percentile—commonly known as the "middle 50 percent." While there may be variability in the way data were reported from one institution to another, the middle 50 percent provides a useful guideline for IT managers. Institutions that fall below the 25th percentile for these costs are likely candidates for further study in hopes of identifying best practices, while institutions that fall above the 75th percentile might consider their service offering in light of other alternatives. Perhaps the high cost of the service is reflective of high quality, or perhaps not. The point is that a college can use these ranges as a basis to look more closely at its own IT services.

Desktop Computer Repair

Given the pervasive use of personal computers on college and university campuses, this service is offered, in some manner, by all institutions. The results of the analyses indicate that, on average, large institutions are able to achieve economies of scale based upon the larger computer population on their campuses. For purposes of the analysis, small institutions are ones with FTE student enrollment less than 3,000. Table 6-A summarizes the analysis of the unit cost of delivering the service per institutional computer.

When one looks at the comparison between the unit costs of small and large institutions the large institutions show costs that are on average 50 and 60 percent lower. This finding supports the economy of scale hypothesis—places with more equipment are able to achieve lower unit costs through more economical use of resources.

TABLE 6-A

DESKTOP COMPUTER REPAIR—ANNUAL COST (IN DOLLARS) PER INSTITUTIONAL COMPUTER

Institution type	25th Percentile	50th Percentile (Median)	75th Percentile
Small (55 institutions)	59	112	174
Large (37 institutions)	40	62	96
Overall	44	86	141

Full or partial outsourcing is often used to provide IT repair services. We defined an institution as doing significant outsourcing in this area if more than 25 percent of the total cost of the service was paid to an outside company. Institutions with significant outsourcing ranged from 25 percent up to full outsourcing (100 percent).[7] We compared the costs of repairs among institutions that outsourced to a significant degree and those that did not. The results

(Table 6-B) support the hypothesis that outsourcing is an economical strategy that reduces the unit cost of providing this service, especially for small institutions. The data also provide insight into the number of computers that can reasonably be supported per full-time-equivalent staff member. Small institutions, for example, average less than two full-time staff to provide this service while averaging over 650 computers per institution.

TABLE 6-B

DESKTOP COMPUTER REPAIR—ANNUAL COST (IN DOLLARS) PER INSTITUTIONAL COMPUTER OUTSOURCING VERSUS IN-HOUSE SERVICE OFFERING

Institution type	25th Percentile	50th Percentile (Median)	75th Percentile
Small (in house)	60	133	180
Small (outsource)	43	86	110
Large (in house)	39	67	103
Large (outsource)	41	43	69

What about the quality of the service offered? Understanding the cost of delivering a service does not provide insight into the quality of the service provided. A low unit cost will be of little value if the user community feels that the service is unacceptable. Assessing quality remains a challenge currently beyond the overall scope of the COSTS Project, but exemplars can be identified and further research can be done.

Some institutions are using periodic surveys to determine user satisfaction. With the pervasive use of electronic mail on college campuses, it is relatively easy to send periodic short electronic surveys to a sampling of users of the service. Such surveys often rate the degree of agreement between what the service promises and what it delivers and the manner in which the service is delivered. For computer repair, this can mean things like how quickly the service provider responded to the request for repair, how quickly the equipment was repaired, and the courtesy shown by the provider. It is important that, prior to measuring quality, there be agreement on expectations for the service. For example, will the technician contact the person within 24 hours of the call? Will the equipment be repaired within 24 hours of the first visit, or replaced with equivalent equipment? Expectations play a significant part in assessing service quality.

Network Services

The data network is the central part of the information technology infrastructure on college and university campuses today. Delivering timely, high quality network services is critical to providing access to electronic resources, both on and off campus. The COSTS study sheds light on typical annual expenditures for replacement of equipment, staffing levels, and professional development needs for this important service area.

Most IT managers realize that the electronics and central servers that drive the campus network need replacement on a regular cycle, similar to desktop computer equipment. Participants were asked to estimate the cost and cycle for replacing these items. The COSTS data indicate that on average IT managers plan to replace servers on a four-year cycle and network electronics every five years. However, when asked, few institutions that submitted data actually budget for these replacement costs on an annual basis but rather depend on the approval of special requests. A few institutions are now renting/leasing this equipment as a way of assuring these annual commitments for upgrading the network. The data indicated that if upgrade costs were budgeted on an annual basis, they would represent 35 percent of the annual network budget. The data also indicate that the average annual upgrade cost of servers and electronics per active network port is $79. Active ports are ones that are connected to electronics and can immediately support a computer or printer. The middle 50 percent ranges for these annual costs provide rough planning ranges for IT managers developing campus network strategies. Table 6-C summarizes the key data elements with respect to replacement costs for network electronics and servers.

TABLE 6-C

NETWORK SERVICES—ANNUAL REPLACEMENT COST OF SERVERS AND ELECTRONICS

Data element	25th Percentile	50th Percentile (Median)	75th Percentile
Replacement cost per active port	$47	$65	$93
Replacement cost as Percent of total network budget	26%	35%	43%

It is well known that there is a shortage of qualified IT services staff and that shortage is even more acute in the network services area. It is therefore important for senior administration to have a sense of how many staff it takes to support a high-speed campus data infrastructure. The COSTS data point to several key staffing ratios that shed light on this question. The key components of the campus network are the wiring/fiber, the electronics that move the data over these wires, and the servers that provide the essential data that is moved. Each of these components has associated staffing needs. Complicating the process of understanding staffing needs are the variety of expectations with respect to service delivery. With the network as the central "glue" that holds information technology use together, expectations for the availability of network resources are approaching 24 (hours per day) and 7 (days per week), without corresponding increases in staffing levels. Recent surveys indicate that institutions are attempting to meet these expectations by having existing staff carry pagers, cell phones, or other devices that effectively extend their work days.[8] The COSTS data indicate that among participating institutions the middle 50 percent range for the number of active ports per staff member is between 475 and 1,000 with a median of 674. For a college in the planning stages for the creation of a campus data network with 2,000 active ports, this translates into needing between two and four staff people to support network operations. There is, of course, considerable variability in the complexity of network environments, including the number of servers, the number of operating systems supported, the speed of the network connections, and the variety of approaches being taken to deliver data service, including wireless.

Finally, IT staff need a continual commitment to professional development if they are to remain current and able to implement the constant change that is the norm. How are institutions doing with respect to providing for these staff needs? In the network services area, the average annual allocation for professional development, per staff member, is approximately $2,200. Table 6-D summarizes professional development allocations for the middle 50 percent.

TABLE 6-D

NETWORK SERVICES—ANNUAL COST OF PROFESSIONAL DEVELOPMENT OF STAFF

Data element	25th Percentile	50th Percentile (Median)	75th Percentile
Professional development expenditures per staff member	$867	$2,000	$3,011
Professional development as a percentage of network budget	0.7%	1.5%	2.2%

Helpdesk Services

As the first point of contact for IT services on many campuses, the helpdesk is the emergency room of the IT department, dealing with the urgent/important problems that affect campus users. What types of staffing levels are appropriate? Are staffing needs related to the diversity of the support environment? And how do the professional development needs of staff compare with other IT service areas? These are all areas where COSTS data can help IT planners.

Helpdesk service is generally provided over the telephone supplemented by use of electronic communication through e-mail and the Web. Staffing is generally provided through a combination of professional staff and students. In some cases, students are the front line with professional staff handling only questions that students can't solve. In other cases, professional staff members are the front line with students being dispatched for on-site visits. A third variation separates helpdesk support into two services, one specifically for students and one for faculty/staff, with separate telephone numbers to call and different hours of operation. Combinations of these three approaches are being tried at institutions worldwide.

The middle 50 percent range for the total number of users supported per staff member is between 1,100 and 4,069 with a median of 1,935. By "total users," we mean the total number of employees and students. This definition is a rough approximation, assuming that most employees and students are users of information technology in some way, whether they have a computer at their desk, in their residence hall room, or use a public access computing lab. This range is wide and suggests that there might be significant variability in the quality of services provided. There are several possible quality measures available in the helpdesk service, such as the number of calls resolved, number/percentage of unresolved calls per day/month, and the average length of time to resolve a call.[9] Most institutions do not collect this kind of assessment data in a systematic manner, and many tasks are performed by harried employees who are caught while on the run between one computer and another.

An interesting question explored in the COSTS study was the effect of the diversity of the support environment on the cost of providing the service per user. As a measure of the diversity of the support environment, we used the percentage of computers whose platforms were Macintosh versus Windows. This measure reflects the fact that the current IT environments on college campuses tend to be some mix of Macintosh and Windows. This measure is admittedly crude, since many other factors come into play in determining support needs for the helpdesk, including the complexity of the network, the number of services offered (e.g., backup, centralized storage, etc.), and the degree to which IT has been integrated into the academic program. Nevertheless, the COSTS data did not indicate that support costs were significantly higher in a mixed Macintosh/Windows environment. This finding is consistent with a similar study by the Gartner Group.[10]

Finally, how do the professional development expenditures for the helpdesk staff compare with those of the staff for network services? The data in Table 6-E indicate that institutions are not spending as much on the professional development of their helpdesk staff as they do in the network services area. Perhaps the data merely reflect the higher cost of network training courses.

TABLE 6-E			
HELPDESK SERVICES—ANNUAL COST OF PROFESSIONAL DEVELOPMENT OF STAFF			
Data element	25th Percentile	50th Percentile (Median)	75th Percentile
Professional development expenditures per staff member	$332	$750	$1,667

BEYOND PILOT EFFORTS (1999-)

The initial results and analyses from the pilot project were encouraging. Participating IT directors appreciated and used the data, and financial officers asked their IT directors to participate. At the same time, there were two key barriers to the project's success. First, unless we asked schools to divide up *all* their IT expenses into service categories, we could not be sure that people were including reliable amounts for a particular service. We therefore decided to expand the survey to include "all" IT services. Second, different organizational models meant that some schools might include significant expenses that would not be included by others because they were not in the "central" IT organization. For example, the Webmaster may report to IT ("central") at one school, and to the publications office ("non-central") at another. Other departments, such as the library, might have a person whose primary role is IT support for that department. The focus of the COSTS Project *is* primarily on *centrally provided* IT services. This focus creates a particular problem for larger institutions, which tend to provide these services in a decentralized fashion, making it more difficult to account for costs that are not part of the central IT budget. Even among smaller institutions, some decentralization is common. In the future, COSTS will try to capture important IT expenses that may be budgeted outside the central IT organization.

In moving to capture all IT services, the project defined 12 core IT support services. The advantage of this approach is that additional services can be added as they evolve in the future. For example, distance learning would be considered a recent addition for many and may not be a category at all for some. The core services are the following:

1. *Administrative Information Systems (INFO):* Support provided for centralized information systems that are used by the offices of the college, e.g., Admissions, Financial Aid, Registrar/Student Affairs, Business Office (General Ledger, Accounts Payable/Receivable, Payroll), Human Resources, Alumni/Fundraising, and Inventory/Work Control.

Typical services provided in this area include systems analysis, programming, and assistance with reporting and operations.

2. *Helpline Services (HELP):* A call-in problem-solving service designed to provide help to staff and students experiencing problems of an immediate and important nature with information technology resources. Although the telephone is the primary means of accessing this service, other forms of communication (e.g., e-mail, the Web) may also be used. Callers either have their problems resolved over the phone, by visits to offices, or by referral to other parts of the organization.

3. *Desktop Computer Repair (REPAIR):* Repair of college-owned desktop/ laptop computers and printers, excluding only central servers that are reported in #9 (NET). Typical services provided in this area include diagnosis and repair of hardware problems and related software problems.

4. *Training (TRAIN):* Activities related to helping members of the institution learn to use information technology resources. Typical services provided in this area include scheduled classes, small group and individualized learning, creation of documentation, and provision of self-paced learning materials.

5. *Curricular Support Services (CURR):* Support provided to faculty in connection with teaching (and research, if provided by IT). Typical services in this area are consulting, assistance in locating and testing instructional hardware and software, help in the creation and use of multimedia materials, and instruction in the use of these technologies.

6. *Hardware and Software Installation and Renewal (INSTALL):* Activities related to the periodic installation and replacement of college-owned desktop computer hardware and software. Typical services provided in this area include selection of replacement systems, installation of new hardware and software, and transferring of files from old to new systems. Includes moneys budgeted for computer replacement.

7. *Web Support (WEB):* Activities related to the support of the college's Web efforts, including use of the Web in connection with traditional courses and the operation of the central Web server. Typical services provided in this area include the design and creation of Web pages and consulting with departments on how to use the Web.

8. *Student Support (STUDENT):* Activities related to the support provided directly to students other than through a centralized helpdesk. Typical services provided in this area include the operation of public computing facilities and the servers that support their operation, and direct support to students living in residence halls.

9. *Network Services (NET)*: Maintaining the infrastructure (wiring, fiber, hubs, etc.) and the general-purpose central servers on the campus network, including the connection to the Internet. Typical services provided in this area include administration of campus-wide servers (e.g., electronic mail, print, file storage, DNS/ DHCP), and maintenance of wiring and electronics.

10. *Distance/Asynchronous Learning (DIST)*: Activities related to supporting programs that use videoconferencing, courses delivered substantially on the Internet, or other forms of learning that are primarily focused outside the traditional classroom. Typical services provided in this area include operation and maintenance of distance learning technologies and assistance to faculty teaching with these technologies, e.g., instructional design.

11. *Administration and Planning (PLAN)*: Central coordination and management of the IT organization, research and development, and long-range planning. Activities not related to providing direct day-to-day technical support.

12. *Other (OTHER)*: If all the FTE staff and budgets from Central and Non-Central IT support services do not fit in the first 11 services, the remaining amounts are classified under OTHER.

SURVEY DESIGN

The current COSTS survey consists of 25 questions that capture demographic information, data about the technical environment, and a short spreadsheet (see Table 6-F) to collect the information on expenditures by type of service. The basic demographic data serve to help create ratios that are comparable across institutions. The characteristics of the IT environment further help to normalize the data and make inter-institutional comparisons possible. In an effort to extend the results of early IT service studies, the comprehensive template was created to develop a high-level look at all services at one time.

Institutional Demographic Information

1. Name of institution
2. Number of FTE (full time equivalent) students
3. Number of FTE faculty
4. Number of FTE non-faculty staff

Information About the Computing and Networking Environment

5. Name of vendor(s) providing primary business system software
6. Annual number of service requests to your helpdesk for general desktop support
7. Number of institutionally owned desktop/laptop computers
8. Estimated number of student-owned computers
9. Estimated percentage of institutional computers that are Macintosh
10. Estimated percentage of institutional computers that run some form of Windows
11. Estimated percentage of student-owned computers that are Macintosh
12. Estimated percentage of student-owned computers that run some form of Windows
13. Average total replacement cost of a desktop/laptop computer system, including monitor, which you use for planning purposes
14. Average replacement cycle for a computer system, in years, which you use for planning purposes
15. Estimated annual number of new computers installed
16. Estimated annual number of computers "cascaded" (moved from one user to another) or significantly upgraded
17. Average number of hours per installation of a new computer system, including transfer of files
18. Estimated total replacement value of all central campus servers
19. Estimated average replacement cycle for central servers in years
20. Total replacement cost for network electronics (hubs, switches, etc.)
21. Replacement cycle for network electronics, in years, which you use for planning purposes
22. Number of active network ports (i.e., connected to network electronics)
23. Number of network ports in use (i.e., actually have a computer/printer connected to them)
24. Estimated FTE staff outside of central IT organization who provide IT-type support
25. Estimated total budget for IT-type services provided by areas other than central IT

TABLE 6-F

The COSTS Template (Actual template is available on the COSTS Web site as an Excel spreadsheet.)

Budget Categories	Budget	The 12 IT Support Services											
		1	2	3	4	5	6	7	8	9	10	11	12
FTE Staff													
Non-student Salaries													
Student Salaries													
Contractual Consulting													
Hardware Lease/ rent purchase													
Hardware Maintenance													
Software Purchased													
Software Licenses													
Professional Development													
Other													

Detailed information about the current COSTS template and instructions for completing it can be found on the Web at <http://www.its.colgate.edu/kleach/COSTS/costs.htm>.

LATEST RESULTS

The task of moving from compiling data for one service to try to understand all services has been difficult even though the data set being collected is limited. IT managers, already dealing with information and expectation overload, are reluctant to take time to develop the data that could be used to compare their environment to others even though most acknowledge that much could be gained by doing so. This reluctance is particularly true at large, complex universities where IT support services are highly decentralized and costs are hard to capture.

By looking back at the early results, the value of the comprehensive approach to understanding IT services costs is clear. The new information gives a more complete picture of IT services and will increase the reliability of the information and the resulting benchmarks. It will also allow IT managers to see relationships among services.

Spending per student is a common benchmark for traditional budget categories and the COSTS data begin to reveal ranges of spending for IT per student. The middle 50 percent range for central IT budgets per student is $409 to $908 with a median of $569 per student. This ratio provides a crude measure of the level of IT expenditures that can be compared across institutions. As more institutions participate in the COSTS Project, it will be possible to stratify the data, for example, by the Carnegie Classification of the institution.

IT managers are also interested in whether they are devoting appropriate portions of their budget to things such as salaries, hardware purchases, and professional development of staff. When looking at the particular budget components, the latest COSTS data show that for the middle 50 percent salaries comprise 43-59 percent of the total budget. The middle 50 percent for spending on professional development of staff is 1-3 percent of the total central IT budget.

Other information that can enlighten the planning and management process is the proportion of resources devoted to particular service areas. For example, the COSTS approach shows that the middle 50 percent devote 4-8 percent of total staff to instructional support; the middle 50 percent range for average salary of these instructional support staff is $35,000 to $44,000.

The COSTS data also open the door to understanding the patterns of resources devoted to each service area. The percentage of spending on each service as shown in Table 6-G provides a first insight into the way central IT budgets are allocated and the relative costs of providing the services.

THE FUTURE

Studies such as the COSTS Project can help institutional and IT planners develop a common language to promote understanding of the costs and benefits of information technologies. Given the importance of these technologies to achieving institutional missions, and the significant amounts of continuing expenditures that will be necessary to support these technologies, it is urgent that we make these investments wisely.

As more institutions participate in the comprehensive COSTS survey, it will be possible to develop a clearer understanding of IT investments. Moreover, annual participation will result in longitudinal data showing changes over time. This is an opportunity to develop benchmarks and seek best practices for spending on IT services. Astute institutional leaders will not miss this opportunity.

TABLE 6-G

SERVICE COSTS AS A PERCENT OF TOTAL IT BUDGET

Service category	Average distribution (service costs as a percent of IT budget)
Info	23%
Help	6%
Repair	5%
Train	3%
Curr	6%
Install	19%
Web	3%
Student	7%
Net	17%
Dist	2%
Plan	7%
Other	2%

ENDNOTES

1. Richard Katz, "A Time to Assess," *Educom Review* 34, 2 (March/April 1999): 56.

2. John M. Berry, "Study Predicts Sustainable Growth," *The Washington Post*, September 9, 1999: E /01.

3. Edward Teach, "Setting up Cybershop," *CFO Magazine* (October 1999).

4. Total spending on information technology as a percentage of total education and general budget. Median of all schools reporting that year.

5. C.S. Peebles, and L. Antolovic, "Cost (and Quality and Value) of Information Technology Support in Large Research Universities," *Educom Review* 34, 5: 20-23, 46-49.

6. The Total Cost of Ownership (TCO) is an estimate of the purchase price plus operating costs of a computer system. Included in operating costs are such items as maintenance, software support, configuration time, etc.

7. The data further indicate that as the percentage of outsourcing increases, the gap between in-house and outsourced costs become wider.

8. Rob Whitnell, "Summary, On-Call Policies," CIO Listserv, September 30, 1999.

9. Emily Paulsen, "What Does Support Really Cost," *Support Management* 1, 2 (May/June 1997): 14.

10. Gartner Group, "Technical Support Costs and Dual-Platform Desktops: Managed Diversity," technical report issued to subscribers, (November 1995).

CHAPTER

Assessing Educational Quality Using Student Satisfaction

James Caplan

Information on costs may often be best viewed through the lens of quality. Traditional budgetary processes resolve into the tradeoff between costs and quality. In education, the trend has been toward assessing quality in terms of student outcomes and those have been essentially achievement-based. Examples include course grades, test scores, retained knowledge, student retention, certification rates, rates of seeking advanced training, graduation rates, and professional salaries.

One of the key elements of service quality, often ignored in higher education, is consumer satisfaction. This chapter attempts to remedy that shortcoming. In our *Change* article,[1] Carol Frances, Richard Pumerantz, and I challenged the notion that there were no significant differences in educational outcomes between class-based and technology-mediated learning. We found that when student options were taken into consideration, subjective outcomes, i.e., satisfaction with the learning experience, differed significantly while objective outcomes, i.e., grades, showed no significant differences.

COMPARISON OF INSTRUCTOR-PRESENT TEACHING WITH TELECONFERENCING TECHNOLOGY

The 165 participants in this study came from a total enrollment of 197 students in a two-year, certificate-granting physician's assistant program offered by a California health professions institution. Students received identical curricula with the same faculty, books, schedules, assignments, and grading standards on two different campuses. On the "main" campus, 101 participants took courses with live faculty, while on the "remote" campus, 64 participants viewed the same lectures and participated in class discussion via videoconferencing technology. Both groups had opportunities to ask questions and interact with the faculty in real time.

The two groups were demographically identical except for ethnicity. Those differences had no effect on results.[2] Determination of which students attended which program was primarily based on individual preference. However, once the slots at the main campus were filled, students were directed to the remote campus. No numbers are available for this, but informal discussion with staff suggested that the percentage not receiving their first choice was small. The group included 58 percent first-year students and 42 percent second-year students. All individuals received their training at the same site, i.e., there were no crossovers.

A survey instrument was developed to evaluate student perceptions of different aspects of the educational program, especially satisfaction. Questions were also asked about prior experience with technology and perceptions of the costs and economic value of the program. Over 80 percent of the students from both campuses completed and returned the questionnaires. Identification was coded and controlled by the program to protect the confidentiality of participants. Grades and demographic information were provided to the researchers by code number, which allowed us to match survey responses with student records without knowledge of individuals. To achieve adequate numbers, students from the first and second year of the program were combined, after assuring that they were comparable.

To make sure that any differences we might find were not due to familiarization differences, we asked a number of questions that dealt with prior familiarity with technology. The results are shown in Table 7-A.

TABLE 7-A

Prior Familiarity with Technology

1=No Experience; 5=A Great Deal of Experience	Campus		
	Main	Remote	Signif.
Experience using PCs	3.09	3.08	ns
Experience with Internet browsing	2.89	2.80	ns
Experience with Internet chatting	1.75	1.75	ns
Experience with e-mail	2.99	2.95	ns
Experience with other instructional technology	2.40	2.14	ns
Experience with remote instructors	1.54	1.56	ns

Another possible source of contamination was differences in how much participants used technology in their everyday lives. Table 7-B shows the differences in use of technology outside of class.

TABLE 7-B

COMPARISONS OF CURRENT TECHNOLOGY USE

1=Not at all;	Campus		
5=A Great Deal	Main	Remote	Signif.
To what extent do you use the computer lab?	2.03	2.19	ns
To what extent do you use your own pc?	3.13	3.59	p<.01
To what extent do you send e-mail to students?	2.29	2.87	P<.005
To what extent do you send e-mail to faculty?	1/62	1.82	ns

In contrast to students' experience prior to enrolling in the program, students at the distance-learning campus tended to be more familiar with computers and to use them more outside of class, especially to e-mail other students. This familiarity difference, should it prove contaminating, should bias responses at the remote campus *in favor* of technology.

Finally, as a check on our system and to assure that respondents were using the terminology as we intended, we asked how much respondents used instructional technology in their classes and to what extent they anticipated using information technology (IT) in their careers. The results are shown in Table 7-C.

TABLE 7-C

COMPARISONS OF PERCEIVED USE OF IT IN PRESENT CLASSES AND FUTURE CAREERS

	Campus		
1=Not at All; 5=A Great Deal	Main	Remote	Signif.
To what extent do your classes use instructional technology?	3.45	4.24	P<.0001
To what extent do you believe you will use computers or other information technology in your professional career?	3.66	3.78	ns

This result demonstrates that participants interpreted the teleconferencing used for classes at the remote campus as instructional technology. Likewise, use of technology outside of class or classroom exposure to technology did not predispose participants to see technology as a tool for their careers.

FINDINGS

We compared student grade point averages for the courses that used both instructional methods. That typically meant 6 courses for the first-year students and 11 courses for second-year students. Table 7-D shows GPAs for the main and distance-learning campuses by class year. Like hundreds of previous studies, we found no significant differences.

TABLE 7-D

GPA Comparisons Between Campuses, Considering Class Year

GPA Class year	Campus			
	Main	Remote	Both	Signif.
1999	3.3233	3.4564	3.3754	ns
2000	3.1346	3.1404	3.1368	ns
Combined	3.2131	3.2737	3.2366	ns

SATISFACTION MEASURES

We were curious to see how students at one campus compared their experience to the other campus. This goes to the question of whether students were familiar with how the instruction was conducted on both campuses and whether programs taught by on-site instructors were perceived to be more desirable than the ones using videoconferencing. We asked participants a variety of questions comparing their programs and facilities. The results are shown in Table 7-E.

TABLE 7-E

STUDENT COMPARISONS OF THE TWO CAMPUSES

1 = Your campus is much worse; 5 = Your campus is much better	Campus		Signif.
	Main	Remote	
How would you compare the overall quality of education?	4.08	2.84	p<.0000
How would you compare total education costs?	3.33	2.39	p<.0000
How would you compare student academic ability?	3.86	3.51	p<.05
How would you compare quality of clinical training?	4.02	2.51	p<.0000
How would you compare your enjoyment of the learning process?	4.01	3.15	p<.0000
How would you compare access to instructors?	3.99	1.73	p<.0000
How would you compare access to information?	3.74	1.97	p<.0000
How would you compare quality of classroom facilities?	3.55	2.00	p<.0000
How would you compare living accommodations?	2.03	3.49	p<.0000
How would you compare the quality of student life?	3.43	3.65	ns

Although the distance-learning campus was seen as having better living accommodations and comparable quality of student life, it trailed in all other comparisons. Even student academic ability on the remote campus was perceived as lower, although, based on undergraduate GPA, it was practically identical. Clinical courses on the main campus were perceived as better, despite the fact that they were both taught by in-class instructors. There was no "grass is greener" phenomenon. Students at both sites preferred the classrooms with live instructors.

We attempted to understand what differences might exist between live and remote classrooms. Table 7-F provides a list of some questions used to measure student perceptions of the learning experience and the mean response ratings between the students in the same classroom with the instructor and those in the distance-learning classrooms.

TABLE 7-F

Average Ratings of Various Satisfaction Items Provided by Students Receiving Classroom and Teleconferenced Instruction

5= Highest 1= Lowest	Mean Rating with Instructor Present (N=101)	Mean Rating for Televised Instruction (N=64)
How satisfactory is your communication with your instructors?	3.99	2.87*
How satisfactory is your access to information (Internet, library, etc.)?	4.01	3.15*
How would you rate the degree of privacy you feel when interacting with instructors or other students?	3.76	3.03*
How would you rate your campus environment in being conducive to helping you learn?	4.12	3.21*
How would you rate the student activities and social life on your campus?	3.63	3.75
How would you rate the degree of student support services (counseling, advising, etc.)?	3.87	3.10*
How would you rate your classroom lectures and discussions?	4.18	3.31*
How motivated are you by the manner in which your classes are taught (instructor present or video conferencing)?	3.85	3.42*
How would you rate the quality of the feedback you get from instructors?	3.78	2.57*
Rate the degree to which the PA program is meeting your educational expectations	4.24	3.28*
Overall, how would you evaluate the PA program?	4.39	3.45*
Compare your overall quality of education	4.08	2.84*
Compare your total education costs	3.33	2.39*
Compare your academic ability of the students	3.86	3.51[†]
Compare your quality of the clinical training experience	4.02	2.51*
Compare how enjoyable the process of learning is	4.01	3.15*
Compare your access to instructors	3.99	1.73*
Compare your ease of getting access to information (reference material)	3.74	1.97*
Compare your quality of classroom facilities	3.55	2.00*
Compare your living accommodations	2.03	3.49*
Compare your quality of student life	3.43	3.65

* Significant, p<.001; [†] Significant, p<.01

DISCUSSION

In almost every aspect, students were simply not as satisfied with the program at the distance-learning campus that used videoconferencing. Unlike comparisons of GPAs and the perceived dollar value of the certificate earned, the subjective measures of satisfaction with the program showed large differences between the two campuses. Students using IT were apparently learning as much but enjoying it less. They clearly felt that the quality of the educational experience was inferior when taught via videoconferencing.

While many studies have found no differences in student satisfaction between traditional and distance learning methods,[3] ours was unusual in several regards:

1. An entire program of study was compared as opposed to a single course.
2. Extraneous variables were reduced by having the same instructors, materials, tests, grading standards, and course schedules. Only the presence or absence of the instructor in the actual classroom varied.
3. Differences in backgrounds, abilities, or demographics between groups were carefully evaluated and found not to be factors.
4. Satisfaction was defined from a consumer viewpoint. Most studies of student satisfaction rely on course evaluation questions, which seldom assess how satisfied students are with the instruction. Most evaluations focus on materials, instructor, and information transfer. Some measure attitudes toward the content. Our study asked students to rate how much they learned and how motivated they were as a result.

These factors answer most of the objections to previous research on the effectiveness of distance learning published by The Institute for Higher Education Policy.[4]

ASSESSING PERCEIVED COSTS AND BENEFITS

In an earlier study,[5] we found that prospective students were more influenced in their willingness to borrow money for education by how much is at risk rather than by anticipated return on investment. During this current study, we had the opportunity to extend research using dollar value as an index of perceived importance by looking at a wide range of perceived subjective values associated with education as well as anticipated return on investment to assess how higher education is valued in dollar terms.

Comparing education expressed in dollar terms with more traditional evaluation scales gives us new insights into the motivations students have to continue their formal learning. Post-graduate certificate programs are a quick way to immediately enhance earning potential. In our present study, participants believed that program completion would add an average $30,000 to their annual salaries within five years of completion. This belief has implications for recruiting, retaining, and converting students into dedicated alumni.

From a measurement perspective, comparing scales using subjective ratings with those using perceived dollar value gives a new dimension for evaluating student satisfaction. It also fits extremely well into considerations of quality because a direct comparison can be made between actual dollars spent and perceived dollar value received.

In the most recent study, the following questions were devised for assessing perceived financial value:

- To what extent will participating in this program help you find a better job?
- Estimate the *difference* (not the total income, only the difference) a PA certificate will make in your *annual income* after working five years: $ _____ (check one: ❑ More ❑ Less) per year difference
- How would you rate the *overall expected future value you will receive* from your total education costs for the PA program?
- Estimate how much you could have earned this year, working full-time instead of going to school: $ _____

One of the key aspects of the study was to compare estimates of costs with perceived value. We did this (1) by asking for estimates of how much completion of the program would increment annual income, and (2) by asking participants to directly rate the value of their training. (We also gathered extensive data on costs, including lost opportunity costs, for later use in following up with these participants.) The results are shown in Table 7-G.

TABLE 7-G

PERCEIVED VALUE OF THE PROGRAM

Class year	Main	Remote	Signif.
To what extent will attending this program help you find a better job? (1 = not at all; 5 = a Great Deal)	4.10	3.79	ns
Estimate how much you could have earned this year, working full-time instead of going to school	$36,955	$31,185	ns
Estimate the difference in your annual income after five years	$30,600	$28,333	ns
Rate the overall expected future value received from education costs	4.35	4.30	ns

Starting salary differences between campuses most likely represent prevailing job market conditions between the northern and southern portions of the state, rather than educational values. With the advanced certificate, students fully expected to almost double their salaries after five years. Clearly, they looked upon this program as a means to an end. When that end (approximately $30,000 per year greater income) is made explicit, how students learned made no difference.

PERCEIVED EXPENDITURES

As part of this study, we asked participants to provide detailed estimates of their expenditures for each academic year to complete the PA program. The average estimates for the expenditures by campus are shown in Table 7-H.

TABLE 7-H

MEAN ESTIMATED PROGRAM EXPENDITURES

Estimated Annual Expenditure	Main	Remote	Signif.
How much will you spend on tuition?	$13,102.63	$14,104.53	ns
Spend on books, equipment, and supplies?	$1,548.97	$1,125.00	ns
Spend on computer hardware, software, and other tech?	$437.53	$600.00	ns
Spend on computer fees?	$110.62	$122.31	ns
Spend on communication with students/faculty?	$280.33	$153.98	ns
Spend on training-related transportation?	$749.38	$1,207.41	ns
Spend on interest related to borrowing for school?	$1,217.26	$2,195.37	ns
Spend on other school expenses?	$2,024.23	$2,868.52	ns
Spend on all expenses?	$19,470.94	$22,397.57	p<.05

Individual expenditure estimates are not significantly different but the small differences accumulate. Students at the distance-learning site see themselves spending $3,000 more per year, a statistically significant difference. We have verified with the institution that tuition, fees, books, and supplies are the same for the two locations.

SOURCES OF FUNDING

We asked all participants to indicate the detailed source of funds used to pay for their program. The mean amounts by campus are shown in Table 7-I.

TABLE 7-1

MEAN AMOUNTS AND SOURCES OF FUNDING FOR PROGRAM EXPENSES

Source of Funding	Main	Remote	Signif.
Funds from personal assets	$5,462	$3,386	ns
Funds from spouse or partner—no repayment	$3,836	$2,800	ns
Gift from family/friends	$1,621	$1,436	ns
Scholarship/grant/direct stipend—not repaid	$2,538	$1,610	ns
Part-time work	$2,161	$712	ns
Full-time work	$425	$.00	ns
Student loan	$14,160	$20,580	p<.01
Borrowed from family/friends	$1,589	$1,068	ns
Funds from other sources	$1,185	$406	ns
Total revenues	$31,906	$31,998	ns

Students at the two sites reported almost the identical amount of total funding per year. The difference between funding and school expenditures presumably went toward personal living expenses. One wonders why students at the distance-learning site showed greater personal incomes in view of the fact that the cost of living is actually lower there. Perhaps childcare or some other expense accounted for the difference.

Additionally, the large difference (actually statistically significant) in amount borrowed through student loans is interesting. The disproportionate amount of part-time work clearly accounts for some of it. One finding from this study was that even if institutions believe that conducting distance learning costs less than traditional classroom-based teaching, the savings are not being passed on to the consumers, at least not in this instance.

HOW TO MAKE DISTANCE LEARNING MORE COMPARABLE TO CLASSROOM INSTRUCTION

In our *Change* article, we revisited the research, reported by Harry Harlow and associates in the late 1960s. In his work, which would now be considered unethical, he created surrogate caregivers, one made of soft cloth and the other of chicken wire. Soon after birth, baby rhesus monkeys were taken from their mothers and exposed to these surrogates. The baby monkeys universally preferred the "cloth mothers" even when the wire mothers provided the food. Harlow referred to this as "contact comfort." Presumably, baby primates need the comfort and support of another to smooth the emotion created by new and strange surroundings.

I once attended a colloquium given by Harlow where he related an anecdote that has not, to my knowledge, been published. It seems that one grouping of monkeys raised by the surrogate mothers developed normally without the antisocial and pathological behaviors characteristic of the others once they matured. Harlow decided to investigate and visited the lab late one night. He found a first-year graduate student who was responsible for evening shift at the Primate Center with all the baby monkeys from that study sitting on the floor playing with her and each other. She was clearly providing the contact comfort of which the others were deprived. While unintended, these results may provide a legacy that we can use. A major conclusion from the Institute for Higher Education Policy study of distance learning was that technology has not replaced the human factor in higher education.

This conclusion leads to the following set of research questions that should be investigated as a prerequisite for creating distance learning conditions that produce the same level of student satisfaction as instructor-present courses:

1. What is the role of student-teacher interaction in making the learning process more satisfying? Could a trained proctor or teaching assistant perform the same role?

2. What is the role of student-student interaction? Should structured methods of creating discussion groups or study groups be considered?

3. How effective would peer mentors be to deal with questions and problems outside the formal classroom?

4. Can instructors be trained to better use technology to overcome some of the problems?

Some of the same measurement methodology that is currently used to pretest entertainment product could lend itself readily to research on the human factor in higher education. Television producers routinely ask test audiences to respond to content on a moment-by-moment basis with input devices that gather individual reactions via button or dial. Real time monitoring of class response would be useful in trying out methods and techniques, as well as content and humor. Another proven technique used frequently in marketing research is the focus group. Students would be given the opportunity to discuss the reasons why they aren't as happy with remote learning.

Finally, we believe that student options are important in assessing student satisfaction. Some of the prior attitude research that reported no significant differences was conducted on students for whom distance learning was their only access to higher education. It is hard to believe that, given no other options, students would be unhappy with distance learning. Our results were based on participants whose preferences were considered in making placements (with the exception of an unknown but small number who were assigned to the remote site because the main site was full), but there is no indication that these students had no other options.

Student satisfaction is an important indicant of the value of learning. We must work at developing better measurement tools and track this factor as rigorously as we do grades, dropout rates, or course evaluations.

ENDNOTES

1. C. Frances, R. Pumeranz, and J.R. Caplan, "Planning for Instructional Technology: What You Thought You Knew Could Lead You Astray," *Change 31* (July/August, 1999): 24-33.

2. For a detailed report of the results see J.R. Caplan, "Instructional Technology Cost and the 'No Significant Differences' Phenomenon." Presented to the Executive Forum on Managing the Cost of IT in Higher Education, Princeton, NJ, April 16, 1999.

3. See, for instance, K.J. Paulsen, K. Higgins, S.P. Miller, S. Strawser, and R. Boone, "Delivering Instruction via Interactive Television and Videotape: Student Achievement and Satisfaction." *Journal of Special Education Technology 13* (Spring, 1998): 59-77.

4. R. Phipps, R. Merisotis, and J. Merisotis, *What's the Difference? A Review of the Contemporary Research on the Effectiveness of Distance Learning in Higher Education.* Washington, DC: The Institute for Higher Education Policy, 1999.

5. J.R. Caplan, "Willingness to Borrow for College as Influenced by Perceived Income and Risk." Paper presented to the annual meeting of the American Association for Public Opinion Research, Fort Lauderdale, FL, May 1995.

CHAPTER

Courseware for Remedial Mathematics
A Case Study in the Benefits and Costs of the Mediated Learning System in the California State University

Frank Jewett

CONTEXT

California State University (CSU) consists of 22 campuses located throughout the state.[1] The campuses enroll over 350,000 students and offer degrees in over 200 subject areas. The CSU system includes urban institutions serving large, primarily local, inner-city populations as well as suburban and rural institutions drawing their enrollments from throughout the state. Undergraduate students are admitted if they are in the upper one-third

Contributor's Note: This chapter is an edited version of a case study done by the author as part of a project entitled *Case Studies in Evaluating the Benefits and Costs of Mediated Instruction and Distributed Learning.* The project was funded through a Field-Initiated Studies Educational Research Grant by the National Institute on Postsecondary Education, Libraries, and Lifelong Learning, Office of Educational Research and Improvement, U.S. Department of Education, with additional funding provided by Information Resources and Technology in the Chancellor's Office of the California State University, and jointly sponsored by the California State University, the National Learning Infrastructure Initiative of EduCause, and the State Higher Education Executive Officers.

A California State University (CSU) ad hoc committee was appointed to oversee this case study. The committee's advice and contributions are gratefully acknowledged. Marshall Cates, professor of mathematics at CSU Los Angeles, provided a useful paper on both the earlier implementation efforts and the follow-up studies on the performance of students in later courses in mathematics that was incorporated in the report. Support, assistance, and advice were also provided by members of the benefit cost project's Steering, Review, and Oversight Committee: Tony Bates, director of Distance Education and Technology, University of British Columbia; Dennis Jones, president of NCHEMS; Jim Mingle, executive director of SHEEO; and Tom West, assistant vice chancellor for information resources and technology, CSU Chancellor's Office.

of their high school graduating class or transfer as upper division students from community colleges. CSU has had programs for testing the proficiency of entering undergraduate students in English since 1977, and in mathematics since 1983. Students who fail the proficiency examinations are placed in remedial courses in the first term of their enrollment. Students who do not make adequate progress in their remedial work are expected to enroll elsewhere. The number of freshman students requiring remedial courses became a source of system-wide concern in the 1990s; typically, over 50 percent of incoming freshman fail the entry level mathematics examination. CSU is operating under a 1997 Board of Trustees mandate to reduce the percentage of students requiring remedial work in mathematics to 42 percent by 2001, to 26 percent by 2004, and to 10 percent by 2007. A similar provision is in place for English.

Academic Systems Corporation's Mediated Learning System courseware was developed to provide multimedia instructional materials in campus computer labs.[2] In fall 1994, two campuses, CSU LA and California Polytechnic State University San Luis Obispo (Cal Poly), began working with Academic Systems to implement MLS as a component of their instruction in remedial mathematics. The intent was to exploit the potential of the computer to provide more flexibility for individual pacing, to better accommodate different learning styles, and to allow for increased time on task. It was also hoped that the introduction of more real life examples would improve student motivation to study elementary mathematics. Because English is a second language for many CSU LA students, ways also had to be found to deal with understanding written mathematics. MLS courseware was chosen because it seemed the most sophisticated multimedia program available. It emphasizes use of video and sound-animated text, is highly interactive, and provides several layers of student feedback. MLS comes equipped with a management system that captures student responses to questions and records time on task, thus allowing the instructor to monitor each student's progress and identify those students having problems.

The first two campuses to experiment with MLS courseware, Cal Poly and CSU LA, are different. Cal Poly is a polytechnic university with programs in agriculture, architecture, and engineering. Located on the central California coast, it draws its students from throughout the state. CSU LA is a comprehensive urban university with large programs in business, teacher preparation, and engineering. It is located in east Los Angeles and draws its students primarily from the local region, which has a high proportion of Hispanic, African American, and Asian households. Both campuses had been using regular lecture classes to teach remedial mathematics and both had senior faculty who were interested in experimenting with computer-mediated learning. Academic Systems worked closely with each campus to implement MLS. Beginning in 1995, six other CSU campuses joined the experiment.

The CSU ad hoc committee appointed to oversee the project agreed to report a common set of data elements for evaluating the impact of MLS courseware on learning outcomes in introductory and intermediate algebra courses. The data included an entry-level measure of mathematical skills, the MDTP test. Exit-level performance was measured by final exam scores, course grades, and course completion rates. Because some campuses were just beginning to use MLS while others had two to three years of experience, it was decided not to identify campuses by name. The campuses are labeled here A through H. Numbers of course sections and total enrollments for both MLS and classroom versions of elementary and intermediate courses appear in Table 8-A. At the elementary level, Site B had no regular classroom (control) sections, Site C had 14 classroom sections compared to 8 MLS, and Site F had 2 MLS sections compared to 17 classroom sections. At the intermediate level, Site A had 3 MLS sections and 13 classroom sections, Site B, again, had no classroom sections, Site C had no intermediate sections, and Site F had 2 MLS and 27 classroom sections. In total, almost 4,700 students were enrolled in 155 sections of elementary and intermediate remedial mathematics. Approximately 34 percent of enrollments were in MLS sections, 66 percent in regular classroom sections.

MLS courseware was employed differently across campuses. Some campuses had been using MLS for several terms; some had just implemented it. Based upon the experience of the longer users, there is a learning period during which the course configuration is likely to be changed somewhat in response to the particular campus needs. One of the campuses that had used MLS for several terms has adopted it for all remedial mathematics instruction. In some cases, MLS was used entirely as a supplement to regular weekly course meetings; in other cases, it was used as an integral part of the course in the sense that its use replaced some, but not all, regular class meetings. At some sites, the MLS was used to essentially replace regular class meetings and became the principal mode of providing instruction. These different uses are summarized in the campus sections below where the amount of regular classroom time that was displaced by the courseware is estimated. For all campuses, even if the entire course was scheduled to be delivered using the courseware, instructors would still call groups of students out of the lab for short "chalk talks" on particular topics as the need arose. In most cases, students were expected to spend time, in addition to the regularly scheduled class hours, in the MLS labs doing homework or otherwise using the courseware.

In addition to the number of course sections and enrollment data, each site reported scores on the CSU-UC Mathematics Development Project Test (MDPT), which was used as a pre-test for students enrolled in both elementary

TABLE 8-A

Number of MLS and Classroom Sections and Enrollments by Site and Course Level, Fall 1996

		MLS sections		Classroom sections	
Sites/course levels		Sections	Students	Sections	Students
Site A	elementary	3	88	4	101
	intermediate	3	80	13	337
Site B	elementary	5	265	0	0
	intermediate	5	253	0	0
Site C	elementary	8	225	14	475
	intermediate	0	0	0	0
Site D	elementary	3	90	3	129
	intermediate	4	118	5	210
Site E	elementary	4	70	5	75
	intermediate	5	83	4	67
Site F	elementary	2	46	17	415
	intermediate	2	55	27	931
Site G	elementary	3	80	3	95
	intermediate	3	64	3	118
Site H	elementary	2	47	2	81
	intermediate	2	50	1	39
Total	elementary	30	911	48	1,371
	intermediate	24	703	53	1,702
Total	all levels	54	1,614	101	3,073

Total enrollments   4,687
Total sections   155

and intermediate sections of the courses. Four outcome results were reported in the original evaluation study:[3] (1) the number of enrollees who took the final (a measure of attrition), (2) average final exam scores, (3) number of enrollees passing the course, and (4) the number who received a final score of 70 or better. The site-specific data reported in Tables 8-B1 through 8-B8 below include average MDPT scores, average section size, total enrollment in the experimental and control sections, percent of students passing the course, and percent taking the final who received a score of 70 or better.

COMPARING LEARNING OUTCOMES ON EIGHT CAMPUSES

Site A: Approximately 75 percent of course work was based on MLS courseware at this campus. All sections were taught from a common syllabus. Course pacing was standardized. All students took instructor-designed, coordinator-approved weekly quizzes and two midterms. Daily homework was required and graded. The regular classroom/lecture (control) sections were scheduled for four hours of lecture/discussion per week with some minimal use of small groups at the discretion of the instructor. The MLS (experimental) sections had one hour of lecture per week in a classroom and three hours of class time online, supplemented as necessary with one-on-one or small group instruction.

Elementary Level: In terms of the MDPT pre-test scores, the two groups were essentially equal. Eighty percent of the MLS students successfully completed the course compared to 71 percent in the regular classroom sections, a differential pass rate for these groups of over 12 percent.[4] The MLS group also had a higher rate, by about 11 percent, of passing the course with final scores of 70 or better. Neither of these differences were statistically significant from zero at the 5-percent level (i.e., neither of the "z" values were greater than 1.96).

Intermediate Level: The pass rate for the MLS sections was over 7 percent higher than for the classroom sections but the difference was not statistically significant. The lecture sections had a substantially higher proportion of final scores of 70 or better (negative percentages shown in the table indicate differences in favor of the classroom sections), and, in this case, the difference was statistically significant and in favor of the classroom group.

TABLE 8-B1

COMPARISON OF STUDENT PERFORMANCE IN MLS AND LECTURE SECTIONS

Course level	MLS	Regular classroom	Percent difference[5]	Difference significant @ 5%? ("z")
Elementary				
Average MDPT score	70	69		
Average section size	29	25		
Total enrollment	88	101		
Percent passing	80%	71%	+12.7%	No (1.31)
Percent passing with score of 70 or better	60%	54%	+11.1%	No (0.89)
Intermediate				
Average MDPT score	57	59		
Average section size	27	26		
Total enrollment	80	337		
Percent passing	59%	55%	+7.3%	No (0.53)
Percent passing with score of 70 or better	15%	30%	-50.0%	Yes (2.74)

Site B: The MLS courseware constituted approximately 95 percent of the course work at this campus. The campus has used the MLS materials for several terms and has adopted it for all remedial mathematics instruction in its two courses. All courses are three-quarter units and are taught by graduate assistants under the supervision of a part-time faculty member. All instruction occurs in a large (60 station) computer lab constructed for the courses. Except for group orientation, occasional small group sessions and explanations, and one-on-one or small-group sidebars, all work was done online. The course pass rates and percent passing with final scores of 70 or better for this site compare favorably with those at the other campuses. The average MDPT scores at this site are in the upper range of those observed at other sites.

TABLE 8-B2

Student Performance in MLS Sections

*"Percent passing with a score of 70 or better" is calculated based upon number of students who took the final. This value can exceed "percent passing," which is based upon total students enrolled.

Course level:	MLS
Elementary	
Average MDPT score	71
Average section size	53
Total enrollment	265
Percent passing	73%
Percent passing with score of 70 or better	73%
Intermediate	
Average MDPT score	57
Average section size	51
Total enrollment	253
Percent passing	74%
Percent passing with score of 70 or better	79%*

Site C: At this site, a four-quarter unit elementary course was offered, but no intermediate course. All course work in the MLS sections was based on MLS courseware. Lecture section students spent four hours in lecture/discussion classes. All instruction for MLS sections took place in the computer lab where students received approximately one hour of lecture/discussion and three hours online instruction per week. Students in the lecture sections had a higher average score on the MDPT test but the MLS students passed the course at a 54 percent higher rate. The MLS students also did better on the final scores, earning grades of 70 plus at a 46 percent higher rate. Both differences were statistically significant.

TABLE 8-B3

COMPARISON OF STUDENT PERFORMANCE IN MLS AND LECTURE SECTIONS

Course level:	MLS	Regular classroom	Percent difference	Difference significant @ 5%? ("z")
Elementary				
Average MDPT score	43	55		
Average section size	28	34		
Total enrollment	225	475		
Percent passing	77%	50%	+54.0%	Yes (6.81)
Percent passing with score of 70 or better	51%	35%	+45.7%	Yes (4.19)

Site D: All courses were three semester units. Lecture sections met in regular classrooms. The MLS courseware constituted approximately 95 percent of the MLS version of the courses. The MLS sections met in a computer laboratory and were assisted by instructors primarily on a one-on-one basis. All MLS section work was done online. All students took a common final examination. Students in the intermediate MLS sections had higher MDPT scores. The passing rate and the percent passing with a score of 70 or better were higher for MLS students in both the elementary and intermediate courses. Although the differences in all the ratios favored the MLS sections, none of the differences were statistically significant.

TABLE 8-B4

COMPARISON OF STUDENT PERFORMANCE IN MLS AND LECTURE SECTIONS

Course level:	MLS	Regular classroom	Percent difference	Difference significant @ 5%? ("z")
Elementary				
Average MDPT score	68	67		
Average section size	30	43		
Total enrollment	90	129		
Percent passing	86%	81%	+6.2%	No (0.95)
Percent passing with score of 70 or better	79%	69%	+14.5%	No (1.60)
Intermediate				
Average MDPT score	52	46		
Average section size	30	42		
Total enrollment	118	210		
Percent passing	70%	60%	+16.7%	No (1.95)
Percent passing with score of 70 or better	46%	40%	+15.0%	No (1.12)

Site E: Both classroom and MLS sections met four times per week for four units. The curriculum for both was paced and required in-class examinations. The MLS courseware constituted approximately 95 percent of the content in the MLS sections. Classroom sections enrolled 15-17 students on average and were taught as tutorials by three student assistants who were supervised by a part-time faculty member. MLS sections enrolled 17-18 students and were taught in a 20-station computer laboratory by two graduate assistants supervised by a part-time faculty member. All work in the MLS sections was done online. MLS students in the elementary course had slightly higher MDPT scores and course passing rates, but an 11 percent lower pass rate with final scores of 70 or better; neither difference was statistically significant. MLS students in the intermediate sections had slightly lower MDPT scores and a course passing rate 21 percent lower than the lecture students. This difference was statistically significant. MLS students had a slightly higher rate of passing with final scores of 70 or better but the difference was not statistically significant.

TABLE 8-B5

COMPARISON OF STUDENT PERFORMANCE IN MLS AND LECTURE SECTIONS

Course level:	MLS	Regular classroom	Percent difference	Difference significant @ 5%? ("z")
Elementary				
Average MDPT score	71	67		
Average section size	18	15		
Total enrollment	70	75		
Percent passing	86%	83%	+3.6%	No (0.50)
Percent passing with score of 70 or better	58%	65%	-10.8%	No (0.87)
Intermediate				
Average MDPT score	48	52		
Average section size	17	17		
Total enrollment	83	67		
Percent passing	65%	82%	-20.7%	Yes (2.32)
Percent passing with score of 70 or better	31%	30%	+3.3%	No (0.19)

Site F: All courses were three semester units. Classroom sections were scheduled three hours per week in a regular classroom. Use of MLS courseware accounted for approximately 67 percent of the course work in the MLS sections. MLS sections were scheduled one hour per week in a classroom and two hours in the computer lab. MLS students at both levels had slightly lower average MDPT scores, higher course passing rates, and a higher percent passing with a final score of 70 or better. None of the differences were statistically significant.

TABLE 8-B6

COMPARISON OF STUDENT PERFORMANCE IN MLS AND LECTURE SECTIONS

Course level:	MLS	Regular classroom	Percent difference	Difference Significant @ 5%? ("z")
Elementary				
Average MDPT score	51	53		
Average section size	23	24		
Total enrollment	46	415		
Percent passing	74%	62%	+19.4%	No (1.54)
Percent passing with score of 70 or better	64%	55%	+16.4%	No (1.17)
Intermediate				
Average MDPT score	40	42		
Average section size	28	34		
Total enrollment	55	931		
Percent passing	71%	64%	+10.9%	No (1.08)
Percent passing with score of 70 or better	64%	55%	+16.4%	No (1.31)

Site G: All courses were four quarter units. MLS courseware constituted approximately 95 of the content of MLS sections. Students in MLS sections spent four hours per week in a lab setting; students in the classroom version of the courses spent four hours per week in lecture/discussion class. Students in MLS sections were also expected to spend an unspecified amount of time in the computer lab. At both course levels, the MLS sections had lower average section enrollments, slightly higher MDPT scores, and higher course passing rates than the lecture sections. At both levels, the lecture sections had a substantially higher passing rate with final scores of 70 or better. The difference in the passing rate for the elementary sections was not statistically significant. The difference in the passing rate at the intermediate level and the passing rate with a final score of 70 or more at both levels was statistically significant.

TABLE 8-B7

COMPARISON OF STUDENT PERFORMANCE IN MLS AND LECTURE SECTIONS

Course level:	MLS	Regular classroom	Percent difference	Is difference Significant @ 5%? ("z")
Elementary				
Average MDPT score	69	64		
Average section size	27	32		
Total enrollment	80	95		
Percent passing	73%	60%	+21.7%	No (1.74)
Percent passing with Score of 70 or better	36%	58%	-37.9%	Yes (2.88)
Intermediate				
Average MDPT score	45	41		
Average section size	21	39		
Total enrollment	64	118		
Percent passing	68%	53%	+28.3%	Yes (2.01)
Percent passing with Score of 70 or better	28%	53%	-52.8%	Yes (3.30)

Site H: MLS courseware constituted approximately 90 percent of the work in MLS sections. All sections were for five semester units that required students to attend five hours per week. All sections required interactive learning. Non-MLS sections (control sections) relied upon collaborative learning and group problem-solving approaches in combination with 10-15 minute instructor-led discussions with the entire class. Elementary control sections enrolled an average of 41 students in a course taught by a graduate teaching associate assisted by two student tutors. MLS sections enrolled an average of 24 students, all repeating the course. Topics not included in MLS courseware were taught in classrooms the same way as in the control sections. Most MLS instruction occurred in the computer lab with occasional group work in an adjoining classroom. Elementary MLS sections had substantially smaller average enrollments than control sections. There was no difference between the MDPT scores. The MLS section had an 11 percent higher passing rate but the control section had an over 81 percent higher rate for students passing with a final score of 70 or better. This latter difference was statistically significant. Intermediate MLS sections had smaller average enrollments and lower average MDPT scores than classroom sections. Both the pass rate and the percentage with a final score of 70 or better were substantially higher for the control sections but the differences were not statistically significant.

TABLE 8-B8

COMPARISON OF STUDENT PERFORMANCE IN MLS AND LECTURE SECTIONS

Course level:	MLS	Regular classroom	Percent difference	Difference Significant @ 5%? ("z")
Elementary				
Average MDPT score	35	35		
Average section size	24	41		
Total enrollment	47	81		
Percent passing	40%	36%	+11.1%	No (0.52)
Percent passing with score of 70 or better	5%	27%	-81.5%	Yes (3.09)
Intermediate				
Average MDPT score	48	53		
Average section size	25	39		
Total enrollment	50	39		
Percent passing	38%	54%	-29.6%	No (1.49)
Percent passing with score of 70 or better	12%	22%	-45.5%	No (1.24)

Figures 8-1 and 8-2 show passing rate data associated with average MDPT scores across the campuses. The hypothesis is that students with higher scores on the MDPT pre-test should have a higher probability of passing the course without regard to whether they were in a classroom or MLS section. The scatter of points representing the average MDPT scores and average passing rates should show a trend from the lower left to the upper right of the chart. To the extent the MLS materials systematically improve course passing rates, the MLS points should lie above the classroom points.

Both of these patterns are present for the elementary course as shown in Figure 8-1. The positive correlation between MDPT scores and passing rates is most obvious for the classroom sections. This same pattern is less clear for MLS sections (it is even less obvious if the single MLS point on the lower left of the chart is ignored). MLS passing rates tend to lie above the classroom passing rates but the tendency is much stronger for the sections with low average MDPT scores. The implication is that MLS is most beneficial to students in the elementary course who are most challenged mathematically.

The patterns for passing rates in the intermediate course shown in Figure 8-2 are more ambiguous. The MLS rates have a slight tendency to lie above the classroom rates for given MDPT scores, but the pattern is contradicted by two outliers, a classroom passing rate above all others and an MLS passing rate below all others.

These results correspond to findings that Professor Marshall Cates of the CSU LA Mathematics Department indicated in a 1998 report, which also touches on a number of incidental benefits. He reports that as a substitute for

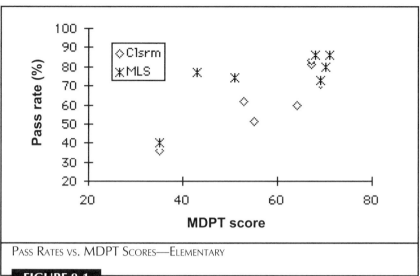

Pass Rates vs. MDPT Scores—Elementary

FIGURE 8-1

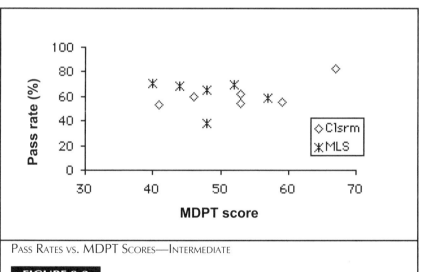

Pass Rates vs. MDPT Scores—Intermediate

FIGURE 8-2

instruction in the traditional classroom setting, MLS courseware has the greatest benefit for students who need remediation the most. Using MLS, these students can repeat a lesson as often as needed. Taking into consideration all remedial students, MLS courseware is neither superior nor inferior. An instructor remains essential for the MLS version of remedial courses, to motivate and provide personal contact. In the most elementary courses, MLS allows larger section sizes without a loss of student performance. Other potential benefits included more flexible use of student time, more time for students on task, more instructional support outside of class, completion of course on a shortened time schedule, greater convenience and a more user-friendly atmosphere for ESL students, and longer retention of the material. Furthermore, the availability of MLS on the Internet supported distributed instruction to off-campus locations.

COMPARING COSTS

For purposes of developing campus cost estimates for MLS and regular classroom instruction, the ad hoc committee agreed to report a set of data relating to the costs of the computer lab where the MLS courseware is available and to the costs of staffing both the MLS and the lecture course. The results, which are discussed below, are based upon data provided by six campuses.

Campuses did not implement MLS courseware in the same way. Differences in use led to differences in costs. This was especially true for laboratory monitoring costs and for fees charged students for MLS workbooks (fee revenue is treated here as an offset against the costs associated with the MLS course). Section enrollments in the MLS version of the course varied between 15 and 50. In some cases, enrollments were restricted because of existing computer lab capacity. In others, large labs had been specifically designed to allow the courseware to serve as the basis for a substantial amount of the actual coursework, with instructors primarily responsible for monitoring student progress and intervening only as necessary.[6]

Costs of MLS versions of courses were estimated based on three versions of a basic model that relates costs to annual course enrollments. The cost parameters of the model shown in Tables 8-C, 8-D, and 8-E are based upon data supplied by the campuses. The basic cost model combines characteristics of the actual course offered but does not exactly represent any specific course. The three versions of the model were based upon MLS computer labs designed for 20, 35, and 50 stations, a range that encompasses the actual enrollment levels observed across the campuses. The average section size for all classroom sections offered was 30. This enrollment value was used for classroom sections in the three cost comparisons shown below.

The MLS version of the course requires that students have access to a multimedia laboratory where the courseware is available on a local area network (later versions of MLS materials are available on the Internet). The capital costs of creating such a lab are detailed in the top panel of Table 8-C. These initial capital costs are converted to annual costs based upon estimates of useful lives of the various assets. The second panel of Table 8-C shows lab monitor and maintenance estimates. The third panel shows the estimated annual costs for three different size labs.

TABLE 8-C

ESTIMATED COSTS FOR MEDIATED LEARNING SYSTEM LAB

Cost items	Initial cost	Useful life	Annual cost
Capital costs:[7]			
Computer workstation	@ $2,000	4 years	$500
Facility remodel	$15,000	25 years	$600
Furniture	$10,000	10 years	$1,000
Value of room	90,000	30 years	$3,000
Operating costs:			
Lab monitors			$ 21,000
70 hrs./wk. @ $10/hr. for 30 weeks			
Lab maintenance			$ 2,000
Estimated annual costs for:			
20 station lab			$37,600
35 station lab			$45,100
50 station lab			$52,600

Table 8-D provides the elements for estimating the annual direct costs of both the MLS and the lecture versions of the course. The site license fee is a major component of MLS costs. Section staffing costs are relatively low due to use of part-time faculty to teach the course (the same staffing costs are used for both the MLS and classroom sections). The lab cost for the MLS course is the estimated annual capital cost from Table 8-C adjusted upward as the capacity of a lab is reached. For the MLS course, a fee representing the net revenue from the sale of the workbooks (supplied as part of the site license) is treated as an offset against expenses.

The capital cost of the classroom is based upon an estimate of $90,000 to construct and a 30-year useful life spread over an estimated capacity of 24 sections per term per room. A tutor/grading cost, estimated at $17.50 per student, is added to the classroom costs because several of the campuses used student assistants for this purpose.

TABLE 8-D

ESTIMATED DIRECT ANNUAL COST ELEMENTS FOR REMEDIAL MATHEMATICS

MLS version	Item
Site license	$72,500
Section staffing	$2,400
Lab costs	(see Table 8-C)
Less revenues	@ $35/student

Classroom version	
Section staffing	$2,400.00
Estimated capital cost per section	$125.00
Estimated tutor/grading cost per student	$17.50
(1.75 hrs./student @ $10 per hour)	

Finally, lab capacity must be calculated because once the capacity of a lab is reached, an additional facility has to be added. The calculation, shown in Table 8-E, is based upon the assumption that a student enrolled in an MLS section will, on average, spend five hours per week in the lab. The 70-hour week represents the CSU's standard classroom schedule requirement of 8 AM-10 PM, five days a week. Labs could be available more than 70 hours per week by scheduling on weekends (scheduling during the summer months could also increase lab availability).

The combined cost estimates from Tables 8-C and 8-D are used to generate the graphs of the cost schedules relating estimated direct costs to annual course enrollments for both MLS and lecture sections of the course. The lab capacity data in Table 8-E are used to adjust the MLS cost upward when the capacity of a lab is reached. In actual practice, the labs might be phased in (or shared with other courses) so that the "steps" shown in the graphs below might not have such sharp corners. Nevertheless, the general shape and position of the graph still provides a relatively good indicator for comparison purposes.

TABLE 8-E			
ESTIMATED MLS LAB CAPACITY			

hours per week per student	lab hours per week	students per station per term	students per station per year
5	70	14	28

	Stations per lab: Small lab 20	Intermediate lab 35	Large lab 50
Students per lab	560	980	1,400

The Small Lab Case illustrated in Figure 8-3 shows MLS courseware is implemented in a lab that limits section enrollments below those of the classroom sections.[8] In this case, the MLS course costs more than the classroom course at all levels of enrollment even though the incremental (or marginal cost) per student enrollee is less for the MLS course than for the lecture course (because the $35 workbook revenues offset some of the staffing costs). The MLS costs are always greater than the lecture costs because the capacity of the lab is reached before the MLS cost graph intersects the classroom cost graph. The additional lab costs shift the MLS graph in such a way that the MLS costs are always above lecture costs.

The Intermediate Case shown in Figure 8-4 has the MLS lab section with an enrollment of 30,[9] the same as the classroom section size. Here the MLS incremental costs per student are lower than in Figure 8-3 because of the larger section size. The two graphs are converging but the intersection occurs at an annual enrollment level above 2,500. (If MLS section size were 35, an intersection—a crossover or breakeven point—occurs at an enrollment of 2,000.) This is an important result because annual enrollments in the remedial mathematics courses average about 1,000 students across the campuses.

Finally, the Large Lab Case in Figure 8-5 has MLS lab sections with an enrollment of 50. Note that the MLS cost curve has an even flatter slope than in Figure 8-4 because the incremental staffing cost declines again as section size increases. The curves first intersect at an enrollment of 1,000. At about 1,400 annual enrollments, the need for an additional lab causes the MLS costs to shift up but after that MLS costs are less than classroom costs.

If we compare the costs of the two modes of instruction considered here, we can see the following patterns:

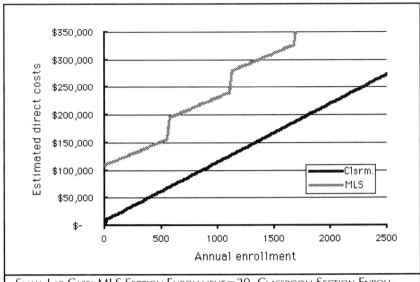

SMALL LAB CASE: MLS SECTION ENROLLMENT=20, CLASSROOM SECTION ENROLL-MENT=30

FIGURE 8-3

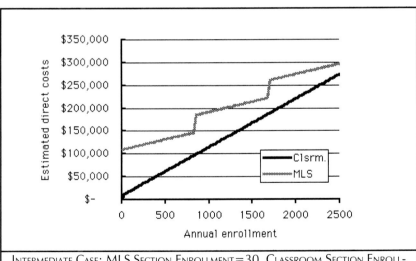

INTERMEDIATE CASE: MLS SECTION ENROLLMENT=30, CLASSROOM SECTION ENROLL-MENT=30

FIGURE 8-4

1. At the lower levels of annual course enrollment, the costs of the MLS version of the course always exceed those of the classroom version. This occurs because of the fixed costs associated with the MLS course, including the license fee and the costs of establishing and operating the initial MLS lab.
2. The incremental (or marginal) cost of additional enrollments in the MLS course tends to be less than those for the regular classroom course (assuming instructor pay rates for the different course sections are the same). This result occurs because the MLS fee revenue offsets some of the course's staffing cost. Incremental costs are also reduced to the extent enrollment in the MLS sections is larger than in the classroom sections.
3. Once enrollment grows to the capacity of the MLS lab, an additional lab must be added, causing a step-up in MLS costs.

At the current levels of annual enrollments in remedial mathematics courses (ranging between 300 and 1,500 students per year per campus), the direct costs of the MLS course with section enrollments of 30 exceed the costs of offering the instruction to students in the classroom course with enrollments of 30.

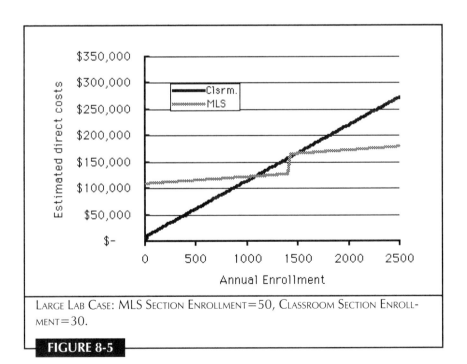

LARGE LAB CASE: MLS SECTION ENROLLMENT=50, CLASSROOM SECTION ENROLLMENT=30.

FIGURE 8-5

However, because the marginal costs of the MLS course tend to be less than those of the classroom version, with sufficient levels of annual enrollment and the appropriate combination of cost and fee factors, the MLS costs can be less than that of classroom courses. For example, increasing MLS section size to 50 results in a crossover point at an annual enrollment of 1,000 students. These results are dependent upon all the assumptions and estimates used in the cost model. A sensitivity analysis focused on the MLS section with 30 students, equal to the classroom section size, suggests that reducing the site license fee by half shifts the MLS cost schedule so that the crossover point is at an annual enrollment of approximately 2,000 instead of 2,500.

Another factor at work here is that the staffing costs for all remedial course sections are low because of the use of part-time faculty. The result is that any savings from increasing MLS section size are minimized because the staffing costs are small relative to the fixed costs of MLS. Again, focusing upon the intermediate lab case shown in Figure 8-4, holding staffing costs at $2,400 and increasing MLS section size to 35 results in a crossover point at an enrollment of 2,200. If section staffing costs are set at a higher rate (e.g., $7,750 based upon an average salary of $62,000 for full-time faculty and eight courses per year), the crossover for an MLS section size of 35 occurs at an annual course enrollment of 1,100. If MLS section size is increased to 50, the crossover occurs at an annual enrollment of 600.

The overall results of this two-pronged case study at CSU, comparing the teaching of remedial mathematics in traditional lecture classes and in classes using courseware, might then be summarized as follows: The evidence did not yield a definitive conclusion that the learning outcomes of IT-supported instruction are either better or worse than regular classroom instruction. There was some indication that the use of courseware improved the passing rate for students who experienced the most severe problems with mathematics, those who can benefit most from extensive drill and practice. Incidental benefits of IT-supported instruction included lower attrition rates, more user-friendly learning situations, and an opportunity for students to become more familiar with computers.

The total direct costs of the IT-supported version of courses exceeded the costs of the traditionally taught versions at the levels of enrollment that were observed. The cost data also suggested that incremental cost—the cost of enrolling additional students—was less for the IT-enhanced than for the regular classroom version; the classroom version was less expensive at the observed enrollment levels because of the relatively high fixed costs of the IT version. Because of the economy of scale effect—spreading fixed costs over larger and larger numbers of enrollments—at sufficient levels of enrollments, IT-enhanced instruction can cost less than regular classroom instruction.

ENDNOTES

1. A twenty-third campus, CSU Channel Islands, is under development.

2. After this study had started, Academic Systems announced that the courseware, "AcademicOnline," would be available for wide area networks and the Internet.

3. See J.R. Frankel, *Academic Systems Corporation Interactive Mathematics Evaluation of Learning Outcomes.* San Francisco State University, June, 1997.

4. The difference between the two rates is 9 percentage points (80-71). The relative difference, using the classroom rate as the base, is 12.7 percent (9/71 = 0.127).

5. As discussed in the previous endnote, the percent difference in this series of tables is calculated as follows:

((MLS% - Regular classroom%)/Regular classroom%).

A positive percent difference indicates the MLS value is greater, a negative difference indicates the classroom value is greater.

6. Cal State LA had experimented earlier with an MLS section without an instructor. The conclusion was that this was not a feasible way to offer the course.

7. These capital costs are estimated as though the lab was used exclusively for the MLS courses. If other courses could use the lab, e.g., on a 50-50 basis, then the lab costs should be reduced proportionately. For MLS courses with relatively small annual enrollments, such sharing represents a good way to reduce lab costs.

8. This reflects the experience of several of the campuses in the case study. It is likely the enrollment difference is the result of a start-up situation constrained by inadequate lab facilities rather than a policy decision to have lower section enrollments in the MLS course. It is a good example to model, however, because it illustrates an expensive implementation of the MLS technology.

9. The reported average section size across all MLS sections in fall 1996 was 29.

CHATER

How Much Does It Cost to Put a Course Online? It All Depends

Judith V. Boettcher

The costs of putting a course online are of universal interest because practically every institution of higher education is involved with some online offerings. This chapter describes three basic models of online courses and the costs, resources, and time associated with their design and development, including strategies for low cost development.

The basic conclusion about the costs of putting courses online is that an institution can spend as much or as little as it desires. The courses that result from the funding of Web course projects, however, can be dramatically different in their effectiveness and return on investment. And, of course, the correlation between cost and effectiveness is not exact. Costs depend on institutional variables, such as mission, information technology infrastructure, course design, student audience, and faculty and student characteristics. In other words, it all depends. In real estate, how much a house costs is highly dependent on location, location, location. In instructional programs, how much a course costs is highly dependent on students, faculty, content, and location. The question of how much it will cost in time and money to develop an online course has no simple answer.

Recently, some new comprehensive online service companies have been suggesting that an entire virtual campus, not just a course, can go "online" in 60 to 90 days. Outsourcing the conversion of existing courses to go online is an option that is worth considering, particularly in the area of information technology (IT) delivery infrastructure. It may fit into who and where an institution is at the time. However, the first step in going online is an analysis of an institution and its mission and goals. The aim of this analysis is to answer the following questions: "What programs do we want to offer online?" "To which students will these programs be attractive?" and "What type of course environment do we plan on having?"

With the advent of the new information technology environments, all our comfortable assumptions about teaching and learning are being challenged. When talking about a course in academic circles, it was once safe to assume that everyone was thinking about more or less the same construct—a three-credit course, spanning a 15-week period during which students spent about three hours per week in a classroom with a faculty member. In addition to the "class time" (also called "contact hours" or "seat time"), students were expected to spend time outside class reading, writing, studying, and doing projects.

We are now witnessing the evolution of the classroom into a myriad of new teaching and learning environments. Some are similar to the traditional classroom course; some are more like traditional distance learning courses delivered via broadcast TV or videotapes; and some have little resemblance to anything that has gone before. The evolution of these environments has been underway for some time, but the recent emergence of the World Wide Web as the primary focus for much of this activity has created the sense of a "rush to the Web."

THE WEB AS A PRIMARY SITE OF ORGANIZED INSTRUCTION

The Web is a new space, and a new place, for teaching and learning that is already working well for many faculty and students. While this does not mean that the classroom will disappear, it does mean that the day of the classroom as the primary site of organized instruction is over. We will see the Web emerging as another primary place, in some cases the core place, where faculty and students gather for organized instruction.

We are just beginning to grasp the potential of the Web for providing new teaching and learning environments. The classroom used to be the "place" where a course began and ended. The classroom was the place where faculty and students gathered for the first day of class, for the overview of the course, for a preview of the teaching and learning activities in that subject area for 15 weeks. The classroom was also the place where final exams were completed. The classroom was the center of the "course community." Now we are seeing course Web sites become the new gathering place for this community of learning.

Figure 9-1 shows a possible mid-state of the evolution of this teaching and learning environment. It shows the Web as the new focus of organized instruction. It is also the core of the learning community, serving as the communication hub. The new paradigm of the Web as the course center will begin as a shift in an emphasis of meeting places, but it will change almost everything, including the economics and business models of instruction. Although it is obvious that we will need campuses and classrooms into the foreseeable future, the long-run effect of the Web on the traditional campus and classroom environment is difficult to predict.

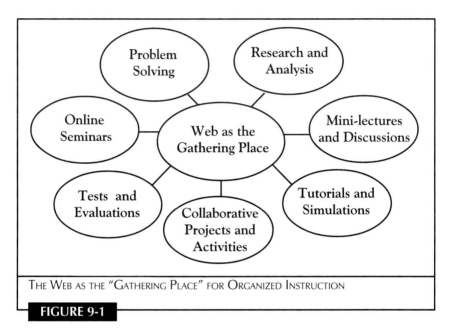

THE WEB AS THE "GATHERING PLACE" FOR ORGANIZED INSTRUCTION

FIGURE 9-1

In her book, *The Last Word on Power*, T. Goss[1] stated that "When you declare a new context, you create a new realm of possibility, one that did not previously exist" (p. 19). As an example of the power of a new context, she uses the example of the new context created by John F. Kennedy when he said that the United States would put a man on the moon by 1970. With this commitment, Kennedy created a context in which getting to the moon was believed to be possible. He, and the American public by agreeing to it, created a belief system that made it possible. Resources and talent were allocated on the basis of this belief system, and the goal was achieved (p. 123). Of course, rocket and space science had also been developed to a sufficient stage to enable the project.

The power of a new context is having an effect in higher education today. Many institutions are moving courses to the Web, some on a larger scale than others. A few dozen are mandating and enabling 24-hour student access to computing and networking.[2] The Web creates a context for teaching and learning in which traditional processes and assumptions change. This new communication context supports the fundamental processes that occur in teaching and learning: communication, dialogue, knowledge creation and sharing. But how much will online courses cost? The first step in costing is to design an online course.

WHAT IS A COURSE? WHAT IS A WEB COURSE?

How will a Web course be similar to a traditional classroom course? How will it be different? Guidelines for designing Web courses are essential to ensure that, as we change the environment for teaching and learning, we design quality into it. Web courses must be based upon sound instructional methodology and strategies.

We begin by analyzing how classroom courses are structured: What are the essential components of a three-credit course. One important element is the amount of time students are expected to spend in class, often referred to as "contact hours" or "seat time." Web courses that reduce the time of classroom meeting may run counter to state requirements, curriculum policies, and accrediting guidelines. These requirements are being updated, but still must be considered.

The basic measure of academic activity for students, faculty, and administrators is the credit unit. A four-year college degree requires 120-128 credit units; a master's degree is about 30 units and undergraduate students are considered full-time students if they carry at least 12 units per semester. The three-credit semester course is one of the most common formats of instruction. But what does the three-unit course imply?

A three-credit course can be viewed in the following ways:

1. We can approach it from the perspective of student time or student competency. How many hours "make up" a three-credit course? And what knowledge, skills, and attitudes will a student be expected to acquire in such a course?

2. From the faculty viewpoint, the questions cluster around such measures as how much time does it take a faculty member to "teach" a three-credit classroom course, including preparation of materials, presentation of materials (in the classroom), interaction with students regarding the course materials (both in and outside the classroom), testing, assessment, and assignment of grades? A closely related question is how much time does it take to design and develop a new course, whether in the classroom or online?

3. From an administrative viewpoint, the question becomes one of managing resources (e.g., faculty positions and space) to offer courses that meet

student needs within the curriculum and that return some amount of tuition/state subsidy.

4. At the institutional level, the question might be how any particular course contributes to the basic mission of the campus and the maintenance of a quality institutional image.

From the perspective of student time, a three-credit course is assumed to require 135 hours of effort. Classroom courses meet 3 hours a week for 15 weeks, a total of 45 contact hours. In addition, students are expected to spend time outside class. I have been asking faculty and higher education administrators the question of how much time outside of class is expected of students for the last 10 years or so, and the most common response is that students are expected to devote two hours outside of class for every hour in class.[3] If we use this ratio of two-to-one, students are expected to devote an additional 90 hours (45 hours times 2) to studying in addition to the scheduled class time. This study time can be accomplished in many ways, either individually or in a group, using a variety of content resources, such as books, journals, library research, etc. Adding 90 to 45 gives the norm of 135 hours for the course. As we begin designing courses for more flexible environments, this time perspective can provide a touchstone of constancy and assurance that we are not changing things too dramatically too quickly.

From the perspective of student competency, faculty teaching regular classroom courses maintain that their courses are not simply based on contact hours or seat time, the courses also require competency, as demonstrated through projects, examinations, and other assessment activities. In traditional distance learning course models, there is less focus on time expectations and greater focus on competency, i.e., whether or not students achieve a stated set of goals and objectives.

Let's examine the implications of these two perspectives for course design. Given the difficulty of providing objective measures of achievement for all courses, many state regulations and accreditation agencies require a certain number of contact hours for a three-credit undergraduate course. The time-based model does have a certain amount of validity because learning requires time, but regulations based primarily on time rather than competency may contribute to outcomes only indirectly and superficially.

If we know the desired learning outcomes, and can measure those outcomes, we can be comfortable requiring individuals to pass a competency test, such as a driver's test, real estate appraisal test, etc. However, when the desired learning objectives are a set of complex cognitive, behavioral, and attitudinal outcomes, we have traditionally relied on a time-based model in conjunction with competency exams and other evaluation exercises, as appropriate.

The time-based model can be rationalized as follows:

We are not certain about the exact nature of the educational outcomes desired, and we are not certain how to measure these outcomes, but we are certain that students need to develop and acquire a complex and rich set of skills and experiences. If students have taken the required set of courses in which they spent the expected amount of "time-on-task," had appropriate interaction with knowledgeable faculty and access to other resources (e.g., library), and demonstrate satisfactory performance on exams and other evaluation measures, they have satisfied the requirements for a degree and can be expected to function in an acceptable fashion as members of society and in their working careers.

Given the difficulties of assessment and accountability in the higher education and professional arenas, we often rely on a time-based experience coupled with a competency-based demonstration, e.g., the bar exam, the nursing exam. In other fields, we combine a time-based experience with a set of products, such as the series of innovative research projects that are required for a Ph.D. in science, or a portfolio of art or writings for other bachelor's or master's degrees.

The relevance of this analysis is to provide a basis for the redesign of on-campus and Web courses. We need to design instruction with the knowledge that while time for learning is necessary, time alone is not sufficient to ensure success. We also need to design instruction in such a way as to ensure a focus on the more important goals of learning. We need to design instruction by specifying a body of knowledge, skills, and beliefs that students are to learn in some given period of time and by specifying how that learning will be evaluated. As we move to designing courses for the Web, a viable approach, for now, is to continue to combine both time-based and competency-based components.

DESIGNING A COURSE FROM THE STUDENT TIME PERSPECTIVE

Table 9-A applies this analysis to a practical situation to illustrate how a Web course might look if we align it with components similar to those of a traditional lecture course. It is apparent that the majority of student effort is spent outside the classroom even for traditional lecture-discussion courses. Only one-third (45 of 135 hours) of the hours represent "contact" time, the other two-thirds of the time is outside-of-class learning activities that take place away from the presence of the instructor. Viewed this way, distance learning and Web learning represent only degrees of difference from the classroom approach.

TABLE 9-A

CLASSROOM AND WEB COURSES: STUDENT TIME PERSPECTIVE

Course Components	Classroom course hours	Web course hours
Primary focus is the classroom lecture and faculty-led dialogue. In the Web environment, this component is replaced with a variety of activities, including interactive software, mini-lectures, online seminars, and threaded discussions.	30 (in classroom)	20
Reading books or journals, other study assignments using other resources, including the Internet, group interactions	30	40
Individual (or group) paper or study project	30	30
Testing and other assessment activities plus preparing for these assessments. Final evaluation can be via projects or proctored testing.	30 (10 in classroom)	30
General administrative and management tasks	15 (5 in class)	15
Total hours (three-credit course)	135	135

The one classroom activity that is difficult to envision immediately on the Web is the faculty lecture. The lecture has been under review in the recent past as we search for data that support and validate lecturing as an effective learning strategy for students. The pedagogical research that encourages active rather than passive learning suggests that we find ways to increase student mental activity during lecture time. This active learning movement suggests that lecturing may be effective part of the time, but that we need to link faculty talking to student learning more consistently. In other words, just because an instructor is lecturing—and even lecturing well—is no assurance that the students are learning. Faculty lecturing requires much brain activity by the lecturer, but not necessarily by the student. Principles on making lectures more effective and particularly the classroom environment more learner-centered are available from a number of sources. The principles and sources are summarized in a small monograph by K. P. Cross.[4]

TOOLS FOR SUPPORTING TEACHING AND LEARNING ON THE WEB

The technology tools to support teaching and learning on the Web are quickly evolving, and with this evolution, the time and skills needed to move a course to the Web are changing. Some of the tools will decrease the time invested by faculty; other tools will increase the level of expectations of Web courses, and put more pressure on the time and skills needed by the faculty and on the infrastructure to support the design, development, and delivery of Web teaching and learning.

Presentation software is a good example of improved tools. The most recent releases of presentation packages, such as PowerPoint 98 and 2000 have made putting lecture slides on the Web almost straightforward. However, it still takes time. The next improvement that faculty are looking for is audio to incorporate voiceover with the slides, simulating the delivery of a lecture. (Which brings us back to our query of whether lectures are effective student learning tools.) New plug-ins and peripheral tools are paving the way for voice capability, and we may find that it supports newer techniques for teaching and learning, other than lecturing. Tools such as QuickTime, RealAudio, RealVideo, and voice applications with mail packages are bringing audio to the Web environment. I have experimented with the voice application with my e-mail. The next wave of improvements in these categories will enable easier, lower bandwidth transmission of a video of the faculty member as well, if we want it. Another recent development is the proliferation of course templates, which make the initial conversion, or transfer of basic course documents to the Web, much easier than in the past. The impact of these tools on the cost of courses has three dimensions. An infrastructure is needed to support them for faculty and student use; the faculty member needs time and money continued over time for acquiring, learning, and integrating the tools; and the students need to be enabled and supported in their use of such tools for learning.

The design of the Web course used as an example in Table 9-A suggests a shift away from "lecture" type instructional methods toward more time devoted to methods focusing on individual study and inquiry, group study and inquiry, and assessment, and on time spent interacting with other students and faculty. The biggest challenge in designing and developing courses for the Web is in addressing the redesign of lecture/discussion time. For the delivery of courses, the two most significant design challenges are the testing and assessment component and managing the interaction component within reasonable time limits. Learning how to use the tools and operate in the new environments are challenges for both faculty and students.

"A COURSE ON THE WEB"

The phrase "course on the Web" means something to almost everyone, but the meaning is not necessarily the same in the minds of faculty, deans, campus executives, and legislators. It is difficult to manage expectations when there is such ambiguity. What does it mean, for example, if one hears in the hallways that a technically experienced faculty member "put her course on the Web last weekend?" Expectations may develop that the entire 135-hour course is on the Web and that all faculty can easily put their courses on the Web. Often, "putting a course on the Web" means that some course documents, such as a syllabus, bibliography, a course calendar, and a class list for communications are available on the Web. Although the statement of putting one's course on the Web over a weekend may be impressive and true at some level, it is more likely to be the cause of great confusion. Statements such as these gloss over big issues, such as the campus infrastructure, equipment, and skill training necessary to support this type of activity.

Table 9-A implicitly assumes only one example of one type of Web course. This Web course example does not use a classroom for any synchronous class meetings, assessments, or social gatherings. However, getting to this type of Web course, which means redesigning all 45 hours of class time for the communication, discussion, projects, and testing to be done on the Web, is a major task. Many faculty have started putting their courses on the Web by building Web sites to support their regular classroom courses. Other faculty have moved a portion of their class time to the Web, and reduced the number of class meetings. The amount of time and support needed to do Web courses varies greatly with course type.

TYPES OF COURSES ON THE WEB

An important first step in a campus analysis planning phase is to clarify which types of Web courses fit a programmatic need so that we can manage expectations, time, and resources. All Web courses are not equal. The Web courses and course Web sites that faculty have been designing over the last few years are generally one of the following four types[5]:

- *WebCourses* are available anywhere and anytime via the Internet.
- *WebCentric courses* shift focus from the physical classroom to the Web as classroom.
- *Web-Enhanced courses* look similar to campus courses, but make significant use of the Web, including a well-organized course Web site.
- *Course Description Web sites* provide programmatic and faculty information and are used primarily for marketing and informational purposes.

For purposes of costing the move to the Web, it is useful to focus on the first three types of courses that are structured for the design of teaching and learning. Each of these different types of courses make different uses of the Web and have different requirements for campus infrastructure and equipment and types of support needed for faculty and students. Thus, the costs in moving a course to the Web vary according to the type of Web course being planned.

WEBCOURSE

A WebCourse is truly and completely available on the Web; it can be accessed anywhere and anytime via the Internet and a Web browser. The times and places for interaction and communication are flexible and generally asynchronous. Synchronous class meetings are few or nonexistent. Any course today that is fully available on the Internet generally makes use of one of the popular Web browsers, such as Internet Explorer or Netscape Navigator. The course experience begins and ends on the Web. All instructional strategies are planned and executed around the communication capabilities and content resources available on the Web.

The primary characteristic of a WebCourse, that it is fully available on the Web, means that the faculty member teaching the course and the students taking the course can literally be anywhere in the world. It also means that there is generally no requirement for location-based activities, such as class meetings or gatherings at physical seminars or conferences. All these characteristics will have exceptions. The use of synchronous videoconferencing makes some location-based activities feasible in WebCourses. The new Webcasting delivery modes can also encourage synchronous, although flexible, meeting places, sometimes across multiple time zones.

Many remotely delivered degree programs represent a slight variant of the WebCourse by focusing on students within, say, 300 miles, which enables students to gather for one- or two-day events in conjunction with the course or the program. But the idea of a globally available WebCourse means no requirement for students to physically gather regularly anywhere.

The WebCourse makes significant use of Web applications to support the teaching and learning that make up the instructional activities of the course, including e-mail, chat rooms, bulletin boards, online conferences to support discussion, and social communication among the students and between faculty and students. The WebCourse also uses Web applications to provide access to electronic resources, such as interactive tutorial courseware, databases, simulations, current news, course book sites, and digital libraries. These tools and resources help support student-centered learning by individual students and among groups of students. The use of a balanced set of communication tools supports the creation of a learning community similar to the bonding that occurs with regular class meetings.

WebCourses that are part of a larger program, such as certificate sequences, seem to be more effective if they are cohort-based (a group of students that stay together through a series of courses) because the community and the relationships that are created during one course can continue and deepen during subsequent courses. Many online courses that are components of a degree program have provision for "physical gathering" activities to enable students and faculty to develop as a learning community. It is usually more comfortable for individuals to communicate electronically if they have met and talked in person. The online synchronous and asynchronous communication activities support both social and intellectual networking and bonding. On-campus graduate programs often use these social gathering strategies. For example, many online MBA programs have beginning and ending weekend components.

WEBCENTRIC COURSE

A WebCentric course has made the shift away from the classroom as the primary site of organized instruction. As with WebCourses, the WebCentric course experience is likely to begin and end on the Web. The faculty member introduces the course on the Web, specifies what is to be done and learned, and with what resources and tools. Testing and evaluation can be accomplished with check tests, projects, and reports. Like the WebCourse, the WebCentric course makes significant use of Web technology and Web applications to create an online community for teaching and learning.

Even though a WebCentric course has shifted its communications center from the classroom to the Web, it also has a series of regularly scheduled meetings, either on- or off-campus. However, to meet the needs and convenience of working professionals, the length, frequency, and content of the class sessions may be different from regular on-campus courses.

Synchronous meetings of a WebCentric course may total 15 to 24 hours. Regular three-unit classroom courses have about 45 hours of meetings scheduled over 15 weeks. A WebCentric course may have as few as one to three meetings, but each meeting may be from five to eight hours. The classroom time is concentrated, reducing the number of times students must travel to physically gather together.

WebCentric courses can also be cohort-based but, because they include more physical meetings, a cohort-based design is not as critical a factor as for WebCourses. WebCentric courses can also be made available only within a fairly limited geographic area, such as a campus or a city. But, again, this is not necessarily the case. Working adults will often travel farther if a particular program is available in a desirable format. WebCentric courses may include use of other gathering events, such as intensive location-based launching activities, weekend seminars, and celebratory events. Depending on the frequency and length of class meetings, WebCentric courses can look a great deal like regular campus classroom courses with heavy reliance on Web technology.

WEB-ENHANCED COURSE

A Web-Enhanced course is first and foremost a classroom course. It uses the Web to enhance and support a traditional campus course. Faculty use Web technology to present the usual course administration components, such as a syllabus, bibliography of resources, course and project requirements, and project consultation. The Web is also used to support the faculty-to-student dialogue and communication, often supplementing or replacing office hours with e-mail communication and interaction. The Web also provides access to content and dynamic subject matter resources most easily available online.

Designing, developing, and delivering Web-Enhanced courses can be an evolutionary step for many faculty, gradually removing the dependency on synchronous meetings and paper-based materials. A Web-Enhanced course can also help a faculty member migrate from a lecture mode of presentation toward more interactive and collaborative learning. It represents a step away from the current classroom model towards a WebCentric Course. As such, it can be an effective change strategy for both faculty and administrators.

Moving to a Web-Enhanced course provides a transition step from the traditional models of classroom learning to the newer models of information age learning. If this transition is done over time, and with good infrastructure support, it makes the paradigm shift less costly. This is a good strategy if one has the time and a plan to support it.

For faculty who want to experiment with technology, the best choice is probably a Web-Enhanced course. Moving to a Web-Enhanced course is a low-cost strategy, but it is not free from an institutional perspective. It requires technologically competent and experienced faculty backed with departmental resources and adequate campus infrastructure. Development of Web-Enhanced courses requires a realistic look at the time and the resources needed to complete the shift effectively. However, a campus-wide initiative in this direction has many benefits.

COURSE DESCRIPTION WEB SITE

A Course Description Web site provides programmatic information about a course that is generally found in the course catalog plus faculty information. A Course Description Web site might have pictures and biographies of the faculty who teach the course, course outlines, bibliographies, course requirements, and prerequisites. A Course Description Web site may evolve to feature comments and evaluations from students who have taken the course. This type of Web site can give important, key courses a Web presence for programmatic purposes while the courses are transitioning to the other types of Web course formats. A Course Description Web site can be created quickly because it is basically a compilation of existing materials.[6]

A Course Description Web site can evolve into the communications hub of the course. Some of the new course management templates support this type of use. The Course Description Web site may evolve into an instructional vehicle, supporting the dialogue and interaction of the students, thus becoming the course Web site for a Web-Enhanced course. The primary differentiation is the involvement of the faculty member. In other words, administrators can decide that every course will have a Course Description Web site, but faculty involvement is needed for a Web-Enhanced course.

The hours of Web-based instruction vary for each of the three types of courses just described. Table 9-B provides estimates of the number of classroom hours that need to be replaced by online materials that can be delivered by one of the Web applications. The table is based on the assumption of 45 hours of in-class time and 90 hours of work outside class expected for a three-credit course. Table 9-B illustrates the three types of Web courses. While these examples are not the only possible alternatives, they can serve to illustrate program planning, design, and cost analysis. Many other alternatives are possible. One of strengths of the Web environment is that the basic model can be modified to produce numerous alternative course designs. Each of these designs can be tailored to provide course content based upon specific needs of students and faculty by varying the proportions of synchronous and asynchronous components, and the number, length, and timing of the scheduled class meetings.

TABLE 9-B

AMOUNT OF CLASSROOM TIME DISPLACED BY TYPES OF WEB COURSES

Type of Course	Class time moved to Web	Class time retained	Course hours outside of class time	Total hours
WebCourse: 100% on Web	45	0	90	135
WebCentric: 33-50% on Web	15-23	22-30	90	135
Web-Enhanced: 25% on Web	11	34	90	135
Classroom course with Course Description Web site	0	45	90	135

Another analysis of the number of hours to be converted from classroom mode to distributed mode (Web courses) has recently been published as part of a cost simulation model developed by Frank Jewett.[7] Jewett bases course design upon how a typical student's effort would be distributed over 135 hours for a three-unit semester course. One example in the model is based upon an estimate of 51 hours of instructional material that needs to be prepared for a course. This number is obtained by adding an estimated 45 hours of student activity that uses "interactive courseware on a server" plus 6 hours of "quizzes, tests, and examinations." Note that the 45 hours of "interactive courseware" is in alignment with the number of classroom/lecture hours used in Table 9-B. The BRIDGE model converts the 51 hours of instructional materials into an estimate of the professional effort (faculty and media specialist positions) needed to produce the instructional materials.

This list of course types helps refine our original question: "How much does it cost to move a course to the Web?" into "If this is the kind of online course we want, how much professional effort will it take and what will it cost?" Two follow-up questions also must be addressed: "How much will it cost to deliver the course, once the materials have been produced?" and "How much will it cost to maintain the course materials in future years?"

PLANNING A MOVE TO THE WEB

Before deciding to move courses or programs to the Web, faculty and administrators should consider the following general questions:

- What kind of Web course (or program) is needed, would it attract students?
- What kind of Web course can we design and develop?
- What tools and resources are needed to support this project?
- What resources should faculty have to support effective use of the Internet and the Web for teaching, learning, and research?
- How can the campus, college, or department support the first set of Web course projects?
- How much time for design and development is needed for this project?
- What technical infrastructure needs to be in place for students, faculty, departments, and the campus?
- What changes will be required in campus policies?
- Will this online program be delivered once or many times?
- Is there potential to produce instructional materials that can be licensed to other institutions for their courses?
- Is it an objective of this program to remove the primary faculty expert from the delivery process and hire others for course delivery and student interaction?

Many times we just want to "get started." Sometimes, this approach is best. But planning makes it easier to avoid the potholes and helps to create more reasonable expectations. Realistic answers to these questions will make any move to the Web more manageable and realistic. In fact, that might be the most important outcome of the planning process, helping to manage expectations about what *can* be done, how *quickly* it can be done, with what *resources* it can be done, and how Web courses respond to institutional mission and the curriculum needs of the institution.

STEPS IN MOVING A COURSE TO THE WEB

The following brief overview covers the steps that should be considered in preparing to move a specific course to the Web. The intent is to ensure an effective instructional experience for students by focusing on developing structured instructional materials. Following a similar process would probably also improve existing classroom courses.

Before moving a course to the Web, faculty and the campus must be prepared with both software and adequate infrastructure. The speed at which this readiness can be attained varies with the technical skills of the faculty members and with the resources and tools available in the campus infrastructure.

Readiness Phase

Faculty who will be teaching on the Web need to develop a basic set of computer tools and resources. Essential skills include the following:

- Electronic mail and bulletin boards
- Personal productivity software, such as word processing, spreadsheets, and databases
- Internet resources, including a WWW browser, such as Netscape, ftp, etc.

Knowledge of the following tools is highly desirable:

- Presentation software
- Discipline-specific software
- Custom software for course objectives

With this skill base, and the availability of the appropriate equipment, the process of moving a course to the Web can begin using the following five steps:

Step 1: Define Goals and Objectives. Examine the current and desired course content. Determine the essential skills, knowledge, and attitudes that students need to develop, learn, and experience to achieve the goals and objectives of the course. Ask the following question: "What do students need to know, think, experience, and be able to do as a result of completing this course?"

Step 2: Search for Content Materials. Search out possibilities and ideas. Identify content materials for achieving objectives. Select materials, processes, and projects for the course. Consider what is possible when many or most students have access to a networked multimedia computer. Consider the implications of the anywhere, anytime, virtual educational environment.

Step 3: Reexamine Course Goals, Course Units, and Evaluation Processes. Reexamine the goals of the course in light of the materials and opportunities that are available and the new material that might be developed locally. Based upon this re-evaluation, define the scope of the course: Should the current course credit value remain the same or be changed? Is there a need to redesign the processes by which student performance is evaluated?

Step 4: Design the Course and Acquire and Produce the Materials. Design the component parts of the course. Develop the course outline, including live meetings, student activities, and a bibliography. Specify the teaching activities and the student learning materials and activities. Determine the specific online materials that will be used. Use of existing materials (whether or not already available online) must be in conformance with copyright law. New materials must be developed locally (with an awareness of copyright law). Specify the processes for faculty communicating with students and for students communicating with other students. Specify the computing and communications resources that will be used. Plan and develop the examinations, projects, and other components by which students will be evaluated.

Step 5: Implement and Evaluate. Offer the course. Involve students with an evaluation of the course as it is being delivered. Consider how the evaluations and experiences of the course can be used to improve the course the next time it is offered.

Following these steps should result in an improved instructional experience for students. But the process also takes more time than provided for in the bundled model. If the goal is to simply get a course into the Web environment as quickly as possible, there is a faster way to do it. That approach is summarized later in this chapter.

A principle to be incorporated into all course planning is that "program design drives costs." This principle helps clarify why there is no hard and fast rule about how much it costs to move a course or a program to the Web.

A second planning principle is to budget for each phase of a program. When planning for an educational program to be offered in any environment, it is good practice to build a budget for each phase of the program. In economic terms, each program can be conceptualized as a small business with the following four phases:

- Phase I is the needs analysis and scope of the program.
- Phase II is the design and development of the program (including acquisition and production of course materials).
- Phase III is the marketing and initial course/program delivery.

- Phase IV is the ongoing maintenance, evaluation, and updating of the program.

This type of phased planning and budgeting for new programs is somewhat difficult to do within the context of our current academic structures and programs. For the existing, ongoing programs, the classroom model bundles all the phases together by assigning courses to faculty. This approach is efficient from one point of view. When a faculty member is assigned the responsibility of teaching a course, that individual is responsible for all the phases, including design and development, production of instructional materials, marketing (getting the word out via the course catalog listings and occasional flyers), delivery of the course (including interaction with students), maintenance of the course materials, and evaluation and assessment of student performance.

With online learning programs, especially those that are designed as degree or upper division major programs, these tasks and phases need to be "un-bundled." Distance learning programs, at least most of those offered before the Internet became widely available, often were able to lower costs by taking the highly paid, expert faculty out of the delivery (classroom presentation) phase of the program, and delivering the course to hundreds or thousands of students. The Open University of the United Kingdom uses this well-recognized un-bundled model. Faculty experts are assigned the responsibility for preparing and packaging the course content (design and development). When a student registers for a course, the full package of course materials is provided. The student completes the course by interacting with the materials and with a tutor (an individual who specializes in student interaction).

Taking content expert faculty out of the "delivery" phase of a course is a change in instructional delivery that has important implications for costs. If the faculty member who is designing and developing a Web course is also respon-sible for delivering the course, design and development costs may be signifi-cantly lower because many, if not most, of the costs are borne by the individual faculty. If the Web course is intended as a departmental offering delivered by many different faculty or by an adjunct who will only support the interactive but not the instructional content component, the design and development costs will be higher, often much higher. The trade-off is between lower devel-opment costs and a smaller student audience (the bundled model) and higher development costs and a larger student audience (the unbundled model).

The Infrastructure for Online Learning

Another principle for planning is that "Every medium requires its own infra-structure." Traditional on-campus courses are often designed around two primary media: classrooms (or labs) with synchronous lectures and interac-tions, and print materials, including textbooks and access to a library. Most of the Web course models are also being designed around two primary media: Web and related digital resources, and print materials. The Web also provides a broad range of choices for instructional activities, including asynchronous mini-lectures, digital libraries and databases, e-mail, subscription online resources associated with a printed book, and other social and intellectual virtual spaces. Web courses also have the option to use analog and other media for personal communication and interaction, including meetings, telephone calls, and faxes.

Campuses have developed a physical plant that provides for teaching and learning spaces for faculty and students, and supports other processes and procedures that are part of the classroom mode of instruction. Online and Web learning require a "digital plant" to support the places, processes, and procedures for online teaching and learning. Costs of this digital plant infrastructure are also part of the costs of moving a course to the Web. A well-developed digital plant infrastructure will support basic processes, such as recruiting, marketing, admissions, counseling, assessment, library resources, and the other application media used in online instructional programs.

ESTIMATES OF TIME AND COST

The above analysis of what makes up a three-credit course identified the number of hours of instructional material that must be converted, redesigned, and produced for the three types of Web courses. To arrive at cost estimates, we need the number of hours it takes to design and produce an hour of instructional material. Using that value in conjunction with salary figures for faculty and other professionals, we can estimate personnel costs of producing Web courses.

Based on much anecdotal evidence gathered over the last 20 years of building computer-based material, a reasonable starting estimate is that it takes an average of 18 hours of faculty effort to create learning materials for an hour of student instruction on the Web.[8] Mixed reactions to this estimate should come as no surprise. The cost consequences are problematic. Multiplying 18 hours of design/production time by the 45 hours of class time shows that it takes an investment of 810 hours of faculty time to move a course to the Web. If we assume some additional time for learning the new technology and new skills in teaching and learning (possibly complicated by unstable infrastructure and inefficient support), we quickly approach 1,000 professional hours for moving a course to the Web.

Previous studies on the time for development of course materials are consistent with the 18-hour estimate, e.g., Rumble,[9] provides the data shown in Table 9-C for the hours of academic effort required to produce one hour of student learning materials in different media forms. All such numbers need to be viewed with caution because the variables in course production are almost infinite. While the actual number of hours to produce each type of media needs to be further verified, the relationship of the amount of effort to the different format and media provides a good starting point. Similar outcomes were reported from a study of "academic production" effort for various types of courses at the Open University in the mid-1970s.[10] Extrapolating from the data, it appears that one hour of independent learning required between 32 and 60 hours of faculty time in the Open University model.

TABLE 9-C

ACADEMIC WORK TO PRODUCE ONE HOUR OF STUDENT LEARNING

Instructional Medium	Hours of academic effort
Lecturing	2-10
Small group teaching	1-10
Videotaped lectures	3-10
Teaching text (i.e., book)	50-100*
Broadcast television	100*
Computer-aided learning	200*
Interactive video	300*

*Requires additional support staff.

Source: G. Rumble, The Costs and Economics of Open and Distance Learning. London: Kogan Page, 1997, p. 79, based upon estimates from J.J. Sparkes, "Pedagogic Differences in Course Design." In A. W. Bates, ed. The Role of Technology in Distance Education. London: Croom Helm, 1984.

A somewhat different approach to this problem is provided in the BRIDGE cost model mentioned above. Here the user can set the "days of effort" to produce one "interactive lesson hour." Examples used in the model are in the range of 2 to 5 days, which translate into (normative) values of 16 to 40 hours. The BRIDGE model also includes the assumption of unbundled faculty effort.

The assumption of 18 hours of effort for one hour of interactive instructional materials is used below to illustrate how costs can be calculated. A range of 5 to 23 hours probably captures reality better because the hours of effort can differ substantially even within the same subject matter, with the same faculty and the same group of students. This is a broad range, just as with the range of 2 to 10 used for lecturing. As faculty become more experienced and comfortable with the new Web environment, the number of hours required may go down as long as the bundled strategy is in place.

Table 9-D shows the faculty hours and costs for producing materials needed for the three types of Web courses, based upon 18 hours of development for one hour of online lesson materials (values for the 5-to-23-hour range are also shown in parentheses). The faculty salary cost of $50 per hour is based upon an annual salary of $68,000 (including fringe benefits), assuming 170 workdays (two 17-week semesters with 85 workdays each) and a nominal 8 hours per day. Faculty typically report an average workweek greater than the nominal 40 hours used here. In particular, faculty involved with online courses indicate that the instructional workload increases over that generated by classroom instruction. The 40-hour value is used here because, since the annual salary value is fixed, to use a larger value for hours would have the effect of reducing the per hour cost (e.g., using a 60-hour workweek results in an hourly rate of $33). The $50 per hour faculty salary is relatively modest. Higher salary values will, of course, increase the costs.

TABLE 9-D

REDESIGNING CLASS-TIME FOR WEB COURSES—FACULTY HOURS AND COSTS

	Lecture hours to be redesigned	Average design/ development hours per hour (range 5-23/hr.)	Total hours	Average salary per hour	Faculty cost
WebCourse: 100% on Web	45	18 (range 5-23/hr.)	810 (225-1,440)	$50	$40,500 ($11,250-$72,000)
WebCentric: 50% on Web	23	18 (range 5-23/hr.)	414 (115-529)	$50	$13,248 ($5,750- $26,450)
Web-Enhanced: 25% on Web	11	18 (range 5-23/hr.)	198 (55-253)	$50	$6,336 ($2,750-$12,650)

A relatively common practice is to provide a faculty member release time from one course for one semester to convert a course for the Web. How does this assignment compare with the values shown in Table 9-D? Again, using a nominal 40-hour week, the release time amounts to about 136 hours. This can vary substantially across institutions—the 136 assumes a 17-week semester (15 weeks of instruction plus a week before and after), and averaging 8 hours per week (20 percent of effort[11]) working on the conversion. This is within the range of hours needed for a Web-Enhanced course but less than 70 percent of the 198 average hours estimated to put up such a course. It is less than 17 percent of the 810 hours estimated for a WebCourse.

If moving courses to the Web is this time intensive, how are the faculty who have not received any significant release time or support doing it? There are at least two answers.

1. Faculty who are interested in moving courses to the Web are enthusiastic and work many additional hours to accomplish the job (based upon the discussion above, this also includes faculty who do have release time). Faculty regularly self-report working 60 to 80 hours a week while making the transition from classroom to Web materials.

2. The faculty member is still working on the design/development process involved with making the move and the work is not yet complete.

Most of the materials produced are being used solely by the individual who produced them, and not by other faculty. This fact suggests that the "bundled" instructional teaching approach, where a single faculty member is responsible for all aspects of a course, is moving from the campus classroom to the Web environment.

Retaining the current bundled model in the Web environment is certainly one alternative, if that is part of the expectations. If this happens on a widespread basis, we could evolve to a new form of online and distance learning in which the percentage of pre-packaged materials is less than is currently being used. At the same time, we may be moving to a new form of course in which the Web becomes the classroom. Retaining the bundled model (i.e., concentrating on the Web-Enhanced and WebCentric courses) reduces development costs, but moving to the Web, even in the bundled model, still requires some investment.

If we want to maximize the power of the electronic media, we should design and develop complex instructional materials. This process generally requires the skills of professional support staff in addition to effort by faculty. The figures in Table 9-D reflect only the faculty effort required to produce online materials. For complex media, such as computer simulations, animation, and digital video, professional support staff are also required. The amount of support staff effort needed will vary, depending upon the design decisions made during the planning process. If the goal is to develop instructional materials that can be delivered multiple times and independent of the designing/developing faculty member, then costs will be dramatically higher than for building materials to be delivered in a "bundled" context.

Table 9-E1 converts the hour estimates of faculty time in Table 9-D to days and adds estimates for all other personnel needed to produce online instructional materials to be used for WebCourses and WebCentric courses that are intended to be delivered to hundreds or thousands of students and where the design and development faculty are not necessarily "teaching" the course, i.e., the instructional activities are unbundled.

Of course, every campus is different; many have resources that can be leveraged. Students, for example, are often the best source of support for building Web courses. Most projects benefit from a mix of full-time professional and part-time project team members. Another caveat is that much of these data come from a time "before the net" and "before good tools." Good tools for creating Web pages and interactive online materials are now available to reduce the time and skill and support for moving courses to the Web. The use of these tools in conjunction with the improved infrastructure support that is evolving could substantially reduce the time for developing Web courses. (Expectations are likely to go up in parallel, however.)

TABLE 9-E1

ESTIMATED FACULTY AND SUPPORT STAFF DAYS FOR DESIGNING AND DEVELOPING WEB COURSES

	Project Mgr.	Faculty 8-hr. day	Inst. Designer	Tech. Support	Other*	Total Days
WebCourse: 100% on Web (45 hours)	45	101	54	45	115	360
WebCentric: 50% on Web (23 hours)	20	52	20	25	25	142
Web-Enhanced: 25% (11hours)	0	25	6	0	6	37

*Other support personnel include content researcher, graphic design, editing, production, and clerical.

Table 9-E2 applies salary estimates to the staff position estimates in Table 9-E1 and adds an "other cost" factor to cover operating expense, special equipment, copyright, software licenses, and other overhead. Subject matter faculty, project managers, and instructional designers (all of whom may hold faculty appointments) are all costed at the same $400 per day rate as used in Table 9-D. Technical support and other staff are all costed at $320 per day, 20 percent less than faculty, to recognize the fact that some of these positions are paid less than faculty (but not that much less on average because some of the technical support can be relatively expensive). A factor to recognize non-personnel costs is needed. The 40-percent value used is a reasonable estimate and can be considered as a placeholder (40 percent of personnel costs means that these other costs represent about 28.5 percent of the total cost). Below the point estimates of total cost shown in the last column of the table, a range is provided to acknowledge the substantial amount of variability in costs among different situations and campuses. The range is roughly derived from the ranges shown in Table 9-D. The lower value is half the point estimate; the upper value is twice the point estimate.

Designing and developing good content is essential for good teaching and learning, and this has always been costly. In the 1980s, when full sequences of computer-based lower division courses were being developed by companies such as Control Data Corporation, the cost of a three-credit course was about $1 million. This cost covered all aspects of the development process, including an advisory board, content experts, content selection, course design, development, production, and testing. Recent discussions with colleagues in distance learning and publishing firms confirm that these numbers have not changed significantly. Fully pre-packaged developed distance learning courses can cost $2-3 million dollars. CDs of well structured, complex media cost between $400,000 and $900,000. The conclusion remains that the design, development, and production of high quality instructional materials is expensive.

TABLE 9-E2

ESTIMATED COSTS OF PRODUCING A WEB COURSE

	Prof. staff (days) @ $400	Support staff (days) @ $320	Total staff costs (days)	Other cost operating expense, equip., copyright, software licenses, & overhead @ 40% of staff costs	Total cost (rounded)
WebCourse: 100% on Web range	$80,000 (200)	$51,200 (160)	$131,200 (360)	$52,480	$184,000 $92K-368K
WebCentric: 50% on Web range	36,800 (92)	16,000 (50)	52,800 (142)	21,120	$74,000 $37K-148K
Web-Enhanced: 25% on Web range	12,400 (31)	1,920 (6)	14,320 (37)	5,728	$20,000 $10K-40K

This reality, regarding the time and costs of doing significant Web-based content development, was rediscovered during the period 1995-98. By that point, the wave of enthusiastic innovators was over, and early adopters and ordinary mortals were being asked to "put their courses on the Web." It was at this juncture that the fruits of creative faculty and commercial vendors started to make a real impact in providing tools and resources to make it easier to move courses to the Web.

Impact of Course Type on Cost

The effect of course type upon costs is, of course, substantial. Table 9-F provides a rough look at the relationship among the variables of course model, the investment, the number of students likely to be reached, and the maintenance costs that must be incurred annually to keep the materials current (derived by dividing the production costs by years of useful life). The economic viability of these courses depends significantly on annual student enrollments. The larger the enrollment, the lower the imputed start-up and maintenance costs are on a per-student basis.

These numbers are intended only to provide a quick insight into this relationship. The numbers in this table show again that development of well-structured effective content is costly in terms of professional effort and dollars.

It is one reason that I think we will continue to adopt prepackaged materials for a long time to come, and probably increase our use of such resources as they improve.

TABLE 9-F

Rough Relationship of Course Model to Initial Start-up Costs, Number of Enrollments per Year, and Useful Life of Materials

	Initial investment	Students (per year)	Useful life of materials (years)
Packaged materials, i.e., Web resources, books, etc.	$3,000,000	20,000-40,000	5 yrs. ($600,000/yr. to maintain)
WebCourse	$92K-386K	2,000-5,000	3+ yrs ($31K-128K/yr. to maintain)
WebCentric	$37K-148K	200-500+	3+ yrs (maintenance becomes part of normal course preparation workload)
Web-Enhanced	$10K-40K*	20-40	2+ yrs (maintenance becomes part of normal course preparation workload)

FASTEST WAY TO THE WEB

What is the fastest way to move a course of any type to the Web? We can abbreviate the process to the following three steps:

1. **Select a Course.** Identify the Web course model that fits the program needs and gather the resources and the tools for this type of course. For a Web-Enhanced course, this can be a one-semester release time project with support. The course to be moved should be selected with some care. Ideally, it should be a course for which digital and Web materials are readily available. It should also be a course that is important and visible in the department offerings. Such a course will ensure support at both the departmental and school levels.

2. **Adopt a Course Management Tool.** If the institution already supports a course management tool, accept that tool as a starting point. More support will be available in the learning experiences of the other faculty and students. And support will be more readily available for the students. Most of the more popular course management tools have their origins in templates designed by and with higher education faculty. These tools are getting more flexible and improving every year. Several of the course

management vendors offer free Web hosting or trials for faculty just starting to put courses on the Web. Participation of this type is often associated with an opportunity to affect the future design of the tool. It is possible to use selected components of a tool. Some faculty, for example, are using the communications modules of a given tool and linking to existing course sites for other resources (see #3, below). Some faculty have suggested keeping digital originals of course materials someplace other than in the course management tool to make moving or upgrading to a new tool easier.

3. **Adopt a Book or Set of Course Materials That Have Accompanying CD Materials or a "Booksite."** The content Web sites offered by publishers are rapidly evolving. These Web sites often started out as digital twins of the analog textbook and faculty resources. The faculty resources at one time consisted of overheads, PowerPoint presentations, test banks, and student problems and assignments. Book Web sites have now evolved into sites offering interactive tutorials, animations, simulations, and real audio and video content. Such Web sites are quickly becoming even more dynamic, with links to related Web resources, hosted events and contests, and contributing editors, who are almost like journalists, always on duty. The book Web sites also offer virtual spaces where faculty who are teaching in similar areas can network and share resources online rather than waiting for annual conferences.

BEYOND THE COURSE

All the discussion of online materials in this chapter has used the three-credit course as the unit of analysis. The results are easily extended to courses that are offered for more or fewer credits. An avenue yet to be explored is whether the course and the course credit will continue as the basis for measuring educational achievement and progress toward a degree (there is a question as to whether degrees will continue to have relevance). To put this another way, we may want to rethink whether the course (of however many units) is the appropriate basis for the delivery of online instruction.

If instructional software is developed that is truly learner centered, able to start with what each individual student knows, capable of discerning individual learning styles and problems, and charting a route through the instructional materials that will provide the individual student with the highest probability of learning success, the "course," which is designed to provide instruction for a group of students, will disappear and be replaced by customized individual learning programs that behave like a highly skilled, knowledgeable, and full-time tutor. Significant components of these programs may be shared among many individuals but the pace and the strategy of each program will be different.

ADDENDUM: INTERESTING DATAPOINTS

- We estimate the cost of developing a fully stand-alone three-credit course to be delivered independent of an experienced faculty member can range between $100,000 and $400,000 depending on the selected media and the digital plant infrastructure. In the 1980s, the figure was generally estimated at $1 million dollars.
- The cost of a PBS/Annenberg course that uses student and personality talent, and requires on-location photographic shoots, ranges between $2 and $6 million for a series of 20 to 26 half hour programs.
- A one-hour television episode of *ER* is budgeted at $13 million. This figure was announced in January 1998. Other one-hour shows are budgeted at between $2 and $3 million per episode.
- An Open University Course (somewhat larger than our three-credit course) generally costs between £2 and £3 million.
- The CREN TechTalks, 50 minutes of synchronous, live Webcasts, cost about $7,000 each. This cost includes the Web Event page, outsourcing of media services, transcription, editing and indexing of text, and archiving of text and audio files. Some of the cost and time is leveraged through volunteers and almost volunteers.

ENDNOTES

1. T. Goss, *The Last Word on Power*. New York: Doubleday, 1996.

2. K.C. Green, *The 1999 National Survey of Information Technology in Higher Education: The Continuing Challenge of Instructional Integration and User Support*. October 1999. <www.campuscomputing.net>.

3. The responses to this question have ranged from between four hours at the high end to about a half hour or even less at the low, depending on the institution, the faculty's experience, and general optimism or pessimism.

4. K.P. Cross, "Opening Windows on Learning," in *League for Innovation in the Community College, Educational Testing Service*. Vol. 2. The Cross Papers, Number 2. Mission Viejo, CA: League for Innovation, 1998, p. 24.

5. J.V. Boettcher, "Communicating in the Tower of WWWebble," *Syllabus* 11(3) (October, 1997): 44, 46-47, 61; J.V. Boettcher, "Distance Learning: Another Look at the Tower of WWWebble," *Syllabus* 13(3) (October, 1999): 50-52. See also J.V. Boettcher and Conrad Rita Marie, *Faculty Guide for Moving Teaching and Learning to the Web*. Mission Viejo, CA: League for Innovation, 1999 and G.T. Sherron and J.V. Boettcher, *Distance Learning: The Shift to Interactivity*. Vol. 17. Boulder, CO: CAUSE, 1997.

6. A campus-wide example of Course Description Web sites occurred at UCLA as described in the *Chronicle of Higher Education* (August 1997): A21. The article, "UCLA's Requirement of a Web Page for Every Class Spurs Debate," promoted the goal of "a Web page for every one of the 3,000 undergraduate courses in the College of Letters and Science." The campus provided support to the faculty by hiring approximately 70 technol-

ogy consultants, many of them students, to construct the Web pages and teach professors how to put up the basic course information (meeting time, course description, and syllabus). A discussion area appears on every Web site, letting students "chat" with each other and with the professors. More information about this program is available at <http://www.college.ucla.edu/>.

7. F. Jewett, BRIDGE: A Simulation Model for Comparing the Costs of Expanding a Campus Using Distributed Instruction versus Classroom Instruction. Report and Computer Simulation. Seal Beach: California State University, 1998, available at <www.calstate.edu/special_projects/>. See also F. Jewett, A Framework for the Comparative Analysis of the Costs of Classroom Instruction vis-a-vis Distributed Instruction. Chapter 5 in this volume is available at <www.shu.edu/depts/itcosts/index.htm>.

8. Mention of this number may produce an "oh, no" or "that's impossible" response on the part of deans, department chairs, and other administrators. However, faculty who have done this kind of work either nod sagely, having known this all along, or nod vigorously as if finally getting confirmation of what they have known all along. Some faculty also breathe a huge sigh of relief, hearing from an outside source that it may not be them after all, that they can stop beating up on themselves for being slow, inefficient, or just not good at this information technology thing.

9. G. Rumble, The Costs and Economics of Open and Distance Learning. London: Kogan Page, 1997.

10. Rumble, The Costs and Economics, pp. 79, 81.

11. It might be objected that a faculty member whose regular load is two courses should spend a nominal 20 hours per week on the assignment. Such an objection neglects the fact that faculty who teach two courses per term are also expected to undertake research activities (40-60 percent of total effort). Whether research is expected or not, all faculty are expected to participate in shared governance, which is also part of the expected workload. The 20-percent value assumes that one course is equivalent to one-fifth of total effort.

CHAPTER

Costs of Ubiquitous Computing
A Case Study at Seton Hall University

Stephen G. Landry

N umerous strategies exist for letting students take full advantage of the learning possibilities the personal computer and the Internet offer. Many campuses are now issuing students personal computers when they enter the institution. The college or university provides for periodic replacement, technical support, and faculty training and selects courses for the use of information technology in class. The New Jersey Institute for Technology embraced that strategy as early as 1985. Wake Forest University made an exceptional effort to support such an initiative 10 years later, and many campuses, both public and independent, have followed suit. While the investment in some cases seems to be extraordinary, some colleges and universities have managed to move with relatively limited resources to a high level of information technology use in teaching and learning. Like most organizations, colleges and universities are reluctant to open their books to the public and provide financial information that is both comprehensive and detailed, an understandable hesitation in an age of intensifying competition between institutions. This chapter considers the issues and costs of introducing "mobile computing" for 4,500 full-time undergraduates at Seton Hall University.

AN OVERVIEW OF UBIQUITOUS COMPUTING

Ubiquitous computing refers to programs aimed at making a computer available to all members of a learning community. The goals of ubiquitous computing are to ensure that everyone in the learning community has access to the necessary learning materials (many of which are computer- or networked-based) and instructional software "any time, any place." Practically, these programs usually involve ensuring that all students have some form of laptop computer and access to the Internet.

Ubiquitous computing programs have been around for more than a decade. These programs are heavily supported by computer vendors, initially Apple Computer, but more recently by IBM and Compaq. In spring 1999, IBM Corporation identified 36 colleges and universities implementing IBM's Thinkpad University Program. A study carried out in fall 1998 by Valley City State University in North Dakota identified some 84 campuses with ubiquitous computing programs, with several hundred more in active planning for implementation.

Why Ubiquitous Computing?

The instructional uses of personal computers are broad and diverse. The potential benefits of incorporating instructional technology into teaching and learning are documented elsewhere, including the overview in Chapter 1 of this book. However, institutions face significant barriers to fully incorporating information technology (IT) into teaching and learning.

One of the biggest potential obstacles is *access* to technology. Commuting and nontraditional students often do not have the access to computer labs or networks necessary to support extensive use of instructional technology. In addition, the traditional computer lab model does not reflect the way students typically work and learn. Surveys show, for example, that student use of network-based instructional resources peaks in the late evening and early morning hours, when most campus facilities are either closed or closing. The ability of information technology to bridge this gap between faculty and student work patterns is often cited as one of the most significant benefits of campus IT investments.

A major concern for higher education is the "digital divide," that is, the potential for instructional technology to widen the societal gap between the "haves" and the "have nots," and specifically between those that have anytime, anywhere access to technology and those that do not have such access. As IT becomes an increasingly important means of delivering and enhancing higher education, lack of access to technology will become a significant barrier to full participation in our learning communities. One of the goals of ubiquitous computing programs is to ensure equal access to these important resources. For example, Seton Hall University's *Mobile Computing Mission Statement* declares, in part, that "[the] University's Mobile Computing Program is designed to break down the barriers of space and time and allow all our students to fully participate in our scholarly community and achieve high levels of performance."

Kinds of Ubiquitous Computing Programs

Ubiquitous computing programs are characterized by the following types of access:

- to a personally configurable computer, 24 hours a day, 365 days a year, capable of running the institution's standard instructional software and capable of accessing the Internet
- to extensive electronic content
- to high quality and easily available technical support

The availability of computers anytime and any place is usually achieved through the use of some form of notebook computer. Within these parameters, however, the implementation of ubiquitous computing programs has varied significantly. Some of the basic choices in ubiquitous computing programs include the following:

- student-owned computers vs. institution-owned computers
- uniform equipment and software vs. minimum equipment and software standards
- fixed upgrade cycles vs. variable upgrade cycles

Mark Resmer, director of EduCause's Instructional Management Standards (IMS) group, has done a study of the various types of ubiquitous computing programs and has identified two predominant models.

- The *Sonoma State University model* requires all students to demonstrate possession of a minimal laptop computer. Students own their own machines, and technical support is often provided through an outsourcing arrangement with a vendor. While some computer models may be recommended by the institution or discounted by the vendor, students typically have significant latitude regarding the hardware and software specifications. Financially disadvantaged students are usually provided financing options or direct subsidies through the institution. Technology upgrades are at the discretion of the student.
- The *Wake Forest University model* provides an institutionally owned computer to all students as part of their tuition and fees. Hardware and software is highly standardized. Support is usually provided through the university, and because the hardware is standardized, high levels of support can be assured. Some institutions have increased the amount of financial aid to students to compensate for the increased cost of attending the university.

Obviously, each kind of ubiquitous computing program has advantages and disadvantages. The Sonoma State University model offers a lower overall cost to the student as well as a great deal of student choice in the selection of the computer. However, Steve Gilbert of the American Association of Higher Education's TLT Group notes that the high level of standardization of hardware and software provided by the Wake Forest University model makes the development of electronic content and curricula easier and can increase the technology options available to faculty. Resmer notes that in practice the decision regarding which ubiquitous computing model to adopt is highly dependant on the campus culture and business practices; he notes that, in general, state institutions have followed the Sonoma State University model while private institutions have followed the Wake Forest model.

Impact of Ubiquitous Computing

A study of ubiquitous computing in higher education conducted by Hochschul Information System in Germany finds that most of the campuses that have implemented these kinds of programs "are unreservedly positive about the use of computers and the related changes in teaching." Campuses that have implemented ubiquitous computing report high student satisfaction, a positive impact on the learning environment, and increased student enrollment. Faculty report that the level and expectation of student work had increased substantially as a result of the increased communication with the students.

However, implementation of ubiquitous computing programs is typically an institutional initiative that includes significantly increased funding for faculty and curriculum development, increased financial aid, the development of online content, and the implementation of online student services. The results cited are not likely to have come about from the distribution of computers themselves; rather, the results are likely attributable to the attention to the learning environment that such programs engender.

SETON HALL UNIVERSITY'S MOBILE COMPUTING INITIATIVE

Seton Hall University, founded in 1856, is the oldest and largest diocesan Catholic university in the nation. Seton Hall's 58-acre main campus is located in suburban South Orange, New Jersey, 15 miles from New York City. The university enrolls some 4,400 full-time undergraduates (half of whom live in the campus residence halls) and some 2,000 full-time graduate students. These students are served by 350 full-time faculty and 600 administrative, professional, and staff employees.

Seton Hall made a major commitment to information technology as part of the university's 1996 Strategic Plan, which included a strategic technology plan and long-range technology budget. Seton Hall made a major commitment to information technology in the university's planning and budgeting processes. Seton Hall initiated a strategic planning effort in 1993. Early in the development of the university's Strategic Plan it was determined that "providing a technologically advanced learning environment for our students and faculty" would be one of the six strategic objectives of the university's Plan. By 1995, the university's Strategic Plan included a Technology Plan and by 1996, the Strategic Plan included not only the Technology Plan but also a long-range technology budget.

The university has a strategic alliance with IBM Corporation to implement the university's vision for the use of technology in support of its mission. As a result, Seton Hall was ranked the 16th most wired campus in the May 1999 *Yahoo! Internet Life* survey of the 100 most wired colleges. More recently, Seton Hall was awarded the 1999 EduCause Leadership Award for Networking Excellence.

Seton Hall's Strategic Technology Plan

Seton Hall's technology plan was developed by a cross-functional team of faculty and administrators sponsored by the university's chief academic and financial officers. The planning team received extensive feedback and support from the university community, including significant release time to work on the plan, and the team was assisted in its efforts by a technology planning consultant from IBM Corporation.

The university's overall technology strategy is to develop and implement a learner-centered, network-enabled, distributed learning environment with a robust set of digital information resources in support of teaching, learning, scholarship, and the administration of the university. Critical to the success of this planning effort was the support of the university's executive team, the engagement of the faculty, and the focus on the use of technology to better serve teaching and learning.

In support of the strategic technology plan, Seton Hall also developed a long-range technology budget, calling for $15 million in new technology spending over five years. This long-range technology budget shifted the university's technology spending from capital to operating budgets. In implementing the technology plan, the university changed the way technology was budgeted and supported, creating new support services and leasing rather than purchasing most of the technology equipment used on campus.

Seton Hall's Mobile Computing Program

One of the cornerstones of the university's strategic technology plan is Seton Hall's ubiquitous computing program, known as the Mobile Computing Program. Seton Hall's Mobile Computing Program is primarily viewed as an *academic* program combining ubiquitous access to technology, integration of information technology into the curriculum, and infrastructure and services

that enable the effective use of information technology in teaching and learning. As part of this program, the university licenses to each incoming undergraduate student the use of a current IBM Thinkpad computer, preloaded with
a variety of instructional and professional software (including the MS Office
productivity suite, Lotus Notes, the Maple V symbolic and graphical calculator
package, and SPSS for statistical analysis). The computer is replaced every two
years. The current technology fee is $650 per semester, which covers hard-
ware, software, and insurance.

Teaching, Learning, and Student Services

Critical to the success of the university's strategic technology plan and the
Mobile Computing Program is faculty incorporation of information technology
into the curriculum. The university developed a number of new support
services, including a technology help desk and the Teaching, Learning, and
Technology Center (TLTC). Instructional technology consultants in TLTC
assist faculty in the adoption and use of information technology in teaching and
learning. The TLTC's *Curriculum Development Initiative* provides multi-year
support to academic departments undertaking systemic integration of information technology to enhance teaching and learning.

Through special projects in English, mathematics, and Freshman Studies,
the use of information technology has become a significant part of the first-year
student experience. Additional Curriculum Development Initiative projects
include art and music, biology, business, chemistry, history, physics, religious
studies, and the social sciences. With support from IBM Corporation, and in
partnership with the American Association of Higher Education's TLT Group,
Seton Hall has also undertaken a comprehensive, long-term assessment of the
impact of information technology on the university's learning environment.
Preliminary results indicate that the university's Mobile Computing Program
has had a significant positive impact on indicators of effective learning, such as
time on task, communication with the instructor, and prompt feedback on
assignments.

The University Libraries have also leveraged the campus network environment, implementing a new Web-based integrated library system and shifting
resources from acquisitions toward access to Web-based information services.
The University Libraries are active leaders in New Jersey's Virtual Academic
Library Environment (VALE), a consortium of 39 colleges and universities to
provide Web-based databases. In addition, the libraries have implemented
electronic reserves, making reserve material available to the university community via the Web.

In conjunction with the Mobile Computing Program, the university has also
made efforts to enhance student services. The offices of admissions, the bursar,
financial aid, and the registrar, previously in separate locations and reporting to

different parts of the organization, have been combined into a single Office of Enrollment Services, providing one-stop shopping for most student services. The university has also Web-enabled its administrative systems, allowing Web-based application, registration, drop/add, and access to academic progress and financial aid information. As part of the effort to enhance student services, the university increased the amount of financial aid available to students and redesigned the way in which financial aid was distributed.

SetonWorldWide

Seton Hall University is making use of information technology to deliver graduate degrees and professional certification through SetonWorldWide. In partnership with e-college (formerly Real Education), SetonWorldWide delivers online degree programs to several hundred students in the fields of corporate communications, counseling psychology, education, health care administration, and taxation and accounting. Additional online programs and certificates are under development and continually expanding the reach and scope of Seton Hall's educational offerings.

Infrastructure and Support Services

Seton Hall has made a major investment in the technology infrastructure and support services upon which the university's teaching, learning, and technology initiatives rest. The university's residence halls are fully wired with voice and data connections for each student. Approximately one-third of the classrooms are "mobile ready," with multimedia projection facilities and power and data connections to each desktop. All classrooms have Internet connections available at the instructor's station. The university also has wired a number of public spaces on campus, including study carrels in the University Library, the Pirate's Cove Coffee Shop, study lounges in the academic buildings, and even the benches on the University Green.

Lotus Domino is one of the foundations of the university's network services, providing messaging, scheduling, document management, and workflow services to the campus. The university has adopted Lotus LearningSpace as the primary tool for online course development and delivery. Several hundred undergraduate courses, including the Freshman and Sophomore English (writing and literature) course sequences, actively use Lotus LearningSpace for delivery of course content and to support communication and collaboration between students and faculty.

The university runs Lotus Domino on an IBM RS6000 SP2 complex. The university's SCT administrative applications run on an IBM S/390 Enterprise Server. Network file and print services are provided through the IBM S/390 using Novell Netware and IBM's LanRes. The university employs a number of

Web servers running on a combination of AIX, NT, and Linux. Several Web authoring tools are supported, including Microsoft FrontPage.

The campus has an ATM backbone using IBM ATM equipment. Connections between academic buildings on the main campus run between 155 Mb/s (OC3) and 620 Mb/s (OC12). Connections to remote sites are via T1 connections. Network services within academic buildings on the main campus are largely switched 10Mb/s to the desktop, with some legacy shared 10 Mb/s Ethernet segments still remaining. The university employs IBM's Tivoli (NetView) for network monitoring and management. The campus has multiple T1 connections to the Internet providing a combined bandwidth of 6 Mb/s. Access to the campus network is managed using the Checkpoint firewall product with the Netscape proxy server. The goal of the university network is to provide a single point of authentication for all standard network services.

Seton Hall students have a critical role in supporting the university's technology initiatives. The university's Student Technology Assistants (STA) Program recruits and trains students to be effective instructional technology consultants to the faculty and their peers. Innovative aspects of this program include an emphasis on student management of the program as well as "intellectual barter," whereby as part of the students' support contracts with faculty they receive mentoring from the faculty member in his or her area of expertise. Indeed, the STA Program has become a national model for the effective use of student workers in support of instructional technology.

The university's technical services have evolved considerably over the past several years to support Mobile Computing and the university's teaching, learning, and technology initiatives. The Division of Technology currently employs a professional support staff of approximately 90 professionals and has an annual operating budget of approximately $12.6 million (now approximately 12 percent of the $108 million General and Education budget for the South Orange campus). A significant part of this budget is supported by student fees. While support services are centrally managed, they are distributed in several academic buildings, and the inefficiencies in such an arrangement are more than offset by the advantages of providing convenient support to users.

Successes and Challenges of Mobile Computing

Seton Hall has achieved much during the past several years as a result of its strategic plan and commitment to technology. In particular, student enrollments have increased while at the same time the average SAT scores for incoming students have also increased. Seton Hall has succeeded in engaging the entire campus, including faculty and students, in rethinking the role of technology in support of teaching and learning.

As noted above, the university's assessment data indicates that technology has had a positive impact on the learning environment. The university has found that technology is a powerful lever for change, and has been successful in using that lever effectively. Some of these changes have been cultural. For example, at a faculty roundtable in 1998, a senior faculty member in English noted that prior to the university's technology initiatives there was little discussion among faculty regarding teaching and learning, while now there is a vital campus discourse about teaching and learning, what it takes to develop an educated leader for the twenty-first century, and how the current undergraduate core curriculum might be structured to support that vision.

Clearly, however, such change has not come without challenges. The university has made a significant commitment of its financial and human resources to this effort, and this has come as a result of both increases in tuition and fees as well as internal reallocation of resources. Despite the clear advantages of standardization of technology and centralization of support services, the difficulty and cost of providing the necessary infrastructure and support have been greater than anticipated. Nevertheless, we have found the successes, particularly the enhancement of the learning environment and the qualitative improvements in the campus culture, have outweighed the problems encountered.

Centers of Excellence

As a result of implementing the Mobile Computing Program, Seton Hall has developed core competencies in the areas of strategic technology planning; faculty engagement and support; using technology to enhance teaching and learning in select academic disciplines (for example, English and mathematics); using select technologies in teaching and learning (for example, Lotus Domino, Lotus LearningSpace, SPSS, and Maple V); and assessing the impact of technology on the learning environment.

Through its partnerships with IBM Corporation and the American Association of Higher Education's Teaching, Learning, and Technology Group, Seton Hall University has formed the Institute for Technology Development (ITD) to promote the effective use of information technology in teaching and learning. A particular mission of the institute is to assess the impact of information technology on the learning environment. One of the goals of the ITD is to develop a national repository of assessment data from campuses actively engaged in using technology to transform teaching and learning.

THE COSTS OF IMPLEMENTING UBIQUITOUS COMPUTING

Seton Hall University has a General and Education (G&E) Budget for the South Orange Campus (excluding the Law School, Seminary, and graduate medical education) of approximately $108 million. The University's *central* technology budget for fiscal year 1999-2000 (covering the period from July 1, 1999, through June 30, 2000) is $12.6 million, or 11.6 percent of the total G&E budget. An overview of Seton Hall's technology budget for fiscal year 1999-2000 is provided in Table 10-A, below. This overview does not include the budgets for Legal Computing at the University's Law School, SetonWorldWide, or the University Libraries, nor does it include departmental expenditures on technology (some departments, for example, support their own specialized computer labs or servers).

Table 10-A clearly shows that a large part of the technology budget goes toward personnel; personnel costs (excluding benefits) comprise approximately 43 percent of the total technology budget. Nearly half of the personnel budget

TABLE 10-A

Summary of SHU's Technology Budget for Fiscal Year 1999-2000

	Amount (000)	Percent of Budget	
Salaries and Wages	$ 5,362	43%	
Office of Technology			6%
Applications Support			5%
Systems Support			6%
Operation Support			3%
Telecommunications			4%
PC Support Services			12%
TLT Center			8%
Operating	4,693	37%	
Computer Leases (Faculty)			5%
Computer Leases (Staff/Admin.)			4%
Library Automation System (hardware lease and maintenance)			1%
Other Network Server Leases			3%
Computer Leases (Public Labs)			2%
ATM (Network) Equip. Leases			2%
TLT Center (incl. CDI, Media Equip., etc.)			5%
Telecommunications			8%
Computing Operations			4%
Other Noncategorized Expenses			3%
Mobile Computing Program (student laptop leases, software, etc.)	2,560	20%	20%
Total	$ 12,615		100%

(20 percent of the total technology budget) goes toward supporting PCs (PC Support Services) and faculty and classroom technology (the TLT Center). A large part of the budget also goes toward maintaining laptop computers for faculty and students and desktop computers for administrators and computer labs (together these account for approximately 31 percent of the total technology budget). The university replaces the faculty and student laptop computers, as well as the desktop computers in the public computer labs, every two years. Desktop computers for staff and administrators are replaced every three years. Maintaining the university's voice and data networks, including leases on the university's network switches and hubs, the university's local and long distance telephone services, and the campus connection to the Internet, comprises approximately 13 percent of the total technology budget.

Funding Seton Hall's Technology Initiatives

The university's technology budget was not always funded at this level. For example, in 1994, prior to the implementation of the university's strategic technology plan, the *central* technology operating budget was approximately 2.8 percent of the G&E budget. Significant additional funds were spent from capital funds and the operating funds of other academic and administrative units; nevertheless, the overall technology expenditures of the university have increased significantly since that time. These increases in the campus technology budget came about through careful planning and were implemented over several years. Funding for these initiatives came from a variety of sources, including the following:

- **Reallocation.** Prior to implementing the university's technology plan, technology budgets were highly decentralized. The technology plan called for central funding of basic infrastructure, including centralization of network funding and regular replacement of the university's computer stock. The development of the central technology budget was achieved in part by reallocation of these formerly decentralized technology funds.
- **Tuition and Fees.** Seton Hall University is a tuition-driven institution, that is, the bulk of the institution's expense budgets are funded from student tuition and fees. To fund the technology initiatives, Seton Hall implemented a $650 per semester Mobile Computing Technology Fee for undergraduate students. In addition, a significant portion of the university's tuition increases over the past several years have gone toward the central technology budget.
- **One-Time Infusion of Capital.** Seton Hall University recognized that an initial investment in the technology infrastructure was necessary to begin the Mobile Computing Program. To "jump start"

implementation of the technology plan, the university's Board of Regents allocated $5 million in capital from the university's quasi-endowment. This was used to provide laptop computers for all faculty, upgrade the campus network, and begin funding faculty and curriculum development.

- **Cost Cutting in Nonacademic Areas.** During implementation of the technology plan, the university also reengineered the campus procurement process and negotiated preferred vendor relationships that somewhat reduced operating costs. To recoup those costs, all nonacademic operating budgets (excluding personnel) were reduced by 5 percent.
- **Partnerships with Vendors.** Seton Hall University negotiated a comprehensive strategic alliance with IBM Corporation. As part of this agreement, IBM made significant investments in campus infrastructure. Seton Hall agreed to use IBM Corporation as the preferred technology vendor and to demonstrate the use of IBM products and services in higher education.

The most significant change in the technology budget is the shift of almost all the funding of technology from capital to operating budgets. Little of the technology is now funded through capital budgets. Shifting funding from capital to operating budgets has significant benefits. It has allowed Seton Hall to lease, rather than purchase, most of the equipment used on campus, and has allowed the university to plan regular refresh cycles for various technology components.

The importance of leasing in implementing Seton Hall's technology plan cannot be overemphasized. By way of example, the technology plan called for a $1 million upgrade to the campus fiber optic backbone in 1997. This upgrade was funded in the technology long-range budget beginning at $300,000 per year starting with the 1997-98 fiscal year. As a result, the university leased a state-of-the-art high speed campus backbone. The resulting three-year lease dramatically reduced the entry cost of implementing such technology.

Just as important, however, leasing from operating budgets recognizes the rapid obsolescence of technology. In early 1999, University Computing Services noted congestion at the core of the network backbone. Network traffic between academic buildings in 1999 had grown beyond the capacity of the state-of-the-art 1997 equipment. In response, University Computing Services negotiated an early end to the lease and replaced the core network equipment after only two years. Not only did this allow the university to upgrade to state-of-the-art 1999 equipment, but the monthly lease payments on the new equipment are actually lower than on the 1997 equipment.

Despite the concerns of many at the university that Seton Hall could not afford the level of investment required for its technology plan, other areas of the campus—particularly the academic area—also experienced significant growth during implementation of Mobile Computing. For example, the number of full-time faculty increased by 15 percent during implementation of the Mobile Computing Program. Average undergraduate class sizes were reduced, in part allaying faculty concerns that the Mobile Computing Program would result in the replacement of faculty by computers. SetonWorldWide was launched and new programs were initiated in diplomacy and international relations and graduate medical education.

LESSONS LEARNED

The university has learned a number of important lessons through implementation of its technology plan and Mobile Computing Program. These lessons include the following:

- Develop a plan focused on the use of technology in teaching and learning. Make sure to look at the student experience in using technology.
- Executive sponsorship is critical. The president, chief academic officer, and chief financial officer must all be on board. Seton Hall University is fortunate to have had the continuing support of the individuals in these key positions.[1]
- Faculty engagement is equally critical. Most faculty are eager to use technology, but the integration of technology into teaching in really effective and meaningful ways is difficult and takes time. Find multiple ways of engaging and supporting faculty.
- Develop a long-term budget for technology. Recognize the rapid obsolescence of computers and networks by establishing regular replacement cycles for technology. Consider leasing rather than purchasing technology.
- Provide high levels of support. As in Maslow's hierarchy, it is difficult to consider the use of technology to improve teaching if your network connection isn't working.
- Forge partnerships with vendors. The benefits of long-term vendor support outweigh the relatively small cost benefits of individual transaction-based technology decisions.[2]

ENDNOTES

1. Monsignor Robert Sheeran is president, and Dennis Garbini is vice president and CFO. In addition, we owe a debt of gratitude to former provosts Bernhard W. Scholz and Peter Ahr and former CFOs James Allison and Kimberly Cline for their staunch support of the university's technology plan.

2. For more information regarding Seton Hall University's teaching, learning, and technology initiatives, see the campus Web pages at <www.shu.edu> or Seton Hall's Teaching, Learning, and Technology Center Web pages at <tltc.shu.edu>.

CHAPTER 11

Procedures for Calculating the Costs of Alternative Modes of Instructional Delivery

Dennis Jones and Frank Jewett

INTRODUCTION

The methods of instructional delivery in higher education are changing rapidly as a consequence of developments in information technology (IT). The advent of the Internet, the World Wide Web, the CD-ROM, and reliable, high quality interactive video technologies has created an explosion of experimentation with, and commitment to, alternative modes of instructional delivery. This explosion is partly a consequence of such high-profile

Contributor's Note: This material has been extracted from the preliminary draft of a costing manual under development as part of the Technology Costing Project funded by the Fund for Improvement in Postsecondary Education (FIPSE) and sponsored by the Western Cooperative for Educational Telecommunications (WCET). The manual has gone through a review by the project's advisory board and by a group of participating campuses. It is still a work in progress but the rationale and methodology for course costing presented here are sufficiently well defined to merit widespread distribution and discussion. Several topics in the manual that are *not* included here are alternative unit(s) of analysis (an academic department or a media center rather than a course), conventions for data exchange among institutions, and technical appendices on the Program Classification Structure, definitions of activities, and objectives of expenditures. Case studies are currently underway at participating campuses that have agreed to apply the costing methodology to a set of selected courses. The project is scheduled to conclude in 2000. To the best of our knowledge, only two other projects have some overlap with this one: "Modeling Resource Use in Teaching and Learning with Technology," S. Ehrmann and J. Milam, The TLT Group (1999), the long awaited costing study from the Flashlight Project, and "Costs of Networked Learning," Paul Bacsich, et al., Hallam Sheffield University (1999), a study of information technology costs from Great Britain. These efforts exhibit major elements of similarity. The Flashlight handbook differs in being somewhat less structured and more focused upon how a campus might organize and plan to undertake its own cost study. The British study focused more upon social issues, such as the "hidden" costs of information technology to students and faculty, and developing a planning schema rather than proposing a comprehensive basis for cost analysis.

organizations as the University of Phoenix and the United Kingdom Open University successfully demonstrating that there is a substantial market for instruction delivered in ways that most educational administrations and faculty would find unconventional, and perhaps even unacceptable.

This diversification of delivery mechanisms also is a function of greater responsiveness to client expectations and needs. Higher education students are increasingly place-bound, largely because effective performance on the job (and as a member of society) requires learning throughout life. Once settled with work and family obligations, individuals have limited ability to go to providers of higher education. If these students are to be reached, the providers will have to go to them. While these place-bound adults are expanding the domain regarding *where* learning opportunities will be delivered, all clients are pressing provider organizations on the issue of *when* these opportunities will be offered. Many colleges and universities find that a preponderance of students who are enrolled in distance-delivered courses are simultaneously enrolled in on-campus courses, making time, rather than place, a critical variable for these clients.

Whatever the motivation, the volume of instruction being delivered either off-site or on-site, but with considerable technology enhancements, has reached a level at which both educational and managerial questions are being raised. Among academics, the debate rages about the effectiveness—or quality—of such instruction. While the debate will continue, it is too late to turn back. Recent history suggests that both the variety of offerings and the number of individuals availing themselves of these alternative forms of learning will not only increase but will increase dramatically. The alternatives are entering—and in some circumstances becoming—the mainstream.

As these alternative forms of instructional delivery become more common, they cease to fly under managerial radar. At many institutions, these alternatives historically have been treated as "experimental" or "demonstration" approaches to the delivery of instruction. As such, they were frequently ignored in a managerial context. Alternatively, they were treated as "projects" funded from special allocations of resources, often from sources outside the institution. Such funding created a fiduciary interest in accounting for associated costs, the kind of interest associated with responsibly reporting to the funding agency the costs incurred in the context of any grant or contract. However, as these new forms of delivery have become more commonplace, decision-makers are, understandably, asking a series of fundamental questions not previously asked.

1. What are the per-student costs associated with alternative forms of instructional delivery? How do costs of alternative methods compare to more traditional, face-to-face classroom instruction?

2. Under what conditions, if any, do alternative delivery mechanisms become cost-effective? For example, are there enrollment levels at which certain instructional methods become much more cost-effective than other approaches?
3. What are the learning results? Are they as good as those achieved through classroom modes? Does the widespread finding of "no significant difference" hold in this particular case? Are learning outcomes different, not just in level but in kind?
4. What are the levels of user satisfaction, from the perspective of both clients and faculty?

These reasonable questions have too few answers. Certainly, the empirical evidence is not sufficient to yield rules of thumb that can inform managerial choices. This is not to say that *no* data are available about the costs of alternative methods of delivery. Many ongoing alternative delivery activities have developed cost or expenditure data of some form. Further, efforts have been undertaken to capture some of these fugitive data, to develop comparative statistics regarding the costs of various modes of instructional delivery,[1] and to model cost behavior of different instructional modes at different enrollment levels.[2]

These studies have made enormous contributions to an understanding of cost variations across different modes of delivery. However, as significant as the contributions of these studies are, they suffer from the limitations of the data on which they are based. For the comparative studies, the authors had little choice but to use whatever data were readily available. As is common in such instances, the available data resided in record systems kept in accordance with different data categories, definitions, and data entry protocols. As a consequence, the authors were required to adjust these data as best they could to achieve some measure of comparability. Such post facto adjustments were pragmatically necessary if their studies were to proceed. They, of all people, would be the first to argue for standardization in the data on which their work relied.

In the case of Frank Jewett's work in modeling the costs of alternative delivery in the eight case studies, the data used were those available in the budget and accounting systems of the various campuses involved, augmented by information about faculty workload policy and salary schedules, equipment inventories, and special communications costs. For the BRIDGE cost simulation model, Jewett used default values based upon system-wide data from the California State University. While these data represent a significant sample of higher education institutions, it is also true that the data reflect the experiences—and the idiosyncrasies—of a single system of institutions. A good deal more credence could be accorded the results if they were benchmarked against the experiences of other institutions operating within a different set of internal rules and regulations.

These comments and observations are not intended to denigrate in any way the pioneering work that these studies represent. The intent is to make a case for more—and more comparable—data about the costs associated with delivering instruction in various ways.

Decision-makers need internal data that allow the costs of alternative modes of delivery to be compared. Calculating costs of instruction under an assumption of traditional classroom delivery has a long history. In the generally recognized approaches to costing, mode of delivery is almost never explicitly considered; the assumption is that instruction will be conducted on-campus, in a classroom or laboratory, using face-to-face methods of instruction. Given the emergence of alternative delivery modes, there is a need for costing methodologies that make delivery modes explicit and consider the full range of costs associated with each mode so that valid comparisons can be made. One of the major objectives of this chapter is to present a costing methodology that responds to this internal need.

The development of consistent internal cost data is a necessary first step for decision-makers. However, they also need a context within which they can interpret the results—they need "benchmark" information. Only by compiling data from many more of the "natural experiments" now underway will it be possible to develop a body of conventional wisdom about the patterns in variation of costs across different modes of delivery and different enrollment levels within each of the different modes.

By accumulating such data over time, general rules will likely emerge—rules of thumb such as those regarding differential costs of classroom instruction in different disciplines and at different levels that emerged from cost analyses conducted in years past. These rules of thumb (such as those that help us understand the typical relative costs of lower-division versus graduate-level instruction in a given discipline or of upper-division instruction in psychology versus that in engineering) do not provide precise guides. They do, however, provide decision-makers with information that serves them well when more detailed analyses are either not possible or not warranted. For instance, most decision-makers expect lower-division nursing courses to cost roughly twice that of lower-division social science courses. The same level of intuitive understanding does not exist regarding the relative costs of delivering a 30-student lower-division social science class by regular classroom instruction and by interactive video. The objective is to work toward a situation in which this level of understanding is widely shared.

This internal costing methodology objective could be pursued along two paths. The first is to devise and use a common record-keeping system in which those wishing to conduct cost analyses would keep their operating (transactional) data. Data kept in a standard way, if analyzed using similar procedures, would yield the kinds of comparable information that policymakers constantly seek. While this alternative has many desirable characteristics, it is rejected as infeasible. Institutions have made substantial investments over the years in data systems designed to serve their day-to-day operational needs. These data systems differ considerably for a variety of reasons, not the least of which are the accounting and reporting requirements of state and local governments that provide the largest share of funding to many institutions. Given the competition for scarce revenues, there is almost *no* chance that institutions will abandon these data systems and adopt a replacement that would simplify some analyses but complicate the majority of their day-to-day transactions.

The outright rejection of one alternative leads to the second alternative to be investigated here, which is based upon the following considerations:

- Institutions continue to keep their basic budget and expenditure data in existing, diverse record-keeping systems.
- These data are translated into a common set of data structures and categories. This translation step itself will typically require some form of analytic activity.
- Data in these common data structures are manipulated/analyzed in accordance with a set of "conventions" designed to produce the comparative cost information deemed most useful to policymakers and other users.

The two alternatives are described diagrammatically in Figure 11-1.

The second major purpose of this chapter is to propose a set of procedures by which data from multiple institutions can be placed in a reasonably common framework and exchanged or compared. Based upon these objectives, the following materials were developed to provide (1) a proposed common data structure, (2) definitions of the data categories and elements identified as necessary within this structure, and (3) specifications of the conventions and common procedures required for converting these data into the kinds of cost information relevant to decision-makers.

Given that each institution will start the process from its own unique point of departure, it must devise its own procedures for making the conversion to the common data structure as indicated for Alternative 2 in Figure 11-1. While these conversion routines cannot be specified, hints as to how these translations might be done are provided wherever possible. These conversion routines will most likely be implemented through use of a series of look-up tables—for example, tables that describe the translation of the institution's departmental numbering scheme to the Classification of Instructional Programs schema recommended for use in inter-institutional exchange.

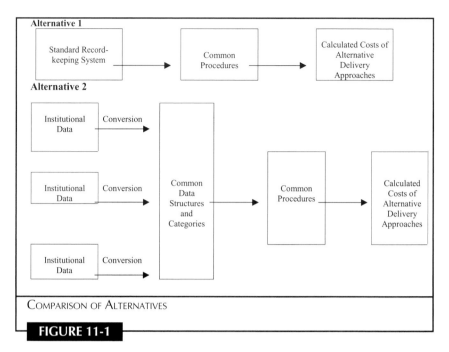

COMPARISON OF ALTERNATIVES

FIGURE 11-1

In developing the costing procedures described later in this chapter, two important choices have been made regarding (1) the types of costs that are calculated or derived from the basic data and (2) the specific categories of cost data that we want to collect.

The first choice reflects a decision about *type* of costs to be calculated. Higher education has a longstanding practice of calculating and reporting *historic, average costs*, e.g., total campus expenditures in a given year divided by FTE to obtain average cost per FTE. Average cost data have worked relatively well in the past for describing and comparing costs because of the relatively simple cost structure of classroom instruction. But average cost calculations, by themselves, are not sufficient for analyzing the costs of delivery modes based upon information technology because these modes have fundamentally different cost structures. Many (if not most) forms of IT instructional delivery have a significant fixed cost component (related, for example, to specialized equipment, communication, or production costs) that is not present in classroom instruction. In addition, the variable cost component of IT delivery may also be substantially different from that of classroom delivery. Thus, for these alternative modes it is essential that we attempt to identify and estimate both the fixed and variable components of costs prior to calculating average costs.

The second choice, discussed more completely later in this chapter, relates to the handling of so-called "indirect" costs, which are *directly* associated with campus support functions of various kinds but only *indirectly* associated with instructional activities.

For an instructional cost center, common costing parlance would have

direct costs of instruction + indirect costs = full costs of instruction

indirect costs = allocated share of direct costs of support activities

In this chapter, the decision has been made to focus upon the direct costs of instruction whether those costs are incurred in the instructional program or in one of the support programs (of the Program Classification Structure) where these support program costs can be identified (see below). It has also been decided *not* to attempt the allocation of indirect costs to achieve a full cost estimate.

The "model" that underlies the costing schema proposed in this chapter borrows from Jewett's work. It simply comprises the following:

- *Course-related costs*—the (operating and capital[3]) costs associated with offering the course, regardless of the number of students enrolled.
- *Enrollment*—the (operating and capital) costs that vary in accordance with the number of students enrolled in the course.

A simple form of this model is illustrated in Figures 11-2A to C. As defined here, the underlying model we are working with should be considered a hypothesis whose usefulness will be confirmed by how well it assists in the cost analysis. Without such an hypothesis as a guide, it is difficult to organize the analysis or to define useful data. As with all hypotheses, this one is subject to revision or refutation as new information and findings become available.

Panel A: Regular Classroom Instruction. Students meet in a scheduled room with an instructor. If total course demand exceeds some pre-set enrollment limit, additional course sections are added. The cost of a section is basically the cost of putting the instructor in the classroom, e.g., if a full-time faculty workload is eight course sections per year, the cost of a section is 1/8th of average faculty salary. The imputed cost of the classroom is relatively small, about $150 compared to $7,000-8,000 for faculty cost. As shown below in Panel A (Figure 11-2A), direct costs rise (step-up) in proportion to the number of sections offered.

PANEL A: MULTIPLE CLASSROOM SECTIONS

FIGURE 11-2A

Panel B: Large Lecture, Quiz Sections. A variation on classroom instruction involves a single large lecture section for all students enrolled in the course plus separately scheduled quiz/discussion sections that are usually staffed by graduate teaching assistants. The cost of the large lecture is "course related"; it is only incurred once as a consequence of offering the course. The quiz/discussion section costs are related to the number of students enrolled (which determines the number of quiz sections needed). In Panel B (Figure 11-2B) the

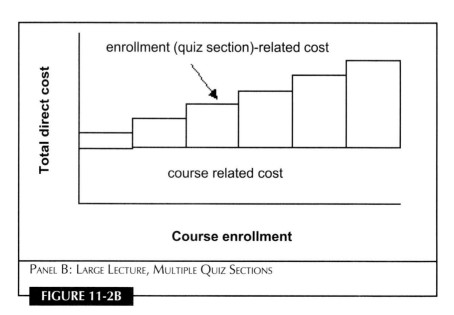

PANEL B: LARGE LECTURE, MULTIPLE QUIZ SECTIONS

FIGURE 11-2B

course-related costs are shown as a constant to which the enrollment-related quiz section costs are added. Because of the constant, costs do not rise in proportion to enrollment.

Panel C: Internet Course. Internet, online, or Web courses may have high (course-related) development costs but, under certain circumstances, additional students can be added individually for the costs of interaction and evaluation. As shown in Panel C (Figure 11-2C), the production costs are treated as a constant to which enrollment costs are added as a smooth line because individual students can be enrolled without consideration of "sections."

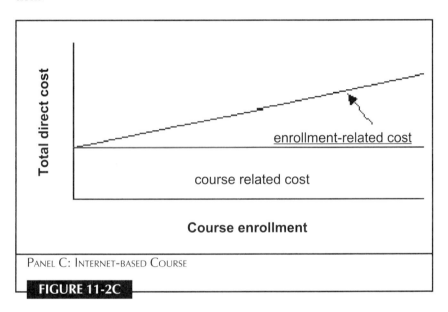

PANEL C: INTERNET-BASED COURSE

FIGURE 11-2C

The working model also recognizes that both course- and enrollment-related costs for a single course can occur in multiple locations simultaneously. This phenomenon is illustrated in Figure 11-3.

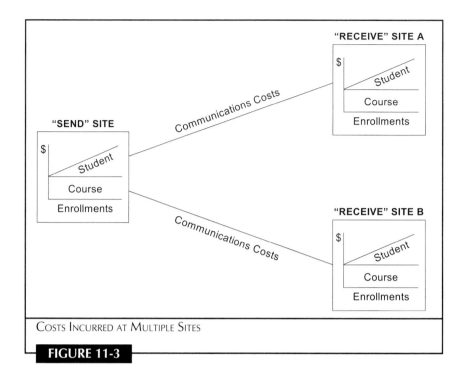

Costs Incurred at Multiple Sites

FIGURE 11-3

COST CALCULATION PROCEDURES INTERNAL TO THE INSTITUTION

The purpose of the procedures presented in this section is to provide decision-makers with information about the costs associated with alternative methods of delivering instruction at the course level within the context of their institution. By inference, the procedures are not intended to cover all facets of an institution's operations. While the procedures have to be developed, and used, within the broader institutional costing context, the procedures presented herein are not intended to be substitutes for this broader set of costing methodologies. Similarly, while the procedures must be conceptually consistent with procedures used to calculate cost information intended for exchange, there is no imperative that common data structures and definitions be used.

Basic Assumptions

Given this particular objective, several principles that shaped the nature of the procedures presented below require explicit treatment. Among the key considerations are the following:

1. The procedures are analytic, not accounting procedures. The objective is not to create a record-keeping system (although the result may be to influence the content of record-keeping systems in some instances). Rather the agenda is to suggest analytic conventions and approaches that can be used to organize data in a way that informs internal decision making.

2. As a corollary, the intent is to produce results that have utility for decision-makers rather than results that conform to accounting and auditing standards and principles. Thus, the goal is to develop conceptually sound, meaningful estimates rather than numbers that fully reconcile to accounting records. This is not an excuse or argument for sloppiness; rather, it is a recognition of the costs associated with transforming data into information and the rapid escalation in costs associated with marginal (and usually unnecessary) improvements to precision in this regard. The intent is to generate results that are considerably better than back-of-the-envelope estimates, but not as precise as those that could be obtained if all transactional costs were accounted for at the course level.

3. The procedures constructed must be applicable to all kinds of instructional delivery, from the most traditional face-to-face classroom instruction to asynchronous learning through courses delivered over the World Wide Web. Indeed, a primary objective is to calculate the costs of "non-traditional," "non-classroom" delivery methods relative to the costs associated with delivery in a regular classroom setting.

4. Since the criterion is managerial utility, the eventual need is to have a costing framework that allows capturing data on both method and scale to shed light on the question of whether there are conditions under which a seemingly cost-effective approach loses its comparative advantage vis-à-vis other approaches (and vice versa). While a single institution can develop data on alternative methods using only data originating from within, most institutions will be unable to estimate scale effects over a sufficiently wide spectrum to be useful. In this arena, comparable data from multiple institutions—data developed in conformance with a common underlying model—can have their greatest utility.

5. The unit of analysis is the course. Determining the unit of analysis is perhaps the most vexing issue in the entire conceptual scheme. Historically, costing methodologies have disaggregated institutional cost data to the discipline and course level, allowing the calculation of the cost per student credit hour for teaching lower-division math, for example. But historically, one did not have to make distinctions among delivery modes to get managerially useful information. Face-to-face classroom instruction so dominated the scene that any variations were basically anomalies

that did little more than provide a little noise in the system; the variations simply did not rise to the level of materiality.

Although new modes of instructional delivery are expanding rapidly, few guidelines exist to indicate the path that might be most usefully followed in breaking away from the history that has governed calculation of higher education costs. To understand cost behavior in ways that have managerial meaning, and to protect against charges of inappropriate comparison, the methodology arguably must recognize distinctions in all the following areas: academic discipline, level of instruction, delivery method (e.g., classroom, TV, computer network), and scale (variations in course enrollment levels that may affect cost per student).

At this point, one can argue that to start with existing (top-down) costing methodologies and drive the analyses to increasingly finite levels of detail (delivery method and scale within the framework of discipline and level) is likely to be extraordinarily cumbersome and yield a large analysis with many "empty cells" in the final report. While alternative means of delivery are attaining greater acceptance and becoming more prevalent, they are still much in the minority at most institutions. Consequently, the procedures laid out below start from the position that, at this time, they should reflect the reality that they will be applied to a small fraction of instructional activities at most institutions. This position translates into a conclusion that they be applied at a *course* level. In a later section of the costing manual (not included in the material excerpted in this chapter), approaches to costing are discussed for those instances in which an institution has made a major commitment to a particular alternative form of delivery—instances where the overall costs of the delivery mechanisms are known and the question becomes one of disaggregating to disciplines and course levels.

Even specifying that the unit of analysis is the "course" results in ambiguity, especially because of the difference between *course section* (a given course scheduled at a given time and place) and *a course* (the aggregation of all course sections associated with a given course title and number, e.g., Biology 101). For purposes of informing decision making, it is useful to calculate costs for individual course sections and the aggregate of all course sections *for which the mode* of delivery is the same. In the final analysis, it is this latter unit of analysis that is the most useful in that it gets at the two most important variables—mode of delivery and scale (e.g., number of students enrolled per year).

6. Initial attention should be given to the *direct* costs of instruction rather than to full costs, that is, that indirect costs not be allocated back to individual courses. This is because of the technical problems associated with such allocations as well as practical questions of utility. It is the *direct* costs that are managed, and adding indirect costs into the mix often

confuses more than it enlightens. And, especially if cost comparisons between delivery modes are to be made, inclusion of allocated indirect costs will not affect the comparison because they will be entered on both sides of the comparison.

7. Costs are calculated on the basis of assets and consumables actually used. Costs of unused capacity are *not* allocated to functions or activities. For example, the entire cost of an interactive video classroom or origination site is *not* allocated to the one course that happens to be using the facility for its intended purpose. Still, the costs associated with under-utilization of (particularly expensive) assets need to be recognized. As an alternative, the procedures presented recommend that the costs associated with unused capacity be made explicit.

Procedures for Calculating Costs at the Course Level

With these basic assumptions as guidance, procedures for calculating costs at the course level consist of the steps described below.

Step 1. Identify Courses to Be Costed

Identify courses for which cost calculations are to be made. Initially, this selection should reflect choices based upon the following:

- **Importance to Decision-makers.** Are there impending decisions concerning further utilization of the method of delivery represented?
- **Need for Baseline Data.** When dealing with cost issues, it is important to have a control/comparison group that allows the resulting cost data to be placed in a broader perspective. In the longer run, it is the intent that these procedures support the ability to trade cost data across institutional lines—to have external comparisons for costs associated with delivery of particular kinds of courses delivered in particular ways. In the short run, and for many decisions, the need is for an internal comparison of teaching a course in the traditional face-to-face classroom mode relative to the costs associated with alternative delivery formats.
- **Materiality/Relevance.** Analytic time and energy should not be wasted on the small stuff. For most institutions, this will mean identifying a relative handful of courses and an associated control group of courses, if at all possible. In this discussion, the term "course" should be interpreted as being a "unit for which learning is certified/transcripted upon successful completion." Because the objective is to identify cost patterns associated with alternative modes of delivery, a course (an entity with a particular identifying number) should be treated holistically. A "course" comprising a lecture and numerous discussion and laboratory sections should be viewed as a single course

with multiple components to its method of delivery. Similarly, courses with numerous stand-alone sections should also be treated as a single course with a particular mode of delivery.

Complete steps 2-5 below for each of the courses.

Step 2. Write a Description of How the Course Is Delivered

Write a prose description of the delivery mechanism being used and the kinds of resources being used. This step has two purposes. First, it provides the basis from which others—including those in other institutions if data are exchanged—can understand the results of the cost calculation. Second, it helps ensure that the cost calculations will encompass the full range of appropriate items. The description should help frame the subsequent analyses by providing an understanding of the following:

- The activities being conducted to deliver the course
- The organization or organizational units (whether inside or outside the institution) responsible for the activities
- The resources (both capital and operating) used in performance of the activities

This description should be inclusive of required support services (such as technical support for technology-intensive courses) as well as resources required at remote sites, if any.

Step 3. Specify Elements of the Activity Structure Associated with the Course

Establish the activity structure that describes the course. This procedure is a critically important step in the process. Table 11-A lists the set of potential choices. It also draws attention to the fact that courses consist of a variety of activities and that various support activities can be associated directly with some courses. The activities identified within the instruction function are the following:

- Course planning, specification, and design of instructional materials
- Instructional materials development/production/acquisition
- Delivery/presentation of instructional materials
- Tutoring/interaction with students
- Assessment/evaluation/grade assignment

With regard to these activities, the only question is whether they have to be separately identified. For courses in which a single individual is responsible for all the activities and delivery is face-to-face in a traditional classroom setting, these distinctions are not necessary. For many courses, however, including those taught in a combination of lecture and quiz/discussion modes, different resources are associated with these different activities and, to the extent possible, they should be recorded separately.

Beyond the Instruction Function level, however, questions about whether or not to include Functions/Activities in the calculation become less black and white. A particularly relevant example involves the distinction between direct and indirect costs and between variable and fixed costs. Indirect costs are costs associated with some aspect of institutional operation but are not directly associated with instruction, i.e., are not sensitive to changes in the volume of instruction—the president's salary is an example. Direct costs are a measure of the resources that are required to actually provide the instruction, e.g., the instructor, studio, technical staff, and broadcast equipment for live TV delivery. In this example, the studio is a direct input to instructional delivery and is appropriately included as part of the direct costs of instruction. Because the studio is a fixed asset whose cost was incurred in the past, the need arises to impute or allocate a share of its total cost to the instructional activity (approaches to the imputation process are discussed below).

TABLE 11-A

COSTING ACTIVITY STRUCTURE

Code	Title
Course Number	An identifier that typically indicates both discipline/department and course level
Course Activities 1. Course Planning, Design of Materials 2. Materials Development/Production/Acquisition 3. Delivery/Presentation of Course Materials 4. Tutoring/Mediation/Interaction with Students 5. Evaluation/Assessment/Grade Assignment	
Academic Support 1. Computing Support 2. Telecommunications Support 3. Library/Information Support 4. Assessment Support 5. Academic Logistical Support 6. Academic Administration 7. Academic Personnel Development	Academic Support
Student Services 1. Academic Advising 2. Counseling and Career Guidance	Student Services
Institutional Support 1. Advertising and Marketing 2. Recruitment 3. Admissions 4. Financial Aid 5. Student Records	Institutional Support Student Access

The situation with indirect costs, the costs of campus resources that are not directly required for instruction, is different. If indirect costs are to be "charged" to the course, they must be assigned or allocated based upon some allocation method that will necessarily be somewhat arbitrary, e.g., per FTE or per student enrollment. Moreover, no matter what allocation method is used, the result will allocate the same amount of indirect cost to FTE or student enrollments on both the classroom and mediated sides of the cost comparison. Based on these considerations, indirect costs, whether fixed or variable, can probably be ignored in the cost calculations.

While, in the end, decisions to include or exclude certain items are necessarily judgment calls based upon practical reality, the following considerations can help inform that judgment:

- **Ability to Specifically Assign Costs.** Direct costs are best conceived as those that can be explicitly tied to a specific course, while indirect costs can be assigned only on the basis of some pro-rata share. Thus, if a faculty member makes use of the educational media center to get advice about how to develop a Web page for a course, this "training" cost would normally be considered an indirect cost. If, however, the educational media center undertook a project to develop courseware for a particular course on a "project" basis, that cost would appropriately be considered a direct cost.

- **Materiality/Relevance.** In many situations, much effort is required to relate costs directly to cost objectives, with the results not being substantially different from the identification of cost as indirect. Therefore, an important factor for consideration in the assignment of costs is the added expense of identifying costs as direct rather than indirect. The expense of making a precise assignment of costs as direct must be weighed against the precision required in satisfying the purpose for which the cost information is to be used.

If costs are direct but particularly difficult to estimate (or allocate), it may be useful to arbitrarily assign a modest amount—e.g., $100—as a placeholder. This act ensures that the item is not ignored and provides an estimate that can be improved later if additional precision becomes important.

Step 4. Assign Activity Costs to Expenditure Program Categories

Table 11-B is used to assign costs associated with various objects of expenditure to the elements in the activity structure. The double column under Instruction allows separation of course-related from enrollment-related (student) costs for various forms of mediated instruction. For example, curriculum planning and materials development are course-related; depending upon how the content is delivered, it may be course-related, or enrollment-related, or both; tutoring/

interaction, evaluation, and assessment are enrollment related. This separation of costs is not necessary if all the listed activities are the responsibility of an individual faculty member (whether the course is in a classroom or based upon some form of mediated delivery). Although not shown in Table 11-B, the distinction between course- and enrollment-related costs may apply in the other program categories as well, e.g., duplication of materials, licenses, and postage in the Institutional Support program may be highly dependent upon enrollment. The list of expenditure items is not exhaustive; other items can be added as needed.

In simple terms, the task is to add cost information, *as appropriate*, to the matrix shown in Table 11-B. "As appropriate" is emphasized to reinforce the point that, for many courses, many or even most of these rows and columns will not have entries. Because the procedures are analytic rather than accounting devices, several shortcuts and conventions should be considered in making entries into this format.

Faculty Compensation: Suggestions in this arena include the following:

1. Use assignment data as the basis for the calculation unless the institution already has a fully functioning faculty activity analysis system in place. If, for example, the institution has a four-course teaching load for each of two semesters, assign each course one-eighth of an individual's load for the year. If the normal tracking load is two courses per semester, but 50 percent of the faculty member's time is allocated to research and public service, then each course would still represent one-eighth of an individual's load for the year. The same algorithm applies for graduate students.

2. Be primarily concerned that the total resources commitment of an individual is reflected and less concerned about distribution of effort across activities. As a device, it may be useful to enter the cost estimate in a total column and simply indicate the activities (by a check mark, etc.) primarily covered by this expenditure level.

3. Provide entries for such items as materials development only if there is a clearly established basis for determining costs, e.g., faculty members are given release time to develop course materials or assessments. If the materials developed are intended to have a useful life of more than one year or they are to be used in teaching the course multiple times, an appropriate allocation must be made. Suggestions in this regard are treated in the part of the capital section dealing with acquisition/development of courseware. In the absence of identifiable time (and, therefore, costs) that can be associated with the creation of an asset, there is little need to cost these elements separately.

4. Use average compensation by type of personnel when making cost calculations. Because overall costs are so heavily influenced by the personnel

TABLE 11-B

Prototype Cost Assignment Summary

	Programs:				
Objects of Expenditures:	Instruction course related	Instruction enrollment related	Academic support	Student services	Institutional support
Operating expenditures					
Compensation					
Faculty					
curriculum planning					
materials development					
content delivery					
tutoring/interaction w/ students					
evaluation/assessment/grade assignment					
Graduate students/paraprofessionals					
curriculum planning					
materials development					
content delivery					
tutoring/interaction w/ students					
evaluation/assessment/grade assignment					
Support personnel					
curriculum planning					
materials development					
content delivery					
tutoring/interaction w/ students					
evaluation/assessment/grade assignment					
Supplies and Expenses					
Media/communications/computing					
voice/video/charges					
data connect time/server charges					
satellite transponder charges					
ITFS/cable/TV/broadcast feeds					
computer lab/server charges					
Duplication of course materials					
print					
audio					
video					
Licenses for the use of:					
courseware					
software					
databases					
Postage and other distribution services					
Travel					
Contract services					
consulting					
purchased services					
Rent					
Other operating expenses					
Capital costs (imputed)					
Facility charges					
Equipment charges					
Other capital charges					
Totals					

component, using actual compensation of the specific individual teaching the course may yield a result that is attributable more to the accident of personnel assignments than to actual costs. Using averages (or, better yet, medians) serves to remove this source of variation. This procedure will lead to greater comparability of results, both inside and outside the institution. In instances in which faculty are paid a "premium" to teach using alternative delivery modes, the value of this premium should be reflected.

5. Keep track of FTEs of human resources used as well as the dollar cost. This tracking allows elimination of salary differences in making comparisons.

Compensation of Other Employees: Suggestions in this arena include the following:

1. For technicians and other support personnel, include costs only for hours that can be tied directly to the course in question. For example, it is usually possible to specifically identify hours devoted by technicians operating the equipment for interactive video communications. In calculating costs, it is recommended that costs be calculated as follows:

$$cost = (assigned\ hours) \times (average\ compensation/hour)$$

Costs of staff who keep the computer systems running, but cannot be tied explicitly to the course, should be treated as direct costs of academic support (an "indirect cost") rather than as a direct cost of instruction.

2. Clerical and other support staff would normally be considered as part of the indirect cost component. The only exceptions would be instances when staff are explicitly assigned to projects associated solely with a single course. An alternative is to prorate departmental support staff across faculty positions. As a consequence, each faculty position, or fraction thereof, comes "fully loaded" with its own share of clerical staff and related office expense.

Supplies and Expenses: Categories include the following:

1. *Office and Instructional Supplies:* Include expenses directly attributable to the course. Where costs cannot be directly assigned to a course, it is often possible and practical to estimate per-faculty costs for course-related (office) supplies and to estimate per-student costs for instructional supplies and then to use these costs in the calculation routines.

2. *Travel:* Again, only expenses directly related to the course should be included. Typical in this category are expenses associated with faculty traveling to an off-campus site to teach a class or to meet occasionally

with a group of students. For ease of calculation, it is appropriate to estimate as follows:

travel costs = costs/trip x number of trips required

3. *Communications:* These costs on a per-course basis are usually determined on the basis of cost per hour of connect time or of transponder time. Again, for analytic purposes, it is appropriate to estimate this cost as follows:

course communication costs = cost/hour x number of hours

For transponders, it may be appropriate to estimate per-course costs by calculating as follows:

lease cost of transponder per year/number of courses *at capacity use*

In any event, it is not necessary to obtain this number by actual compilation of accounting data.

4. *Duplication of Materials:* Many alternative forms of delivery rely on use of materials—print, audio, video, CD-ROMs, etc.—specifically designed for the course. This cost component includes the cost of reproducing the materials for student use. Costs of developing the materials in the first instance are not included here (they are included as a capital item). Calculation of the cost in this area is appropriately done by estimating cost per unit and multiplying by the number of units.

5. *Postage and Distribution Services:* Include here the estimated costs of mailing or otherwise distributing course materials identified in #4, above. Again, the costs included are only those directly attributable to the course; other postage costs are appropriately considered an indirect cost.

6. *Contract Services:* This category includes costs of consultants and purchase of services under contract. It excludes purchases of services of part-time faculty members, a cost treated as part of personnel compensation.

7. *Licenses:* Included in this category are fees paid for the use of proprietary courseware, software, and databases. For inclusion in this category, expenditures must be made solely for purposes of supporting the course in question, for example, software designed and used expressly for teaching a basic accounting course, calculus, etc. In some instances, license fees are established on a per-student basis. In this case, the cost estimate is simply the product of cost per student and the number of students. In other instances, site licenses are granted without reference to the number of users. In this case, costs are determined by calculating the per-student costs (including students in all sections of the course for which cost

estimates are being developed) and multiplying by the number of students.

8. *Rent:* This category includes costs of using space in facilities not owned by the organization providing the instruction. Typical would be rents associated with delivering a course at a high school or other off-campus site. The calculation is as follows:

$$\text{cost} = \text{annual cost/square foot} \times \text{number of square feet} \times (\text{hours of use/total hours per year of availability})$$

Capital Items: Historically, capital costs have not been calculated as an element in higher education cost studies. This is particularly true of facilities costs, but can also be true of equipment costs and costs associated with acquisition of courseware and course-specific materials that have a multi-year life. However, one of the hallmarks of many of the alternative modes of delivery is the substitution of capital for labor, that is, the use of technology to do some part of the instruction function that had typically been done by a faculty member. As a consequence, meaningful comparisons of alternative delivery mechanisms require explicit recognition of capital costs. This requirement applies regardless of mode of delivery. The general rule is that costs of *all* capital items should be converted to an annual cost, no matter how access to them is obtained (purchase, lease, or home grown).

1. *Facilities:* Almost all forms of delivery require some type of facilities. Further, many alternative forms of delivery require either the construction or use of special purpose facilities (e.g., television studios or "smart" classrooms) or a direct expenditure for lease/rent of off-campus facilities. Rental costs were discussed above in #8 under "Supplies and Expenses." To keep the comparisons on a level playing field, facilities costs associated with traditional classroom instruction should be included in the calculation. The calculation of capital costs of owned facilities can take the following alternative forms:

$$\left[\frac{construction.cost.per.sq.ft.}{50}\right] \times \left[sq.ft.of.space.used\right] \times \left[\frac{hours.used}{hours.of.capacity}\right]$$

$$\text{OR}$$

$$\left[\frac{\frac{replace.value.of.facility}{total.assignable.sq.ft.}}{50}\right] \times \left[sq.ft.of.space.used\right] \times \left[\frac{hours.used}{hours.of.capacity}\right]$$

In both of these equations the number 50 is the suggested convention for number of years of useful life over which capital cost is spread. In this calculation, hours used is calculated as the number of hours per week times the number of weeks the class meets. In those instances where facilities are provided "free" by a third party, it is recommended that either a rental value be established or an estimated annual capital value be calculated in accordance with the formulas described above. These costs should be treated as "costs borne by others" (see below).

2. *Equipment:* As noted earlier, it is most useful to consider costs of equipment in aggregate, rather than per unit, terms. For example, there may be a need to calculate the costs of equipping a send-site interactive video facility, a receive-site interactive video facility, or a computer lab (perhaps of various standard sizes used on the campus). The cost calculation is as follows:

[cost of the facility/years of useful life] x [hours used/hours of capacity]

Hours of use for computer facilities should be estimated on the basis of the number of hours (total for the courses) in which a class physically meets in such a facility (recognizing that this number may well be zero) plus the estimated number of hours a typical student would use the facility outside of formal class.

3. *Courseware/Software:* In the case of software/courseware, costs should only be included if the following situations apply:

- The material is expressly for the course for which cost calculations are being made. Thus, costs associated with acquiring general-purpose software, e.g., e-mail, word processing, spreadsheets, etc., would not be included, even if they are used regularly by students in the class.
- The expenditure covers a multi-year period. If costs are limited to year-to-year expenditures for licensing, the costs should be reflected under licenses in the Supplies and Services category.

In addition, these particular assets can be acquired in multiple ways, including purchase, lease, and local development. In instances where courseware/software is locally developed, an overall development cost should be calculated. This is only true, however, if the material was developed as part of a "project" that received a specific allocation of personnel, technical support, etc. If the material was developed without explicit recognition—no release time for faculty or assignment of time of graduate students, technicians, etc.—the developmental costs should be ignored. Where costs are identifiable, through purchase or local development, they should be assigned in accordance with the following algorithm:

$$\left[\frac{acquisition.cost}{yrs.of.useful.life} \right] \times \left[\frac{course.enrollment}{no.annual.users} \right]$$

For purposes of these calculations, and in the absence of more definitive institutional data, the convention of a useful life of four years should be assumed.

Costs of Underutilized Capacity: Course cost calculations as specified in the previous steps include costs for facilities and equipment for only those hours actually used for delivery of the course in question. If the facilities and equipment are fully used (or nearly so), this yields a result that is not misleading for decision-makers. However, if these resources are severely underused, the resulting course cost as calculated can provide decision-makers an incomplete (and understated) picture of the costs associated with alternative modes of delivery. The following two ways are suggested to address this potential problem:

- *Alternative 1: Calculate the Costs of Unused Capacity.* In this alternative, the costs of unused capacity are calculated and appended to the cost of delivery calculations as additional information to be considered in the decision-making process. The calculations are the same as those indicated in Step 4, #1 or #2, under "Capital Items," except that hours the facility is *not* used (hours of capacity minus total hours used) is substituted for hours used in the calculation.
- *Alternative 2: Distribute Total Costs Over Hours of Actual Use.* Another approach is to allocate the total costs of the resources to those courses (and other activities, if any) using them. In this instance, the right-hand component of the cost calculation would be altered to the following:

[hours used for course/total hours used]

The result would typically be an increase over the costs calculated in Step 4. Alternative 1 is probably more appropriate if full utilization can be reasonably assumed in the short run. If this assumption cannot logically be made, Alternative 2 is a more appropriate path to information useful in a decision-making context. The cost of unused capacity is appropriately calculated for on-campus classrooms as well as the more specialized facilities used for alternative modes of delivery.

The issue here is how useful actual data are for planning purposes. If the decision is to allocate all the costs of the media center to the single course that uses it, a mistake was probably made sometime in the past when it was decided to build the center (the implication is that another center is not needed). If a new facility is being planned, it will only be feasible at some reasonable level of use (and the implicit costs per course at that level of use). One implication is that a sound market analysis should underlie the original planning process. Another implication is that one should apply Alternative 1 calculations for data from recent start-ups that have not yet reached capacity but that have a good expectation of doing so in the near future (2-4 years).

Costs Borne by Others: In many instances, some of the costs associated with delivering a course are borne by parties other than the organization providing the instruction, as for example, in the following:

- A statewide agency may cover all communications expenditures without charging costs back to the provider.
- A "receive-site" organization may provide space and equipment free of charge.
- A vendor may provide courseware at no cost (or at a substantially reduced cost) in return for the provider serving as a beta test site for the product. In some instances, this arrangement is complicated by quid-pro-quo arrangements, e.g., a receive site provides space free in cases in which the sending institution pays for equipping the room. In such instances, it is suggested that the sending institution calculate the amortized cost of equipment and include this figure in its costs and that the rented (or amortized) cost of the "free" space be calculated as suggested above and treated as a cost borne by others.

These costs borne by others should not be included in the summary of the costs of delivering the course. However, it is recommended that the true costs of these free or reduced rate components be calculated according to the procedures identified above and recorded separately. This procedure will serve two purposes. First, it will provide decision-makers within the institution an indication of their "exposure," i.e., —the additional costs they would have to incur if the ground rules changed and they wished to continue with the activity. Second, providing estimates of the total cost, will aid comparisons in instances where the comparison provider is not receiving the benefits of reduced rates.

Step 5. Summary of Data and Calculation of Average Costs

Enter course information in Panel A of Table 11-C. Enter cost totals from Table 11-B in Panels B and C (course-related and enrollment-related costs will not be available for courses delivered via regular classroom instruction, and may not be available for mediated courses). Enter information on underused capacity and costs borne by others in Panel E. Panel D provides basic management information about average course costs. "Average cost per (student) enrollment and "average cost per SCU" (student credit unit) are the average cost data that have been used historically as cost indicators for classroom instruction.

If total course-related and enrollment-related costs are available, calculate "average course-related cost" and "average enrollment-related cost." Course-related costs correspond to "fixed costs," which are not sensitive to enrollment changes. Average course-related cost is an estimate of "average fixed cost" (the cost that declines as course enrollment grows). To the extent fixed costs constitute a substantial cost of the mediated course, the cost structure of the course is characterized by economies of scale. Enrollment-related costs correspond to "variable costs," which are sensitive to enrollment changes. Average

TABLE 11-C

COST DATA SUMMARY AND AVERAGE COST CALCULATIONS

Panel A Course Information

Course title, number and abbreviation, course units (semester or quarter)	e.g., Intermediate Microeconomic Theory, Econ 100, 3 units, semester
Year and term	e.g., fall 2000
Course delivery mode	e.g., 25% classroom lecture, 75% Internet
Course enrollment	e.g., 45
Course student credit units (SCU) (course units x enrollment)	e.g., 135 (=3x45)

Panel B Cost Data from Table 2

	Programs			
	Instruction	Acad. support	Stud. Serv.	Instit. support
Total direct costs				
Total course related direct costs				
Total enrollment related direct costs				

Panel C Totals from Panel B

Direct cost, all programs (sum of costs across programs)	Course related costs (sum across programs)	Enroll. related costs (sum across programs)

Panel D Average Costs Calculated from Panels A and C

Average cost/stud. enrollment	Avg. course related cost/stud. enrollment	Avg. enrollment related cost/stud. enrollment
Average cost/SCU	Avg. course related cost/SCU	Avg. enrollment related cost/SCU

Panel E Supplementary Cost Information

Estimated costs of unused or underutilized capacity from Step 4, "Costs of Underutilized Capacity"	
Estimated costs borne or contributed by others from Step 4, "Costs Borne by Others"	

enrollment-related cost is an estimate of "average variable cost," a proxy for incremental or marginal cost, the cost of adding an additional student to the course.

ENDNOTES

1. See, for example, A.W. (Tony) Bates, *Technology, Open Learning, and Distance Education*. London: Routledge, 1995; Greville Rumble, *The Costs and Economics of Open and Distance Learning*. London: Kogan Page, 1997; and Sir John S. Daniel, *Mega-Universities and Knowledge Media*. London: Kogan Page, 1996.

2. See the following studies:

a. Frank Jewett, "Courseware for Remedial Mathematics: A Case Study in the Benefits and Costs of the Mediated Learning System in the California State University."

b. ———, "Teaching College Literacy: A Case Study in the Benefits and Costs of *Daedalus* Courseware at Baruch College."

c. ———, "The Education Network of Maine: A Case Study in the Benefits and Costs of Instructional Television."

d. ———, "The Master's Degree in Social Work at Cleveland State University and the University of Akron: A Case Study of the Benefits and Costs of a Joint Degree Program Offered via Videoconferencing."

e. ———, "TELETECHNET—Old Dominion University and 'Two Plus Two' Programs at Community Colleges in Virginia: A Case Study in the Benefits and Costs of an Intercampus Instructional Television Network."

f. ———, "The Human Computer Interaction Certificate Program at Rensselaer Polytechnic Institute: A Case Study in the Benefits and Costs of a Joint Industry/University Designed Program Featuring Integrated Delivery Methods."

g. ———, "The WESTNET Program—SUNY Brockport and the SUNY Campuses in Western New York State: A Case Study in the Benefits and Costs of an Interactive Television Network."

h. ———, "Course Restructuring: A Case Study in the Benefits and Costs of Restructured Courses Following an Instructional Development Initiative at Virginia Polytechnic Institute and State University."

All case study reports were completed in 1998 and published by the CSU Chancellor's Office, Seal Beach, California. Jewett has also developed a simulation model (called BRIDGE) to compare the costs of expanding a campus using mediated instruction versus using classroom instruction. Copies of the case studies and the BRIDGE model are available at the benefit cost project Web site at <www.calstate.edu/special_projects/>.

3. Although capital costs are usually considered as "fixed," they can also represent direct costs of instruction. For classroom instruction, the room itself is a direct cost; for TV delivery, the studio and the cost of distributing the signal are direct costs; for online courses, the server is a direct cost.

Part 3

• • • • • • • • • • •

Caveats and Options

CHAPTER 12

Wide-Angle View of the Costs of Introducing New Technologies to the Instructional Program

Richard Pumerantz and Carol Frances

IDENTIFYING THE COSTS

New information technologies (IT) are sweeping over the traditional classroom model of teaching and learning that has characterized higher education for centuries. Comparisons of traditional face-to-face instruction with the innovative, computerized modes of delivery are encouraging educators everywhere to take a fresh look at the courses, the curriculum, and the instructional system. The arrival of IT is stimulating—even forcing—change, reform, and improvement in education. Good cost data are essential to the management of the process of changing from the old to the new technologies.

The first stage in the comparison of costs of different technologies is carefully documented in Chapter 11 by Dennis Jones and Frank Jewett. Their unit of analysis is the individual course, which is certainly the place to begin. If, however, management wishes to track and estimate the overall costs to the entire institution of the transition from the existing way of teaching to fully using the potential of the new information technologies, then a broader,wide-angle view of costs is helpful. The wide-angle view described in this chapter is, at this point, not rigorously developed and speculative, but it is offered as a next

Acknowledgments: We wish to acknowledge the insightful comments and helpful suggestions for improvements of Sara Lundquist, Keiko Khoo, Robert Risko, Nana Osei-Kofi, and Donna Standlea, members of the Claremont Graduate University seminar on the economics and finance of higher education. We are indebted to Frank Jewett, as a pioneer in the field, for generously sharing his wide knowledge of IT economics, and for his critical comments on earlier versions of this chapter.

step toward a more *dynamic* view of the costs of *changing* technologies, as well as toward more comprehensive, *static* comparisons of the costs of different technologies. The framework in Figure 12-1 constitutes a checklist of the types of activities that might be involved in a radical restructuring or re-engineering of the educational processes, and the concomitant re-organization of the educational institution; it will also serve as a reminder to recognize the associated costs.

Most fundamentally, the introduction of new IT could involve a reconsideration of the mission of a college or university, resulting in a decision to serve a new clientele, or attract students from a different geographic area, or to fundamentally revamp the academic program. New approaches to recruiting faculty and students may be required. Serving a new market will likely involve developing and testing new marketing strategies, which could be costly. Academic and financial planning and budgeting may need improvement.

A major commitment to introducing new information technologies will almost certainly require substantial funds. As a consequence, special efforts will be required to develop substantially more financial resources, by raising new funds in a capital campaign, or borrowing from quasi-endowments, or negotiating joint ventures with corporations providing the technology. It will take money to raise money.

In addition to the investment in facilities and equipment, an entire cadre of technical support people must be recruited or trained and positioned either centrally or distributed across campus to help faculty and students use the new information technology.

Intellectual property issues will have to be addressed, fair use policies will have to be developed—and funds budgeted for litigation. Faculty hiring, promotion, and tenure policies will have to be reviewed and adapted to the new technological era. Institutions will need to develop policies for faculty release time to implement IT approaches, and faculty workloads may need to be redefined to take into account the time involved in meeting students' rising expectations of continuous, direct contact with faculty via e-mail. Faculty and staff salary scales and benefits packages may need to be adapted to react to competition from the business world for technical professionals.

Vast investments will be necessary to redesign and restaff libraries to make full use of digital information resources. Bookstores will need to be reorganized and stocked differently.

The definition and measurement of academic quality may need to change, and time—which is costly—will need to be invested to develop new assessment policies and procedures. New diagnostic tools may be needed to help match teaching to students' preferred learning styles. Additional research may be required to learn more about the factors affecting students' satisfaction or

	Faculty / Staff Costs	Technology Costs	Other Costs

One-Tme Start-Up Costs

Re-examining and Updating the Mission / Strategic Plan
Analysis / decision to implement IT
Revising planning and budgeting processes

Management Re-organization

Marketing Program
Release-time of current faculty and staff
Recruiting of new faculty and staff

Securing Additional Funding
Current budget reallocations
Special development efforts to raise additional funds
Salary
Non-Salary

Negotiating Contract and Partnership Agreements

Professional Development
Faculty
Professional development
IT presentation skills development
IT support staff
Management briefing on IT potential

Educational Program Redesign
IT curriculum development
IT course development
IT materials development

Student Support Services
Purchase/lease/on-campus student access to hardware / software
Student training
Student financial aid / including IT costs in base budgets
Identify and develop responses to student needs
Undergraduate students
Graduate students
Disabled students

"WIDE ANGLE" FRAMEWORK FOR IDENTIFYING THE COSTS OF INTRODUCING NEW INSTRUCTIONAL TECHNOLOGIES

FIGURE 12-1

	Faculty / Staff Costs	Technology Costs	Other Costs

Human Resources Management
Review old and adopt new hiring, promotion,
  and tenure policies and procedures
Review and re-negotiate collective bargaining agreements
Review faculty work-load, release-time, and sabbatical policies
Develop and implement incentive policies to encourage
  appropriate utilization of IT

Adapting and Expanding Physical Infrastructure
Physical plant
  Capital investment
  Purchasing / processing
  Borrowing / debt service
  Space rental

Equipment
  Computer equipment - administrative and academic
  Telecom line installation charges
  Video conference equipment
    Purchase / lease

Providing On-Line Access to IT in Dormitories
and Student Centers

IT Property Management
  Set up inventory system by remaining useful life
  Set-up cycle for refreshing and/or disposing of equipment
  Negotiate insurance coverage
  Establish stronger security policies and procedures

Re-structuring of Library Operations
  On-line access to books / periodicals / abstracts / data bases
  On-line research capabilities
  Training of library technical support staff

Re-configuration of the Bookstore
  Negotiation of re-seller contracts
  Inventories of hardware / software
  Training of technical support staff
  Offering classes to new purchasers of computer hardware/software

Legal Costs
  Establishing intellectual property rights, policies, and procedures
  Protecting the intellectual property of institution, faculty, and students
  Establishing and implementing fair-use policies
  Setting up profit-oriented e-commerce ventures
  Litigation

"WIDE ANGLE" FRAMEWORK FOR IDENTIFYING THE COSTS OF INTRODUCING NEW
INSTRUCTIONAL TECHNOLOGIES

FIGURE 12-1 (continued)

	Faculty / Staff Costs	Technology Costs	Other Costs
	_____	_____	_____

Ongoing or Recurring Costs

Management
Overhead - General
Overhead - IT

Instructional Costs
Defining, measuring, controlling academic quality
Curriculum development
Course development
  Initial design
  Up-date and re-design
Development of course web-site
Development of course learning materials
Instruction
  Salary and fringe benefits
    Full-time
    Part-time
Faculty / teaching assistant / student interaction / contact hours
  In class
  Outside of class
    Responding to students' questions and comments
    Tutoring
    Advising
Evaluating academic performance
Teaching supplies
Office supplies, printing, copying, postage

Faculty / Teaching Assistant Support Costs
Release-time for IT implementation
Travel / conference fees to maintain / upgrade competencies

Assessment of Student Progress
  Development of diagnostic assessments / tests
  Administration of diagnostic assessments / tests
  Report results
  Interacting with students
  Feedback into course design

Student Support Services
Student advising
Student tutoring
Student retention programs
Development of opportunities for student work experience
Job placement of graduates

Equipment Usage
Computer usage / maintenance / repair
Telecom usage / maintenance / repair

"WIDE ANGLE" FRAMEWORK FOR IDENTIFYING THE COSTS OF INTRODUCING NEW
INSTRUCTIONAL TECHNOLOGIES

FIGURE 12-1 (continued)

	Faculty / Staff Costs	Technology Costs	Other Costs
Financial Accounting / Auditing of Costs			
Departmental and Funded Research to Improve Teaching and Learning Using IT			
Technological Forecasting / Environmental Scanning			
Total Costs			

Potential IT Benefits
  Enhanced student learning experiences
  Additional students served
  Educational quality enhancement
  Cost savings / revenue enhancements

Opportunity Costs
  Non-IT projects not launched
  Staff not hired
  Salary and fringe benefit increases not provided
  Students not served

Note: Costs intended to be one-time costs often become recurring costs. This format can be used to collect information in dollars or percentages; on a per student or per faculty member basis; or to compare conditions before and after introducing IT.

"WIDE ANGLE" FRAMEWORK FOR IDENTIFYING THE COSTS OF INTRODUCING NEW INSTRUCTIONAL TECHNOLOGIES

FIGURE 12-1 (continued)

dissatisfaction with IT classes, and how to restore to IT classes the aspects which students value in the face-to-face interactions in effective classrooms.

The framework, or checklist, displayed in Figure 12-1 gives an initial impression of the depth and breadth of change that can take place in the course of fully incorporating IT into the educational processes, and the activities that will consume resources in the course of managing the technological change. These costs may be characterized as the costs of change, not the costs of IT, but they nevertheless require resources.

DATA ON THE COST OF INTRODUCING NEW INFORMATION TECHNOLOGIES

Information on the costs to institutions of changing from classroom technology to new digital technologies is needed not only to decide which technology to use, but also to manage the overall process of change. However, such cost data are rare because they are difficult to generate. Standard accounting practices were not originally developed to collect educational cost data by type of technology used. Some form of activity-based cost (ABC) accounting is more helpful.

The framework shown in Figure 12-1 is a generic, first-cut—but quite comprehensive—ABC checklist for generating comprehensive data on the costs of introducing new technology. This framework differs from that in Chapter 11 in several ways. First, the unit of analysis is an entire two-year program involving about 20 courses, not just one course. The course cost comparison includes only operating costs while the program cost comparison attempts to include more of the transformational costs of change. Some overhead costs are also included, which involved selecting cost drivers and allocating these overhead costs to particular instructional activities. If a single institution is comparing costs of different technologies, and allocation of overhead would essentially increase the costs of all the different technologies in about the same way, then management decisions would not be affected by ignoring the overhead costs. If, however, the cost comparisons are across institutions, and some institutions have much greater overhead than others—which may not always be justifiable—then the benchmarks should come closer to full costs, including overhead, as a better basis on which to make management decisions.

The course cost collection format facilitates making a useful analytic distinction between costs that are related to the course and *do not* vary with enrollment, and costs that *do* vary with enrollment. This information is essential in examining economies of scale and deciding which technology is less costly depending on the numbers of students enrolled. This is not, however, the same as identifying the marginal costs of a particular technology. If an institution offers a course in a traditional classroom and then televises the course for viewing at another site, the cost of the television is a marginal cost, although it does not vary with the number of students enrolled at the remote site.

COST COMPARISONS

Working with Western University of Health Sciences in Pomona, California, we adapted the wide-angle framework to compare the actual, documented costs of one form of IT, interactive tele-video or ITV, with the costs of traditional classroom teaching. We used this framework to compare the costs of a physician-assistant certificate program that was delivered simultaneously via a traditional classroom on the Pomona campus and to a remote classroom site in Chico. The Chico site was designed to respond to growing health workforce needs in rural communities. Expanding the program to a rural educational setting had been determined by the program director and the dean of the college to be the best way to encourage health professionals to return, after graduation, to practice in these underserved regions.

The type of IT used, interactive tele-video or ITV distance education, was purposefully selected to meet the accreditation requirement of providing substantially the same educational process and clinical opportunities for each group. Note that to meet the current accreditation standards, this physician-assistant program was required to be delivered to students at both sites in classrooms.

Students with similar characteristics, drawn from the same applicant pool, were offered a faculty-based classroom in southern California or an ITV-based classroom in northern California. The classroom lectures were delivered via video conferencing technology. The students in both groups simultaneously heard the same lecture and could interact with the professors before, during, and after the lecture.

The process of developing the comparative cost data is described here in some detail to indicate how much work is involved and to lend credibility to the results. Well over 100 hours of staff time were involved in interviewing the chief financial officer, treasurer, chief information officer, academic dean, program director, faculty, and staff to identify activities connected with the program and estimate the direct time and expense involved. In addition, great care was used to develop and apply appropriate cost drivers to allocate indirect, or overhead costs, to the relevant site. Depending on the specific cost item, the drivers considered included staff head count, staff time, student head count, or square footage of facilities.

This cost study included only the current operating costs. It did not include the considerable capital costs of renovating facilities or installing the video-conferencing capacity. The fundamental decision rule was to allocate *all* basic costs to the Pomona classroom site because these costs would be incurred whether or not there was a remote Chico classroom site, and to allocate only marginal costs to the remote site.

Approximately 175 budget line items were examined in eight budget units for each of three semesters for a total of close to 525 separate line items. Cost data were developed independently for the three semesters and averaged, because of the variation in outlays, over the three semesters in 1998-1999.

The results of the comprehensive, detailed cost comparison are presented in Table 12-A, below. As shown, the marginal operating costs of the remote site were close to the full operating costs of the main site. On a per-student basis, the costs of the remote ITV site were greater than the costs of the main traditional classroom site simply because there were fewer students at the remote site.

In the program we studied, the ITV-based classroom had fewer students (76) than the faculty-based classroom (120). Because the average per student cost of the programs depends to such a great extent on the numbers of students enrolled, the IT-based classroom with fewer students was more expensive per student than the faculty-based classroom, even though we counted only the marginal costs of the ITV-based classroom.

Thus, the scale of the operations is critical to the cost comparisons. For future planning purposes, the feasibility of achieving the required scale is thus also a critical consideration. Reaching the required number of students may involve large marketing expenses that would also have to be factored into the cost comparisons.

In making these cost comparisons, we uncovered several additional issues that require further exploration. First, what is the appropriate allocation of direct operating and overhead costs between the two groups? In this typical case, distance education lectures could not have existed without the faculty-based classroom lectures to televise. Counting all the costs toward the faculty-based classroom overstates the cost differential. Counting only the marginal costs of serving the IT-based students probably understates the cost differential. Conservatively, we chose to include only the marginal costs of the IT-based classroom in making our cost comparisons.

At both sites, the annual tuition was $12,500 (exclusive of fees), which meant that both the main and the remote programs were running an excess of revenue over expenses. Thus, the decision rule for using IT is not necessarily to employ it only beyond the cross-over point at which it costs less than traditional classroom technology. IT might also be used to enhance educational quality or broaden access as long as revenues cover expenses, even if IT at a particular scale below the cross-over point costs more than traditional classrooms.

Our study confirmed the larger per-student costs created by the non-economies of scale. To serve the additional students, the northern California group required an administrative structure that duplicated that of the southern California group. Additionally, more servers and high-speed data lines were needed, as well as larger service and maintenance contracts, and more software licensing agreements. The overall university IT capacity required added infrastructure, including installation of fiber optics and networks systems.

Faculty professional development was needed, along with extra time to redesign/redevelop the courses and curriculum. Achieving the potential of IT required adoption of new teaching styles. Training was also needed for students and the IT staff. Access to the instructor did improve via e-mail, increasing the educational interactions for those students who may not previously have been able to speak with the instructor. However, the impact on the instructor's time was enormous, which meant less time was spent on research/scholarly activity.

TABLE 12-A

Comparative Physician Assistant Program Costs

Traditional Classroom-Main Site (120 students)	FY 1998	% of Total
Salary and Fringe Benefits (including part-time and temporary)	$ 471,449	53.86%
Continuing Education and Training (all staff and faculty)	9,414	1.08%
Travel (administrative only)	7,750	0.89%
Stockroom, Office Supplies and General Maintenance	4,437	0.51%
Computer Equipment–administrative use only	2,400	0.27%
Xerox, Postage, and Printing	7,644	0.87%
Teaching Supplies	2,311	0.26%
Clinical Education Site Development and Faculty Recruitment	8,965	1.02%
Telephone	10,635	1.22%
Overhead–general administrative (main campus only)	95,366	10.90%
Overhead–IT (salaries, fringes, operationalized expenses and lab)	93,150	10.64%
Debt Service (main campus only)	161,728	18.48%
Total	**$ 875,250**	
Cost per student	**$ 7,294**	

Remote Interactive TV Site (76 students)	FY 1998	% of Total
Salary and Fringe Benefits (including part-time and temporary)	$ 471,950	58.07%
Student Services (non-salary)	872	0.11%
Continuing Education and Training (all staff and faculty)	4,602	0.57%
Travel	51,232	6.30%
Advancement Expenses (non-salary)	21,355	2.63%
Stockroom, Office Supplies, and General Maintenance	15,838	1.95%
Computer Equipment – administrative use only	3,600	0.44%
Xerox, Postage, and Printing (primarily educational)	26,617	3.27%
Teaching Supplies	5,786	0.71%
Clinical Education Site Development and Faculty Recruitment	7,029	0.86%
Rental Expense (building was leased, not owned)	72,259	8.89%
Multimedia Personnel (salaries and fringes)	2,400	0.30%
Telecom Usage and Line Charges	23,259	2.86%
Video Conferencing Equipment (lease and service contract)	11,000	1.35%
Telephone	12,927	1.59%
Overhead–IT (salaries, fringes, operationalized expenses and lab)	62,100	7.64%
Outside Contracts and Agreements (including library and legal)	19,962	2.46%
Total	**$ 812,789**	
Cost per student	**$ 10,695**	

The second issue is that the full costs of instruction include not only the initial costs but also the costs over time. The recurring costs of the new IT are much greater than the recurring costs of traditional classroom teaching. IT costs recur because even the best equipment requires maintenance, repairs, and replacement. IT infrastructure, however, hardly ever requires replacement because it has worn out or failed. Replacement is required due to the stunning, accelerating pace of technological innovations. The upward spiral of technological capability is compounded by "quality" competition among educational institutions responding to students' continually rising expectations that they will have access to "state of the art" technology.

Third, even when IT is scaleable, the marginal costs cannot be fairly represented by a smooth straight line sloping slightly upward. The marginal costs actually come closer to a stair-step function with fairly steep steps representing additional infrastructure capacity and technological advances.

Fourth, the expectation of lower costs for IT depends essentially on the economics of scale. However, we have all heard that faculty-student interaction via e-mail can become overwhelming with large numbers of students, and faculty insist that teaching would be more effective with fewer students. A major component of cost-effective IT is thus organization of communication and time-management skills.

Additionally, spreading the higher initial capital costs of IT over time is often difficult because of the technological advances that require expensive upgrades and replacements of capacity. It is also difficult because the accessibility to new information created by IT results in much more rapid outdating of the educational content of many courses that then require renewing much sooner. Thus, the potential economies of scale and lower costs of IT may often be more hoped for than actually realized.

The fifth issue relates to the other costs, which are generally not included in cost accounts. Students may have direct costs arising from required purchases of hardware and software, as well as academic computing fees. There are also indirect costs to the students and the institutions. From our survey, we learned that the students receiving their instruction via IT were much less satisfied, in this particular case, with their experience. A high correlation exists between student satisfaction in their program and their future involvement with their institutions. Dissatisfied students are not as likely to become generous donors. The present value of lost future support would probably result in a much higher long-term cost of IT than anyone originally contemplated. Without question, the most widely recognized reason a donor will provide major support for an organization is the relationship(s) developed with the people. People give primarily to people. This is not to say that relationships could not be developed via technology, nor is it to contend that relationships are not developed after graduation. It is rather to point out that less satisfied alumni are less likely to stay involved and be agreeable to cultivation. This group is not likely to provide significant future financial support.

Finally, the largest of all the costs of IT may be the opportunity costs, which are generally unrecognized in conventional cost comparisons. Educational institutions, with limited budgets, which are spending money on IT, are not spending on other things, in particular, on faculty and faculty development. IT spending appears to most heavily impact faculty salaries, and possibly the number of faculty hired. A disaffected faculty, with technophiles pitted against technophobes, may result in considerable unforeseen costs. The allocation of financial resources that is, or could be construed as, not aligned with the institution's mission could result in a loss of faith by the constituencies.

The costs, and benefits, of adopting new instructional technology should be evaluated not only in the short run but also in the long run. If, in the long run, the new instructional technology results in significant increases in teaching and learning productivity, then additional resources could be made available to increase faculty salaries and invest in quality improvements.

MAKING TRADE-OFFS BETWEEN FACULTY AND IT

Comparing the results of the surveys of students at the main and the remote sites indicated that face-to-face interaction with the faculty appeared to be a significant factor in the students' satisfaction with their educational experiences. IT has great potential to enhance education, but over-reliance on IT results in student dissatisfaction. Thus, a combination of face-to-face interaction and IT offers the greatest potential for student learning and satisfaction.

Conventional economic models, developed simply to compare the costs of an all-classroom delivery with an all-IT delivery at different scales of operation, provide no effective means for analyzing the decision process for achieving the optimal mix of technologies. The conventional economic model has no way to examine the trade-offs between direct human interaction and the electronic instructional technology to enhance learning and student satisfaction.

A second generation economic model is needed to help answer the key question: What is the appropriate allocation of resources between faculty and technology? This question is central to both annual budgeting and to the strategic planning that will help shape the future of college education.

CONCLUDING QUESTIONS

Questions About Using the Conventional Economic Model for Making IT Decisions

IT is used in higher education for the following three purposes:

1. To expand access

2. To enhance quality
3. To cut costs

The conventional economic model used to illustrate the cross-over point at which IT costs less per student than traditional classrooms is not adequate for making critical decisions about when to use IT.

1. When IT is used to expand access, particularly when distance education using IT is the only option because student presence in the classroom is not an option, the decision to use IT is not based on the finding that IT costs less than conventional classrooms beyond some scale of operation. The decision is based instead on a determination that IT costs less than the *revenues* available to pay for it—or that for educational reasons, it is worthy of subsidy.
2. When IT is used to enhance the quality of education, whether the teaching is on-site or at a distance, the decision is not to use the conventional modes of delivery *or* IT, but what is the most effective *combination* of human and technological resources. For this decision, a model that helps to make trade-offs to arrive at the most effective combination of resources is more useful than the conventional economic model, which treats the quality of education as an assumption, or an exogenous variable determined outside the model.
3. When IT is used to cut costs, the conventional economic model is useful in understanding, conceptually, the way in which economies of scale could produce lower costs. However, to use the conventional economic model to make actual decisions, it is necessary, first, to determine the actual scale and cross-over point (measured by the numbers of students served) at which delivery becomes less costly using IT than traditional classrooms, and second, to consider the feasibility and costs, both financial and educational, of achieving that scale.

Furthermore, because the use of IT to cut costs is done primarily by substituting technology for faculty, it is also necessary, in a straightforward way, to identify how the educational process must be unbundled and restructured. Thus, to use the economic model to make actual decisions about how to cut costs using IT, it is necessary also to identify the types of education—by field, by level, or by type of student—where the substitution of IT for faculty is a positive option.

Questions to Address as We Go Forward

As leaders and policy makers in higher education, we are faced with many opportunities, questions, and challenging decisions respecting the use of technology in higher education. Pressing questions arise in three domains— the educational, the financial, and the managerial.

Educational Questions: Large numbers of studies conclude that there are "no significant differences" in learning outcomes and student satisfaction between traditional and IT educational experiences. On the other hand, some more recent studies come to different conclusions, finding that student dissatisfaction is specifically related to lack of face-to-face, human interaction. (See Chapter 7 by James Caplan.) This leads to two fundamental questions: What are the essential elements of effective face-to-face teaching that students value? and Is it possible to put these elements back into the IT teaching and learning experience?

Financial Questions: We must answer questions about resource allocations to assure that they will have long- as well as short-term benefits. The vast majority of chief financial officers, deans, and department chairs are overspending their IT budgets—and find that, so far, there are no significant gains in educational productivity. In fact, IT is now taking much more administrative and faculty time. Faculty are required to spend more time on curriculum development and new course preparations. Faculty must take time to learn how to use the new technology and deal with the frustrations of their own and their students' technical problems. Faculty must devote significantly more time to interacting with students via e-mail. As a consequence, the real wage per hour of faculty time has actually gone down over the past several years.

One final, overarching financial question for colleges and universities is therefore: Where will the money come from to buy more information technology? Given the current budget constraints, increasing expenditures for IT will most likely come out of faculty salaries and fringe benefits. This will manifest itself in smaller salary increases and the filling of vacated tenured faculty positions with adjunct or non-tenure track faculty.

Many decisions to buy IT are the result of determination by colleges and universities to meet or beat competition in education markets and to respond to students' expectations, or demands, for access to state-of-the art technology. The idea that the faculty are the institutions' most valuable asset has faded. Somehow, without our noticing, it seems that microchips have become more valuable than the intellect of our faculties and the richness of our curricula. The consequence, seen on many campuses, is the great consternation of the faculty, and a renewed interest in collective bargaining.

Managerial Questions: We must understand that just because we can do something, does not mean we should do it. Translated to higher education, this means that just because we can use technology, does not mean we should. The basic managerial question is, How can we best integrate technology into the educational process? Or, much more fundamentally, How can the availability of technology be used to cause a complete rethinking of educational processes, both traditional and innovative?

Any new IT program should be given a reasonable amount of time to prove its efficacy and thereby justify its existence. To make informed decisions, however, we must weigh all the costs that may directly, or indirectly, affect our institutions, our faculty, our students, and our constituencies.

Furthermore, if an institution aspires to lead in new directions, and to promote innovative uses of new instructional technologies, its administrative and educational leaders must also be willing to acknowledge when the results do not meet their expectations. And they must be able and willing to take appropriate actions. These actions may range from minor redesign of the program, to cutting losses and closing the program. It is not legitimate to continue a sub-par IT endeavor that is not fulfilling the institution's mission, especially if the mission emphasizes excellence of programs as an educational goal.

We have promised to deliver both a quality education to the student and a well-educated person to our communities. Both public and private, institutional leaders also have a fiduciary responsibility to deliver the education in a cost-effective manner without sacrificing quality.

Therefore, it is imperative that we as educators take the time to more fullyunderstand the costs and benefits of using IT. Educators are all charged with the duty of questioning decisions—and, most important, we must question our own decisions relating to IT. We should endeavor to make decisions that are aligned with our respective missions, and in the best interests of our students, our constituencies, and our communities, but mostly our students.

CHAPTER 13

From Managing Expenditures to Managing Costs

Strategic Management for Information Technology

George Kaludis and Glen Stine

INTRODUCTION

It has been two decades since Howard Bowen[1] initially posited the first law of higher education financial management: "Raise all the money you can; and spend all the money that you raise." In the intervening period, institutions of higher education have been generally loathe to defy *Bowen's Law* and have sought to develop better processes for controlling expenditures (often enabled by new technologies) rather than attempting to control *actual costs*. Perhaps nowhere has this approach been more perfectly operationalized than in campus budgeting for information technology (IT), whether for instruction or other purposes (see Chapter 3, "What Is Information Technology in Higher Education" and Chapter 6 "Understanding the COSTS of Information Technology (IT) Support Services in Higher Education"). Yet institutions now face a world where policymakers, trustees, and students are applying increasing pressure to hold the line on costs.[2] More immediate for many institutions, new competitors for students, including for-profit providers, and other market forces may force reductions in price for certain programs or services, requiring institutions to change their cost structures to remain competitive.

In this context, it is critical to draw the distinction between the *management of expenditures* and the *management of costs*. For the most part, colleges and universities have managed expenditures through budgeting and other fiscal controls like procurement procedures within the institution. Managing costs, however, encompasses broader issues like depreciation, assets and liabilities, and activity measurements and opportunity costs. Strategic management of costs may require analysis of economies of scale, return on investment measurement, and scalability of the technology being implemented.

If one assumes that personal computers and the Internet are transformational, even "disruptive" technologies, then, for many institutions, a substantial part of the technology infrastructure has become a "utility" much like electricity and the heating plant, some portion of which can be capitalized while others are an ongoing operating expense. These infrastructure costs include the development of campus networks and the provision of minimally configured personal computers, network connections, and e-mail technology with appropriate network servers. For some institutions, the utility infrastructure will include the provision of a purchased or licensed platform through which to offer Web-based courseware. These utilities are generally "managed" through direct subsidy of the departmental budget or through some charge-back/cost recovery mechanism. As a utility type of expense, management of the costs will depend heavily on institutional policy and plans for provision and expansion of the utility, and will be partly driven by other issues like the needs of administration and institutional economic factors like indirect cost recovery and research funding. That is, does the method of charging for the infrastructure allow for the recovery of the expenditure through either direct charges to grants and contracts or by applying those expenditures to the institution's indirect cost rate?

The basic approach to controlling costs is to *limit access to the utility*; and when access control is not feasible or functional, institutions must find ways to absorb the expansion costs. The relatively unplanned and non-integrated set of decisions to develop the infrastructure means it occurs without substitution for other areas of expense. Over time, the use of PCs has changed the way most faculty and other staff conduct their business and may have led to cost substitution, but few institutions were either able to recapture the savings or to plan systematic reinvestment. An example of the change in the way work is conducted can be seen in the fact that faculty and staff now produce finished papers rather than using secretaries to meet these needs. In the main, this change in work has not been recaptured by a systematic budgetary approach.

The following three basic and unavoidable principles apply when managing the cost of information technology:

1. The uses of instructional technologies will only increase costs of instruction when that technology is used to supplement existing activities or be an add-on to current courses.
2. The cost of instructional technology must be measured as part of a whole process or activity, not as a stand-alone cost. That is, the development and use of instructional technologies will inevitably require new expendi-

tures to acquire those technologies; cost savings, if any, must come in the application of the technology to other activities associated with the use of IT, e.g., course delivery costs.

3. Instructional technology works well for certain activities, but cannot readily be used for other activities, no matter what costs are incurred. For example, instructional technology generally works well for large courses with multiple sections. It works less well where interaction in class is essential to achieve the course purposes.

Each of these principles challenges current management thinking and the state of current management practice at most colleges and universities. We treat each of the principles and the management challenges it poses below.

THE CHALLENGES TO MANAGEMENT

Data from the Campus Computing Survey (see Chapter 3) show that most campuses are employing information technology in the instructional program to supplement and enhance traditional course offerings. This strategy allows institutions to use traditional faculty and department structures as the primary mode of operations. Costs are not likely to be the primary consideration and rates of expenditures will be based on the availability of the support infrastructure and marginal allocations of funding through regular budget processes. More faculty are interested in learning to develop information technology applications for part or all of their courses, and institutions are likely to be limited by the availability of technical talent to support both the needed technology infrastructure and the faculty support functions. This situation will limit institutional expenditures, but may not actually manage costs. The approach, however, will limit institutional goals to what Dr. William H. Graves, the president of Eduprise.com, calls "random acts of progress" which he distinguishes from "global progress."[3]

Under this strategy or scenario, the task of management is essentially to manage the expenditures of the utility, which now includes course development support and new instructional support functions. Costs are high because expenditure management is the resource allocation tool. Many new kinds of *proactive* management decisions may more effectively manage costs. What and how many courseware systems will be licensed? Will the institution do its own Web hosting or purchase the service? How will student enrollment transactions be handled within the technology-enhanced courses? How will faculty support functions be developed and managed? Issues may arise concerning faculty seeking significant support or even supplemental salary for course development, intellectual property ownership and royalties owed, and responses to individual faculty initiatives to develop distance course offerings.

Typically, these questions will be handled within the traditional decision and resource allocation process of the institution. The overall result is likely to be high cost and low impact, with incremental expenditures and incremental unplanned progress. Lots of different "experiments" will occur, driven by individual faculty interest but with little thought to issues of replication and scalability of the experiment. Institutions are attempting to build in technology fees to pay for the infrastructure and technology course fees to pay for the added expenditures of delivery.

Institutions have faced similar situations in the implementation of Enterprise Resource Planning (ERP) client-server software systems for administration.[4] The expenditure for the systems and their implementation usually is in the millions of dollars and the level of technology support to maintain them and install frequent upgrades essential for the long-term maintenance of the systems is usually significantly higher than for existing fully depreciated legacy systems.[5] (The Y2K problem highlighted some of the hidden costs of legacy systems that are not accounted for by traditional expenditure control processes.)

Institutions choosing to implement new ERP systems *with the same administrative and management procedures* were then faced with extraordinary expenditures for changing the systems and their implementation to handle the old processes and higher costs for maintenance and renewal. Institutions willing to dramatically redesign their administrative transactions processes and activities to take advantage of the ERP systems' power often lowered their overall cost of a transaction. They also created significant new management opportunities to take advantage of, for example, e-commerce, such as the availability of Web-based procurement systems linking the institutional customer directly to a vendor of a needed product or service. The costs were lowered by reducing redundant control steps, multiple points of data entry and by using technology to handle the repetitive transactions and reducing the needed "shadow systems" to capture data.[6] Impact on both the new process and the administrative culture of the institution was high and the initial expenditures for implementing the process changes were high. Costs had to be considered across the whole process and, to be worthwhile, the process change had to yield substantial cost and time savings. The basic question became, how does the institution produce the maximum rate of return on its investment in the new ERP system, given that the investment is essential?

There are a number of clear parallels to the case of managing the costs of instructional applications of information technology. Institutions tied to traditional time issues (e.g., semesters), customized course and program offerings, a "not made here" approach and traditional cost measures (expenditures per student) will neither manage costs nor take advantage of high return on investment opportunities. Institutions allowing "producers" rather than "customers" to determine programming, particularly within the distance and off-campus learning program, will not be able to manage costs. Institutions that do not seek to deal with economies-of-scale issues and build scaleable, replicable technology uses will find escalating costs. Institutions that are not able to deal with issues like the continuing debate over the ownership of intellectual property for courses and courseware will be left with high costs and low returns on investment.

Particularly when dealing with Internet delivery issues, institutions must understand that the new customers for purchasing products and services using the Web are looking for "deep markdowns, razor thin margins and the commoditization of goods and services."[7] By being customer and market focused, institutions can avoid courses or curricula that have high costs that too few customers are willing to purchase. For example, a course that costs $100,000 to develop and can only be delivered to an average of 20 students once a year has a much higher cost than the same expenditure of $100,000 for a course delivered five times a year to an average group of 200 students.

Information technology can effectively handle certain approaches to courses, classes, and course delivery and potentially reduce, and certainly allow for, the management of costs. While potential savings can be realized from reductions in the need for new class space by allowing a portion of a course to be taught asynchronously and in virtual form, the more important management of costs will be done understanding the issues of scaleability and replication. In one way or another, about 25 courses constitute over one-third of all course credits delivered to undergraduates at colleges and universities in the U.S. The sheer volume of these courses, and, perhaps, of the next 25 largest courses, makes them suitable subjects for managing IT costs with high educational impact. Distance and off-campus learning opportunities are clear candidates to pro-duce courses and, potentially, curricula where costs are managed. Courses and programs offered on-campus to few students are unlikely to be attractive to off-campus students either and will not meet acceptable management criteria for scalability and replication. Off-campus courses offered or facilitated by infor-mation technology with standard time and instructional practices are unlikely to achieve the essential economies of scale and to meet scalability standards to "manage costs."

For a few wealthy institutions that desire to be on the "bleeding edge" in information technologies, these issues and principles will not matter because maximum return is achieved by being out ahead of others and defining a new institutional competitive niche. Most other institutions need management strategies to deal with these cost issues or should attempt to at least control the resources allocated to information technology, so that small decisions do not inadvertently and dramatically increase long-term costs.

COMPREHENSIVE ENTERPRISE PLANNING (CEP): A STRATEGY FOR MANAGING ENTERPRISE, INVESTMENTS, AND MISSIONS

The costs of information technology can only be *managed* to the extent that an institution understands its technology-enabled educational objectives and places them in the context of overall institutional mission. Information technology-enabled improvements are potentially available at many levels and parts of the institution. Some colleges and universities, however, will be neither willing nor able to achieve the fundamental shifts in thinking necessary to manage the cost of information technology. Many do not have an integrated, purposeful plan for applying information technology to new delivery systems and new customer markets. They will treat such efforts through separate organization, using separate faculty policies and approaches and generating separate revenue streams and investment decisions. Traditional students may or may not be included in any redesign of the learning delivery process. Some institutions have made and must continue to make their reputation on course delivery mechanisms that do not allow economies of scale essential to manage technology costs. Further, the introduction of certain technologies creates significant links and ramifications to and with other administrative systems, resource planning and allocation policy, libraries, student services activities, alumni management, and degree and course certification. Without critical enterprise-wide thinking and strategic agenda setting, the costs of instructional technology are essentially an unmanageable process. We have labeled the process *Comprehensive Enterprise Planning (CEP)*.

The CEP planning model identifies the following five critical areas of concern for every institution:

1. What are the key characteristics of the institutions as they relate to the use of instructional and other technologies?

2. What is the institution's current and desired future market position in terms of instructional applications of information technology? Going into distance learning, for example, on a small scale will be extremely costly because shared technologies and overhead costs cannot be leveraged.

3. How ready is the campus in terms of the physical, policy, and management infrastructure to apply information technology to the instructional program? Campus attitudes are also part of this question.

4. Is the institution ready to deal with management issues like activity-based costing, multi-year capitalization of losses, and a broader view of strategic asset management?

5. What are the critical determinants for the institution's reputation and current market position?

A critical mission element to consider is what portion of an institution's mission includes services to non-traditional students. For the most part, this means working students, older students, and students for whom convenience and price are primary considerations. The higher the mission importance of these students, the less likely traditional delivery systems are going to work in the future and the greater potential for instructional applications of information technology. A second mission element to consider might be the role research, particularly research in the use of information technology, plays at the institution. A few institutions will play leading roles in the development and implementation of instructional applications of IT as a spin-off of their research roles. Current institutional economics should also contribute to the analysis. Small institutions may have to join together or make greater use of outsourcing services than institutions that can absorb short-term investment costs within their existing revenue streams. Institutions with large numbers of high enrollment introductory classes and sections have significantly greater use of technology opportunities than institutions that limit class size.

Institution-wide goals for the instructional use of information technologies need to serve as a benchmark against which to test plans and activities. For example, an institution that seeks to develop new and expanded markets using technology needs to act considerably different from an institution that plans to develop, protect, and perhaps expand on-campus or existing continuing education markets. Even within on-campus markets, institutions having enrollments of traditional undergraduate students are likely to need to invest differently from institutions with large non-traditional or graduate enrollments. Finally, technologies can be fully developed by the focal institution or can be used only after a fully tested purchasable product is available. Institutions will face different "management of cost" issues by deciding where they want to fit on a continuum from "bleeding edge" to "total non-participant" in the instructional applications of information technologies. Even within the distance learning arena, institutions can be content producers, course distributors, learning support centers, or course and degree providers, depending on their enterprise strategy.

The desire, even with much of the technology infrastructure in place, may not be enough to allow an institution to become a major competitive force in distance learning. In a long prospectus touting e-knowledge businesses using the Internet to deliver services as a fundamental and major opportunity for investors, Wit Capital Corporation provides the following admonitions about what *value* will require in the market:

1. The focus on "Value Added" content, delivery, or services to sustain a competitive advantage.

2. The use of brand and reputation not just for narrow audiences, but for all that must evaluate the service (including students, employers, parents and businesses who might want to purchase services). Since location will be less important, establishing reputation will depend on type, level, quality, and price of services, not faculty reputation.
3. The development and maintenance of a strong management team, management processes, and management action that can move quickly and decisively to have a winning approach.
4. First movers have advantages, but these advantages are based on quality relationships, particularly corporate and strategic alliance relationships. Few companies (or institutions) will be able to provide a comprehensive set of services.

Wit Capital indicates that traditional higher education currently offers weak competition to emerging for-profit providers in the major growth of e-knowledge commerce because of higher education's inability to leverage capital and confront these issues.[8]

Alternatively, focusing on on-campus uses of IT, Carol A. Twigg identifies the following eight criteria against which an institution can assess its own readiness to reduce costs and enrich learning through information technology:

1. The institution must want to reduce costs and increase academic productivity.
2. The institution must view technology as a way to achieve strategic academic goals rather than as a general resource for all faculty and for all courses.
3. The institution's goal must be to integrate computing into the campus culture.
4. The institution must have a mature information technology organization(s) to support faculty integration of technology into courses or it must contract with external providers to offer such support.
5. A substantial number of the institution's faculty members must have an understanding of and some experience with integrating elements of computer-based instruction into existing courses.
6. The institution must have a demonstrated commitment to learner-centered education.
7. The institution must have established ways to assess and provide learner readiness to engage in IT-based courses.
8. The institution must recognize that large-scale course redesign using information technology involves a partnership among faculty, IT staff, and administrators in both planning and execution.[9]

Conditions and issues such as the ownership of course materials, the role of non-faculty in course delivery, and faculty compensation management must be addressed by most institutions to successfully manage the enterprise and associated costs.

ANALYZING RETURN ON INVESTMENT AND STRATEGIC ASSET MANAGEMENT

Because the instructional applications of IT will inevitably require the expenditure of funds, analysis of the return on the investment (ROI) and the use of strategic asset management provide strategies for cost management. ROI, while usually seen in strictly quantitative or financial terms, can use qualitative criteria as well. That is, by measuring the progress an investment returns against a set of stated goals, the ROI can be compared against other investments that the institution might make. This process assumes that an institution can identify and measure the goals or strategic agenda that it seeks to accomplish and is willing to explore a series of investment opportunities for capital or other funds to which it might have access. Investment funds can be generated from many sources, including fund raising, capital funding, debt, or operating funds after fixed costs have been met. The largest allocable resource at most institutions is the time and effort of faculty and staff. Increasingly, institutions are using for-profit corporations as a means of generating equity and potential venture capital for the development of new markets and delivery systems.

Strategic asset management takes a broader view of the assets of the institution than that found in financial statements. For example, intellectual property generated and owned or licensed by an institution has substantial potential value. Many institutions have developed technology transfer operations to deal with the potential value of inventions, patents, and licenses in the institution. By more systematically applying underutilized assets, particularly those with high development and depreciation costs, institutions can better manage the cost of information technology. Different institutions with different cultures are using a number of models for this management strategy. Many outside vendors are also willing to support strategic assets management depending on the model an institution chooses. The point is that institutions need to make overt and significant decisions about deploying their strategic assets as part of a cost management approach.

Truly managing the cost of information technology will also require cost measurement processes and understandings rarely evidenced in higher education. Twigg points out the value of activity-based costing, but only after assignment of certain expenditures to fixed institutional costs.[10] Thus, both measurement methodologies need to be employed. Understanding the half-life of certain technology, certain content and knowledge, and similar issues are essential for building cost strategies based on depreciation. Predicting markets and market responses may also be a significant issue for determining ROI and thus management of costs. Because a large portion of the potential cost reduction from the use of IT will come in the form of time and effort savings of current personnel, institutions will need to understand how to recapture and put to productive use that time and effort.

Beyond the expense in dollars and cents of information technology applications, certain non-tangible costs in terms of an institution's reputation and current market position may be equally significant and will require searching analysis. Large enrollment courses, particularly those with either many sections or several types of delivery activities like labs or discussion sections, present substantial opportunities for reducing instructional cost and improving learning. Institutions whose reputation is built around small sections and high direct faculty involvement will need a high ROI to begin to substitute technology for the small enrollment reputation. Similarly, increasing opportunities will appear for institutions to purchase course content and even outside delivery with potentially significant savings and learning improvements, but institutional reputation must be a significant consideration. Institutions renowned for providing leading self-service technology solutions cannot forego continuing investment in these technologies to support instructional applications of IT.[11] Strategic assets may be sold or licensed to outside businesses, but a cost consideration must include reputation management and current market position management. There may be opportunities to develop economies of scale through institutional consortia or partnership arrangements, but there are likely to be reputation considerations, which can add to or reduce costs.

All these considerations suggest that an institutional investment strategy must also include a corresponding exit strategy, i.e., management processes to avoid costly expenditures. Because institutions are not generally good at eliminating programs and many institutions have current investments in antiquated technologies for instructional delivery, the rate of technology and content depreciation costs are going to increase and this will further outdate existing infrastructure investments. Cost management, thus, requires planned exit and risk mitigation strategies rarely found in the academic management of colleges and universities.

IN CONCLUSION: COST MANAGEMENT REQUIRES A PARADIGM SHIFT

Information technology will strain not only the instructional budgets and current policies of many institutions, but will also strain the management skills and experience of their leaders. As we have suggested, IT costs can go unmanaged, but the costs will be high and are unlikely to meet significant institutional goals. On the other hand, IT presents significant opportunities. Those opportunities will not be realized without management skill in the assessment of technology investments, both from the point of ROI and at levels like buy (and potential outsource) versus build decisions. Partnerships, alliances, and consortia represent potential opportunities to increase ROI, reducing costs of required technologies or achieving economies of scale, but require significant management skill in negotiation and relationship management. The potential for significantly different organizational forms within or around the institution will be critical to most institutions considering new markets or technology-based learning markets.

Cost issues and assessment of outcomes will challenge academic management structures because assessment of programs will need to move from deliverer assessment to learning outcome assessment. Cost issues will also require decisions to be made on what technology standardization is essential for the entire institution to use. Most institutions will not be able to afford IT without having significant standardization of technology to limit various costs, including maintenance and training in the chosen technologies. Exit strategies for programmatic decisions must be developed and used.

Thus, the use of information technology presents institutions with paradigm shifts not only in course and program delivery, but also in the management of costs and in broad management processes. A key is to manage costs, not expenditures. Costs must be managed at the following four levels:

- At the *infrastructure or utility level*, the management of costs is not only to determine whether the expenditures will be made, but also how fast and which technologies provide the greatest functionality at the lowest price to meet institutional needs.
- At the *Comprehensive Enterprise Model planning and strategy level*, institutional positioning, strategy, and technology are brought together in an integrated package. Using technology for experiments and "random acts of progress" can be an expenditure-controlled process, but not a cost management approach. Without a realistic approach to developing the institutional strategy, costs cannot be managed and priorities for enterprise progress established. Because the strategy mix is different for every campus, no singular approach is available to manage the cost of IT, even within institutions that appear fairly comparable. Indigenous enterprise planning must be a key element.
- At the level of *institutional management*, practices and policies will need to be transformed to accomplish the set of desired global or enterprise-wide progress outcomes. Institutions unwilling to trans-

form current practices and approaches to instruction and service delivery will not find ways to manage costs for new types of IT.

- Finally, at the level of *strategic investment*, appropriate assets deployment and measured return on investments and new management processes skills and experiences will be essential. The technologies have great potential for transforming instruction, cost structures of institutions, and institutional opportunities to manage overall costs.
- The deployment of information technologies will have a high impact on the institution. Lowering costs (or insuring net returns) will require that other activities and management practices within an institution be transformed as well. Thus, for many institutions, a conservative approach to investment makes the most sense. For a few on the "bleeding edge," costs will not be a primary consideration. For all others, management of costs, investments, assets, and relationships present tremendous challenge and opportunities, the level of which depends on institutional goals, competition, and strategic agendas. Cost management is an active process, certainly not integrated into the current practices of many institutions, and best not left to chance.

ENDNOTES

1. Howard R. Bowen, *The Cost of Higher Education.* San Francisco: Jossey-Bass Inc., 1980.

2. National Commission on the Cost of Higher Education, *Straight Talk about College Costs and Prices.* Washington, DC: U.S. Department of Education, January 21, 1998.

3. William Graves, "The Instructional Management Systems Cooperative: Converting Random Acts of Progress into Global Progress." *Educom Review* (November-December, 1998): 33-36, 60-62.

4. ERP systems are used by colleges and universities as well as other for-profit and not-for-profit enterprises to manage transactions and store data and information related to those transactions. Institutions usually have ERP system applications in the financial, human resource, and student management areas. These applications are licensed for institutional use from large software application providers, but the applications are fit to the institutions.

5. Legacy systems are also transaction management systems for payroll, accounting, registration, and other similar functions. The software architecture and technology for these systems is out-of-date and, in many cases, no longer supported by the original software vendor.

6. Shadow systems are record systems that organizational subunits create to track their business that operate in parallel to formal organization-wide systems. For example, if accounting statements are routinely late, inaccurate, or do not include up-to-date financial commitments, institutional units will "keep their own books."

7. Jeremy Seigel, "Are Internet Stocks Overvalued? Are They Ever." *The Wall Street Journal* (April 19, 1999): A-22.

8. Wit Capital Corporation, *The E-Knowledge Industry*. (August 11, 1999):

9. Twigg, Carol, *Improving Learning and Reducing Costs: Redesigning Large-Enrollment Courses*. Philadelphia: The Pew Learning and Technology Program, 1999, pp. 5-7.

10. Twigg, *Improving Learning and Reducing Costs*, pp. 18-22.

11. Self-service technology solutions allow, for example, students to be admitted, plan their major, audit their progress, register for courses, apply and receive financial aid, and pay bills through technology rather than standing in lines or having to obtain unnecessary signatures.

CHAPTER 14

Faculty Costs and Compensation in Distance Education

Christine Maitland, Rachel Hendrickson, and Leroy Dubeck

This chapter discusses the role of faculty and faculty work in a technologically changing environment. Each time a faculty member assumes responsibility for a distance education course, it is not cost neutral to an institution. There are opportunity costs that may not figure into an institution's profit and loss calculations. Where there is collective bargaining, these costs become visible. What also becomes visible is the dynamic tension between cost and quality.

We explore a series of questions in this chapter. In this changing environment, what is the impact of information technology on faculty compensation and costs? What is the role of faculty in developing the curriculum and course content of technology-mediated instruction? What have faculty bargained that will ensure the quality of the distance education program? What intellectual property issues arise with the use of technology that concern institutions and faculty? How can an institution estimate the costs of distance education? And finally, the ultimate question: What is the cost of quality?

The creation of the Internet and the World Wide Web in 1990 was but the next step in an information technology evolution that began with the written word sometime before 3000 BCE, the Gutenberg printing press in 1455, the Remington typewriter in 1874, and the personal computer in 1975. The stylus used to imprint cuneiform letters on wet clay was the first step in the development of tools to transmit the products of human intellect. Society went from writing to computers in only about 5,000 years. In 1969, the ARPNET was launched by the Defense Department with the aim of linking computer science labs throughout the country so they could share data. Although not intended to be a message system, it revolutionized communications and gave rise to the global Internet. It is a product of a golden era in American science and technology.[1]

Today's higher education system and its faculty are providing services in a radically different economy and social environment than institutions did pre-Net. Robert Reich, a former secretary of labor and a labor economist, often speaks about the role of education in the new economy.

> Education is a key component of any nation's success in the global economy. In the new global economy, the only resource that is really rooted in a nation—the ultimate source of all its wealth—is its people. To compete and win, our work force must be well educated, well trained, and highly skilled.[2]

In *Shifting Gears: Thriving in the New Economy*, Nuala Beck notes that "in the new economy more Americans make computers than all forms of transport, work in accounting firms than in the whole energy industry, work in biotechnology than machine tools, and work in the movie industry than the automotive industry." Jim Taylor and Watts Wacker, authors of *The 500 Year Delta: What Happens After What Comes Next* (1997), posit that the market economy that we have used for the last 500 years is being transformed by the information economy. They talk about the "unreal realities" that have occurred since 1960, when

- 2.3 million women worked for pay—today over 61 million women do;
- the average person needed to learn one new skill a year to prosper in the workplace—today that person needs to learn one new skill a day; and
- the most important American industry was manufacturing—today the most important American industry is ideas.

The U.S. Census Bureau's *Labor Force, Employment, and Earnings Report* (September 1998) noted that in 1960 only 16 percent of married women with children under six were in the labor force compared to 1997, when there were 64 percent. The existence of e-mail is changing the way we work and communicate.

> Just as the car made it possible for people to live far from work, so e-mail and related technologies let people both live and work anywhere. It's tearing apart the organizational structures of the last century. . . . The Federal Department of Transportation projects that as many as 15 million workers will telecommute in 2002, a gain of 650 percent from 1992.[3]

Richard Saul Wuman, author of *Information Anxiety*, wrote that a weekday edition of the *New York Times* contains more information than the average person was likely to come across in a lifetime in seventeenth-century England; more information has been produced in the last 30 years than during the previous 5,000 years; and the information supply available to us doubles every five years.

In *The Post-Capitalist Society*, Peter Drucker noted the following:

- As recently as the 1960s, almost one-half of all workers in the industrialized countries were involved in making (or helping to make) things.
- By 2000, no developed country will have more than one-sixth or one-eighth of its workforce in the traditional roles of making and moving goods.
- Already an estimated two-thirds of U.S. employees work in the services sector, and "knowledge" is becoming our most important "product."
- This trend calls for different organizations, as well as different kinds of workers.

Higher education and its faculty are at the gateway to this new information economy.

> Today there is an emerging class, known as knowledge workers, who earn their living sharing information and solving problems, usually within an organizational setting. Team members and groups of teams focus on achieving specific outcomes in what appear to be spontaneous ways, frequently with no more instruction from outside authority than a clear statement of the goals to be accomplished and the process to be followed.[4]

Faculty are knowledge workers, struggling to adapt their own traditions and work lives to the demands of that brave new economy at the same time that they are charged with preparing others for their role as knowledge workers. Faculty are teachers and learners, producers and consumers in the knowledge economy.

The term "knowledge work" first appeared in the late 1950s in the publications of economist Fritz Machlup. Peter Drucker popularized the term during the same time period, but Machlup did the analytical work, spending over 30 years studying "knowledge and its creation, distribution and economic significance."[5] In 1962, he published *The Production and Distribution of Knowledge in the United States*, in which he set forth his theory that knowledge was a major production item in the U.S. economy. Knowledge workers have as their stock in trade "information and intellectual activity."[6] In recent times, the expansion of discoveries in science and technology has created new knowledge professions, which increasingly are connected to data analysis and computers. Drucker noted that the knowledge society depends on education. He dated the start of this period to the GI Bill, which provided access to higher education for soldiers returning after World War II and opened higher education to women. He predicted the knowledge transformation will continue until 2010 or 2020, so we should recognize we are in the midst of it and adapt.[7]

According to a survey by Buffa and Hais,[8] knowledge workers share the following three factors:

1. They all use a computer on the job—85 percent do so full-time.
2. They work in unstructured environments where "their judgement and independence is a critical component"—77 percent decide what to do on the job rather than being told.
3. They function as part of a team.

Winograd and Buffa also made the following observations about this new workforce constituency in *Taking Control: Politics in the Information Age:*

> These self-governing teams of knowledge workers serve as the organization model of the information age, creating values and metaphors for Americans that are light-years removed from Henry Ford's assembly line and the pyramidal organization Alfred Sloan created at General Motors.[9] (p. 2)

Charles Handy, in *The Age of Unreason,* noted that work has shifted to the service sector—between 1960 and 1985 the share of workers in the service sector rose from 56 to 69 percent in both the U.S. and Italy. A 1986 study by McKinsey's Amsterdam office estimated that 70 percent of jobs in Europe in the year 2000 would require cerebral skills rather than manual skills. In the U.S., it is expected to be 80 percent. These skills will place increased demands on higher education.[10]

What do these tranformations mean for higher education? More than ever, higher education must deal with the concept of lifelong learning because the workers of the future will need to update their knowledge and skills several times during their careers. Dolence and Norris postulate about the increased need for higher education in *Transforming Higher Education: A Vision for Learning in the 21st Century.* They make the following assumptions: The 1990s marked the beginning of the Information Age which is "being driven by learning and knowledge." Today, workers will need to accumulate learning at a faster pace to maintain basic employment skills and to remain competitive. Each individual worker will "need to accumulate learning equivalent to that currently associated with 30 credit hours of instruction, every seven years."[11] This could mean that each year one-seventh of the workforce will need more education. In 10 industrialized countries, there are close to 700 million people in the workforce, which would produce 100 million full-time equivalent (FTE) learners and would translate into a need for 3,300 new campuses. The costs would be exorbitant.

Does higher education have the capacity to educate these adult students in the workforce in addition to the traditional 18- to 22-year-old students? Between 1998 and 2008, eighteen states will have an increase in their numbers of high school graduates from 16 percent to over 35 percent. In addition, the Dolence and Norris projections indicate that 672 more campuses would be required to educate the adults in the U.S. workforce.

Let us take California as an example. An article in the October 1, 1999, issue of the *Chronicle of Higher Education* noted that the California Postsecondary Education Commission is predicting a 36 percent increase in enrollment by 2010. The projected increase in enrollment of more than one-third means the state will need to accommodate 715,000 more students in addition to the 2 million currently enrolled. "If California were to accommodate these additional students solely by building new campuses, the cost to taxpayers would be staggering." The report recommends increasing the use of distance education and operating campuses year round. Furthermore, a rapid increase is expected among Hispanic and Asian students. Other minority groups will also increase, while the percentage of white students will decline from 47 to 43 percent.

Despite the need to serve vastly greater numbers of college-age and adult students, few new campuses are being built and few full-time faculty are being hired. In the face of limited increases in funding, institutions have chosen the low-wage route. While trying to meet burgeoning educational needs, they are limiting personnel costs by hiring a large number of part-time faculty, most of whom are paid much less than full-time faculty and receive none of the regular retirement or health benefits.

In 1970, part-time faculty accounted for 22 percent of the total number of faculty. By 1997, part-time faculty had increased to 41 percent. Even more disturbing are the data on recent hires. In the fall of 1997, 51 percent of the newly hired full-time faculty were in temporary positions.[12] In the U.S. labor force, over 30 million people work part-time—about 23 percent of the total workforce. The percentage of part-time workers in higher education is almost double the percentage in the U.S. labor force as a whole. Higher education has become a prominent employer in the contingent economy.

Handy believes that in the future less than half the work force in the industrial world will be in proper full-time jobs; the rest will work part-time, in temporary positions, because they chose to or because they cannot find full-time work. Core workers will be supported by outside contractors and temporary workers. This trend is already the case in higher education in the U.S.

FACULTY USE OF TECHNOLOGY

Faculty members are both the inventors of and users of technology. Scientists from academe and the military invented the Internet. The speed and capacity of modern computers enable faculty to observe, quantify, and analyze much larger data sets. New knowledge is exploding in many fields, and established principles are being reexamined in light of new data.

The Hubbell Space Telescope is creating so much new information about the universe that astronomers have to "constantly update" the content of science books. "Hubble is turning in discovery after discovery about how the cosmos works. There's a major turnover in information, and Hubble is becoming embedded in that."[13] The Mars Pathfinder produced millions of gigabytes of information that was posted on the Internet and made available to scientists, students, teachers, and the public on a global basis. The mapping of human genes is leading to new medical diagnoses and treatments. New discoveries are being made and published every day in psychology, education, and history, thus creating the need to revise the curriculum on an ongoing basis. One of the myths about distance education is that courses can be taped and played over again with no need for a permanent faculty. But if the teaching material has a short shelf-life, faculty in the disciplines will be needed to keep courses current.

Many faculty members use technology daily, for teaching, to communicate with students and colleagues, and for research. In a May 1998 National Education Association (NEA) phone survey of its members, virtually all faculty reported that they had access to a personal computer, e-mail, and the Internet on campus. In fact, 70 percent of faculty have a computer at home as well as on campus. Access to computer technology is high among all faculty subgroups, i.e. part-time, tenure-track, and tenured. E-mail is the most accessible and frequently used of the new technologies, with two-thirds of faculty using e-mail to communicate with students.[14]

In the NEA survey, one-fourth of the faculty reported teaching via distance education and 27 percent reported using a Web site for their classes. Senior faculty members and full professors are more likely than junior faculty to teach a class using distance education.

In a recent Higher Education Research Institute Faculty Survey, *The American College Teacher: National Norms for 1998-1999*, faculty reported that "keeping up with information technology" has been stressful for them during the past two years (67 percent), ranking above teaching load (62 percent), research and publishing demands (50 percent), and the review and promotion process (46 percent). The vast majority of faculty, however, believe that computers are educationally beneficial, with almost 90 percent agreeing that "student use of computers enhances their learning" (p. 5). The study argues that stress levels are a reflection of the time faculty invest in using technology. Almost 90 percent communicate using e-mail at least twice a week, and 85 percent use the computer to write memos and letters. The following table from *The American College Teacher* shows the percentage of college faculty in 1998–99 that used a computer at least twice a week to accomplish the listed tasks.

TABLE 14-A	
COMPUTER USE AMONG COLLEGE FACULTY (% USING COMPUTERS AT LEAST TWICE A WEEK TO DO THE FOLLOWING:)	
Communicate via e-mail	87
Write memos/letters	85
Work from home	55
Conduct scholarly writing	54
Create presentations	38
Conduct research using Internet	35
Conduct data analysis	27
Participate in on-line discussion groups	11

Source: The American College Teacher: National Norms for the 1998–99 HERI Faculty Survey, Higher Education Research Institute, University of California, Los Angeles.

QUALITY ISSUES AND POLICY

The National Education Association (NEA) represents 2.5 million members— the knowledge workers who staff the education system of the United States. Close to 100,000 of these NEA members are in higher education. While its higher education members have been grappling with issues of distance education for some time, these issues are increasingly affecting K-12 members as well. In response to concerns raised by its membership, the NEA determined to set the standards for quality in distance education. The resulting discussion was both faculty-focused and student-focused. As an advocacy organization, the NEA needed to deal with technology because so many of its members are being impacted by changes in their workplace and are using new technologies to teach their students and conduct research.

However, there was also a concern that institutions might be asking students to trade quality for access and that the decision to take a distance education course over a traditional campus course might not be cost-neutral for the student and might even be part of the invisible costs of distance education. Students taking distance education courses face additional expense because they need to have the necessary computer equipment, including modems and an Internet service provider, and the technical skills to use the equipment. E-mail is not a substitute for real-time interaction. At a distance, students may feel isolated and disconnected from the campus and the instructor. Keeping materials up to date and adapted to the distance learning environment is a challenge.

In 1999, the NEA developed and formally adopted a distance education policy to guide members who were concerned that quality was giving way to expediency in the introduction of distance education on campuses and in school districts. The provisions of the NEA distance education policy (Section B-62) include the following:

> The National Education Association believes that quality distance education can create or extend learning opportunities not otherwise available to all students.
> The Association also believes that, to ensure quality, distance education courses must—
>
> a. Be at least as rigorous as similar courses delivered by more traditional means
> b. Meet accreditation standards
> c. Have content that is relevant, accurate, meets state and local standards, and is subject to the normal processes of collegial decision-making
> d. Meet the objectives and requirements outlined in the official course description
> e. Have the student/faculty ratios that ensure the active engagement of students and high academic achievement
> f. Have appropriate procedures mutually agreed upon by the instructor and the institution for evaluation and verification that the student is submitting his/her own work
> g. Have instructors whose qualification are the same as those of instructors teaching in traditional classes and who are prepared specifically and comprehensively to teach in this environment
> h. Be integrated into the mission and consistent with the overall offerings of the institution
> i. Provide fair use exemptions for participants' access to copyrighted materials for educational purposes.
>
> The Association further believes that the institution offering the courses must provide—
>
> a. Adequate infrastructure
> b. Appropriate facilities and equipment
> c. Libraries and laboratories as needed
> d. Adequate support and technical personnel on or off campus.
>
> The Association believes that the rights of the education employees delivering and monitoring the courses must be protected through the normal process of collegial decision-making and, when relevant, collective bargaining. The intellectual property rights of instructors should be protected and should include the introduction, use, and impact of distance education as well as the revenue, revisions, reuse, and duration of the courses.

The Association also believes that the rights of the students taking the courses must be protected. These rights must include, but not be limited to—

a. Appropriate equipment, technical support, libraries, and laboratories
b. Appropriate student services
c. Accurate course descriptions and expectations prior to enrollment
d. Individualized interaction with their instructor
e. Opportunities for appropriate student-to-student interaction.

IN THE CONTRACTS

Have faculty and institutions addressed the quality concerns raised in the above policies? The NEA maintains a database of over 500 contracts in the Higher Education Contract Analysis System (HECAS), a CD-ROM with full-text retrieval software that contains contracts representing the collectively agreed-upon working conditions of approximately 80 percent of faculty on organized campuses in the United States. With approximately 50 percent of the faculty in public sector institutions organized and one-third organized overall, these contracts represent the working conditions of a significant number of the academic knowledge workers of the United States. An analysis of HECAS contracts suggests that the process is well on its way, but that faculty and their institutions are still struggling with the integration of distance education on campuses.

Using HECAS, NEA staff began to note trends in collective bargaining with respect to distance education in 1994. The initial attempts to deal with the issue usually focused on a recognition that some questions needed to be addressed, often through a task force, but seldom grappled with those questions, recognizing that the parties did not have enough information to take into account rapidly changing technology. By 1999, the contractual situation had changed dramatically. More than 125 U.S. faculty contracts and an additional 15 Canadian contracts contained sections or articles addressing issues of technology introduction, distance education, and intellectual property as it related to distance education.

CLASS SIZE

With the absence of reliable information on the effects of class size on quality distance education, faculty and institutions have used relatively traditional standards to negotiate issues of class size. What is not contained in the contracts is the link of class size to quality education. Indeed, the compensation structure often works to encourage increased class size, raising the concern that quality will diminish with the increased work. As the following examples show, the compensation level is often specifically linked to the number of students in a class[15]:

> The maximum class size is 35 students. Once the maximum size is reached the following rate shall go into effect for every student over 35. (*Atlantic Community College, NJ*)
>
> The maximum telecourse class size shall be 75 students per section. (*Belleville Area College, IL*)
>
> In a general instruction-type course, the goal for class scheduling shall be a 25 per student class average. The maximum class size will be thirty (30) students. . . . Exceptions to this maximum are open labs, seminars, teleconferences, and those classes which are organized as combination large lecture with small laboratory or discussion groups. In those instances, the small groups shall not exceed the maximum. (*Blackhawk Technical College, IL*)

The Chemeketa Community College (OR) allows for an increase in class size of 200 percent over usual departmental practice provided there is up to 100 percent extra pay. Such a bonus would still not offset the cost to the institution of hiring a new employee to accommodate an increased enrollment, and therefore would not discourage the college from packing a class, although the contract offers splitting a section as an option, in addition to hiring a teaching assistant or adjusting the full-time workload. In contrast, Glen Oaks Community College (MI) has the following provision:

> Full enrollment in a distance learning course will reflect exactly the caps of regular on-campus courses. For example, if a section of the regular, on-campus course is capped at 25, that shall be the cap for the distance learning section of that course.
>
> If enrollment in a distance learning course exceeds the enrollment cap, then a new section of the course will be opened with the professor/instructor having the privilege of first refusal for teaching the new section.

In other cases, additional compensation is linked to the number of remote sites rather than the number of students: "Faculty teaching on interactive distance learning will be compensated at the rate of $250 per remote site" (*Nebraska State College, NE*).

WORKLOAD AND DISTANCE EDUCATION

Initially, distance education courses were primarily presented in the contracts as overload, rather than integrated into normal faculty activities. In a whole series of contracts, participation in a distance education course remains voluntary.[16] In other distance education articles, the faculty member has the choice of accepting the class as in-load or treating it as overload. In short, approaches to handling the issues of workload and distance education have been inconsistent. The parties often have chosen to address the issue through labor/management committees whose responsibility is to monitor the implementation of distance education programs on the campuses and to handle issues on individual bases.

In the following statement, Clackamas Community College (OR) recognizes the impact distance education can have on faculty workload:

> Distance learning may involve significant increases in tasks such as class exchanges, conferences with students, and evaluation of student work. Therefore, a faculty member who teaches a distance-learning class shall receive an additional one half of compensation associated with the distance learning class for each 75% of student enrollment above the non-distance learning class size associated with that course.

COURSE DEVELOPMENT

While workload is treated inconsistently in the contracts, the issue of course development is not. There is a clear assumption that the development and production of a distance learning or technology-enhanced course is more time-consuming than that required for a traditional course. Preparation is frequently tied to faculty compensation. At Tompkins-Cortland Community College (NY), the contract stipulates that "appropriate and timely training for faculty and staff involved in distance learning activities" in both technical and pedagogical areas shall be provided at the expense of the institution. The Tompkins-Cortland contract also provides for specific compensation for various phases in the development and production of a distance learning course: $2000 for the creation or adaptation of a course to a Web-based platform and $1500 for the same faculty member for a second course, assuming the same technology is used. At Western Michigan University, the faculty member is paid $2000 for the initial preparation or substantial revision of an electronically purveyed course. The Florida State University System recognized need for "Compensation, including recognition in an employee's assignment or provisions for extra State compensation, for appreciably greater workload associated with the assigned development and use of instructional technology/distance learning."

At Glen Oaks Community College (MI), the faculty member receives $500 per credit hour for the development of a distance learning course. In return for that payment, the faculty member agrees, among other things, to attend a training session provided by the college to "modify the course's instructional design in order to build in student interaction and involvement in the course," and to "prepare a syllabus that defines the course objectives as presented in a distance learning environment."[17] Other contracts provide a system of released time in lieu of compensation for the development of a course.

> The District will provide reassigned time to a faculty member for the initial development of a course that the faculty member will teach in the distance education mode. The course must be either fully interactive or must be based primarily on electronic material that has been developed by the faculty member. (*Cuesta Community College, CA*)

> To facilitate the conversion of any course to a distance learning mode, the first time an individual instructor is assigned to teach a particular distance learning course, that instructor will be granted released time equal to the contact hours of the assigned course. The released time will be granted in the semester prior to the assigned course. (*Alpena Community College, MI*)

STUDENT CONTACT

Gerald Van Dusen enumerates four kinds of interaction possible in a virtual learning situation: learner-content, learner-instructor, learner-learner, and learner-interface.[18] According to Van Dusen, "In the virtual classroom, learner-instructor and learner-learner interaction are problematic considerations. Lacking traditional face-to-face contact, educational success in a virtual environment is critically dependent upon methods of instruction and the ability to exploit characteristics of available technologies."[19] A critical quality question is whether faculty contracts have built in conditions that can lead, at least, to learner-instructor interaction.

Traditional collective bargaining agreements in higher education contain clauses on office hours and other forms of student contact. Are there adaptations to these traditional approaches that suit the need for contact and interaction for distance education students? In general, the contracts recognize the need for instructor-student contact, but tend to handle it in traditional, prescriptive ways, for example, by enumerating the type and frequency of contact.

> The instructor must communicate with the students by telephone or mail at least twice monthly. (*Schoolcraft Community College, MI*)

Fox Valley Technical College (WI) has the following extensive section on interactivity:

> To help bridge the distance between instructor and learner, all Distance Education course instructors are required to have an interaction

plan with students on file with the division dean. Possibilities for interaction activities include:

a. 1-hour orientation with students (required)
b. telephone contact
c. on-campus sessions as needed to assure course competencies
d. test review sessions (pre-post) or other means of communicating information to students (i.e. test reviews and test results with comments, to help students learn from their mistakes, mailed or presented over ITV). . . .

Instructors are expected to provide students with their contact information (office hours, telephone number, mailing address) and maintain communication with them.

There are more contracts addressing interaction for telecourses than there are for other forms of distance education. Cabrillo Community College (CA) requires that faculty spend a minimum of seven hours with students in group settings, communicate individually with students, and hold meetings at a variety of times to accommodate the scheduling needs of adult learners.

FACULTY EVALUATION

Little evidence indicates that the evaluation process has been altered to accommodate the idiosyncrasies of distance education. Several contracts specifically prohibit or limit taping or monitoring of courses for purposes of evaluation. In most cases, where evaluation is discussed in the contract, the clause is prescriptive and limiting, that is, it describes what must *not* be done, rather than what should be done.

Evaluation of instruction shall occur at the sending site and shall not be accomplished through electronic monitoring or taping unless both parties are aware of such methods prior to classroom evaluation. (*Cloud County Community College, KS*)[20]

All courses which use as a primary delivery method the technologies described above shall be administered and evaluated by academic employees with appropriate subject matter expertise and experience. (*Lower Columbia College, WA*)

One contract prohibits the use of Web materials in evaluation without consent.

Course materials published on the Internet/Web shall not be used in the evaluation of a faculty member without that faculty member's consent. (*Oakton Community College, IL*)

The Burlington County College (NJ) agreement discusses the evaluation of a faculty member's proficiency in technology, but does not indicate how the evaluation will be accomplished: "The College encourages the use of high technology or innovative instructional methodologies in the classroom and will consider a faculty member's proficiency in and use of such strategies in the classroom as part of the evaluation process." The Spoon River Community College (IL) contract links evaluation to training: "The College will develop or adopt a formal training program, which will include an evaluation component, to prepare selected faculty to become competent in offering instruction in a telecommunications mode."

The faculty contract for the Pennsylvania State College System provides for the development of an evaluation process specific to distance education: "For distance education courses, an appropriate student evaluation instrument shall be developed by local APSCUF (Association of Pennsylvania College and University Faculty), the University management and the appropriate student government body as designated by the President, and approved by local APSCUF and the University management." Further, the contract recognizes the learning curve associated with learning to teach in distance mode and stipulates a formative, rather than summative, evaluation process, one geared to improve the ability of the instructor to offer distance education instruction and to improve the quality of the educational experience as a whole.

> Unless hired specifically to teach through distance education, in instances where the faculty member has not had three (3) or more semesters of experience in teaching distance education courses, evaluation of teaching effectiveness in a distance education course shall be utilized for self-improvement and course refinement and not for renewal, tenure or promotion decisions unless requested by the faculty member.
>
> The faculty member shall write an evaluation of his/her experiences in the distance education course and suggest measures which may be taken to improve the quality of distance education in the future. Additionally, the faculty member should include any student perceptions regarding learning through distance education which may be helpful in improving the quality of the course offerings.

TRAINING

The inclusion of training in distance education in the contracts is a significant change. In academe, the assumption is that faculty know how to teach and to do research. They developed their skills as graduate students and carried them over into their independent professional lives. Thus, while faculty development centers may exist on campuses, they are seldom institutionalized in contracts. The introduction of distance learning and technology-mediated instruction has brought training into the contracts as institutions recognize that the traditional pedagogical skills needed by the campus lecturer do not necessarily translate to the new media. In *What's the Difference*, the authors point out that "Faculty involved in distance education find themselves being a combination of content experts, learning process design experts, process implementation managers, motivators, mentors, and interpreters."[21] The report further states that, in reviewing the effect of technology on student learning, what became clear is that the technology itself "is not nearly as important as other factors, such as learning tasks, learner characteristics, student motivation, and the instructor."[22] Providing adequate training for the instructor goes a long way toward providing quality distance education for the student.

Training for delivery of distance education courses encompasses two different areas: technical and pedagogical. An instructor needs to understand how to manage the equipment used in developing and producing an interactive distance education course and the techniques of instruction. The contract for the Nebraska State College System is comprehensive, containing the following provision for both technical training and pedagogical development as well as provision for infrastructure support:[23]

> Faculty members who are assigned to teach courses via telecommunications delivery will be provided prior training in the operation of the technical equipment to be used for such courses. Technical assistance in the preparation of materials will be provided. Logistical support will be provided for distribution of instructional materials and testing at each remote site. . . . Each college shall provide a professional development fund [to include]. . . . Development of new distance learning courses.
>
> The intent of these funds is to facilitate the broadest, creative applications for the improvement of instruction.

The contract for the Pennsylvania State System of Higher Education contains the following similar provisions for both technical and pedagogical training and development in a section titled "Quality Control":

1. Professional Development: Prior to teaching a distance education course, a faculty member shall be afforded the opportunity for appropriate training in distance education instruction or the use of a technology used by his/her University to offer distance education as determined by the University/State System.
2. Technical and Instructional Support: The University shall assure the availability of technical support personnel and materials appropriate to

the principal technology and consistent with the faculty member's prior training and experience.

Other contracts address training needs. The Florida State University System contract calls for "Training and development resources available to employees who have been assigned to provide instruction through the use of instructional technology, including distance learning." Chemeketa Community College (OR) created the following comprehensive vision statement for distance learning:

> All of these teaching methods need collective commitment across the College to quality, resources, etc. We recognize that using alternative methods requires new skills and learning; therefore, appropriate support and training must be available to faculty. In many cases the methodology also requires additional support and commitment from others. . . . Through all of our delivery methods, we have both the opportunity and the obligation to assure that what we are teaching is current. Distance learning is not just important as a learning modality of the future, but also as an emerging workplace competency.

The institution agrees to "develop mentoring/teaching process (for example, manual/video) for faculty learning new teaching modalities" and to "improve overall technology, monitor the computer system on a regular basis to make sure it is working, and provide technical support for faculty and students."

While contract clauses addressing the development needs of faculty respecting delivery of distance education are by no means wide-spread in the contracts as a whole, those that do exist point to an important commitment by institutions and faculty to ensure quality in distance education.

INTELLECTUAL PROPERTY: A TECHNOLOGICAL BATTLEGROUND

Three hundred years after the invention of the printing press, Immanual Kant and every other writer in the German city-states had a problem. The public was suddenly inundated with printed works—plays, poems, novels, and philosophy. Once the works were published in one city-state, they were copied in others without payment to the authors. The debate raged for over 20 years and involved many of the best minds in Germany. Kant wrote in the *Critique of Judgment* (1790) that "Every artistic work consists of a physical object and a piece of its creator's spirit. People can buy the object but not the spirit, for soul cannot be purchased. Thus readers can freely copy books, but only in ways that respect the writer's integrity." This idea grew into the current European system of copyright.[24]

The protection of copyright in English and American law has a 300-year history. At its earliest conception in England it was viewed as a natural right of authors to protect their written work so they could "reap the profits of their own ingenuity and labor."[25]

By the writing of the U.S. Constitution, copyright was recognized as a common-law right that served both to reward an author's efforts and provide an incentive to create original works for public dissemination. The founders believed that copyright was essential to democracy and included it in the constitution. Article I, Section 8 instructs Congress to "secure for limited Times to Authors and inventors the exclusive Right to their Respective Writings and Discoveries." When George Washington asked Congress to enact copyright legislation, he argued that it would increase the national stock of knowledge. And knowledge, he said, is the "surest basis of public happiness."[26]

Like eighteenth-century Germans, we are now experiencing powerful cultural changes. The rise of digital media and the Internet for communication is forcing us to revisit intellectual property issues. In 1998, Congress passed the Digital Millennium Copyright Act, which has important implications for campuses. The law provides a safe harbor for online service providers, including nonprofit education institutions and libraries, and protections for faculty and students "performing a teaching or research function." The registrar of copyrights will recommend to Congress "how to promote distance education through digital technologies," including Interactive Digital Networks, while maintaining a balance between the rights of copyright owners and the needs of users. The act requires consultation with owners and education institutions. Also enacted was the Sonny Bono Copyright Term Extension Act, which extends copyright protection from 20 years to 50 years after the death of the author (or 75 years after publication for corporate authors) and makes it a crime to circumvent copyright protections. The legislation brings the United States into compliance with the terms of the World Intellectual Property Organization Treaty on Copyrights (WIPO).

The NEA's concern in lobbying for this legislation and for WIPO was balancing the protection of the rights of educators to own their work, and the "fair use" of materials for educators. The NEA's policy is that "faculty and staff should own the rights to their intellectual property." The NEA, library groups, and other education groups were successful in setting forth "fair use" criteria, and in preventing a provision that would have established legal protections for virtually any collection of information (databases), even those currently in the public domain.

INTELLECTUAL PROPERTY LANGUAGE IN BARGAINING AGREEMENTS

Distance education and other uses of technology are raising new questions. Who owns the products of distance learning? If a Web site is created for a course, who owns the copyright? If a class is videotaped, who owns the tape? Traditionally, faculty members have owned the rights to their course materials and written works. This ownership was necessary to give faculty the freedom to publish their works to qualify for tenure and promotion. Administrators did not care about owning faculty members' lecture notes or books that sold 500 copies. But the market is hungry for courseware and now those notes suddenly have value, especially when they are in an electronic format. Who owns the electronic course—the faculty or the institution? Institutions are claiming the course is a "work for hire," especially where substantial campus resources were used in the development and production. What are the implications for part-time faculty teaching on several campuses? Who owns student work?

The contract areas on patents, copyrights, and royalties contained in HECAS and the number of contracts containing language and applications to distance education have also increased dramatically since 1994. The issue of intellectual property rights and distance education, as it is handled in the contracts, raises cost questions. A review of the contracts shows several trends in concepts and language dealing with ownership questions.

1. If the research is funded by another agency, then the contract or grant for that research determines the distribution of income from the product.
2. If a faculty member invents, writes, or produces a product without the use of campus resources then he/she owns full rights to the income from that product.
3. If the faculty member uses campus resources there are several options outlined in the contracts:
   a. The proceeds are shared by the individual faculty and the campus—percentages are determined by the labor agreement.
   b. The proceeds are shared until the "fair market value" of the resources has been repaid.
   c. Sometimes there are provisions that students and other faculty on the campus may use the product for no charge. If it is marketed off the campus, then the individual faculty member and the campus share the proceeds.
4. The faculty own the copyright to their classroom lecture notes and materials and to their publications.
5. The administration cannot make signing away rights a condition of employment.

6. There is a growing use of the concept of residuals in dealing with the use and reuse of distance education products.

COST FACTORS AND ANALYSIS

This section describes the costs of distributed instruction, sometimes referred to as distance education; in particular, it focuses on instruction offered over the Internet. Some of the comments will also be applicable to courses offered via television to distant locations. We will focus this review on courses that individuals can take "at home" via a home computer connected to the Internet, which we shall refer to as courses offered via information technology (IT).

Two issues must be considered: the relative effectiveness of "in class" instruction versus IT instruction and the relative costs of "in class" instruction versus IT instruction.

Relative Effectiveness of In-Class vs. IT Instruction: Deferred Costs

Many studies have reported "no significant difference" between students taught using conventional classroom techniques and those taught using IT. The Frances, Pumerantz, and Caplan study[27] examined the case of students receiving an identical curriculum, with the same faculty, but on two campuses. The first campus class met in person with the faculty member, while the class was transmitted via television to the second campus. Although the objective outcome measures for the two classes, such as grade-point averages, were the same for both groups, the level of student satisfaction differed markedly, with the students using IT enjoying the course far less than those taking it in person. A similar response may apply to those taking courses over the Internet. If students are unhappy with the educational experience, they are less likely to continue to take courses at that institution and also will be less likely to be generous contributors to that institution as alumni, which may represent an additional "cost" to the use of IT.

Another indication of student unhappiness with IT is the report from the Institute for Higher Education Policy that there is a dropout rate of 32 percent for online courses, compared with just 4 percent for in-person classes. If students must take a significant fraction of their courses using IT, it seems reasonable to conclude that the retention rate will decrease, thereby costing the institution tuition dollars. In addition, the College Board recently reported that only 20 percent of low-income households own a computer, so online courses may pose a further disadvantage to those who are economically disadvantaged, and thus may adversely affect diversity on campus, an intangible, but disturbing cost.

A second issue to consider in evaluating the relative effectiveness of the two modes of instruction is class size. At smaller class sizes, both IT and traditional instruction may yield similar results. However, as indicated below, traditional in-class instruction is undoubtedly cheaper than IT, except in larger classes. For in-person instruction, teaching techniques that work well in small classes are often impossible to use in large classes. Similarly, just because small in-person and IT classes yield similar objective outcome measures does not necessarily mean that large IT classes will also demonstrate "no significant difference" when compared to large in-person classes. When IT is used to supplement normal classroom instruction, the result may be improved student learning, but it will occur only at the extra cost associated with enhancing a course with IT. This approach cannot save money.

Cost of IT Instruction Compared to Regular Classroom Instruction

Frank Jewett's central premise in Chapter 2 is that up to a certain maximum number of students, traditional classroom instruction is cheaper than IT,[28] while at higher numbers of students enrolled in a given course, IT will be cheaper than in-person instruction. At large enrollment levels, classes using IT will create cost savings by substituting IT for traditional faculty. Jewett notes that the essential characteristic that distinguishes distributed technology from classroom technology is that once instructional materials are prepared and presented, they are potentially available to all students enrolled in the course. Additionally, less expensive faculty/staff may be used instead of the course instructor to do some or all of the work concerned with interaction and evaluation. Once an Internet course is available on a server, the cost of interacting and evaluating students varies in direct proportion to the number of students enrolled. In Chapter 2, Frank Jewett refers to total costs as the sum of staff salaries (including benefits), operating expenses, and only directly attributable overhead costs.

Application of the Cost Model: Pennsylvania

To get a sense of how this cost model might apply to real universities, we used the data from the annual report, *Instructional Output and Faculty Salary Costs of the State-Related and State-Owned Universities* (in Pennsylvania) for the 1997-98 academic year. This report is produced by the Joint State Government Commission based on data supplied by the institutions named in the report. The report covers Pennsylvania four-year institutions, not the community colleges.

The Commission Report states that on average faculty spent 7.9 hours per week in formal undergraduate contact (in class instruction) and 1.9 hours per week in formal graduate student contact for a total of 9.8 contact hours per week while spending 17.6 hours per week on course preparation and student evaluation. Extending Jewett's formula, and adjusting for the actual *total work week* of faculty members at 53.9 hours, class contacts amounted to .18 (9.8/53.9) of a faculty member's entire workweek. This number represents the maximum fraction of time that may be saved by having the course materials on an Internet Web site. The average class size of 24 students per class for undergraduate courses presented in the table is far too small an average enrollment to save money by teaching these courses via IT, except for those courses in which there are multiple sections.

The faculty cost per course is calculated "by dividing the total instructional salaries paid to staff members in the respective ranks by their total full-time equivalency in the instructional function." This calculation of the cost of instruction means that a faculty member teaching a "full load" will have his or her entire salary charged against duties which, on average, took 27.4 hours (9.8 + 17.6) of a 53.9-hour work week. The Jewett model might be interpreted to show a savings of 9.8/27.4 times the faculty salary instead of 9.8/53.4 times faculty salary.

The average faculty salary in the survey of $50,000 per year would require an even larger course enrollment than the example given by Jewett to have the IT course cost less than the in-person course. In Jewett's example, the crossover point is set at about 450 students enrolled. With the lower salary and benefits from the Pennsylvania survey, an even larger enrollment would be needed. The average cost of instruction per student per course is $246, and the faculty cost for course presentation per student is $88 (9.8/27.4 x $246). This is the only certain faculty savings per student per course taught entirely with IT, although there may be some additional savings in preparation time if a course is taught repeatedly.

IT Costs vs. Decreased Faculty Costs

First consider further the faculty cost components. The course preparation effort is much higher for an IT course than for an in-class course. In Chapter 9, Judith Boettcher claims that it takes about 18 hours of faculty time to create an hour of instruction on the Web. This time is far more than the two to three hours needed to create an hour of traditional lecture. Thus, this cost is higher by a factor of six or more for an Internet course than for a traditional lecture course. Therefore, the cost savings for faculty come mainly from course presentation time. Additionally, once an in-person course is fully prepared, the preparation time to offer it again is much smaller than the initial preparation. The preparation time needed to offer a course repeatedly via the Internet will likely remain close to the in-person preparation time since there will need to be constant revisions of an IT course (e.g., some Web sites referred to in the course may no longer exist, new sites may offer more up-to-date materials, or servers may change requiring format changes in Web materials).

Costs of an All-Virtual University

What would happen to costs at a virtual university? A virtual university would not have any classrooms, dorms, or other physical facilities except a computer center, faculty offices, and an administration complex. It would have dramatic overhead savings compared to a traditional bricks-and-mortar university.

In an attempt to estimate the cost savings, we used budgetary information prepared at Temple University when that institution was considering adopting Responsibility Centered Management. Based on data for fiscal 1994-95, we estimated that the total direct expenses for all main campus colleges was about $147 million and the indirect costs attributed to supporting these colleges (including all physical plant, cleaning, security, central administration, and student services costs) were $105 million, or about 71 percent of the direct expenses. With only a minimal physical plant, these indirect costs might be reduced by half, down to perhaps 35 percent of direct instructional costs.

The enhanced computing requirements needed for all online classes would increase computer support costs substantially. However, there might still be a substantial overall reduction in the indirect costs of the institution. One might argue that such a virtual university should be able to offer courses at lower cost than in-person instruction. However, even for such a university, the really profitable courses would be those with large enrollments. The low pay rate for part-time and temporary faculty, not the mode of delivery, might make these courses profitable.

The Open University in Great Britain has class sizes that usually exceed 200. Furthermore, according to David Garson, the Open University uses a model in which many of the higher-paid regular faculty are replaced by lower-paid tutors. Once again, the savings come in substantial part from using lower-paid personnel instead of higher-paid regular faculty.[29]

It is hardly surprising that if an institution pays less to provide instruction to students, the cost is less. But the real question must be the quality of instruction received by the students. Will graduate students/tutors and part-time or temporary faculty, in general, provide learning experiences for students that are as good as regular faculty? A 1998 NEA survey of part-time faculty in a distance environment indicated that they did not have access to the campus facilities, equipment, or time necessary to ensure consistent interaction with students.[30]

Conclusions about Relative Costs

A number of general conclusions can be reached about the relative costs of IT and traditional classroom instruction.

First, for small class size, in-person instruction will always be less expensive than instruction via the Internet.

Second, for any course that can be held in one section, in-person instruction also will be less costly. Consider a 200-student course that is entirely lecture.

The least expensive way to offer the course is that of one instructor in one classroom. Assume a four-credit-hour course with an average tuition of about $700 per student, or $140,000 in tuition received for each such course, without counting any possible state subsidy that is paid to the institution to subsidize tuition. With just one instructor and no support costs (except computer-graded exams), such a course is profitable in-person and more profitable than it would be if given online. The in-person class will be less costly than the IT course of comparable enrollment because preparation time will be less for the in-person course and delivery of instruction will also take less time in-person than interacting individually with 200 students each week via e-mail.

The least expensive way to teach a multi-section course that has three or fewer sections would also probably be to use one instructor in person. One preparation time would be spread across three classes. The nine contact hours saved by offering it over the Internet will probably not compensate for the increased costs of support personnel and the large initial preparation costs.

Only large courses with more sections than one faculty member could teach at one time may offer savings when offered online. The Jewett example calculates a cross-over point of between 450 and 900 students enrolled in a course to make offering it via IT less costly than via traditional classrooms. However, relatively few courses in any university will satisfy this criterion. Hence, even in a major university setting, the possibility of cost-saving using IT applies only to a small number of multi-section courses. Furthermore, any savings an administration claims might occur by teaching the course via IT should be compared to those achieved by simply adding one or two students per section, thereby reducing the number of sections by 5 to 10 percent, and reducing the total cost of the course accordingly.

IT instruction may be useful for students who need to "time-shift" their classes because of business or family commitments. Such instruction may also be helpful to students living in remote locations. However, in most cases, IT should not be adopted "to save money" because it is not likely to achieve that goal.

One possible additional substantial cost associated with IT teaching is mentioned in Chapter 12 by Pumerantz and Frances. Namely, the possible decrease in retention rates for students, because a greater percentage will likely withdraw from IT courses than from in-person courses. This decreased retention rate would mean a smaller enrollment and fewer tuition dollars, unless the institution is already turning away fully qualified students, in which case, the students dropping out would be replaced within one semester by other applicants.

FORMAT FOR COMPARING IN-PERSON COSTS TO IT COSTS

The following simple format can be used to make rough preliminary comparisons of the costs of different instructional delivery modes. However, simplicity is gained at the expense of accuracy. While this format may help institutions and faculty make initial assessments of whether IT will cost less than in-person instruction, the analysis would need to be much more comprehensive to yield more precise comparative cost figures.

Simple Cost Comparison Between In-Person and Instructional Technology (IT) Courses

1. For any course that can be taught by one faculty member in one section, the in-person course will always be less expensive if there is an available classroom large enough to hold the class.
2. For any course with more than one section, but with fewer sections than one faculty member can teach, the in-person course will also nearly always be cheaper than an IT course.
3. For large enrollment courses with more sections than a single faculty member can teach at one time, perform the following calculation:

I. *Maximum possible faculty cost-saving calculation*

A = Average annual faculty compensation (salary and benefits)_____

N = Number of FTE faculty required to teach the course in a given year_____

C = N x A _____

Take 1/3 x C _____

This figure represents the approximate annual savings in faculty presentation time for the course, as well as time spent in course preparation, because all facets of instruction comprise only about one-half of a faculty member's workload at four-year institutions.

II. *Additional costs of IT course*

D = Development costs of the IT course

FTE Faculty required to prepare course_____

A = Average annual faculty compensation_____

A x FTE faculty cost in preparing course_____

FTE staff required to prepare course_____

SA = Average staff compensation_____

SA x FTE staff cost in preparing course_____

Add faculty and staff course preparation costs_____

Estimated number of years course can be taught before major revisions needed___

D=Divide faculty and staff preparation costs by years _____

O=Ongoing additional costs of IT course

A=Additional FTE staff needed to support course_____

SA=Average staff compensation_____

SA x S added annual staff costs_____

H=Hardware and software purchases needed to run the course_____

H/3=Hardware and software depreciated over 3 years_____

O=SA x S + H/3 _____

Take D + O_____.

This figure represents part of the increased costs of the IT course. If the faculty savings of 1/3 x C are less than or equal to D + O, then using IT will cost more money or have a less effective student outcome. Even if the faculty savings slightly exceed the increased cost estimates for the IT course, an IT course will cost more or have less effective student outcomes because of other IT costs not included above and the likely greater student drop-out rate for any IT course.

CONCLUSION

Both faculty and students are indispensable players in this new technologically changing environment. Institutions need to invest in professional develop-ment to train faculty to teach in the distance education setting. Converting traditional courses to online courses takes time and money. We need to ensure that students are not shortchanged in the rush to tap into the distance education market.

Educating the knowledge workers of the future means they will need to be trained to work in teams. How can that be accomplished if the education experience is predominantly through Web-based courses, or one-way video, with no real-time interaction between students and faculty? Evidence indicates that the drop-out rate for students in online courses is usually higher than for traditional classrooms, which would mean a loss of tuition for institutions. For those students with loans, the risk is that they will end up in debt, unable to repay their loans because they cannot find employment. Much can be done to enhance learning through technology, but quality education has both tangible and intangible costs. Campuses need to educate students to work in an environment that uses technology, but this is likely to cost more money, not less.

ENDNOTES

1. Hafner and Lyon, "Talking Headers," *Washington Post Magazine*, August 1996.

2. Robert B. Reich, *Education and the Next Economy*. Report commissioned by the NEA Research Division. Washington, DC: National Education Association, 1988, p. 17.

3. Rachel Adelson, "The Evolution of E-mail." *Forecast* (May/June, 1996).

4. Morley Winograd and Dudley Buffa, *Taking Control: Politics in the Information Age*. New York: Henry Holt and Company, 1998.

5. James Cortada, *Rise of the Knowledge Worker*. Boston: Butterworth-Heineman, 1998.

6. Cortada, *Rise of the Knowledge Worker*, p. 14.

7. Richard Cattani, "The Productivity of Knowledge Work," *Forbes* (October 7, 1996).

8. Dudley Buffa and Michael Hais, "How Knowledge Workers Vote," *Fast Company* 5 (October, 1996): 70; see <www.fastcompany.com/online/05/vote.html>.

9. Winograd and Buffa, *Taking Control*, p.2.

10. Charles Handy, *The Age of Unreason*. Boston: Harvard Business School Press, 1989, p. 34.

11. Michael G. Dolence and Donald M. Norris, *Transforming Higher Education: A Vision for Learning in the 21st Century*. Ann Arbor, MI: Society for College and University Planning, 1995, pp. 7-8.

12. National Center for Education Statistics, *Fall Staff in Postsecondary Institutions 1997*, September 1999. See <www.nces.ed.gov>.

13. *USA Today*, November 5, 1999, p. A1.

14. "A Survey of Higher Education Members and Leaders." Commissioned by the National Education Association, Washington, DC, May 1998 (unpublished).

15. See also contracts from Salem Community College (NJ), Schoolcraft Community College (MI), and Spoon River College (IL); contracts available from NEA Higher Education Contract Analysis System (HECAS), Version 7.1, 1999-2000.

16. See contracts from Tompkins-Cortland Community College (NY), the University of Alaska, Alpena Community College (MI), and Cincinnati State Technical and Community College; contracts available from NEA Higher Education Contract Analysis System (HECAS), Version 7.1, 1999-2000.

17. See also contracts from Clackamas Community College (OR), where faculty receive compensation for the periodic updating of courses; Dodge City Community College (KS), where faculty compensation of $125 per credit hour is given for each preparation of an interactive television (ITV) course; Elgin Community College (IL), where faculty members receive an additional stipend of $200 each for the first two times they teach a distance education course; Illinois Valley Community College (IL), where a $600 one-time stipend is given for adaptation of instruction to distance learning; and Oakton Community College (IL), where the training rate is $20 per hour, up to 20 hours, and $500 in additional compensation is given the first time a faculty member teaches a distance education class through ITV. Contracts available from NEA Higher Education Contract Analysis System (HECAS), Version 7.1, 1999-2000

18. Gerald Van Dusen, *The Virtual Campus: Technology and Reform in Higher Education.* ASHE-ERIC Higher Education Report. Volume 25, No. 5. Washington, DC: ASHE-ERIC, 1997, p. 39.

19. Ibid.

20. See also Portland Community College and Dodge City Community College. However, Tompkins-Cortland Community College explicitly stipulates that "Electronic transmissions of course materials, lectures or chat groups will not be monitored by the College except for purposes of evaluating the faculty member according to the standard procedures."

21. *What's the Difference: A Review of Contemporary Research on the Effectiveness of Distance Learning in Higher Education.* Washington, DC: Institute for Higher Education Policy, 1999, p. 8.

22. Ibid.

23. See also Pennsylvania College of Technology, where faculty are required to "Participate in orientation to instruction for use and integration of new instructional equipment as appropriate." See also Dodge City Community College (KS), where "The College shall provide training in the use of the ITV equipment for all full-time instructors assigned to teach in the ITV classroom. Training shall be provided prior to the first ITV course taught. . ., shall occur prior to the class start date and shall be no longer than 4 hours in length. Upon completion of training, the full-time instructor shall be paid $60."

24. Charles Mann, "Who Will Own Your Next Good Idea?" *Atlantic Monthly* 282(3) (September 1998); available at <www.theatlantic.com/issues/98sept/copy.htm>.

25. "Preserve Copyrights and Protect Us All," *Washington Post*, Outlook Section, November 1, 1998.

26. Mann, "Who Will Own Your Next Good Idea?," p.5.

27. Carol Frances, Richard Pumerantz, and James Caplan, "Planning for Technology: What You Thought You Knew Could Lead You Astray," *Change* (July/August, 1999): 25-33.

28. See Chapters 2, 5, and 8 by Frank Jewett in this book for an analysis of IT cost concepts and definitions.

29. David Garson, "Distance Education: Assessing Costs and Benefits," *Thought and Action: The NEA Higher Education Journal*, National Education Association, XV, 2 (Fall 1999): 105-18.

30. "A Survey of Part-time Higher Education Faculty Union Members and Non-members in Four States." Report commissioned by the National Education Association, December 1997 (unpublished).

CHAPTER 15

The Future of Higher Education in an Internet World
Twilight or Dawn?

Edward D. Goldberg and David M. Seldin

This chapter explores the rise of online, Internet-based delivery systems and suggests the need for higher education institutions to adopt a much more explicit business approach in planning and implementing such an online effort, including possibly seeking an investment of venture capital. While some in higher education think of their institutions as "businesses," and act as if they were, most do not. The dominant view is that colleges and universities are inherently different, not subject to market forces in the same way that businesses are, and not amenable to being managed by business management techniques.

BACKGROUND

Higher education has been intimately involved with changing technologies over many decades, both as a developer of such technologies and as a user. Most of the time, the impact of technology has been marginal on the core educational mission of higher education and higher education has responded, appropriately, in measured ways. It has coped with such technological changes with rates of adoption determined by the relative significance of the innovations, the extent to which early adopters and champions existed at the institution, and by the fiscal circumstances of the institution. Using the rise of the PC as an example of an information technology innovation, we have seen a great deal of equipment added over the last 15 years, but at different rates by year and by institution. The sense was always that if more equipment and its use could not be funded this year, next year would be fine. For example, there would be no major loss to students and the institution overall if delay was necessitated by financial considerations. And, to a large extent, higher education decision-makers were right.

With the rise of the Internet, and its multimedia World Wide Web, we now see a new challenge presented to such decision-makers. For the Internet is not simply "another technological advance" that can be responded to in a typical way; it is a "set of transforming technologies" that impact both the core of the educational process of institutions and the fundamental competitive forces institutions face.

The history of the Internet, from the championship of the Department of Defense through that of the National Science Foundation (NSF), culminates in terms of relevancy for higher education in the development of the World Wide Web and the graphical Web browser. Add to that the rapid rise in number of users worldwide (now well over 100 million), the rapid rise in number of Web sites (anybody can be a publisher), and the rise of groupware functionality (the interactivity) and we have a major force for communicating information, engaging in dialogue, and creating cohesive communities—all processes at the core of higher education. The Internet is a set of truly transforming technologies. It impacts the way students can access higher education and the way teaching and learning can take place, and it significantly changes the competitive landscape for almost all institutions.

For those who have doubts, it is instructive to look at the Internet's transforming impact on some non-higher education activities.

- **Sales of software.** While almost all software was sold in "shrink wrapped" boxes, much is now downloaded from the Internet.
- **Retail trading of securities.** Witness the rise of the online brokerage business and its fast growth.
- **E-commerce.** Christmas 1999 saw roughly a 7-percent increase in store sales, but over a 100-percent increase in online sales. Of course, the base was much smaller, but also witness the rise of such large "e-commerce" companies as Amazon.com as a harbinger of things to come.
- **Employment processes.** Check out the rise of Web sites that bring together people seeking positions with organizations seeking employees.
- **Music.** Witness the use of "MP3 technology" to compress audio and significantly increase the downloading of music.

Examples abound for illustrating that the Internet is simply "not another set of technologies," but a set with potential to fundamentally transform numerous societal activities. It is easy to access, easy to use, and reasonably cheap (both in hardware and access service). It is appealing because of its multimedia functionality. It is not passive; not only can one interact with material and other people, but one can use it to easily publish the output of one's own creativity by building one or more Web sites. And future technological directions favor increased usage and importance.

Two directions warrant mention. First, expect to see the widespread availability of "Internet appliances," integrated systems of inexpensive hardware, software, and access service. These appliances will foster greater use by providing those without full function computers with the ability to use the Internet and those with computers with the opportunity to cheaply add additional ways to use the Internet from different locations. Second, expect to see the spread of broad-bandwidth connectivity to the Internet, via cable modems and DSL (direct subscriber line) hookups. These developments will increase usage by making the Internet experience more enjoyable and productive in three ways: (1) it will allow for the increased use of streaming video, (2) it will reduce the wait for material, and (3) it will allow people to keep their Internet connectivity on at all times, which has the effect of creating much more use for numerous purposes, big and small. Expect to see the continued diffusion and significant impact of the Internet into more societal functions. Expect higher education not to be exempt.

HIGHER EDUCATION AND THE INTERNET

There have been, are, and will be two fundamental public policy issues regarding higher education. They are access (who will have access to higher education, at what price, and with what ease) and excellence (what is the quality of the teaching and learning process as measured by outcomes).

We have seen attention to access in a number of ways over the last 50 plus years: the World War II and Korean War GI Bill of Rights, the rise of the community college, and the rise of federal and state financial aid programs. As society becomes more complex through factors such as globalization and technology, the development of human capital (the knowledge, skills, and abilities of people) becomes important not only from an overall economic development standpoint, but also from the perspective of the individual. Thus, access continues to be an ongoing public policy concern.

We have also seen attention to excellence in a number of ways over the same period—the attention to institutional research and outcomes measurement, the rise of basic skills education, the creation of a nexus between work and academic studies through cooperative education, the assessment movement, attention to the nature of the learning process, and formalization of study abroad programs as one response to economic globalization. Because excellence produces better human capital, it will continue to be an ongoing public policy concern.

We can think of the Internet in terms of how it affects these two public policy goals to better understand its transforming impact. In terms of access, think of several categories of potential part-time commuting students for whom access to higher education has been non-existent or available only with great hardship:

- People who live in parts of the United States where the degrees they seek are not available within easy driving distance.
- People who live overseas who want to study towards a degree from an American university (both U.S. citizens abroad and nationals of other countries).
- People who travel extensively for their work and can't attend classes on, say, Tuesday and Thursday evenings because they are frequently far away from where they might attend a traditional face-to-face program.
- People who work irregular schedules—non-daytime shifts or changing shifts or are required to frequently work long hours without much notice.
- People who have heavy parenting, eldercare, or other personal responsibilities.

These people are candidates for the "anytime, anyplace" Internet delivery of higher education. "Anytime" because the heart of Internet delivery is asynchronous computer conferencing that allows a student to read and contribute to an intellectual dialogue whenever the person logs on. "Anyplace" because Internet delivery allows a person to be anyplace in the world (one place today and another tomorrow) and have access to the course(s) the person is taking. "Anytime, anyplace" higher education greatly increases access.

As to excellence, examples of Internet-based online delivery show great promise in matching and surpassing the quality of traditional face-to-face higher education. If we don't romanticize what really occurs in many of our traditional classrooms, we are faced with some unpleasant realities. Consider the heavy use of adjuncts at some institutions, not because they possess unparalleled specialized expertise, but to save money. Consider the use of the large lecture hall, with unproven teaching assistants handling breakout sessions. Consider the packed classrooms containing 35 students, taught by faculty members ranging from superb to OK who have no ability, because of the large class size, to engage all students in an intellectual dialogue, let alone simply answer all questions. The model of the small seminar, taught by a full-time faculty member who is a good teacher, is not the norm as experienced by most students. While online education can also be poorly implemented, it can be well implemented offering students an educational experience that matches if not surpasses that of the traditional classroom. We have an emerging body of research (no better but no worse than typical higher education research studies) that indicates that students learn as much if not more.

A good way to think about the excellence of online education is to consider that at its best it has strong benefits in terms of information conveyance, intellectual discourse, and even development of learning communities. It can offer heightened student/faculty interaction and active, not passive, learning. Because it is new, online learning also offers the opportunity for each and every institution to rethink how teaching and learning best take place without reference to the "way it's always been done on this campus."

If for no other reasons than increasing access and a fresh chance in striving for excellence, we ought to see institutions actively pursuing the development of online learning efforts. But more is at stake, such as institutional fiscal stability, vitality, and even survival, for online learning radically changes the competitive marketplace for most institutions.

WHAT ONLINE LEARNING MEANS FOR THE COMPETITIVE MARKETPLACE

Higher education has a number of competitive marketplaces because not all the following institutions face the same type of competition:

- A relatively small number of institutions, with strong brand names, attract students from across the United States and from around the world. They can be said to face national, even international, competition from other institutions of the same type. These institutions are stable, usually wealthy as measured by endowment, and strongly committed to excellence. Not much is likely to change because of online delivery unless they utterly fail to bring the same energy and resources to developing and implementing an appropriate online effort.
- Another set of "national institutions," with far weaker brand names and far less wealth, will need to guard against their brand names becoming weaker and less associated with quality, based on the relative quality and scope of their online efforts.
- A larger number of regional institutions (which draw the bulk of their students from a small geographical area) have faced limited competition from a few nearby institutions in the world of traditional higher education, but will face an overwhelmingly crowded competitive scene as the people they have attracted now have access to a large number of competing online programs.

- A large number of institutions have faced limited competition because the geographical area they serve contains zero or only a few alternative institutions. They will now face an overwhelmingly crowded competitive scene.

What impact will the changed competitive scene have for individuals? They will have access to an unprecedented array of educational programs—both from providers in their geographical area and from providers thousands of miles away. Be it degree acquisition or lifelong learning, the individual will be faced with a golden opportunity to frame and satisfy educational objectives.

What impact will the changed competitive scene have for institutions? The result of widespread and rapid growth of online education, over the next decade, is that the Internet will likely create a new national and a world-wide market for higher education. Perhaps the highest quality national institutions have the luxury of assured positions based on current market positions and market perceptions, particularly if they mount a quality and appropriate online effort. All other institutions have a once-in-a-century opportunity to fundamentally change their brand position (the image for which they are known).

There will be big winners and big losers among institutions—at the extreme, the winners will emerge with global brand equity and enormous reach for their educational missions; the losers—now without the safety of geographic barriers—will find their very existence threatened. A unique moment of challenge and opportunity!

THE NEED FOR BOLD INSTITUTIONAL ACTION

We have argued that the Internet is a transforming set of technologies that will allow institutions to extend their mission by opening up further access to what they offer and to seek increased excellence via the new delivery system. We have further argued that the opportunity comes with the challenge of a changed competitive scene that could threaten the vitality and perhaps the survival of particular institutions.

Given these realities, bold action is called for by each and every institution, even though, for the following reasons, bold action is not a hallmark of most institutions of higher education:

- Talented senior higher education decision-makers on each campus are already overloaded with work; the attention demanded by the details of current operating issues tend to preclude, from a time perspective, the planning and implementation of bold new strategies.
- Campus cultures and bureaucratic processes have developed over the years to present checks and balances geared to steady-state delivery, not bold new ventures.

- Bold action requires significant money; new money is in short supply and reallocation brings severe political risks.

Nevertheless, institutions must respond to the opportunity and challenge, with the most significant rewards going to those institutions that are first to market with an online effort congruent with their mission. What to do and how to do it are, therefore, issues to which much thought must be given.

In general, what to do is easy to understand:

- Planning
- Garnering enough support throughout the institution
- Securing resources
- Appointing and empowering a senior change agent
- Encouraging organizational champions to come forward
- Determining the scope of what will be offered
- Deciding on the features of the online effort that will create its competitive advantage
- Investing in high-quality curriculum development
- Dealing with the four key policy issues of (1) ownership and use of the online intellectual property, (2) the role of innovation in online delivery in promotion and tenure decisions, (3) faculty compensation, and (4) outsourcing of certain critical functions

Beyond the above, in getting an effort underway, it is most important to deal with scaling issues. It's easy to develop and offer a small effort, but it's difficult to scale it up and offer it to a significant number of students. Also critical is the marketing of the online effort so that one grabs mindshare, then marketshare, and then achieves a state in which revenue exceeds costs.

But even more difficult is understanding the level of institutional effort required. If an institution cannot mount the effort itself due to limited human and fiscal resources, an outsourcing strategy must be explored.

THE INSTITUTIONAL EFFORT NEEDED FOR A SUCCESSFUL ONLINE PROGRAM

To understand what is needed, one must break down online activity into two categories: (1) supplemental to face-to-face delivery and the delivery of individual online courses and (2) the delivery of full online degrees and a comprehensive set of non-credit offerings. The following categories have differential resource requirements:

- **Supplemental Online Activity and the Delivery of Individual Online Courses.** These efforts, while educationally important to an institution's face-to-face students, do not require, from the institution, the heavy human and financial resources demanded of the other category of online activity. Of course, the burden on faculty can be high. In supplementing face-to-face instruction, we are seeking to improve, not to invent. Pioneering faculty members, and good technical support for other faculty members, can go a long way in creating Web sites for face-to-face courses. Likewise, the delivery of individual online courses is not a heavy resource-demanding effort because this approach flows from a desire to overcome space limitations on campuses, as a convenience to students who need particular courses during a specific term, and, perhaps, for idiosyncratic reasons. Typically, this effort has as its market existing face-to-face students, thus reducing marketing costs. This effort also does not demand significant and costly attention to achieving high graduation rates.

- **Delivery of Full Online Degrees and Comprehensive Sets of Non-Credit Offerings.** To be successful in this category, one has to be successful in a competitive sense, where one's competitors are institutions across the world, both non-profit and for-profit ventures. While there is a need for heavy curriculum development expenditures, key to understanding the dynamic to being successful is to understand the need to market the online effort—typically in a way much more intensive than higher education has marketed itself, although the entire marketing of higher education services is changing. Think of both consumer marketing to individuals and business-to-business marketing to organizations and business corporations. Institutions of higher education that pursue a strategy of offering full degree programs and comprehensive sets of non-credit offerings are starting an Internet-based business, with all that such a start-up requires, not simply extending their educational missions.

So what is needed to establish a significant and successful virtual university offering full online degree programs and comprehensive sets of non-credit offerings? In general, "jump starting" the institution in developing its version of a virtual university, one true to its mission, yet one that optimizes revenue in the new competitive world of online higher education. And after conceptualization, rapid implementation. In emerging competitive markets, those who arrive early with high-quality products and services significantly increase their probability of success.

What are some of the critical steps that need to be taken? For illustrative purposes, consider the case of a university seeking to develop and offer a significant set of full online degree programs. (This would be in keeping with the educational goals of most of the people who enroll in universities, goals that involve the garnering of a degree.)

The first step is planning. The institution must develop a sharp strategy of building upon its strengths to determine what will be offered, to whom, at what quality level, with what features, and at what price level. Then it must develop a detailed academic and fiscal plan for the virtual university effort. Think of this planning effort as encompassing both strategic and operational planning. In undertaking this effort, one will need to educate many campus constituencies about the opportunities and challenges of Internet-based education. Consider setting up a presidential task force on the establishment of a virtual university and of presenting formal day-long and multi-day seminars on online education and the business of online education.

The next step after planning is to garner widespread support for the plan. Consider facilitating the "buy in" on the part of schools and programs within the institution by presentations to various program officials, meetings with deans and key faculty, and the development of a mini-strategic plan for each school. Also, don't overlook the use of both fiscal and non-fiscal incentives.

The next step is implementation where the goal is to achieve rapid entrance into the market. Consider key steps, such as defining common curriculum/ programmatic features, locating management talent to direct the start-up venture, planning for any unique organizational arrangements for the online effort, and preparing a business plan that, among other issues, deals with the funding of up-front costs either through internal investment or the use of outside funds (grants, short-term loans, or venture capital).

Early in the implementation process, four critical policy issues will need to be considered. First, the university must decide on its policy regarding "intellectual property" ownership and use. This decision is important as one considers scaling up from a small online effort to a larger effort. The upfront curriculum development costs are so high that it is important that the intellectual property ownership and use policy allow each course developed to be provided to each and every faculty member who will be teaching that online course as part of the offering of an online degree program. While sharing of course material and lecture notes may take place in traditional higher education delivery, in the online world, each faculty member teaching an online course must be able to use what has been developed through the large expenditure made for course development. The traditional model of curriculum development, where each and every faculty member "prepares" each and every course he or she will be teaching (generally without any extra compensation and under loose institutional policies that give them complete ownership and rights to use), needs to be changed.

Second, tenure and promotion policies as they relate to online education must be reviewed. Junior faculty members must be part of the online effort. But it must be safe for them to be involved. Changing tenure and promotion policies to explicitly recognize innovations in online education is one of the ways to enlist their energies without placing them at risk. Making such changes will be easier at some institutions; harder at others. But even those institutions with policies geared to or centered on a "traditional emphasis on refereed print scholarship" must exhibit some flexibility or see only senior faculty members involved in its online effort. If the policies are not supportive of the involvement of junior faculty members, one will lose some of the people most capable of contributing to excellence in online education.

The third policy issue deals with how to compensate faculty members for their participation in the online effort. One could assert that any energies expended were simply part of the workload for which they draw their regular salary. While this might be an effective approach at some institutions, it seems to ignore a number of institutional needs and seems to be somewhat unfair to faculty. In getting the online effort underway, two driving forces suggest that compensation to faculty be over and above base pay. The first is the speed with which one would want to get to the marketplace. Speed in getting to marketplace suggests that we want a heightened faculty response, an intense effort, and that such faculty contributions over and above normal seem, in fairness, to demand compensation over and above normal. The second is the institutional need to scale up the effort, which necessitates institutional ownership or exclusive use of the intellectual property created through its investment in the curriculum development of online courses that are part of its offering of online degrees. Such ownership/use requires compensation to faculty, in fairness, over and above normal compensation. (Consider three approaches to compensation for intellectual property. The first provides a stipend upon completion. The second provides a royalty each time the course is taught. The third is a hybrid approach.) One should argue that, to the extent the new online effort is to be "run like a modern business," faculty should share in returns at least through increased compensation.

The fourth policy issue has to do with outsourcing, a classic "make or buy" business decision dealing with what universities should do themselves and what they should purchase. Outsourcing is not new to universities; witness its heavy use in the arenas of bookstores and food service. But universities have not extended outsourcing to functions closer to their core mission of education. In quickly starting the online "business," universities need to think through outsourcing of two major functions even though they may already have some institutional capacity in operating the functions.

The first area for outsourcing is to secure the learning software, hosting service for online courses and instructional support for faculty from an outside vendor. While institutions have this capability at some level, they typically have neither the excess capacity to handle the new online effort nor the reliability of service needed when both students and some faculty are thousands of miles away from campus.

The second area for outsourcing is to secure consulting or management services to plan, implement, and operate the new start-up. Again, it is not necessarily that universities do not have the talent, but that they do not have excess capacity. Because all current managers have a full workload, it might be far better to secure, under contract, such management services than to build one's own staff in an employment marketplace that has only a limited number of people who have actually built an online educational business.

With planning done, with policy issues addressed, and with rapid implementation underway, marketing must immediately begin to ensure successful entrance into the market. A marketing plan for the online effort needs to be developed; it should consider the use of online banner advertising; radio and cable TV advertising; collateral material; exhibits at conferences and trade association meetings; all forms of public relations, including online PR; print advertising; face-to-face selling; telephone and Internet support once potential students express interest; and a campaign to mobilize the university's contacts. The saying "build a better mousetrap and they will come" is completely false as a guiding rule. In the competitive marketplace, institutions will face in the online world, information must rapidly get out to the various market segments to prevent failure and ensure success.

Finally, institutions serious about success in the online world will need to build a set of strategic partnerships. Use the general rule that no one institution can go it alone and succeed. Consider content, producer, and marketing alliances. Content alliances refer to arrangements with owners of both broad-based and niche content. One would want easy access to such content at a reasonable cost. Producer alliances are with other institutions whose online effort is complementary (they serve different students and their array of disciplines is significantly different). Marketing alliances are with organizations that can facilitate access to various markets. Consider overseas organizations, professional/trade associations, and marketing firms and unions.

COST ISSUES IN THE DEVELOPMENT, MARKETING, AND DELIVERY OF QUALITY ONLINE DEGREE PROGRAMS

Like any type of educational offering, an online effort can be implemented at various quality levels. While quality is not entirely a function of resources, in general, expenditure level is a major determinant. One, of course, needs excellent management expertise, great faculty, and solid support services for quality to be achieved. But management, faculty, and support services are related to resource level.

Consider the implementation of a plan to offer 10 online graduate degrees, with a year of development prior to enrolling the first students. Expenditures might be made according to the following schedule:

Expenditure	Starting Date	Magnitude
General management	Immediately	Medium
Academic management for each program	Immediately	Low
Curriculum development costs	Immediately	High
Marketing	Immediately	High
Teaching of courses	When classes start	Medium
Program support	Some soon and some when classes start	Medium

Such a schedule suggests heavy expenditures six months to a year before the revenue begins and a different pattern of expenditures than for traditional face-to-face programs (the differences primarily are seen in the heavy upfront curriculum development and marketing costs).

To get a sense of the specific expenditures that will need to be made, consider some of the details for each major category of expenditures.

General management

- Senior manager (dean equivalent) to function as the chief executive of the effort and support for his or her office
- Deputy
- Director of administration
- Chief academic person (for the online effort)
- Chief marketing person
- Chief customer service person, including financial aid administration

Academic management for each program

- Academic director with overall responsibility for the development and offering of each program (could be a faculty member making this a major undertaking that would be their only non-teaching assignment under a 12-month contract)
- Assistant academic director to provide administrative support, but also substantive support to the academic director
- Instructional design support, including training of faculty members

Curriculum development costs

- Faculty members, perhaps on an overload basis, to develop the content of each course
- Intellectual property purchase (either existing works or the commissioning of new works)
- Creation of multimedia content, including streaming video

- Pilot testing of the curriculum
- Long-term and continuous evaluation and redesign/redevelopment

Marketing

- Development of collateral material, print ads, online banner ads, the online venture's Web site, and radio and TV ads
- Placement of ads
- Face-to-face selling at exhibitions associated with professional and trade associations, college and graduate fairs, and corporations and organizations
- Closing of sales through e-mail and phone outreach

Teaching of courses

- Faculty costs
- Hosting costs
- Costs of using learning software

Program support

- Admissions processing
- Financial aid processing
- 24/7 help desk

The price tag for the various expenditures will vary as a function of the number of months the venture has been underway, the number of students, pay levels at the institution, and each institution's definition of the quality level it wants to achieve. The biggest expenditure categories will be curriculum development and marketing (assuming one simply does not want to define the market as those students currently enrolled in face-to-face programs).

While there is no typical budget, we provide the following rough proportions as a broad guideline:

Expenditure Category	Percent of Total*
General management	10%
Academic management	5%
Curriculum development	30%
Marketing	30%
Delivery/Teaching	10%
Program support	10%
Other	5%

*Assumes no allocation of indirect costs

One should note the potential folly of starting with a small effort and either staying small or growing slowly over time. First, one would not be able to take advantage of significant economies of scale, for example, in marketing. Second, with a small number of programs (with or without a slow build-up) the marketplace (generally and niche by niche) might be captured by a set of educational providers who entered early with a critical mass of programs.

Assuming that a significant investment is needed, the questions become what are the sources of funds and how can one garner them? In reflecting on this, it is useful to think about internal and external sources of funds.

Internally, three possible sources exist for such a large investment—none of the sources being particularly feasible for most institutions. Reallocation within the operating budget is always a political minefield. Dipping into an institution's endowment raises questions for trustees about their fiduciary responsibility. A special fund-raising campaign presents difficulties in that there are always other needs, perhaps more pressing or more politically sensitive.

Externally, there are also three possible sources. Foundation grants are a possibility, although not too many foundations are supporting online education and the size of the grants is far short of what is needed. Government appropriations are a possibility for perhaps a few public institutions, but such appropriations, in the typical zero sum game that is public support of higher education, would see less money provided for other programs. Venture capital is a strong possibility for some institutions in that it can provide the amount of investment dollars needed. The following will focus on the world of venture capital.

Sources of venture capital have prided themselves on fueling innovation, and particularly, these days, Internet-related innovation. The basic underlying transaction is that the venture capitalists put up the money and take the risk in return for a sizable proportion of ownership, which gives them a claim on revenue, profits, and eventually capital gains if and when the venture being funded goes public through an IPO (initial public offering). In addition to the money, such sources of funds also provide expertise and contacts to help the fledgling venture.

It is easy to understand the transaction from the venture capitalists' perspective. Risk taking is their business and risk taking has the potential for big financial returns. The uncertainty of success of any particular investment becomes less important, particularly if the venture capitalists have a diversified set of investments. Some failure can be tolerated because a few "wins" can lead to overall success.

What is the general utility of the transaction from the perspective of an institution of higher education? On balance, it might be positive. In its most basic terms, an institution without other sources of funds to invest in its online effort will find that ending up with a less than 100-percent share of revenue from a large and successful online effort is far superior to maintaining a 100-percent share in a small, less than fully successful effort.

One of the many possible arrangements might look like the following:

Factor	Venture Capitalist	Institution
Bearing of risk	Bears financial risk	Bears reputational risk
Split of tuition	Bulk to the venture capitalist	Fixed return to the institution
Expenditures	Costs borne through use of the investment	Minimal costs borne
End game of IPO if successful	Significant ownership accruing to the capitalist	Institution adds significant value to its endowment

As institutions consider the venture capital option, many will not have had experience in seeking and negotiating an arrangement with such sources of funds. For those, note that there are really two starting points. The first involves doing a full business plan (a narrative and a set of financial projections) that demonstrates to the potential source of funds that the university knows what it's doing and that the proposed online venture has a possibility of making a more than adequate return on investment. Universities do not typically develop full-fledged business plans for new ventures; perhaps they should. But, given the lack of experience in doing such plans, and the importance of the business plan in interesting sources of capital, consideration should be given to the use of a consultant to help fashion the business plan.

The second involves searching for sources of funds. The institution's key bank, the firm that handles investment of the university's endowment, business school faculty, alumni, and staff are all sources of leads. Also, in today's world, some companies specialize in providing management expertise and investment capital to the online ventures of universities. Seek them out.

What will the venture capitalist look at in the plan? In a sense, everything in a well done business plan is important because eventual profitability of the proposed online venture may hinge on any of the factors described in the plan. But several factors warrant mentioning. First, the quality of the management chosen to lead the online venture will be viewed as critical. As an Internet start-up venture, it will be hard to anticipate every decision a priori and there will be a significant number of opportunistic possibilities. Only seasoned managers can provide some level of confidence that potentially wise decision-making will take place. Second, an understanding of competitive forces, the niche markets the university wants to compete in, and the competitive advantage(s) it plans to bring to those markets, will be looked at carefully. Clearly, an understanding of the marketplace is a basic underpinning to eventual profitability. Third, the projected financial statements will say a lot, not only about whether the possible investment has promise of meeting the minimum performance standards the venture capitalists insist on, but the statements will also speak volumes about whether the university is realistic in estimating how much of an investment will be required and realistic in understanding the balance between expenditure categories. All in all, the narrative and financials of the business plan must give the potential investors a strong sense of confidence in the university's capabilities.

A standard business plan outline should be used to facilitate review of the venture by both those within and outside the university. Starting with an "executive summary," the opening should stress the objectives to be sought by the online venture and the major keys to success. As a guide to those not accustomed to developing business plans, the following outline is suggested:

- Primary scope of the venture (the major products or services to be offered, description of how they will be delivered, at what quality level and at what price)
- Secondary scope of the venture (the other products and services to be offered, description of how they will be delivered, at what quality level and at what price)
- Characteristics of the venture, including unique features of the products and services, that are designed to lead to success
- Analysis of the markets within which the venture will be competing, including an analysis of demand and of competitors
- The process of curriculum development and delivery, including discussion of the technologies to be used and the issue of outsourcing
- Description of marketing strategy and tactics
- Description of the management of the venture, including the background of key personnel
- Description of any partnerships or alliances the venture has established or will establish
- A five-year fiscal plan, including student enrollment projections, revenues, and expenditures

What are the greatest roadblocks to securing an outside investment? Two of them flow from some of the strengths of universities, which under conditions of rapid change can turn into weaknesses as outside capital is sought. First, all universities have some form of shared governance; that is generally a good thing, but the slowness of those processes could work against securing an outside investment. Second, the culture of many universities is typically conservative and risk aversive. Such a culture can work for the good when it provides the necessary stability useful in facilitating scholarship and good teaching over time. But adherence to a culture that produces stability can work against securing an outside investment because it can produce slowness of decision-making. As a general rule, universities that can demonstrate speed and decisiveness of decision-making (within their particular culture) will secure outside capital if they want it.

Of course, the decision to seek/accept outside capital needs to be grounded in an analysis of the details of any arrangement. The source of capital will push for control to increase the probability that the online effort will become a successful business. The institution will want to change as little as possible from normal processes, particularly given its perception, right or wrong, of what's needed to satisfy licensure and accrediting agencies. While arrangements exist between the for-profit world and the academy, definition of the shape of those arrangements continues. Still, where the for-profit world can invest in and use the intellectual capital and brand of the academy and the academy benefits, we have a classic "win-win" situation. We believe this is the case in regards to large scale, high-quality online educational ventures and we expect to see many universities considering this source of funds.

TWILIGHT OR DAWN?

The Internet is here to stay, transforming many societal functions. Higher education is not immune from the opportunities or challenges the Internet presents in opening a new approach to the delivery of education. Online delivery has great potential to increase access and provide a new opportunity to strive for greater excellence.

The key question is how institutions will respond to the new set of technologies as the Internet ushers in a radically changed, competitive marketplace for higher education. What is clear is that there is no stopping the diffusion of the technologies and online education. At issue is whether existing institutions or new institutions will be the innovators and market leaders.

It is not certain that existing institutions will be up to the challenge. Cultural barriers and bureaucratic processes will preclude some from effective implementation of an online effort because traditional ways of doing things on any particular campus can distort the online effort and dampen its chances of success. Risk aversive leaders will also hinder bold strategies. We also have seen that the financial investment needed to mount a significant online effort, one which can take advantage of economies of scale and become a presence in the marketplace, may be beyond the capability of many institutions. Fortunately, the ability to garner venture capital is possible these days, offering institutions a new, but creative way to enter the Internet world in a way that helps ensure success. But to seek such venture capital will require strong institutional leadership because the culture of most institutions holds as novel, and perhaps as inappropriate, the idea of joint ventures with the for-profit world.

In thinking about whether to seek venture capital, institutions need to turn to a fundamental concept from economics—the concept of opportunity cost.

Simply put, it asks decision-makers to calculate the cost of not doing anything, of what we lose when we do nothing. In the face of the transforming technologies of the Internet, doing nothing can bring with it high costs. The new competitive marketplace poses the risk of threatening the financial stability, the vitality, and even the survival of institutions that are too passive and risk aversive. Such a potential outcome should prompt presidents, faculty members, and board members to focus on the development of a planned, systemic response to the Internet. It will not be sufficient to rely on the fine creative work we see being done by individual faculty members across the country who frequently are working in isolation without the benefits of an overall institutional strategy.

Particularly, presidents will need to involve board members, perhaps earlier then usual, in the process of reviewing the need for outside capital. This review will be particularly useful when the institution has no history of joint venturing in a significant way with the for-profit sector.

Twilight or dawn for higher education institutions? Both. Some will enhance their mission, increase their financial stability, and ensure their vitality and survival. For them, it will be the dawn of a new, exciting era. For other institutions, it will be twilight. Memories of a beautiful day may persist, but the cold of darkness will be settling upon the enterprise.

CONCLUSIONS

WHAT WE HAVE LEARNED

When all is said and done, we can be sure of two things. First, we can be sure that information technology's penetration into the collegiate teaching and learning process will only accelerate. Our confidence is based on the projections for a growing bulge in the traditional 18-22-year age cohort—the sons and daughters of baby boomers who are also the *first* Internet generation. They will no more be able to conceive of higher education without the Internet than many of us in the baby boom generation were able to conceive of higher education without video. Also contributing to our confidence is the future for "anytime, anyplace" learning in a global, knowledge-based economy There will be explosive growth in the demand for such education and training; higher education will either compete in that area or abandon it to the for-profit sector. To the extent that both these growing learner populations require and demand it, and to the extent higher education seeks to serve either or both of these populations, then information technology (IT) is only just beginning to make its presence felt in the academic program.

The increasing ubiquity of IT will, at least in the short term, bring with it increased cost pressures for colleges and universities. Such pressures are inevitable insofar as what is a recurring capital expense of *unknown dimensions* is paid for on the sly with operating funds and continues to eat up whatever slack can be found in campus operating budgets. And that escalation will only be compounded insofar as the dominant applications of IT are to *supplement* rather than replace traditional classroom instruction.

To the extent that IT serves as an adjunct to traditional classroom instruction, it will increase the unit or per-student costs of instruction. If faculty labor costs ("a") remain constant and are added to the capital costs, training costs, and maintenance and support costs of information technology ("b"), then the total ("c") must be greater than "a." The cost increase is only aggravated by the lack of available "benchmarks" for the unit costs of support, maintenance, and training!

To the extent that public policymakers and campus leaders seek to reduce college costs and enhance affordability while exploiting the learning potential of IT, they will need to begin thinking in new ways. All available analysis leads to the inevitable conclusion that cost savings can be achieved *only if* several key conditions are met. First, the basic principle of *substituting capital for labor* means that for IT to reduce costs traditional instructional labor costs *cannot* be held constant. They must be reduced. To do so will require re-examination of the traditional components of the instructional role and of how these components are organized. We alluded earlier to the traditional "bundling" of the various instructional roles—preparation, delivery, interaction with students, and assessment. Each of these components has traditionally been integrated into the work of a single person, the professor, who performs *all* functions independently for *all* student groups taking a course. To reduce costs, we will need to find ways to *unbundle* these functions so that we reduce duplication of effort, and thus reduce labor. *Course preparation* is probably the function that at once promotes the most "duplication" of faculty effort and can yield the most cost savings through elimination. This is, of course, the rationale of the model of *distributed technology* described most fully by Frank Jewett in Chapter 5. As with any restructuring or reconfiguration of "production processes" in any industry, enormous barriers must be overcome. Dissociating the components of the academic role that have crystallized over the past century in the American context is no mean challenge.

While reducing labor costs through substitution of capital is requisite to reducing costs, it is *not* sufficient. The second basic law of cost reduction is the *law of scale*. Because so much of the capital costs associated with IT are fixed, much of the labor costs must be substituted for to achieve real unit cost savings. This need for substitution means that there must be a sufficiently large number of substitutions of units of labor. Every cost study of every non-traditional technology for teaching and learning reaches the same conclusion: substitution must be achieved at a sufficiently large scale to reduce unit costs. Thus, *scaling*, as well as *role restructuring*, is required for cost savings. The possibilities for achieving economies of scale are not equally promising for all academic fields and program levels and types. The promise is greatest for large enrollment courses, which themselves have historically been successful in reducing unit costs through the use of teaching assistants in large lecture sections or part-time adjunct faculty for small sections (although it's not clear what additional *rate* of cost reduction can be achieved by IT beyond that offered through the multiple course section model or the adjunct faculty model). Moreover, it seems likely that economies of scale are subject to the discipline-specific constraints related to the "shelf life" of content and the need to update and revise instructional materials.

Substitution (of capital for labor) and economies of scale may together be insufficient to reduce unit instructional costs in the absence of a third principle—*institutional ownership of course materials.* To the extent institutions "own" the course materials used, they can exploit substitution with scale. To the extent that they do not control course materials, however, the costs of intellectual property become a variable that may affect instructional unit costs.

So intimately bound up with issues of costs are issues of quality because cost savings can only be judged relative to some minimally acceptable level of quality. That is, cost saving at the expense of quality is unlikely to be a trade-off that will be acceptable for either individual institutions or the higher education system in the long run. Therefore, measuring quality and, based on such measurements, maintaining or increasing quality, while substituting capital for labor and achieving economies of scale, is the goal. Measuring and maintaining quality, of course, raise complex normative issues of what is acceptable quality and complex measurement issues of how you assess it. As we have noted, the available evidence suggests that there is no significant difference associated with the particular *technology* of instruction *per se* in the achievement of basic content knowledge. That is, well designed and delivered instruction tends to support student learning of content while badly or carelessly designed and delivered instruction tends to undermine student learning of content—whether the technology be correspondence, video, digital, or traditional classroom. As James Caplan suggests in Chapter 7, that does not mean there are no differences in the quality of the learning experience as perceived by students or in their relative satisfaction, or no differences for particular groups of students or in particular fields. We still have much to learn here.

What do these basic conclusions mean for higher education? Do they mean much at all? We would argue, and the essays in this volume confirm, that they have profound implications for campus administrative leaders, faculty, students, and public policymakers.

For institutional leaders, these conclusions mean that they have some planning to do. Given the costs we are talking about and the sorts of realignments in campus budgets that will be required, and given too that everyone will not be able to do everything, institutions will need to think through what kinds of IT investments make the most sense relative to their mission, their program mix, and their student body. In what ways is the institution willing to add costs to instruction? In what areas can they really save? Or, are there any? Are the applications they have in mind scaleable? Are we prepared to invest in small-scale "pilot" projects that almost certainly will cost more than current practice?

To plan, institutions will need better data. They will need most fundamentally to be able to identify the actual costs of IT in the instructional program, and they will need assessment data. They will need to think about how to get the most instructionally from a given IT investment (for example, leasing may prove more attractive than ownership) and they will also need to be creative about raising large amounts of money. That may mean the exploration of alternative sources of venture capital or instructional collaboration with other institutions. Most broadly, institutions will need to think about their niche in the "new educational marketplace" that is emerging in the Internet world.

For faculty, the implications are enormous. In the short term, tremendous stresses and pressures will be associated with increased workload. Such workload increases include time invested in learning new technologies and applying them in one's courses, and the increased demands of 24/7 availability to students electronically. Clearly, higher education has adapted to the budgetary demands of the new technologies by demanding more of faculty with no concomitant increase in compensation or at least no increase commensurate with the effort. In the long term, there are major implications for the definition of faculty work. To the extent that teaching roles are unbundled, there will be many more opportunities for "specialized" teaching roles (be they providing content, delivering content, or interacting with students and assessment), and that means many more opportunities for "partial" contributions to teaching (reinforcing the explosive growth of part-time faculty).

The transition from the primary role as "content provider and gatekeeper" to "facilitator and guide," may at once strengthen faculty-student relationships in the service of learning, but will no doubt be a source of great discomfort for individual faculty and may serve to weaken the historically strong connection between their disciplinary expertise and the facilitation of the learning process using materials developed by others (autonomy). There will be serious issues regarding the ownership of intellectual property; the resolution of these issues has the potential to fundamentally alter the relationship between faculty and their institutions. Thus, for example, to the extent that institutions become the owners of intellectual property, some faculty will relinquish their claims to disciplinary expertise and probably lose the primary foundation for advancing their claims to a role in institutional governance. To the extent that faculty themselves become the owners of intellectual property, they will take on the characteristics of entrepreneurial product developers rather than service providers. This may mean the loosening of institutional ties and the emergence of a transinstitutional class of academic entrepreneurs.

To the extent that IT supports real productivity improvements, they may provide a source of funds to increase faculty pay (insofar as those improvements are not simply "sucked up" by the computing services monolith; in the short term, IT will more likely be a competitor for resources against faculty salary increases). Such improvements are more likely, however, to result in faculty jobs expanding at a slower rate than enrollment growth and fewer faculty jobs if higher education enrollment is stable or declining.

For students, IT will involve some additional costs in the form of technology fees, the purchase of computer equipment, or tuition increases spurred by institutional investments in IT. Against these relatively minor costs will be set clear and enormous benefits. Instructional applications of IT, including TV and media as well as networked computing, will increase access to higher education for those individuals who are remote from traditional campus sites. Online instruction will provide more choices for *all* students (be they on-campus, commuters, or remote) regarding when, where, and how they accomplish their academic work. This increased convenience, together with increased access, will expand the market for higher education.

For public policymakers, IT can provide an important lever to reduce costs, increase student access and choice, and maintain quality. They will, however, be faced with a bewildering array of policy choices related to support of campus IT infrastructure, support for the "restructuring" of the teaching role and faculty roles generally, and for rethinking the relationships among colleges and universities (cooperation vs. competition), between traditional higher education and new providers, and between faculty and their institutions. To the extent that they seek cost reductions in higher education through IT, policymakers will need to engage or rather encourage institutions to engage in strategic analysis of public IT investments and the possibilities for at once reducing costs while enhancing quality.

WHAT QUESTIONS REMAIN: AN AGENDA FOR FURTHER EXPLORATION OF IT COSTS

Higher education has embraced information technology in its business processes and in teaching and learning despite the high costs. The expectation is that IT will save money for higher education. The contrast between experience and expectation is disconcerting. At this moment, the major issues of information technology costs in higher education relate to calculating costs, managing costs, and policy on costs. We want to conclude here with a list of eight issues that strike us as critical and deserving of serious and systematic exploration.

1. **Calculating Overall IT Costs.** Can one benchmark the costs of these activities, or characterize the costs of best practices (as distinguished from

benchmark or average costs)? Should we not know more about what institutions are actually spending? Has anybody made a survey of what increases in institutional budgets relate to IT? We don't remember coming across any literature saying what institutions are spending on average on IT. We don't know of any estimate for what higher education is spending on IT in the U.S. in total, at least in terms of percentages. (IT accounts for about 10 percent of higher education expenditures in the United Kingdom.) How much has IT increased cost per student over the last 10 years? How much more are students spending? What are the opportunity costs of spending on IT? What are the costs of teaching in the traditional classroom, as compared with mediated teaching and learning, identifying the separate costs for each of the unbundled activities (curriculum development, course preparation, delivery, interaction with students, evaluation of student performance)? How do costs, and cost-saving potentials, differ by field? How many students do you need to enroll in a course to realize the potential cost-savings *supposedly* generated by the economics of scale alleged to be possible with mediated teaching and learning? (Of course, the number depends on the initial fixed costs, and the pattern of recurring costs, but that is the real question. Then, what are the conditions necessary for achieving these enrollments? Is it feasible to achieve these conditions?)

2. **Managing and Controlling Institutional Costs.** How can we identify all institutional IT cost factors? What are the best models? How can we manage and control institutional costs? What are the successful strategies for getting the most out of every dollar an institution invests in IT? What is the record for institutions that have outsourced most of their IT operations? What kind of cost shifting is taking place from institution to faculty; from faculty to IT professionals, including technical support staff; and from institution to student? Are costs being redistributed rather than cut? If so, what are the implications for education?

3. **Calculating Costs of Online Teaching.** What does online learning cost on various levels—the IT enhanced course, the online course, the online program, the virtual university? Is online learning diminishing the cost advantages of distance education via radio and television?

4. **Faculty Costs and Compensation.** What are the costs as faculty become producers? How are faculty compensated in that role? How do colleges and universities deal with the issues of copyright and intellectual property? How do colleges and universities get faculty to work collaboratively, through project teams, on developing online courses? What does it take to get faculty to use courseware developed by others, e.g., in high-enrollment introductory courses? Similar to what NCES has published on shifts towards more distance learning, would it not be helpful to have an

idea of the number of institutions using courseware in large-enrollment courses? How much are institutions saving on such courses? Can we cut costs by increasing productivity? What is the impact of mediated instruction on productivity? Productivity of faculty? Productivity of students? What do we need to improve our measures of productivity, outputs, and inputs?

Does mediated instruction open up opportunities for greater competition, and greater cost competition, between traditional institutions and non-traditional providers?

5. **Public Funding Sources.** How much have public sources contributed to maintaining IT investment in higher education at a level that will enable colleges and universities to compete? How should IT in higher education be financed where public moneys are involved? What should the federal government do as far as higher education's information technology costs are concerned?

6. **Privatization.** What is the role of privatization in financing the costs of IT in higher education? Is spinning off a for-profit financed by venture capital the most promising way, or is it somehow a surrender?

7. **Collaboration.** How can colleges and universities minimize IT costs through strategic partnerships among each other and with businesses and other organizations? What are the successful collaborative efforts in IT matters among institutions? Isn't it business as usual with institutions preferring extinction over sharing? What are examples of successful partnerships?

8. **Competition.** Are institutions using IT to engage in cost competition? Or cost-quality competition? What must higher education do to compete effectively with corporate and proprietary enterprises, in particular in providing continuing education for the workforce and opportunities for lifelong learning? Is higher education's share of the postsecondary market going to shrink inevitably as private providers of education and training make imaginative and aggressive use of online learning? Some higher education institutions seem to compete successfully in the continuing education market; Stanford online is offering 250 advanced courses in engineering and computer science to a worldwide clientele. Does this suggest that the market for higher education is at the high end?

RESOURCES

Bernhard W. Scholz

This "Resources" section lists and frequently summarizes important contributions to the literature on the costs of information technology in
higher education. A number of continuing projects on information
technology costs are included. No attempt is being made to include in this
section all books, articles, and other studies that appear in the end notes to
each of the chapters.

**Asynchronous Learning Networks, A Program funded by the Alfred P. Sloan
Foundation.** See <http://w3.scale.uiuc.edu/education/ALN.new.html>, <http://
www.aln.org/sloan_aln/index.htm>, and <http://www.aln.org>.

The goal is "to make it possible for any person in the U.S. to learn at anytime and
anyplace, in a subject of his/her choice. . . . ALN combines self-study with substantial,
rapid, asynchronous interactivity with others. In ALN, learners use computer and
communications technologies to work with remote learning resources and other
learners, but without the requirement to be online at the same time. . . . We want to
show that ALN can closely replicate traditional classroom learning to a high degree."
The program constitutes a $26-million commitment to about 35 colleges and universi-
ties for developing and offering courses. It has involved, up to this point, 1,000 faculty
and 20,000 students. Results have been reported at several conferences, for which see
the Web sites mentioned. The 1999 conference included a panel on "Cost Effectiveness of ALN," chaired by Lanny Arvan, University of Illinois, Urbana-Champaign. See
also *JALN*, the electronic *Journal of Asynchronous Learning Networks*.

Bacsich, P., Ash, C., Boniwell, K., and Kaplan, L. "The Costs of Networked Learning,"
Telematics in Education Research Group on behalf of the Virtual Campus Programme
and School of Computing and Management Sciences, Sheffield Hallam University,
United Kingdom. November 1999. See <http://www.shu.ac.uk/virtual.campus/cnl/>.

This is a report on a six-month project to identify the hidden costs of networked learning. The aim was to produce a "planning document and financial schema" to establish the actual costs of networked learning. The activities of the study team included developing an overview of the use of networked learning in UK higher education institutions, in-depth studies based on surveys at seven institutions, a literature review, and the analysis of a student survey focusing on perceived costs of networked learning. The authors believe that educators should not invent "a new vocabulary for finance and planning," but should employ existing tools for dealing with finance and management in universities. Among the conclusions are that students believe that networked learning increases their costs, institutions want to see more evidence of the pedagogical value of networked learning, a hidden cost is staff overtime, and one must identify and evaluate software to be used for activity-based costing. The desired "planning document and financial schema" needs further development and testing but the authors propose key features suitable to operate on different levels, from institution to module within a course. The document considers costs incurred by others than the institution, e.g., staff and students; takes into account the traditional division of faculty time; "takes account of the activities *within* the course development process"; and is flexible with regard to methods of allocating overhead.

Bates, A.W. *Managing Technological Change: Strategies for College and University Leaders.* San Francisco: Jossey-Bass Publishers, 1999.

The new technologies—e-mail, presentational software, videoconferencing, World Wide Web, multimedia, and CD-ROM—allow for more access, greater flexibility, and better teaching and learning. They will not reduce costs but can improve cost-effectiveness, provided institutions are re-structured as postindustrial organizations. In planning and managing courses and programs that rely on new technologies, a project management approach is preferable to the laissez-faire approach where the individual instructor develops the technology-based course with the help of a small grant and some technical assistance. Project management offers the chance of a better use of resources, learning from outside of higher education, and higher quality. The author argues for a mix of centralized and decentralized support services. A central unit should offer not only technology support but also faculty and curriculum development and other services. He presents a model of support services costing $10 million for a university with 30,000 students. Technology-based teaching on an extensive scale will require radical re-structuring from the academic department to the central administration. Research into and evaluation of technology-based teaching are indispensable, with special attention to be paid to the unique features of such teaching, which should perhaps be carried out by a central academic technology unit. Research might focus on cost-benefit analysis, indirect benefits, suitable teaching software, the proper structures for technology-based teaching and learning, and assessment of outcomes. Institutions will be increasingly differentiated by the extent of their use of technology-based teaching. Students will insist on learning with technology, and institutions that only add technology to conventional teaching, rather than transforming teaching with the help of technology, will be expensive.

————. "Assessing the Costs and Benefits of Telelearning. A Case Study from the University of British Columbia." 1998. See <http://research.cstudies.ubc.ca>.

————. "The Impact of Technology Change on Open and Distance Learning." Paper delivered at Queensland Open Learning Network Conference "Open Learning: Your Future Depends on It," 4-6 December, 1996. See <www.tellinet.org/Telelearn/ Info_Resources/info_resources.html>.

It is wrong to assume that technology can simply replace labor and thereby reduce educational costs. Applying technology in teaching and learning cannot reduce labor costs without reducing the quality of learning (which in its turn would lead to a less-skilled workforce). Learning materials can go only so far as a substitute for the interaction between a learner and a real teacher. Learning based on machines cannot anticipate all the questions and ideas students might raise. What wise use of technology can do is broaden access and improve the quality of teaching as well as the cost effectiveness of education. Reducing costs and increasing cost effectiveness are not the same.

Benjamin, Roger. "Looming Deficits," *Change* 30, 2 (March-April 1998): 12-17.

Review of *Straight Talk about College Costs and Prices,* which is listed below under the National Commission on the Cost of Higher Education.

Bork, Alfred. "The Future of Learning: An Interview with Alfred Bork," *Educom Review* 34, 4 (July-August 1999). See<http://www.educause.edu/ir/library/html/ erm9946.html>.

Bork argues for the use of highly interactive computer programs that individualize learning and keep track of and respond to students' learning problems. The focus must be on discovery and mastery learning, not on information delivery. Highly interactive computer-based learning is the superior learning mode in any course that has more than 15 students. The future is in distance learning, although at this time Bork sees little use for the Internet in learning. Distance learning with highly interactive computer-based programs will be best applied in large beginning classes. In such courses, costs could be lowered, if the high costs of development ($30,000 per student hour) are compensated by large numbers of students using these programs, including high schools students and students around the globe. Trials should be funded by government and foundations but ultimately such programs should be produced commercially. Highly interactive computer-based learning materials might replace the system of tutors that has added significantly to the costs of distance learning in the Open University.

————. "Is Technology-Based Learning Effective?" *Contemporary Education* 63, 1 (1991): 6-14.

Can technology improve education? Existing evidence for evaluating effectiveness is inadequate. Detailed studies of a few students can lead to useful statements on learning behavior, but they yield no statistical results. Small-scale comparative studies, involving a few hundred students, are largely useless. Usually they show no significant difference between learning with and without technology. That is so because of the small numbers of students and the fact that "the differences are simply swamped out by many factors not under the control of the investigators." Meta-analysis, subjecting many comparative studies, usually involving small numbers, to statistical analysis, is not the answer. It is not likely that combining a large number of inadequate small studies will yield reliable results, despite the elaborate statistics.

Large-scale studies, with a wide variety of students, are more promising. An example is an ETS study of *Writing to Read,* a program to teach reading and writing to five- and six-year-olds developed by John Henry Martin and marketed by IBM. The study involved 35,000 students over a two-year period, in many schools and with many types of students (however, there is no certainty whether it was the technology or the underlying philosophy that was responsible for the results of the program). Large-scale studies involving hundreds of thousands with a mix of different students and schools are needed. The author is thinking, e.g., of 20 newly developed full courses taught with interactive technology and comparing them with courses using all other forms of learning. Evaluation would have to include examination of the production processes for these courses. Compelling examples can provide some of the evidence we need, indicating, e.g., "that the computer can bring back an individualized and interactive approach to education."

Boucher, A. "Information Technology-based Teaching and Learning in Higher Education: A View of the Economic Issues," *Journal of Information Technology for Teacher Education* 7, 1 (1998): 87-111.

The paper deals with the economic issues of IT-assisted teaching and learning as faced in the UK, in the context of a publicly funded system. During the 1980s and 1990s the UK experienced a significant growth in students in higher education, from one in fifteen to one in three in the population aged 18 to 21. Funding for higher education in real terms increased by 45 percent; funding per student in real terms declined by 40 percent. At the same time students entering higher education often have advanced IT skills and corresponding expectations for teaching and learning. One proposed solution is to radically change the delivery of teaching and learning and in particular, to embrace IT-supported teaching and learning. Higher education in the UK, nationally and locally, has taken a series of steps in support of the use of IT in teaching and learning, e.g. on the national level by funding a Computers in Teaching Initiative. The principal aim was to use technology to make teaching and learning more productive and more efficient.

It has been difficult to obtain hard evidence on the costs and benefits of IT-based teaching and learning. The benefits tend to be educational and long-term and there is no consensus on the methodology of measuring them. The application of the methodology of cost/benefit analysis to IT-based teaching and learning is discussed. Such application is made difficult because of the problem of assessing accurately costs and benefits. Cost categories have to be established and such costs as "spillover" and opportunity costs considered. Institutions have to develop "more effective cost measures." Methodologies are needed to identify and quantify benefits—educational, institutional, and social—and to attach to them monetary values. Failure to develop measures of output has been one of the flaws of projects researching the benefits of IT-based teaching and learning. Also, there are no agreed-on methods to measure the effective use of IT-based teaching and learning. Introducing IT-assisted teaching is truly a business re-engineering effort and will require a fundamental rethinking of core processes in universities.

Cause Current Issues Committee. "Current Issues for Higher Education Information Resources Management," *CAUSE/EFFECT* 22, 1 (1999).

Regarding network challenges: "Funding and cost-recovery models will have a profound effect on the development and deployment of future networks." Among challenges of a distributed environment: "What are some successful models for apportioning available IT moneys between the central and the distributed service providers?" Challenges of distributed learning include: "How will technology support for distributed students be delivered and financed?" On funding models and cycles: How "to raise awareness at a national level for the need to allocate more funding for technology diffusion and support...? What are some best-practice models for apportioning the optimal share of available IT money to central IT organizations versus departments?" As to equipment replacement cycles, "... how often is cost-effective? How is cost-effectiveness measured? Is leasing a cost-effective alternative?"

————. "Current Issues for Higher Education Resources Management," *CAUSE/ EFFECT* 20, 4 (Winter, 1997-98): 4-7, 62-63. See <http://www.educause.edu/ir/ library/html/cem9742.html>.

The Cause Current Issues Committee offers a list of issues and trends that are important to IT use and management in higher education. They include retaining, retraining, and recruiting IT staff; the growing complexity and cost of enterprise systems; student expectations for technology support and services; distributed learning and distance education challenges; intellectual property issues in a Networked Environment; managing expectations in the face of rising demands and declining budgets; the continuing challenge of information technology support; information access challenges on the networked campus. The following strategies are suggested for dealing with increasing expectations and declining budgets: "Partnering within the institution to ensure buy-in before generating solutions; use of licensing and consortial agreements; presenting new economic models that identify the true costs associated with networked computing; garnering faculty and student agreement on realistic support levels; strengthening communication strategies to ensure that customers understand what services will be provided and at what cost; empowering customers through better training programs; more effective planning and priority setting; finding simpler, less elegant solutions; re-deploying/recycling of information technology on campus."

Chaffee, Ellen Earle. "Finding the Will and the Way," in Mark Luker ed. *Preparing Your Campus for a Networked Future*. EduCause Leadership Strategies 1. San Francisco: Jossey-Bass, 1999, pp. 81-92.

Even relatively small, low-tuition institutions, in this case Valley City State University and Mayville State University in North Dakota, with tuition of about $2,000 a year, can with their own resources manage the step towards universal computing. The two institutions have generated the funds and created the infrastructure, support, and expertise to put notebook computers in the hands of all students, faculty, and staff. The annual expense for the notebook initiative is 10 percent of the institutional operating budget. Computers are replaced on a two-year cycle. A technology fee increased total tuition and fees by nearly 50 percent. Increased cost has not been a barrier to enrollment. While universal computing can achieve administrative and academic efficiencies, costs are not reduced. Small size is an advantage for technological innovation. Standardization, faculty development, staff training are key. Students using technology are more discriminating educational consumers. Their response to teaching with technology teaches faculty how to best use technology.

Chutchian-Ferranti, J. "Activity-Based Costing," *Computerworld* 33, 32 (August 9, 1999): 54.

Defines and describes activity-based costing and activity-based management: "Activity-based costing is a costing model that identifies the cost pools, or activity centers, in an organization and assigns costs to products and services (cost drivers) based on the number of events or transactions involved in the process of providing a product or service." It is a means for IT personnel to understand the true nature of their costs. For more on this issue, see <www.computerworld.com/more>.

Commission on National Investment in Higher Education. *Breaking the Social Contract: The Fiscal Crisis in Higher Education.* J.L. Dionne and T. Kean, Report of the Commission on National Investment in Higher Education. New York: Council for Aid to Education, 1997. See <http://www.rand.org/publications/CAE100/index.htlm>.

In the next 20 years colleges and universities will have to reject millions of students if public funding remains stagnant. The looming deficits in higher education are more critical than the funding problems of the Social Security system. The answer is increased public funding contingent on institutional reform. What should governments do? "States should re-examine their higher education financing systems and develop a strategic plan for allocating their limited resources to best meet educational demands." Government leaders on all levels "should re-allocate public resources to reflect the growing importance of education to the economic prosperity and social stability of the United States." Federal, state, and local governments should reduce the deficit facing higher education by half. What should institutions do? As the business community has done, higher education has to undergo a process of streamlining and re-engineering to improve service, reduce costs, and increase productivity. The governance structure of institutions is outmoded. Therefore, there is a need for "a system-wide process for reallocating resources among departments and other parts of the institution," which implies and improving performance-based assessment, defining and measuring faculty productivity, and improving accountability in financial management. There should be greater mission differentiation between institutions and systems (e.g., major research universities should do research and graduate programs, not remedial education). Sharing arrangements between institutions should be developed to improve productivity, e.g., by joint outsourcing of functions. The Internet will facilitate sharing arrangements between institutions; library resources placed on the Internet could replace physical collections; the age of cyberspace makes physical space less important and combining physical plants possible.

Costs. **Project on IT costs at Colgate University and Hamilton College.** See Chapter 6 and <http://www.its.colgate.edu/kleach/costs/costs.htm>.

Daniel, John S. "Why Universities Need Technology Strategies," *Change* 29, 4 (July-August 1997): 10-17.

There is a crisis of higher education globally. The three key issues are cost, access, and flexibility. The US is not the ideal candidate for leadership in this crisis. We are wedded to the technology of real-time teaching and to "exclusivity of access and extravagance of resource." The world requires mass training and mass education. The traditional model of the university costs too much. We can reduce costs and enhance quality through technology. The academic tradition does not like the substitution of capital for labor and has little interest in what academic activities cost. The environment is competitive, and competitive advantage comes from lower costs and unique attractions. The 11 largest distance education systems in the world, the mega-universities, provide higher education to more than 2 million students at substantially lower cost than conventional universities.

————. *Mega-Universities and Knowledge Media.* London: Kogan Page Ltd.,1996.

The term Mega-Universities refers to 11 distance education systems around the globe that each enroll more than 100,000 students. The focus is on the United Kingdom and its Open University where the author serves as vice chancellor. The book includes these points: The need for vastly expanded higher education, especially in less developed countries, cannot be met by building more campuses. Distance education through the mega-universities, based on such technologies as mass broadcasting and personal media, has reduced the cost of college and university degrees significantly, by 50 percent in the United Kingdom and by even more in other countries, including Turkey, China, and India. Many governments insist that IT is the answer to the demand for more access and lower cost. The challenge to traditional universities is to use IT to raise learning productivity. The challenge to governments is to develop new funding methodologies because the old ones no longer work. One of the main features of the mega-universities is that teaching there is modeled on industrial production, meaning the various functions carried out by the instructor in the traditional model are separated and assigned to several groups of instructional support personnel.

Universities must maintain or enhance competitive advantage, which is achieved through lower costs, differentiation, or focusing on a niche market. The author applies M.E. Porter's theory on competitive advantage to universities and especially distance education. Universities must pay attention to their value-creating activities, and establish a value chain. Technology can be a crucial competitive weapon if appropriate steps are taken, such as selecting a technology strategy that re-enforces the institution's overall competitive strategy. To attract students to new technology one must demonstrate that learning can be more effective and fun, which is best achieved by exposing them to the "whole product that integrates course materials and tutorial support." The new technologies or third-generation distance education technologies are called here the knowledge media; they result from a convergence of computing, telecommunications, and the learning sciences and are expected to make a difference in kind. To prove their worth they must make a difference for life-long learning and the renewal of universities. For traditional universities their impact on learning productivity, student diversity, the notion of academic community, universities' collaborative ventures with other universities and other organizations is critical. The author also predicts that public funding will be a decreasing proportion of support for higher education, with direct grants going to students rather than institutions; governments will want to continue to ensure accountability and quality. In a final chapter the author draws on the experience of the Open University and describes the implementation of a technology strategy. An appendix gives profiles of the mega-universities.

Darby, Jonathan. "The Economics of Open Learning via the Internet." Unpublished paper.

The author is director, Technology-Assisted Lifelong Learning, University of Oxford Department for Continuing Education, UK. This is a paper delivered at a workshop which addressed the issues of cost of developing and delivering Internet-based courses and minimizing these costs, especially for students. His conclusion: "The economics of Internet-based courses make them highly attractive for meeting course needs for 100 to 200 students per year. These numbers are too low to be viable for traditional distance learning approaches, but are also too large to be easily accommodated in classroom teaching. In addition Internet-based courses bypass many of the logistical problems of delivering courses to students in any country of the world."

Detweiler, Richard A. "Leading the Transition to Information Technology, "*Educational Record* 76, 1 (Winter 1995): 53-57.

Colleges and universities must understand that investments in IT may increase productivity and effectiveness but rarely save institutions significant amounts of money.

De Vries, P. "Telelearn: An EU Project on Costing Issues in Flexible and Distance Learning." Pieter de Vries, Project Coordinator. see <http://www.shu.ac.uk/flish/vriesp.htm>.

TeleLearn: An EU Project on Costing Issues in Flexible and Distance Learning was a 1997-99 project executed by researchers from five European countries. The focus was on vocational and adult learning. According to Pieter de Vries, the project coordinator: "The TeleLearn project team has created a corpus of relevant literature and online resources on the costing issue in flexible and distance teaching and learning. Concept management tools were used to organise the data and to optimise access. There was a list of key factors created on the basis of the resources and a series of new and existing case studies. In addition earlier frameworks and models for costs of online training were reviewed and consultation took place with experts and relevant related projects. It is clear that there are far too little accurate costings data yet available. Although 'key cost factors' can now be itemised in considerable detail, at a narrative level, an 'algorithmic' model remains to be built." Two main project reports are available at the Web site <www.ellinet.org/Telelearn/>—*The TeleLearn Project Report* and *The TeleLearn Case Studies Report.*

This paper was presented at the FLISH 1999 conference based on these reports. The interest here is in vocational and adult learning and how costs are affected by "the introduction of telematic-based learning technologies." That managers do not possess enough knowledge about costs is the working hypothesis of the project. The project collected resources (accessible via www.ellinet.org/telelearn/), used or developed two dozen or so case studies, identified key cost factors, created a community of interest for online discussion. The findings include: costing models of other sectors are not necessarily transferable to the area of this project; most studies have been oriented towards courses; the effect of online learning systems on learning outcomes is not clear; access is improved; "an economic analysis of distance teaching and learning can profitably utilise concepts and methods from applied microeconomics." Key cost factors: fixed costs (usually higher) and variable costs, common costs, indirect costs ("The most significant example of indirect costs is the opportunity cost ...."). The author discusses existing models, including Frank Jewett's "Bridge" model, and concludes that there is a need for a more comprehensive model which takes into consideration previous studies in this area. Overall conclusions: "... there are circumstances in which on-line training is cost-effective .... However, there are far too little accurate costings data yet available." The bibliography includes a series of UK studies on the cost-effectiveness of distance education and training published or presented between 1990 and 1995.

Drucker, Peter D. "Beyond the Information Revolution," *Atlantic Monthly* 284, 4 (October 1999): 47-59.

The most revolutionary impact of the information revolution is not the effect on decision-making, policy-making, and strategy but on world-wide distribution of goods and services through e-commerce. The author calls the emergence of e-commerce "a totally unexpected development," which has eliminated distance and created a single economy and a single market where competition is without boundaries. "This is profoundly changing economies, markets, and industry structures; products and services and their flow; consumer segmentation, consumer values, and consumer behavior; jobs and labor markets. But the impact may be even greater on societies and politics and, above all, on the way we see the world and ourselves in it." The relationship between e-commerce and the information revolution is like that of the railroads and the industrial revolution; both e-commerce and the railroads represented relatively delayed applications of the inventions that drove these revolutions; the railroads mastered distance and e-commerce eliminated distance. "New knowledge-based industries will depend on attracting, holding, and motivating knowledge workers. When this can no longer be done by satisfying knowledge workers' greed, it will have to be done by giving them social recognition and social power."

Ehrmann, S.C. "Asking the Hard Questions about Technology Use and Education," *Change* 31, 2 (March-April 1999): 25-29.

See especially pp. 27-28: "How Does Your Use of Technology Affect Costs." Referring to projects at Washington State University, Baruch College, and the Rochester Institute of Technology, the author notes cost per program, cost per student, cost per graduate, and cost of faculty time as measures of IT costs.

Ernst, David J. "Information Resources and Institutional Effectiveness: The Need for a Holistic Approach to Planning and Budgeting," *CAUSE/EFFECT* 19, 1 (Spring, 1995). See <http://www.educause.edu/ir/library/text/cem9514.text>.

Colleges and universities are suffering from an economic squeeze, the number and percentage of students over 25 is increasing, public expectations of higher education are higher. Academic consolidations, administrative restructuring, and new delivery mechanisms are remedies that are being pursued. Institutions are investing in technology to improve their competitive position. Work processes have to be re-designed from the bottom up. That requires investments in technology. Strategic and coordinated planning across the institution is necessary, as is integrated budgeting for academic, administrative, and IT resources. Trade-offs must cut across the entire institution. Assessment, vision, a tactical plan are the key steps.

FLISH (Flexible Learning on the Information Super Highway). "The Business Case for On-Line Learning." FLISH 1999 Conference at Sheffield Hallam University, United Kingdom. May 25-27, 1999. See <http://www.shu.ac.uk/schools/cms/flish/home.htm> or <http://www.shu.ac.uk/flish/>.

The conference focused "on the business viability of online learning, including such topics as quality, time to market and cost effectiveness." The conference was related to a six-months project, headed by Paul Bacsich, to identify the hidden costs of Networked Learning.

Foster, Susan J., and Hollowell, D.E. "Integrating Information Technology Planning and Funding at the Institutional Level," in Richard N. Katz and Julia A.Rudy,eds. *Information Technology in Higher Education: Assessing Its Impact and Planning for the Future.* New Directions for Institutional Research 102. San Francisco: Jossey-Bass Publishers, 1999, pp. 9-19.

IT planning must occur in a climate of consultation and collaboration; it must be based on a clear understanding of uses intended. It should be inclusive and should have both a strategic and a tactical dimension. IT leadership has to be consistent and visible and should be part of the governance structure on the highest level. For a successful IT effort, quality and quantity of resources are key. Participation of the office of institutional research in planning for IT is crucial. Investing in and budgeting for IT must be integrated with the institution's process for creating and managing operating and capital budgets. Life cycle funding plans for IT must be established; guidelines for regular replacement of departmental equipment will facilitate planning and budgeting. IT needs direct and recurring infusing of capital funds, best provided on an annual basis. Reallocating resources will help funding IT expenditures. Examples are student long-distance telephone resale, negotiating lower telecommunications costs in general, savings from operational efficiencies achieved through automation and business process re-engineering, e.g., in the area of institutional procurement. It is difficult to compare costs with those at other institutions. It is possible to spend too much on IT; the challenge is to spend well.

Frances, Carol. *Higher Education: Enrollment Trends and Staffing Needs.* TIAA-CREF Research Dialogues 55. March 1998.

Frances, Carol, and Pumerantz, R. "Costs of Instructional Technology in Higher Education." Paper presented at the 1998 Conference of the Congress of Political Economists. Bridgetown, Barbados. July 15, 1998.

The introduction and diffusion of technology should be managed. The authors identify steps "that need to be taken to catch up with the reality of technology" and examine the forces driving the introduction of technology. For the analysis of the costs of technology they propose the consideration of 16 factors that could affect the measurement of instructional costs: pace of technological change, time frame, course content, life cycle, type of institutions, economies of scale, financing, types of costs, professional development and staff training, gifts of technology from business, cost sharing, perspective, student technological aptitude, rate of innovation, academic labor markets, and competitive strategies.

Frances, C., Pumerantz, R., and Caplan, J. "Planning for Information Technology: What You Thought You Knew Could Lead You Astray." *Change* 31, 4 (July-August, 1999): 25-33.

Most planning in colleges and universities assumes a vast increase in the use of information technology in higher education. At the same time such planning tends to be based on assumptions that are partially or entirely wrong. The assumptions being questioned here are that (1) in the coming years adults will drive enrollment growth; (2) an increasing percentage of new college students will come from previously underserved minority populations; (3) governments are not contemplating significant investments to build new capacity, instead in many cases expect IT to meet a growing demand for college; (4) information technology will save money over the costs of traditional classroom instruction; (5) planning for information technology has been inadequate; and (6) there is "no significant difference" in educational outcomes when one compares conventional teaching with teaching enhanced by information technology. The authors point to demographic trends, the findings of a comparative cost study conducted by the authors at Western University of Health Sciences and the Japanese approach to the use of information technology in business as making these assumptions questionable or invalid.

Graves, W. "Developing and Using Technology as a Strategic Asset," in Richard N. Katz and Associates, *Dancing with the Devil: Information Technology and the New Competition in Higher Education.* A Publication of EduCause. San Francisco: Jossey-Bass Publishers, 1999, pp. 95-118.

Information technology "is a strategic asset that should be utilized by the entire faculty, staff, and student body to increase the productivity of mission-critical academic programs and the administrative services that support those programs. And nothing is more mission-critical in higher education than instruction." Three issues are being considered: (1)What kind of services should be provided by a central IT organization and how should it be organized for maximum effectiveness? (2)What kind of processes, structures, models make for an integrated IT effort to use IT as a strategic asset? (3) What support models does instructional technology require for online learning? The author develops six principles for funding and managing IT resources to maximize return on investment. These include the need for formal institutional processes "for selecting, developing or customizing, and installing any mission-critical application," representing all stake-holders with veto power by the IT organization. Among his recommendations for IT enhanced instruction are the unbundling of basic skills instruction from preparation for the B.A. and of liberal education from mastery in discipline or profession.

Green, Kenneth C. *The 1999 National Survey of Information Technology in Higher Education: The Continuing Challenge of Instructional Integration and User Support.* October 1999. See <www.campuscomputing.net>.

Financing the replacement of aging hardware and software is ranked third-highest (14.3 percent) among concerns on the almost 600 campuses surveyed. User support staff are difficult to recruit and retain, being paid between one-fifth and one-third of earnings in business and industry. More institutions have strategic plans for information technology (61.3 percent) and more have an "acquire and retire plan" for IT (44.3 percent). IT spending in many institutions remains dependent on year-end budget leftovers. Only a small portion of institutions (13.7 percent) have formal programs for rewarding faculty use of IT in instruction.

————. "The Roads Behind and the Paths Ahead." Plenary Session Presentation, Western Cooperative for Education Telecommunications, 1998, Annual Meeting, Reno, NV. October 16, 1998.

————. "Drawn to the Light, Burnt by the Flame? Money, Technology, and Distance Education," *ED Journal* 11, 5 (May, 1997): J1-J9.

Many consider "technology-enhanced distance education to be a low-cost, high-revenue solution to the rising demand for post-secondary education." However, it is not simple or inexpensive: "It is best viewed as a business, one that involves real and recurring costs: money, time, personnel, content, and a significant technological infrastructure…. Only when educational institutions and educational entrepreneurs view distance education as a fully-capitalized business will campuses and private ventures begin to understand the options and opportunities, real risks and real costs." The capacity of technology "must be assessed against the initial and recurring costs." Technology changes the instructional methodology as well as the content, costs, and delivery of distance education. Because of its imminent ubiquity, adult learners are eager to use IT as a learning resource.

Traditional distance education was relatively low-cost and therefore profitable for many institutions. Technology-enhanced distance education, such as online distance education, requires expensive infrastructure, which, in addition, has a very short life cycle. Cost for developing courses and providing support are very high: " … content development begins to look like a venture capital business generally acknowledged as risky business." "Can all campuses and programs build a revenue stream against the real costs of developing commercial quality, technology-enhanced distance education resources? …. If managed as a 'real business' … how many distance education programs … would be both educationally viable and financially profitable?"

Few campuses - one in six - have a formal plan for use of information technology and the Internet for their distance education effort. The author asks if there is "a 'macro' strategy that should guide institutional efforts and planning" in distance education, and argues for a distinct identity for distance education, as a fourth sector of higher education (next to residential colleges and universities, community colleges, and commuter comprehensive institutions): needs and expectations of adult learners are different, markets are different ("programs and personnel live in a real market"), financial operation is more that of business than of a not-for-profit organization. Before launching or expanding distance education, institutions must develop a business plan (defining markets, consumers, products, producers), appreciate the complexity and cost of content development, provide for recognizing and rewarding faculty, and have a solid foundation for funding distance and online education. Current budget models do not adequately consider the real costs of technology. Especially, "amortization, virtually unknown in the campus community but well understood in the corporate environment, must become a critical financial tool for understanding and managing real costs."

Green, Kenneth C., and Gilbert, S.W. "Expectations: Content, Communications, Productivity, and the Role of Information Technology in Higher Education," *Change* 27, 2 (1995): 8-18.

IT is increasing personal productivity, but in such areas as enhancing traditional teaching, changing pedagogy, and changing content, IT makes for improvement and adds value without generating productivity gains. Computers have improved productivity in the administrative area; and resulted in some productivity gains for faculty in the transition "from the computer as a desktop tool to the computer as the communications gateway to colleagues and 'content.'" Major benefits have been created through IT in content, curriculum, and pedagogy without really increasing instructional productivity. Claimed productivity gains or success at cost control usually are in limited areas.

The "Implementation cycle" in the introduction of technology is more complex in academia. "… information technology partisans will mislead campus leaders when they underestimate the real costs, complexity, and duration of the successful implementation process." Infrastructure and user support are the main issues in successful integration of IT in academia. "The successful integration of information technologies is almost always associated with significant *structural* change—the kind of change that educational institutions routinely resist."

Institutions must embrace IT for reasons of competition, teaching-learning-curriculum enhancement, and labor-market preparation. IT secures productivity gains for individual faculty and students. "… the wisest technology advocate or planner cannot anticipate all the ways that new technologies might be used to enhance instruction and scholarship." "What IT does best—or will do better as it improves—is deliver content and provide access to information and other people." "… there is little if any evidence that information technology will reduce faculty involvement in instruction (that is, reduce the cost of instruction) in the next few years." Each institution should "engage in an institutionwide planning initiative that looks carefully at the ways IT can be used most effectively to improve teaching and learning."

Green, Kenneth C., and Jenkins, R. "IT Financial Planning 101: Developing an Institutional Strategy for Financing Technology," *NACUBO Business Officer* 31, 9 (March 1998): 32-37. See <http://www.nacubo.org/website/members/bomag/9803/101.html>.

Institutions by and large don't know what they are spending on IT, one reason being that IT spending is highly decentralized; according to Green's Campus Computing Survey of 97, academic computing accounts for about 30 to 40 percent of total spending on IT. Few institutions have a financial plan to address short-term and long-term IT needs; only half of institutions have a strategic plan for IT, and where institutional plans exist they usually fail to be specific about how IT investments are to improve teaching and learning or academic and administrative productivity. The authors believe an observation of the early 1980s is still true, namely that "Computing and information technology in higher education remain an accidental revolution: unanticipated, unplanned, and unprepared."

The authors propose three steps for financial planning for IT: (1) Colleges and universities need an asset management program. IT assets must be looked upon as different from other physical assets; labor costs must be included. A cost model that identifies, classifies, and manages total technology costs across all departments is necessary. Managing the labor/capital ratio is becoming important. (2) Institutions must use a life-cycle budget process. It will annualize total technology costs "into streams of longer-term perpetuities." The authors provide a sample life-cycle budget worksheet. "The total annual cost is the cost of all equipment and labor amortized over the expected economic life."(3) Institutions must "Identify and match funding sources to meet total annual costs." The authors provide a sample "simplified cost/funding matrix" to help identify potential sources of funds.

"Greenspan Now Positive on Prospects of Economy." *The New York Times*, September 9, 1999, p. C8.

U.S. economic expansion could continue, due to IT. IT through technologies like better software and integrated circuits has "begun to alter, fundamentally, the manner in which we do business and create economic value." As a result productivity has risen: better inventory management, customer service, distribution systems. Therefore there is less uncertainty for management

Halbert, D.J. *Intellectual Property in the Information Age: The Politics of Expanding Ownership Rights.* Westport, CT: Quorum Books, 1999.

Horn, Paul M. "Information Technology Will Change Everything," *Research Technology Management* 42, 1 (January/February 1999): 42-47.

Projecting a world totally changed by IT, the author expects dramatic cost/ performance improvements in technology; everyone and everything will be connected to the Internet. It cost $10,000 to store a megabyte of information 1956 and 10 cents today. ... "the computer will go the way of the electric motor—it is going to disappear." Knowledge becomes the new currency, and all companies become information companies.

Institute for Higher Education Policy. *What's the Difference? A Review of Contemporary Research on the Effectiveness of Distance Learning in Higher Education.* Prepared for American Federation of Teachers and the National Education Association. Washington DC: The Institute for Higher Education Policy, April 1999. 42 pages. See <http://www.ihep.com>.

The report concludes that "the overall quality of the research is questionable and thereby renders many of the findings inconclusive," and identifies a number of shortcomings in the research, e.g., the questionable validity of instruments used to measure student attitudes and outcomes. It suggests gaps in the research that require further investigation, such as outcomes of total programs rather than individual courses, differences among students, a conceptual framework and others. "The research on distance learning has a long way to go, and much of it is inconclusive. On the other hand, technology has helped the academy to continue its focus on the essential goals of teaching and learning."

Jewett, Frank: Evaluating the Benefits and Costs of Mediated Instruction and Distributed Learning. Campus Case Studies and Related Materials. See<http://www.calstate.edu/special_projects/>. A project funded by U.S. Dept. of Education, OERI and sponsored by the California State University, the National Learning Infrastructure Initiative of Educause, and the State Higher Education Executive Officers, Seal Beach, CA, 1998.

    a. "Courseware for Remedial Mathematics: A Case Study in the Benefits and Costs of the Mediated Learning System in the California State University."

    b. "Teaching College Literacy: A Case Study in the Benefits and Costs of Daedalus Courseware at Baruch College."

    c. "The Education Network of Maine: A Case Study in the Benefits and Costs of Instructional Television."

    d. "The Master's Degree in Social Work at Cleveland State University and the University of Akron: A Case Study of the Benefits and Costs of a Joint Degree Program Offered via Videoconferencing."

    e. "TELETECHNET—Old Dominion University and 'Two Plus Two' Programs at Community Colleges in Virginia: A Case Study in the Benefits and Costs of an Intercampus Instructional Television Network."

    f. "The Human Computer Interaction Certificate Program at Rensselaer Polytechnic Institute: A Case Study in the Benefits and Costs of a Joint Industry/University Designed Program Featuring Integrated Delivery Methods."

    g. "The WESTNET Program - SUNY Brockport and the SUNY Campuses in Western New York State: A Case Study in the Benefits and Costs of an Interactive Television Network."

    h. "Course Restructuring and the Instructional Development Initiative at Virginia Polytechnic Institute and State University: A Benefit Cost Study."

Katz, Richard N. and Associates. *Dancing with the Devil: Information Technology and the New Competition in Higher Education.* A Publication of EduCause. San Francisco: Jossey-Bass Publishers, 1999.

    A collection of six essays. James Duderstadt: "higher education is likely to evolve from a loosely federated system of colleges and universities serving traditional students from local communities into, in effect, a knowledge and learning industry." Richard N. Katz: "New competition and information will impel institutions to rethink their instructional products and, in particular, their markets ...." Harvey Blustain, Philip Goldstein, Gregory Lozier "...provide a specific framework for institutions to engage in institutional strategy making." Gregory Farrington assesses the impact of IT on undergraduate residential communities. See also Graves. The authors' joint recommendations: "Engage the campus in a vision .... Develop the capacity for change.... Devise strategies.... Develop the faculty .... Manage IT as a strategic campus asset .... Focus on the assessment of student outcomes," (pp. 121-122).

Kobulnicky, Paul J. "Critical Factors in Information Technology Planning for the Academy," *CAUSE/EFFECT* 22, 2 (1999).

    Investment in IT must be based on a "comprehensive business plan for achieving academic excellence," and guided by the institutional leadership's decision as to what role IT should play in institution's transformation. "... the effective integration of information technology requires process analysis and process re-engineering to enable technology to replace human labor." If IT is to be an instrument for institutional progress, we need to know "what costs are needed for what services, from which budgets those costs will be covered, and that the costs for mission critical programs will be covered completely." As IT services become part of the operation, they must become part of the budget plan.

One has to decide what goods and services are provided centrally and what rules are to be followed for consumption. Central services should be funded off the top, with other units left to fund remaining services independently. "Increasingly, schools and departments will fund their own hardware, software, systems support, and primary user support entirely." Institutions of higher education must seek decreased costs or increased revenues through IT-based transformation. There has been little investigation of "how academic use of technology can lower costs and retain or increase quality." An IT rich environment increases the value (or the perception of the value) of a student's experience justifying higher tuition or more state funding. The processes affected by IT must be analyzed for productivity gains. Productivity gains require standardized processes, but standardization in teaching and learning is uncommon.

Kramer, M. "The College Cost Conundrum," *Change* 30, 4 (July-August, 1998): 44-42.

Review of *Straight Talk about College Costs and Prices*. The report "is a remarkably fine document. It is clear and wonderfully short, and lays out excellent ground rules for our talking about issues without forever talking past one another. The Commission's recommendations are also sensible, if timid."

Leach, K., and Smallen, D. "What Do Information Technology Support Services Really Cost?" *CAUSE/EFFECT* 21, 2 (1998): 38-45. See <http://www.educause.edu/ir/library/html/cem9829.html>.

This article reports on the *Costs* Project, which originated and is maintained at Colgate University and Hamilton College. There are now more than 100 participating institutions. Its aim is to provide comparative data and benchmarks on IT services in higher education. This article reports on results in three support services areas.

Lohr, Steve. "Computer Age Gains Respect of Economists," *The New York Times*, April 14 1999, p. A1.

"Economists starting to see a payoff from technology: For more than a decade, most of the nation's leading economists have questioned the economic payoff from information technology - the billions upon billions spent each year by companies and households on everything from computers to software to cellular phones. But now economists are wondering whether higher productivity growth - averaging about 2 percent in the last three years, roughly double the pace from 1973 to 1995 - is the long-awaited confirmation that the nation's steadily rising investment in computers and communications is finally paying off."

Madrick, Jeff. "How New Is the New Economy?" *New York Review of Books* 46, 14 (September 23, 1999): 42-50.

GDP since 96 has grown at an annual rate of nearly 4 percent, discounted for inflation; labor productivity by 2 percent, 3 percent in the 9 months ending in June. IT is being held responsible. But growth is no faster than in short periods of 70s and 80s; earlier 90s saw sluggish growth. If we are really at a turning point, growth rates should have been higher. Are we just catching up? We have achieved greater productivity in some goods, even some services, though not health or education. Recent positive economic indicators, like low inflation, are possibly a result of depression in Asia; low unemployment reflects high rate of temporary workers, the high rate of incarceration, smaller number of young workers. One encouraging sign for optimists: the high rate of investment in IT. "High technology" may be creating jobs but may not be transforming economy long-term. Some "technological overhaul" of economy may be taking place. IT is having an effect similar to railroads. There are benefits from investing in IT but how significant are they? "[T]here has indeed been an important technological transformation in America, but not necessarily one that will lead to more rapid productivity growth." New economy is a modern version of crafts economy; skills of workers are key. The new craftsmen are not only computer specialists but also business managers, financial experts, consultants. Jeff Madrick, editor of *Challenge* magazine, seems to be a pessimist. See his 1995 book *The End of Affluence: The Causes and Consequences of America's Economic Dilemma*, which argues that slow economic growth, rather than being cyclical, is now endemic and responsible for lower incomes, budget deficits, and other economic ills.

Massey, William F. "Life on the Wired Campus: How Information Technology Will Shape Institutional Futures," in Diana G. Oblinger and Sean C. Rush, eds. *The Learning Revolution: The Challenge of Information Technology in the Academy.* Bolton, MA: Anker Publishing Company, 1997, pp. 195-210.

Substitution of capital for labor traditionally has driven the improvement of business productivity. The technologies of higher learning have remained the same for centuries. IT upsets the basic technology used in higher education. Finally we can break away from the handicraft tradition. IT gives institutions the opportunity to improve the quality of education. IT improves production processes, economic structure, and the quality of faculty work. It provides the impetus for re-engineering teaching and learning. Without re-engineering, IT can increase individual productivity but that does not save money; it adds to costs.

Adoption of IT increases the capital-labor ratio for instruction (even if faculty remains the same size), reducing cost-rise pressures. Teaching and learning becomes more capital-intensive. Because of the high cost of IT, faculty compensation becomes a smaller part of expenditures. Adoption does not produce immediate cost savings (in fact, costs may rise during IT phase-in). Eventually the impact of a larger capital-labor ratio is felt, with IT costs declining as percentage of total costs. Whether IT brings higher or lower unit cost depends on what society wants to spend. IT can be exploited by making trade-offs between cost, quality, and access. Probably only the wealthier institutions can be both IT- and faculty-intensive. Fiscally constrained institutions are forced to reduce faculty to pay for IT.

The job of the faculty changes, from mainly content deliverer to a combination: content expert, learning process design expert, process implementation manager, interpreter, mentor, motivator, model learner. No longer are the repetition and drudgery of content delivery the main tasks of the instructor. Technology takes over some of the faculty work. Much transmission of information and evaluation is done by IT (and less expensive TA's). Faculty are re-deployed to tasks more intellectually stimulating. Faculty has more time for thinking and planning. Faculty can focus more on the processes of teaching and learning (less repetitive drudgery, optimizing time use, and exploiting comparative advantage). Students have more time, their learning receives more attention; therefore, they are better prepared and more motivated. There is less face-to-face contact between faculty and students.

Massy, William F., and Wilger A.K. "Improving Productivity: What Faculty Think about It—and Its Effect on Quality," *Change* 27,4 (July-August 1995): 10-21.

Faculty at 19 colleges and universities were interviewed for this study, a project of the Stanford Institute for Higher Education Research. The usual productivity-improvement methods do not work with faculty. Faculty are interested in results, outputs, especially measurable outputs, and therefore focus on research. Productivity is the ratio of outputs to inputs; or better, the ratio of total benefits to total costs. If we look upon the student-faculty ratio as a measure of productivity, we ignore non-faculty inputs. Gross productivity is the ratio of outputs to inputs without adjusting either for quality. Cost-per-student indicates gross productivity. Faculty object to improving gross productivity, by increasing teaching loads or student/faculty ratios, because larger classes or more classes mean lower teaching quality and less research. Faculty feel that administrators tend to look upon course enrollments as a measure of productivity. All this does not mean that faculty do not care about cost. They try to economize in teaching and research, e.g., by using IT. But the focus of the faculty is on maximizing productivity in matters of research and grants.

Re-engineering of teaching is uncommon. But faculty work very hard, are autonomy seekers, self-starters, feel empowered, and show the kind of independence and drive productivity consultants dream of. While research is necessary for quality teaching, that realization is not necessarily shared on the outside. Outside the academy one asks whether institutions or the public are getting their money's worth for the funds invested in faculty research. Obviously teaching is important; yet faculty seem satisfied with achieving a level of quality but do not want to make the investment to achieve a level of excellence. Faculty by and large are not interested in focusing on the teaching/learning process and applying the insights and findings of past decades that would improve college teaching and learning. Instead they stick to traditional methods and arrangements. They remain fixated on benefits where the outside asks for a balance between costs and benefits. That balance could be achieved if faculty embraced the idea that "the excitement and payoff of applying modern quality principles to education can rival that of traditional disciplinary-based research."

Massy, W.F., and Zemsky, R. "Using Information Technology to Enhance Academic Productivity." Paper sponsored by NLII, Wingspread Conference on Enhancing Academic Productivity, June 1995. NLII Monograph published by EduCause. See <http://www.educause.edu/nlii/keydocs/massy.html>.

IT is changing teaching and learning. Institutions will have to change if they wish to reap the benefits of IT. IT is an economical means to provide post-secondary education, including continuing education. IT could become the instrument in someone else's hands to threaten the monopoly over certification and credentialing that higher education now enjoys. IT offers many advantages, including economies of scale, mass customization, access to large quantities of information, and low cost access to information resources. IT expands the limits of time and space for education, makes possible self-paced learning, gives students greater control over learning, makes assessment easier, increases learning productivity, especially in matters of "codified knowledge and algorithmic skills," and makes the student less dependent on the institution.

Faculty must change. Faculty will not support additional IT expenditures if the result is a reduction in faculty numbers. Institutions offer few incentives for teaching and little effective monitoring of teaching and learning. "… the departmental curriculum as a whole often lacks explicit educational objectives or outcome and performance measures for those objectives." To be effective, IT-based teaching and learning programs require explicit educational objectives and ways to monitor progress and measure success. Because costs must be contained and labor counts for the bulk of operating cost, the only option to enhance productivity is to do more with less. Using IT then means technology must replace some work now done by faculty and support personnel. Capital must be selectively substituted for some labor and the processes of teaching and learning re-engineered. This presupposes an understanding of the costs of discrete teaching activities, in the manner of activity-based costing. The result will be an increase in the ratio of capital cost to labor cost, which has several advantages including greater flexibility.

The authors present a model comparing a course taught in the traditional way with a "studio" course as introduced by RPI, with courseware and more independent work on the part of students and reduced faculty time committed. In the model the costs turn out to be the same but the percentage of cost for labor is reduced. However, "even break-even cost substitution confers economic advantages because it increases the ratio of capital-based cost to labor cost."

Institutions face these alternatives: one is business as usual, meaning staying with the traditional model. An institution can then do good things with IT but at added cost. The core of the faculty loses in vibrancy and creativity. Other organizations begin to exploit the knowledge base developed by higher education. The other one is transforming higher education. In this scenario faculty make the best use of IT, re-engineer teaching and learning, create a balance between teaching and research. This will enhance quality, increase learning productivity, and maintain the knowledge base. This kind of improvement may lead to more services provided by colleges and universities and thus support current faculty numbers. Only if non-traditional learners, despite the improvement in higher education, continue to be diverted to other organizations will faculty size have to be reduced to pay for technology. The authors' conclusion is that "the potential for increased learning productivity through technology is too great for higher education to ignore. If colleges and universities fail to adapt effectively, other kinds of institutions will take up the challenge."

Matthews, Dewayne. "The Transformation of Higher Education through Information Technology: Implications for State Higher Education Finance Policy," Western Interstate Commission for Higher Education. January 26, 1998. See <http://www.wiche.edu/IT&Finance.htm.edu/>. Also in *Educom Review* 33, 5 (September-October, 1998): 48-57. See <http://www.educause.edu/ir/library/html/erm9854.html>.

An economy that is being transformed by IT demands more education and leads to larger number of students, but higher education is constrained by a lack of resources. Other industries have invested in technology to reduce costs and increase productivity. State governments and higher education leaders also count on technology "to reconcile the paradox of exploding demand and constrained resources."

Entirely new forms of post-secondary education are emerging as a result of IT: For learning to take place students and teachers do not have to meet face to face, and complex interactive learning systems will replace direct instruction; distance does not matter and markets will not be limited by geography; the traditional course and classroom will be replaced by media-rich and asymmetrically interactive models; not the content-based disciplines but the characteristics and needs of the student market will determine program structures; delivery will be customized to student needs; keener competition among institutions, including from new private-sector providers and industry-based education, will make learning outcomes - measured by student competencies - the measure of quality; interactive learning systems call for collaboration among institutions both in development and use, in the style of university-sponsored research.

The new environment raises financial issues that states have to address: ways to finance distance education, moved from the margins through IT and formerly ignored in state funding decisions; shifting IT funding from one-time allocations to ongoing expenditures; re-structuring IT financing to support re-engineering of higher education through IT (e.g. replacing "short-term unit cost-based funding" by "longer-term investments in course and program development"); state funding policies as "protectionist barriers" against higher education alternatives; student cost considerations focused on full-time on-campus students; traditional state residency and tuition policies while IT-based instruction asks for collaboration among institutions; counting contact hours versus measuring competency.

The author suggests a series of steps for states to restructure systems of higher education financial planning, budgeting, and funding: Devise new funding models so that institutions will invest in developing courses and programs that enhance productivity; will make strategic use of technology in the non-instructional area to save costs and enhance quality; will collaborate across departments, institutions, and states in developing and using IT mediated programs. Also states should re-consider restrictive residency policies and tuition differentials for non-residents; deregulate higher education to encourage competition, and accept that public higher education is not the only player in the higher education market; base funding on learning outcomes rather than seat-time; retain the ability to make system-wide strategic investments in such areas as IT infrastructure or program development ("Funding structures that allocate all funds to individual campuses do not permit states to act strategically when conditions warrant"); entertain the possibility Carnegie units might be replaced by another way of course accounting based on learning outcomes; and states should pool their efforts to develop new funding approaches.

McArthur, David J., and Lewis, M.L. "Untangling the Web: Applications of the Internet and Other Information Technologies to Higher Education." Sponsored by the California Education Round Table and carried out under the auspices of RAND Education under the direction of Roger Benjamin. 1998 (actually prepared in 1996). 75 pages. See <http://www.rand.org/publications/MR/MR975/>.

The authors are members of the Institute on Education and Training at Rand. In the past distance learning has shown impressive cost savings. The greatest impact of IT on higher education, however, is not going to be in saving money. Above all, IT drives educational reform, by changing the processes and products of learning. Here also lies the real threat to traditional ways and structures in higher education. IT serves first as an enhancing and magnifying agent, later as a transforming agent. IT has streamlined business processes in colleges and universities (much has been written on costs and benefits of IT in that respect). As a result of IT, most learning in the future will be distance-independent. The value of the Internet in that respect is that it encompasses most other information technologies. However, "the newest Internet and Web applications have little evidence to prove, or disprove, their value for higher education." While some of these applications will prove successful eventually, this will take time. Business has been a radical early adopter of IT and has borne the cost of earlier experimentation. Higher education has kept pace with business with regard to using the Internet. The commercialization of the Internet, though deplored by some, should benefit higher education in the long run, due to larger capacity, more hardware and software, and falling prices. More higher education institutions will take on specialized roles (e.g., as brokers of courses and other services or as highly specialized providers).

IT exacerbates competition with new providers. Delivery costs have been reduced. The proprietary sector is heavily into education; thousands such schools exist in California. Their common feature is that tuition and fees must cover costs (and yield a profit). In 1994 business spent $50 billion on training. Examples of providers are: The Teaching Company, and the Learning Tree. The difference between higher education markets and corporate training markets is beginning to blur; swift response to business needs through rapid course production or a focus on higher order learning skills are becoming features of both. For example, Academic Systems provides both corporate training and college-level courses. IT has made offering higher education courses profitable for entrepreneurs due to lower delivery costs. External providers have the advantage of starting with a clean slate, are able to innovate. On the other hand, colleges, especially community colleges, are getting more and more into corporate training. Improved productivity and doing more contract training are ways of strengthening higher education's competitive position.

Melitzky, Lillian. *Bridging the Gap for the Mainstream Faculty: Understanding the Use of Technology in Instruction.* Ph.D. Dissertation, Claremont Graduate University, Claremont, CA, 1999.

This study is based on a survey of 300 full-time faculty at six California State University and six SUNY campuses. The findings include these: There are no typical IT users, and there is little difference between senior and junior faculty. English and Political Science faculty use more networking technologies, Mathematics faculty more computer software. Faculty are undecided as to whether technology improves student learning. Junior and female faculty in particular use technology to advance careers.

Support services are inadequate. Faculty are interested in workshops to advance skills in their discipline, training for collaboration in instructional use of technology, and recognition of technology use in the academic rewards system.

Morris, D.M., and Olson, M.A. *E-Business in Education: What You Need to Know.* NACUBO, 1999. For a summary by the authors, see "Future E-Business Applications in Education," *NACUBO Business Officer* (July, 1999). See <http://www.nacubo.org/website/members/bomag/99/07/ebusiness.html>.

"Electronic commerce in education will enable 21st century learners to participate in a 'distributed learning' environment that mixes physical and virtual learning resources and experiences, in every combination imaginable…. Distributed learning includes the full spectrum of learning experiences, including campus-based and network-centric learning…. For some types of learning and support services, front-end, lump-sum payment will be supplemented by per-use, point-of-sale payment for such things as merchandise, courseware, information and intellectual property, and all kind of services …. Materials from virtual universities, Web-based courses developed by traditional institutions, and the new generation of customizable learningware will all be used by learners in a wide diversity of settings…. E-business will enable a new generation of academic support tools that will be available in-person, online, or through a combination of both." From the Executive Summary: "E-commerce is the marketing, sales, and payment for products, services, and experiences through electronic means…. Pervasive electronic commerce applications will radically transform the manner in which most colleges and universities conduct their most basic business functions… [based on] ubiquitous and uniform access to networked computing, collaborative initiatives among institutions and business solution providers, and legislative reform of key regulatory law. As a result, campuses will reduce operating expenses, enhance service quality, and outsource (or co-source) noncore business operations." "E-business will also transform academic and academic support experiences," through "distributed learning environments," personalized life-long learning experiences, and "communities of practice made possible through E-business." "Developing tomorrow's E-business environments and applications requires an *expeditionary* approach to strategy, planning, and the development of infrastructure, products, services, and experiences."

National Center for Education Statistics. See U.S. Government.

National Commission on the Cost of Higher Education. *Straight Talk about College Costs and Prices.* Report of the National Commission on the Cost of Higher Education. January 21, 1998. Phoenix: Oryx Press, 1998. See <http://www.ACENET.edu/programs/DGR/costreport.html>.

The report discusses trends in costs, prices, and subsidies; trends in college affordability; and "cost and price drivers" in higher education. The authors express a number of convictions, such as that not only prices are rising but institutional costs are going up as well, or that academic institutions must be "financially more transparent" if public support for "a world-class system of higher education is to be sustained." The five recommendations for actions are strengthening institutional cost control, improving market information and public accountability, deregulating higher education, rethinking accreditation, and enhancing and simplifying student aid.

Noble, David F. "Digital Diploma Mills: The Automation of Higher Education." October 1997. See <http://www.journet.com/twu/deplomamills.html>.
Over the last two decades we have seen in higher education a conversion of intellectual activity into intellectual capital and thus intellectual property. The first phase transformed knowledge produced by science and engineering into proprietary products, based on an alliance of business and higher education and changes in federal law, including patent law. The second phase is turning instruction into a commodity, which is promoted, in particular, by vendors of IT technology and products, advocates of corporate training, university administrators, and some foundations and associations. Campuses are becoming the places of production as well as the markets for such products. The implications for the faculty are negative: less control over their work, more monitoring by administration, loss of the products of their knowledge and skills, replacement by less trained workers, and redundancy. The faculty at Canada's York University conducted a two-month strike and secured "direct and unambiguous control over all decisions relating to the automation of instruction, including veto power." There is no evidence yet that students support technology initiatives in teaching and learning. In fact there is evidence of student concern. One must question whether students can afford such "capital-intensive" education. Students in computer-based courses are used for testing products and markets. The question also arises who owns or who has access to student online communications. Digital diploma mills are in the making. Quality education soon will be for the children of the wealthy only.

———. "Digital Diploma Mills, Part II: The Coming Battle over Online Instruction." March 1999. See <http://chass.utoronto.ca/~buschert/noble/>.
University research has been commercialized over the last two decades. Now universities are in the process of commercializing and commoditizing instruction in the same fashion, by becoming producers and distributors of instructional products or by entering into arrangements with private vendors. In the process some institutions are claiming that online courses are their intellectual property, rather than that of faculty involved. As a result copyright and intellectual property are the most explosive issues on campus. The author reviews arrangements between UCLA and the Home Education Network (THEN), UC Berkeley and AOL, and the University of Colorado and RealEducation. He argues that the focus at the beginning is on extension programs but the ultimate target is the entire campus. If faculty do not assert their copyright for materials they place on the Web, "universities will usurp such rights by default," endangering faculty positions and the quality and integrity of higher education.

Oberlin, John L. "The Financial Mythology of Information Technology: Developing a New Game Plan," *CAUSE/EFFECT* 19, 2 (Summer, 1996): 10-17. See <http://www.educause.edu/ir/library/html/cem9624.html>.
The new economics of IT requires new financial strategies to manage investments in IT. Institutions must plan for change, stay "ahead of the technology curve." "The real infrastructure imperative is to create the underlying processes that can produce the standards, architectures, and governance mechanisms to manage the changing technology." It is not the technical infrastructure that is key but the financial, social, and political infrastructure capable of managing technology change. Myths to be abandoned are that falling computer prices will reduce total IT expenditures, distrib-

uted computing is cheaper than central computing and is lowering overall computing costs, marginal costs of supporting another hardware platform or software package are small, IT investments can be managed through ad hoc funding, decentralized computing means less central computing authority and fewer enterprise-wide standards, new technologies and resultant services will be cash cows for colleges and universities, higher education is leading IT industry in setting standards and requirements ("the educational marketplace is only 6 percent of the total technology marketplace").

Strategic cost analysis is necessary to judge the value of technology and make appropriate decisions on IT investment: Where does technology create values? What is the cost structure supporting strategic choices? How does technology impact competitive position? The criterion for IT investment is not cost but cost/benefit. Life-cycle budgeting shifts focus from acquisition to replacement and avoids "expectation inflation" and "investment creep." If institutions want to reap the benefits of IT, they must spend more money on IT. IT "is a long-term investment in the competitive standing and productivity of the institution." It is important to separate short-term decisions on technology from long-term decisions on funding. It is preferable to recycle old technology off campus and this is best achieved by leasing. A greater portion of institutional expenditures will have to go towards IT.

————. "The Financial Mythology of Information Technology: The New Economics," *CAUSE/EFFECT* 19, 1 (Spring, 1996): 21-29. See <http://www.educause.edu/ir/library/text/CEM9616.txt>.

One must understand the economics of information technology to develop sound financial strategies for dealing with IT. IT "will represent the single biggest opportunity to either enhance or damage an institution's competitive standing." Because of falling prices many expect cost savings; these will not materialize. The value of IT to institutions is increasing. The aggregation of users and resources creates an enterprise-wide eco-system whose value in its totality is greater than the value of its parts. Demand for IT is constantly rising. Central computing is now a smaller portion of total campus computing but it is growing absolutely. Prices per unit may be falling but acquisition prices will still remain high because more memory, peripherals and other items are expected. The total cost of owning technology is rising; distributed and more sophisticated systems require more support, training, and time. Technology success always leads to greater expense. At best, institutions can hope for cost avoidance, surely not cost reduction.

Oliver, M., Conole, G., and Bonetti, L. "The Hidden Costs of Change: Evaluating the Impact of Moving to On-Line Delivery." See <http://www.shu.ac.uk/flish/oliverp.htm>.

This paper attempts to evaluate a technology support program at the University of North London, as one example of investing in online learning. The focus is on the professional development of instructors—of both pedagogical and technical skills—over a one-year period. In the process the authors identify the problems one encounters in trying to evaluate costs of IT. These include categorizing, calculating, and comparing costs, measuring efficiency, and considering benefits. Identifying costs raises the issue of scope: "How broad a range of costs should be considered." Benefits "are often qualitative in nature, and may be extremely difficult to identify" or "have no link to the allocation of resources ... and are therefore hard to assign a cost to." The methodology developed for this evaluation distinguished quantified costs (e.g., fixed and variable costs), qualitative costs (intangible and opportunity costs), and distribution of costs, and relied on "qualitative feedback and analysis." To the authors this is a case study that outlines the direct, recurrent, opportunity and 'intangible' costs associated with online delivery.

Orlans, Harold. "Restructuring Higher Education," *Change* 30, 1 (January-February 1998): 4-5.
  Review of *Breaking the Social Contract: The Fiscal Crisis in Higher Education.*

Peebles, C.S., and Antolovic, L. "Cost (and Quality and Value) of Information Technology Support in Large Universities," *Educom Review* 34, 5 (September-October, 1999). See <http://www.educause.edu/ir/library/html/erm9955.html>.
  This article is about Indiana University's University Information Technology Services and gives a break-down of annual costs of more than $4 million and details the factors that go into the calculation of annual and unit costs. (Thus an annual expenditure of $39,532 for Online Information Resources supports 7,200,000 Web hits at a cost of $0.0055 per hit.). The method applied here is based on Activity Based Costing and Activity Based Management. ABC and ABM are designed "to identify processes and products that add value and those that destroy value." "ABC measures and allocates all the costs that are incurred in the production, sale, and after-market needs ... of a product or service." ABM "uses these costs to catalyze quality improvement and cost reduction." The assumption behind measuring the cost of every product and process is that only in this way can unit costs be reduced, quality enhanced, and products and services re-designed or replaced, especially when IT budgets remain flat while more or new services are being demanded.
  Activity Based Costing as applied here is based on the works of Robert S. Kaplan and David P. Norton, *The Balanced Scorecard.* Boston: Harvard Business School Press, 1995; Robert S. Kaplan and Robin Cooper, *Cost and Effect: Using Integrated Cost Systems to Drive Profitability and Performance.* Boston: Harvard Business School Press, 1998, John K. Shank and Vijay Govindarajan, *Strategic Cost Management: The New Tool for Competitive Advantage.* New York: Free Press, 1993; Jeremy Hope and Tony Hope, *Competing in the Third Wave: The Key Management Issues of the Information Age.* Harvard Business School Press, 1997.

Peebles, C.S., Antolovic, L.G., Holland, N.B., Adams, K.H., Allmayer, D., and Davidson, P.H. "Modeling and Managing the Cost and Quality of Information Technology Services at Indiana University: A Case Study," in Richard N. Katz, Julia A. Rudy, eds. *Information Technology in Higher Education: Assessing Its Impact and Planning for the Future.* New Directions for Institutional Research 102. San Francisco: Jossey-Bass Publishers, 1999.
  IT organizations experience growing pressures for greater productivity and accountability. Economists have developed models for organizational effectiveness, response to changing environments, and measuring performance. Activity-based costing and activity-based management, described by Robert S. Kaplan and others, are tools to improve performance, as is strategic cost management, a particular variant of these techniques. At Indiana University the IT organization has used these methods to

improve process design and execution, which includes calculating and managing the costs of IT activities. It employs the four perspectives of the "balanced scorecard"—internal business process, learning and growth, customers, and finances—for improving IT services. Quality assessment is done through the use of "statistically valid and professionally administered" user surveys.

The case study on assessing the cost and quality of student computing focuses on some 1,100 computers in student technology centers. It considers the number of student users and machines and the exact use students made of IT services, such as 1,280 applications of Acrobat Reader in a given month. It calculates such costs, covered from a student technology fee and general academic computing funds, as account administration cost per action, hardware and software costs per seat and per seat-hour, center consultant costs per seat-hour, or online storage cost per user per year.

The IT productivity paradox is best addressed by making the distinction between computing as automation and augmentation, as suggested by T.K. Landauer, *The Trouble with Computers: Usefulness, Usability, and Productivity*. Cambridge MA: MIT Press, 1995. The results as to augmentation remain questionable. The automation component of computing has added value in research and business processes. The World Wide Web aids research and scholarship; its major perils are instability and quality of information. As far as teaching and learning go, "the value of information technology … has neither been rigorously measured nor comprehensively studied."

Policy Panel on Technology. "Technology and Its Ramifications for Data Systems." Report of the Policy Panel on Technology co-sponsored by the National Post-Secondary Educational Cooperative and the George Washington University. August 4-5, 1997, issued in August 1998. Sponsored by NCES. See <http://nces.ed.gov/pubs98/98279.pdf>. The report is summarized in *CAUSE/EFFECT* 22, 2 (1999); see <http://www.educause.edu/ir/library/html/cem9921.html>.

The report focuses on five areas: new institutional and programmatic configurations, faculty roles and work patterns, analyzing student participation patterns, assessment of student progress and learning gains, and analysis of revenue and expenditure streams. Basic assumptions include these: "students will increasingly participate at locations remote from the campus and the instructor… students will be associated with multiple providers and modes of instruction. Educational services will become 'unbundled' with different providers carrying out various functions including curricular development, delivery of instructional modules, provision of student services, student evaluation, and credentialling." With regard to revenues and expenditures, areas that will have to be addressed include collecting tuition and fees from multiple sites, allocating costs to different providers, defining new cost categories, allocating financial aid, and designing new accounting and reporting systems.

Privateer, Paul Michael. "Academic Technology and the Future of Higher Education: Strategic Paths Taken and Not Taken," *The Journal of Higher Education* 70, 1 (January-February, 1999): 60-79.

Technology in itself does not create new ways of teaching and learning. Instructional technologies today usually only replicate educational practices which are in the tradition of industrial management strategies. Traditional classrooms are like production lines. When we just automate old ways of teaching, we ignore new ways of learning. Central to the old kind of learning are information gathering and memory-based examination. The old paradigm, going back to the seventeenth century, is reproduction technology, the replication of information. "The trend to continue automating the conveyance of information produces more of what will be needed least." New digital technologies require new notions of pedagogy. We have to re-think traditional cost/benefit ratios in higher education and re-design instructional technology as a strategic and cognitive tool. Computers can support new kinds of learning, leading students to new skills as workers and citizens. We must think of computers as tools to re-engineer and re-invent curriculum, not to automate the traditional delivery of instruction. Technology now is able to do more than compute, measure, and manage information. It can help us invent "new kinds of information, knowledge, and truth."

For higher education not to lose its position as society's principal "knowledge site," its students must develop their intelligence by drawing on curricula that contain "value-added knowledge" imparting "value-added skills." Higher education will only remain competitive if it is committed to "a balanced strategy that uses technology to invent intelligence and encourage demonstrations of meta-critical reasoning and effective use of symbolic languages and team-based communication skills in solving a range of problems." Instructional technology must be re-invented; it should support the application of learning management strategies. "In essence, every classroom should be a knowledge laboratory using management strategies and complex knowledge matrices that require students to test and apply that knowledge in simulated applications." Colleges and universities must use business process re-engineering to cut IT cost and improve instruction. The strategies suggested here are: streamlining course offerings and course content; lowering costs of developing curriculum and programs; inventing general education requirements that are interdisciplinary-based; maximizing course revenue; giving students new options for taking courses based on new pedagogy.

Rensselaer Polytechnic Institute, Center for Academic Transformation, The Pew Learning and Technology Program. See <http://www.center.rpi.edu/PewHome.html>.

This is an $8 million, 4-year project, announced in June 1999, "to place the national discussion about the impact that new technologies are having on the nation's campuses in the context of student learning and ways to achieve this learning cost-effectively." The project sponsors three activities: symposia on learning and technology, the electronic Pew Learning and Technology Program Newsletter, and, for about $6 million of the project, a grant program in course re-design. About 10 proposals a year are to be funded at an average of $200,000. Proposals are to focus on high-enrollment introductory courses and to include an analysis of "the cost of traditional methods of instruction as well as new methods of instruction utilizing technology."

Ringle, Martin D. "Forecasting Financial Priorities for Technology," *CAUSE/EF-FECT* 20, 3 (Fall, 1997): 22-29. See <http://www.educause.edu/ir/library/html/cem9736.html>.

Many colleges and universities developed financial models for technology at the end of the 1980s. These were based on assumptions then current, such as hardware life-cycles, maintenance contracts, and students owning computers. Assumptions have changed since. In the future, financial strategies will have to be more adaptable. Financial models from over 20 independent colleges and universities have been used to develop a financial strategy for technology at Reed College.

See also the author's "Strategic Technology Issues: A Checklist for Liberal Arts Colleges," which is based on a 1995 workshop at Reed College. Several of the issues identified relate specifically to financing the cost of IT. See <http://www.reed.edu/pcw/>.

Ringle, Martin D., and Smallen, D.L. "Can Small Colleges Be Information Technology Leaders," *CAUSE/EFFECT* 19, 2 (Summer 1996): 18-25. See <http://www.educause.edu/ir/library/html/cem9814.html>.

Small colleges may seem unlikely technology leaders but can support their missions through focused application of IT. The authors discuss costs, risks, and benefits of being technology leaders.

Ringle, M., and Updegrove, D. "Is Strategic Planning for Technology an Oxymoron?" *CAUSE/EFFECT* 21, 1 (1998):18-23. See <http://www.educause.edu/ir/library/html/cem9814.html>.

"It is our contention, in this paper, that there are two distinct aspects of strategic technology planning. One is socioeconomic and the other is pragmatic/technical. The traditional focus on the creation of a planning document tends to merge these aspects and obscure the distinction, often leading to confusion and frustration. The differences between socioeconomic objectives – which are essentially strategic – and technical goals – which are primarily operational – are non-trivial: while the former need to be stable and comprehensive, the latter need to be agile and responsive to rapid changes in technology and in users' needs. We believe strategic planning for technology is not an oxymoron, yet a failure to appreciate the dual character of technology planning can make it seem that way…. Our goal in this study is to bring these underlying practices and perspectives together into an explicit – and relatively simple – model of a good technology planning process."

Rumble, Greville. *The Costs and Economics of Open and Distance Learning.* London: Kogan Page Ltd., 1997.

This volume is by an author connected with the Open University who has dealt with the costs of distance learning since the 1980's. It presents a clear synopsis of the state of knowledge on the subject at the time of publication. A ten-page bibliography listing more than 200 earlier works indicates the considerable amount of previous research on the subject in the UK and elsewhere. The first half of the book deals with the general principles of cost accounting and that portion is probably most useful to those not familiar with this field. The second half has helpful chapters on cost efficiency, cost effectiveness, and costs and benefits. Among the results, demonstrated from numerous studies and summed up in many pages of tables, is that under certain conditions distance education has been proven to be more cost effective than traditional classroom instruction. However, the author makes no great claims for the potential for cost savings from distance learning, and his prognosis is cautious.

———. "The Costs of Networked Learning: What Have We Learnt?" Paper delivered at the FLISH 1999 Conference. See <http://www.shu.ac.uk/flish/rumblep.htm>.

Since IT expenditures in higher education are high—in the UK, it was estimated in 1997 that 10 percent of the total higher education budget was being spent on communications and information technology—there is a need for investment appraisal. The application of cost/benefit analysis is problematic because costs and benefits are difficult to identify and to measure. Studies of the costs of IT-enhanced teaching and learning are rare. Organizations are reluctant to provide the financial information. A useful study was produced in 1998 by Arizona Learning Systems, comparing ITV and online courses. The economics of online education is now the big issue. Up to this moment, online education has been largely small-scale and experimental; it is now becoming an instrument of mass education. We are at the same point with online education as distance education via television was 40 years ago. "First and second generation distance education" delivered economies of scale; online education may not be able to do that. Is there a business case for online learning? We know little about the costs of online learning.

We must first identify cost categories. One approach he cites is looking at "the functional underpinning of costs:" the costs of developing and maintaining online materials, of online activity on the parts of learners and supporters, of managing online programs. Secondly, "the likely level of costs and their behavior" has to be identified. Here Rumble cites a series of cost findings. "The biggest and I suggest the least costed ingredient in the costs of online learning is the cost of supporting learners online." The supporters are spending more time with students than when that support was mainly by correspondence and telephone. It is these costs in particular that in the end might set limits to online learning (or the cost-effectiveness of online learning). Online rather than face-to-face training reduces cost of time and travel to attend, but savings arise in particular "from moving training time out of the employer's paid time and into the employee's free time." In online learning some costs must be shifted to students, which could affect access: "This shift of costs onto the student raises concerns about the ability of socio-economically deprived sectors of the population to participate in online learning." And students must take more responsibility for their own learning.

Rumble sees many good reasons for investing in online learning other than potential cost savings, although these other outcomes "are very difficult to quantify and give a value to." Among concerns he lists: Will students be able to afford online learning? Will overall costs be too heavy for institutions? Will it be possible to identify and control costs? "Costing is not a precise art, and traditional cost systems and management reporting methods are deeply flawed, with the result that information on the costs of products and services is often seriously inaccurate."

Russel, T. *The No Significant Difference Phenomenon.* Raleigh: North Carolina State University Office of Instructional Telecommunications, 1999.

———. "The 'No Significant Difference' Phenomenon, a Review of over 200 Studies on Learning Outcomes Showing No Significant Difference between Classroom and Distributed Instruction Spanning the Period 1928-1996." See <http://tenb.mta.ca/phenom/phenoml.html>.

Sargeant, Donald. "Moving Toward a Mobile Teaching and Learning Environment: Using Notebook Computers," in Diane G. Oblinger & Sean C. Rush, eds. The Learning Revolution: *The Challenge of Information Technology in the Academy.* Boston, MA: Anker Publishing Company, Inc., 1997, pp. 74–91.

This paper describes the introduction of notebook computers for all full-time students at the University of Minnesota, Crookston, beginning in 1993. This had to be done "with limited incremental funds from the federal or state governments." The University's lease of students' computers was financed by a technology fee which qualifies as a financial aid expense; it was $900 in FY 97. On p. 81 the author gives a summary of expenditures. Expenditures went from $128,000 in FY 1994 to $504,000 in 1997.

Schmidtlein, Frank A. "Critical Factors in Information Technology Planning for the Academy: Assessing the Costs of Instructional Technology." Paper presented at the 39th Annual AIR Forum, Seattle WA, June 2, 1999.

This paper considers types of communication technologies and modes of instruction, common assumptions about the use of instructional technologies, including the effects of technology on productivity and on instructional quality, and costs associated with the use of communications technologies (national infrastructure costs, institutional infrastructure costs, hardware costs, software costs, technical support costs, faculty training and opportunity costs, student access and training costs, course design and development costs, administrative and legal costs, less tangible costs, such as lack of human contact and interaction).

————. "A Framework for Examining the Costs of Instructional Technology." Paper presented at the National Institute for Academic Degrees (NIAD), Nagatuta, Yokohama City, Japan. July 24, 1998.

We need "more comprehensive research on the costs of instructional uses of communication technologies" and "a framework for examining these costs." Technology plans have to be changed more rapidly because of new development. There is a "serious lack of research and policy analysis on the nature and full range of the costs involved in instructional technology." "Without in-depth research, there will continue to be a tendency to invest too large a proportion of available funds in infrastructure, equipment and software and far too little into the other costs noted above; particularly course development, training, and technical support."

"One means to address the gap in our understanding of the costs of instructional technology would be for a federal government agency to fund an Institute for the Study of Instructional Technology. Such an agency could provide resources for the cost studies and policy research that are badly needed to guide the millions of dollars being expended in this area."

Sichel, Daniel E. "Computers and Aggregate Economic Growth," *Business Economics* 34, 2 (April, 1999): 18-24.

IT investment in business has been going on for decades but productivity growth until the mid 90s has been low. More recently productivity performance suggests the possibility of IT investments paying off. Calculations show "a striking step-up in the contributions of computers to output growth." This could be a break with past but might also be transitory and due to rapid decline of computer prices and strong economy.

Strassmann, Paul A. "Credit Greenspan, not Computers," *Computerworld* 33, 23 (June 7, 1999).

"The question of whether information technology has improved productivity is now at the center of the economic stage." Did corporations become more effective as a consequence of computerization? The author makes two points: Had interest costs remained unchanged since 1990, there would be no productivity gains. Greenspan's is the cleverest US monetary policy since Alexander Hamilton. And most of the potential gains from computerization were absorbed by the IT workforce, which includes computer professionals, consultants, and lawyers. "The value of IT can be demonstrated only after proving that the increased economic value of an organization wouldn't materialize by other means."

———. "The Search for Productivity," *Computerworld* 33, 32 (August 9 1999). Excerpt from Paul A. Strassmann. *Information Productivity: Assessing the Information Management Costs of U.S. Industrial Corporations.* New Canaan, CT: The Information Economics Press, 1999.

The focus should not be on IT but on information productivity. Diagnose conditions that will improve information management before automating; make management more productive before adding IT. Traditional measures of productivity, like revenue per employee ratios or return on investment ratios, are relics of an earlier economic order. Productivity increases as a result of a combination of many factors of production. Because capital has been less important for some time, "… what matters now is the productivity of information management." Computing information productivity depends on accurately measuring information costs, which includes, according to the author's definition, "all costs of managing, coordinating, training, communicating, planning, accounting, marketing, and research." "If information productivity increases as a result of effective deployment of information technologies, that would be one of the indicators whether one's computers are producing a business payoff." The author includes information productivity rankings and ratios for 1,560 corporations.

See also Strassmann's Web site <www.strassmann.com>.

———. "IT Paradox Number," *Computerworld* 33, 18 (May 3, 1999).

The productivity paradox is "the inability to convincingly demonstrate that our investments in technology have resulted in measurable productivity improvements." Moore's Law would suggest that electronic costs can decline by 33.3 percent a year; the US Department of Commerce assumes an average decline of IT costs at a compound annual rate of 17.5 percent. Calculating the IT paradox number: "It's your company's IT budget today, compared with what it could have been if you had previously bought your computing capacity every year for 17.5 percent less." The discrepancy between potential and reality is explained by bloated software, excessive support costs, negligent systems engineering.

Thompson, Dennis P. "Intellectual Property Meets Information Technology: An Olive Branch in the Debate over Who Owns IT Products," *Educom Review* 34, 2 (March-April, 1999): 14-21. See <http://www.educause.edu/ir/library/html/erm99022.html>.

The author is a professor of government and associate provost at Harvard University and chaired a university-wide committee that spent a year reviewing questions of IT and intellectual property rights.

The controversy about control of IT products is misconceived. While IT raises new problems, there should be changes more broadly in general university policies on intellectual property, not only with regard to IT products. Usually faculty owns work that can be copyrighted, the university owns products that can be patented; the former draws less on specifically assigned university resources. IT products are like textbooks in some respects and like patents in others. Some universities now have rules for "digital" works, claiming institutional ownership in some cases but not in others. The author proposes that we focus not on the nature of the product but the circumstances of its creation. He advocates a general policy applicable to all kinds of products produced by faculty, students, or staff. The basic principle is: "If the university contributes substantially and specifically to the making of a product, the university should share in its profits and have some control over its uses." The university's contribution may be financial, intellectual, or reputational. In regard to the last, the key is meeting the standards of accuracy, appropriateness, and fairness.

Policies dealing with ownership of IT products should go beyond intellectual property. For example, academia should "establish an alternative medium {to traditional journals} for dissemination of research on the Internet, which would include the equivalent of refereed processes" and thus diminish the issue of who owns the copyright of journal articles. "Fair use" legislation vitally affects the intellectual property rights of faculty, as producers and as users. As to courseware used in distance learning and virtual universities, the university should not own Internet courseware produced by faculty, for reasons of lack of a significant difference from traditional courseware, equity, and the risk of providing an incentive to distribute courseware by means other than the Internet.

Thorp, J. "Computing the Payoff from IT," *The Journal of Business Strategy* 20, 2 (May June, 1999): 35-39.

This article is mainly about the Benefits Realization Approach to managing IT investments. Applications of IT today … enable increasingly strategic business outcomes, whose costs are only partially IT costs (5-20 percent), although the outcomes would not be possible without IT. There are no longer IT projects but only business change programs of which IT is a part. IT investments represent now more than 40 percent of the total capital investment of US companies and a significant portion of their operating expense.

TLT Group, the Teaching, Learning, and Technology Affiliate of the AAHE. The Flashlight Program, directed by Stephen C. Ehrmann. See <http://www.tltgroup.org/programs/flashlight.html>.

The purpose of the Flashlight Program is "to work with institutions to explore how technology might improve education." It does so through workshops, consultation, events and tools. It has published the *Flashlight Cost Analysis Handbook* designed to help institutions analyze how the use of technology consumes time, space, money, and other resources, and to develop models to improve on current ways of using resources The model on which the handbook is based was developed at Indiana University and uses Activity-Based Costing. With funding from the Andrew W. Mellon Foundation, the Flashlight Program supports the Flashlight Cost Analysis Awards Program, a "competition for the best studies of resource use in teaching and learning with technology."

Turoff, Murray. "Costs for the Development of a Virtual University," *Journal of Asynchronous Learning Networks* 1, 1 (March, 1997) Based on a 1982 paper. See <http:///www.aln.org/alnweb/journal/jaln_VolIissue1.htm>.

The costs are $15 million for a university of 2,000 students, with faculty and students scattered around the globe.

Twigg, Carol. "Improving Learning & Reducing Costs: Redesigning Large-Enrollment Courses." Report on a symposium of "20 higher education leaders," on Redesigning More Productive Learning Environments. July 15-16, 1999. Roanoke, Virginia. See <http://www.center.rpi.edu/PewSym/mono1.html>.

The goal of the symposium was "to examine the validity of the conceptual framework" of projects that are part of the Pew Grant Program in Course Design overseen by the author. That program is about using IT to redesign large-enrollment introductory courses, both to save costs and to enhance quality. What is needed are "a comprehensive planning methodology" and "examples of practice." The latter were provided here by projects at Virginia Tech, University of Wisconsin—Madison, Rio Salado College, RPI, University of Illinois-Urbana/Champaign. The report provides links to five case studies on the projects at these campuses.

————. "Academic Productivity: The Case for Instructional Software,"Report from the Broadmoor Roundtable, Colorado Springs, CO, July 24-25, 1996. NLII Monograph published by EDUCAUSE. See <http://www.educause.edu/nlii,keydocs/broadmoor.html>.

More productive learning environments require high-quality instructional software. Individual faculty members are not likely to generate "a sustainable, scaleable body of materials" no matter how much support from external sources. What is needed is a commercial market for interactive learning materials. There is no consensus on the obstacles to or the ways for creating such a market. The conference focused on five propositions:

1. Instructional software is needed to solve the productivity problem because 80 percent of costs are personnel costs, Capital has to be substituted for labor to enhance productivity, simply adding on IT applications does not help with productivity. Instructional software promises to make teaching and learning less labor intensive.

2. Targeting areas of high student enrollment promises to have the greatest likelihood of success, because usually a large portion of credits comes from a tiny number of courses taught in multiple sections. These courses usually are in the areas of codified knowledge and algorithmic skills. Faculty are less proprietary about these courses. A mass market is needed.

3. Higher education institutions cannot create software on their own, because "traditional 'soft money' development strategies have failed to produce a scaleable

body of instructional software," and the business of colleges is teaching and research, not development of products and their production, distribution, and marketing.

4. The need is for self-sustained commercialization; "commercialization is the minimum measure of success."

5. Market success depends on instructional software being in modules so users can pick and choose ("Disaggregation enables 'mass customization' where learning materials may be customized by the adopter"). Such instructional software must be usable without intermediary, capable of being applied in different ways for more than one purpose, and designed for higher education as an industry, not for particular courses.

The discussion portion of the paper is about obstacles and avenues in the development and adoption of such software. One point seems to stand out, namely that the software we need may have to be created initially for markets outside of higher education, e.g., for purchase by individuals.

University of British Columbia, Department of Continuing Studies, Distance Education and Technology. "Developing and Applying a Cost-Benefit Model for Assessing Telelearning." See <http://research.cstudies.ubc.ca>.

The project is part of a larger project, *NCE-Telelearning,* funded at $13 million and conducted by the TeleLearning Network of Centres of Excellence. The larger project involves universities, colleges, schools, and other public and private organizations across Canada and is dedicated to studying the effects of telecommunications on teaching and learning. It is headed by Linda Harasim, Simon Fraser University. See <http://www.telelearn.ca/_access/front.html>.

The project at the University of British Columbia is under the direction of A.W. Bates. Its purpose is to "develop and test a methodology that will allow decision-makers to analyse objectively the costs and benefits of using networks to provide education and training." Among the expected outcomes are: "A flexible and relevant methodology for costing telelearning activities" and a "better understanding of the cost structures of different forms of telelearning." Included in the project are six case studies at different Canadian institutions that focus on cost-benefit analysis of seven types of courseware used for course development, such as HyperNews, Lotus Notes, and Virtual U.

U.S. Congress. Telecommunications Act of 1996 and Related Legislation. See <http://www.fcc.gov./telecom.html>.

Legislation is being considered and passed on the state and federal level that affects the cost of IT for higher education. Regulations deal with the cost of telecommunication infrastructure and services. The Telecommunications Act of 1996 has settled many but by no means all issues. Internet capabilities and costs will continue to be impacted by new federal and state regulations, e.g., in matters of access to and distribution of courseware or copyright law. The Web site has the text and related information. Federal activities relating to IT are tracked by the weekly EduCause *Washington Update* <http://www.educause.edu/pub/wu/>.

U.S. Department of Education, National Center for Education Statistics. *Distance Education at Postsecondary Institutions: 1997-98.* NCES 2000-013, by L. Lewis, K. Snow, E. Farris, and D. Levin. Bernie Greene, project officer. Washington, DC: U.S. Department of Education, 1999. See <http://nces.ed.gov/pubsearch/pubsinfo.asp?pubid=2000013>.

This report, updating and expanding a 1997 NCES report on distance learning, provides data on institutions offering distance education, regarding courses, programs, and enrollments. It examines technologies used as well as tuition and fees. It also reports on trends in distance learning in higher education by comparison with 1994-95 data. The report notes that "the advent of advanced information technologies and, in particular, the Internet, has profoundly altered the character of distance education." In the introduction the authors define distance education, institutional motives for using it, modes of delivery, organizational arrangements, effectiveness, and emerging policy issues, such as costs of developing and implementing distance education programs

During the 1997-98 year one-third of 2- and 4-year institutions offered distance learning courses. Another one-fifth planned to offer such courses within the next three years. Eight percent offered full certificate or degree programs, a total of 1,230 degree programs and 340 certificate programs. The total number of distance learning courses in all postsecondary institutions was close to 55,000. Almost 1.4 million students enrolled in college-level credit-bearing distance courses. Asynchronous Internet instruction, interactive video, and one-way prerecorded video served as the principal technologies. Institutions project that Internet and ITV use in distance education will grow more than that of other technologies. Between 1993-4 and 1997-98 distance learning courses and enrollments doubled; the percentage of institutions participating in distance education increased by one third. Among higher education institutions offering distance education the proportion of students using ITV remained the same, whereas the percentage using Internet-based technologies almost tripled, from 22 percent to 60 percent. "… distance education appears to have become a common feature of many post-secondary education institutions and … will become only more common in the future."

Virginia Polytechnic Institute and State University. The Math Emporium. See <http://www.educause.edu/nlii/meetings/orleans99mathemp.html>.

The purpose of the Math Emporium is to enhance student learning, increase access to quality education, and reduce costs. "The Math Emporium is a 500 workstation, student-centered, advanced learning center that provides an active learning environment for more than 10,000 undergraduates….[it] is the first truly large-scale center of its kind. Courses are taught via interactive, self-paced courseware and diagnostic quizzes, and there is strong emphasis on small-group work and faculty/student tutoring…. The center is open seven days a week, 24 hours a day, and is staffed 80 hours a week. Currently, 11 courses are being taught through the Math Emporium, and more are planned." "Preliminary assessment data suggest that the Math Emporium is indeed helping improve student learning and faculty productivity. According to [Ann H.] Moore, [Director of Information Technology Initiatives], the institution is now teaching 30 percent more students with 6 percent less budget. And mean scores in mathematics have risen 17.4 percent while the failure rate has dropped by 39 percent." "From the faculty perspective, [John F.] Rossi, [professor of mathematics at Virginia

Tech], believes the Math Emporium is changing the instructor's job description. Although the number of hours devoted to instruction remains basically the same, he said, the amount of time spent lecturing and conducting office hours has gone down while lab hours and e-mail communications have grown. Instructors in Math Emporium-type environments need to be willing to think differently about their jobs, according to Rossi. 'Some may ask, Am I still a teacher? Or Are my students learning more?' The answer to both questions, he said, is yes."

Western Cooperative for Educational Communications. "Technology Costing Methodology," a project in partnership with the National Center for Higher Education Management Systems, funded by FIPSE. 1999. See <http://wiche.edu/telecom/projects/>.

The objective is to calculate technology costs within and across institutions. At the outset, NCHEMS did not know whether instructional technology can reduce costs in higher education. Costing methodologies derived from single institutions are not sufficient. The methodology to be developed will be based on the 1974 NCHEMS "Cost Finding Principles" that have been widely accepted. The methodology would include procedures to define cost categories, treat capital appropriately for regular classroom and mediated instruction, distinguish between institutional costs and student costs, treat appropriately costs for courseware development. The goal is to develop a methodology for calculating costs to determine within an institution if instruction making heavy use of technology does contain costs, and to compare data across institutions for the costs of using different technologies in instruction. The methodology is to be tested in Montana, New Mexico, Utah and Washington during the 1999-2000 academic year.

Willcox, L.P., and Willcox, Lester S. *Beyond the IT Productivity Paradox.* Wiley Series in Information Systems. New York: John Wiley and Sons, 1999.

Computers and telecommunications investments around the globe make up half or more of annual capital expenditures in most large corporations, and computers and other IT equipment as far back as 1994 represented 50 percent or more of what businesses were spending on equipment, not considering what was being spent on software. The belief that "despite massive accumulated and rising investments in information technology ..., on the whole these have not contributed to significant rises in productivity," has been called the IT productivity paradox. It is difficult to show that the large investments made in IT have improved business efficiency and raised profits. The introduction by the editors and the 13 essays in this book, by the editors and others, are to "enhance our understanding of the relationships between IT investments, productivity and performance and how these can be assessed."

The debate on the IT productivity paradox has been going on for more than 20 years; it was, however, in particular a perception of the 1980s to the early 90s. By and large this book argues that there is no longer a productivity paradox. A key point here is that the apparent lack of reasonable payback is due to some extent to inadequate yardsticks that have been used to measure the payback. Also economists did not give adequate consideration to timing lags or to redistribution (those investing heavily in IT getting a bigger share of the pie). Studies in the 1980s and beyond tended to be done by macroeconomists looking at the total economy. As a result they based their studies largely on the service sector, which is four-fifths of the U.S. economy. IT productivity, however, can be examined more accurately "at the more meaningful intra-organizational level," through microeconomic studies. Some organizations are much better at using IT than others. What is needed is "a multidimensional assessment of IT business value." Strong businesses gain from IT whereas weak businesses seem to benefit less or are even damaged. The notion of the IT productivity paradox suggests that there is a "simple unilinear relation" between IT investments and heightened productivity whereas in reality the linkage between IT use, productivity, and business success is more complex. The role of IT has changed from support to strategy. For business, the primary reason for IT investment is customer service and satisfaction; only after that come cost savings, because "customer satisfaction is the key determinant of economic success… [and] the controlling factor for optimizing an organization." In fact "value creation can potentially improve economic performance far more than cost reductions ever could."

Zemsky, R., and Massy, W.F. "Expanding Perimeters, Melting Cores, and Sticky Functions: Towards an Understanding of Current Predicaments," *Change* 27, 6 (November-December 1995): 40-49.

Colleges and universities exhibit conservative tendencies, are characterized by a commitment to a "sense of sustaining mission" and "a belief that at its core the academy is largely immutable—its costs largely fixed, its purposes well established, its educational and intellectual values well honed." These tendencies are barriers that make difficult the introduction of IT in teaching and learning.

INDEX

by Dottie M. Jahoda

Page numbers followed by *f* refer to figures; page numbers followed by *t* refer to tables, and page numbers followed by *n* and a number refer to endnotes.